CAMBRIDGE SOUTH ASIAN STUDIES

THE DEVS OF CINCVAD

A list of the books in the series will
be found at the end of the volume

THE DEVS OF CINCVAD

*A lineage and the state
in Maharashtra*

LAURENCE W. PRESTON

*Department of Humanities and Social Sciences,
Red Deer College*

L. W. Preston

The right of the
University of Cambridge
to print and sell
all manner of books
was granted by
Henry VIII in 1534.
The University has printed
and published continuously
since 1584.

CAMBRIDGE UNIVERSITY PRESS
CAMBRIDGE
NEW YORK   NEW ROCHELLE
MELBOURNE   SYDNEY

Published by the Press Syndicate of the University of Cambridge
The Pitt Building, Trumpington Street, Cambridge CB2 1RP
32 East 57th Street, New York, NY 10022, USA
10 Stamford Road, Oakleigh, Melbourne 3166, Australia

First published 1989

Printed in Great Britain at the University Press, Cambridge

British Library cataloguing in publication data
Preston, Laurence W.
The Devs of Cincvad: a lineage and the state in Maharashtra
 – (Cambridge South Asian Studies; v.41).
1. Kinship – India – Maharashtra – History
I. Title
306.8′3′0954792   GN487

Library of Congress cataloguing in publication data applied for.

ISBN 0 521 34633 9

TM

for Trevor and Graham

CONTENTS

ILLUSTRATIONS

Figures

Tables

PREFACE

The historian who attempts to write on two great eras continually feels the pull of one or the other. In this history of the Dev lineage of Cincvad village I have often had to resist the temptations and pressures to concentrate on the 'traditional' (whatever that might mean) order of the preconquest Maratha state. Likewise, I have not sought to evaluate, in any usual manner, the impact of the British conquest of India. With a certain deliberation, therefore, I have examined an institution through which the profound political change of the conquest could be seen in a somewhat dispassionate way. The Dev lineage experienced both the old order and the new imperialism. For the Devs, great matters of lineage welfare were equally pressing under the Marathas and the British. In both eras the Devs looked to the state for protection and support while always living in suspicion and respect for the state's power.

My understanding of the conquest and, generally, change in India is conservative. In fact, I am also not at ease with such slogans as 'social change'; Indian society changed rather less than the opportunities for Indian social institutions to act out their constant objectives. The conquest created the need for alternative strategies in devising new solutions for old problems. Of course, social adaptation may be considered as the visible effects of deeper social change. I have no quarrel with the notion that societies do change. But, as I think any acquaintance with modern South Asia would press home, Indian society clings to the past in many of its fundamentals. Historians have rightly given serious attention to the effects of European imperialism on India. Here I have taken a different perspective: social institutions and social structure often dictated how the conquest would affect Indians.

The sources for a history of the Devs of Cincvad have perhaps helped to shape my cautious approach to historical change. Working on one lineage necessarily means searching out local and often humble documents. The great affairs of state and empire yield to the mundane practicalities of revenue documents concerned only with the immediate and particular. When examining either the vernacular or English sources for a lineage such as the Devs, the historian is forced to concentrate on the purpose of the documents, and thus to discern what is common in the sources. My overriding impression of the material I have been able to study in Pune and Bombay – and this is only the most basic sample of what is available – confirms the constancy of purpose of Indian social institutions throughout both the Maratha and British periods. With this understanding I offer the present work.

Although he is in no way responsible for the specific or general conclusions reached in this study, Professor N. K. Wagle has been my first and continuing inspiration to unearth the history of Indian social institutions. Professor Wagle's insistence that historians of early modern India must make use of the plentiful but neglected archival resources available in Marathi has been simple but sage advice. Several others have read and commented on the present work or in other ways offered their encouragement. The many kindnesses of Frank F. Conlon, Peter Harnetty, Milton Israel, Barrie M. Morrison, Ed. Moulton, Günther-Dietz Sontheimer and A. P. Thornton have been truly appreciated.

In India my research was made possible by a fellowship from the Shastri Indo-Canadian Institute. To that sympathetic organization, and to Professor A. R. Kulkarni, my sponsor, I extend my thanks. Much of this work was written at the Australian National University, Canberra. I gratefully acknowledge the incisive comments of the faculty and students of the Research School of Pacific Studies and the Faculty of Asian Studies. A postdoctoral fellowship from the Social Sciences and Humanities Research Council of Canada, as well as facilities provided by the Department of History, University of Toronto, brought this work to a completion.

Finally, the remarkable forbearance of my wife, Jennifer, and my sons, Trevor and Graham, cannot be adequately described.

ABBREVIATIONS

The following abbreviations are used throughout the footnotes:
BA Bombay Archives, Elphinstone College, Bombay
  RD Revenue Department
  PD Political Department
  Citations are thus, BA: RD; volume/compilation, pages
PA Pune Archives ('the Peshva daphtar'), Bund Garden Road, Oppo-
site Council Hall, Pune
  DC Deccan Commission files
  Citations are thus, PA: DC volume/serial number of letter.
  IC Inam Commission Marathi rumals ('bundles')
  SD Shahu daphtar, document numbers taken from M. G. Diksit and
  V. G. Khobrekar, eds. *Shahu daptaratil kagadpatramci varnanatmak
  suci*, 2 vols. (Bombay, 1969–70)
  English files in PA (Inam Commission and Agent for Sardars) are
  cited thus, PA: list number; rumal/file, pages, or folios

INDIAN TECHNICAL USAGES

Indian usage is to note large numbers in terms of units of 100,000 (*lākh*s).
Thus, for example, 1,000,000 is 10,00,000 or ten hundred-thousands.

Because the Indian calendar year does not correspond to the western
calendar, year dates cited from Indian documentary sources are
expressed as extending over two western years. Thus, 1834/5 is the
Indian calendar year (of whatever Indian era) that began in 1834 and
ended in 1835.

Introduction: an inamdar lineage in Indian history

> The opportunity afforded me of visiting the city of Poona, with the embassy of 1800, I eagerly embraced, to obtain information respecting an extraordinary family, which enjoys the distinction of an hereditary incarnation of the divinity, from father to son; and the following is the result of my researches.[1]

So Captain Edward Moor begins the first English account of the Devs of Cincvad, a brahman lineage of Maharashtra that is the subject of this book. By any standard the Devs were unique and visit to Cincvad, a village some 15 kilometers north-west of the Maratha capital Pune (see Figure 1), was considered worthwhile. They were descended from Moroba Gosavi, a seventeenth-century saint famed in Maharashtra for his devotions to Ganesh, that ubiquitous elephant-headed deity so popular in western India. Like a hereditary office or dignity, the senior descendant of the saint was considered a manifestation of the deity; he was *the* Dev of Cincvad (the surname Dev meaning 'god'.) The lineage was wealthy, having rights over many *inām* ('rent-free') villages near Pune, which encompassed some of the best lands in upland Maharashtra. In addition, the Devs coined their own rupees, collected duties from trade in and out of Pune, and received a variety of state allowances. Moreover, the political elite of the Maratha state – starting with the kings, descendants of Shivaji, and continuing under their powerful hereditary ministers, the Peshvas – held the Dev and his kin in great esteem.

With his orientalist and antiquarian inclinations, Captain Moor produced an insightful description of the Devs as they flourished under the Marathas.[2] Several other British travelers followed his lead in the

---

[1] Edward Moor, 'Account of an Hereditary Living Deity, To Whom Devotion is Paid by the Bramins of Poona and its Neighbourhood,' *Asiatick Researches*, 7 (1801), 383. This is the Calcutta edition, which is cited throughout this study. The London edition, under the title *Asiatic Researches* (same volume and date), has Moor's article on pp. 381–95 with slight variations of pagination, punctuation and printing. The London edition of this journal has recently been reprinted.

[2] Moor (1771–1848) authored such forgotten works as *Hindu Pantheon* (1810) and *Suffolk Words and Phrases* (1823) among others. For his life see *Dictionary of National Biography*, XIII, 781–82.

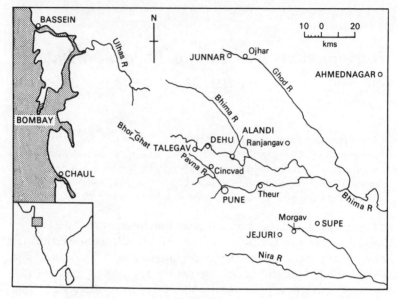

Figure 1. Pune region

first quarter of the nineteenth century. In fact, Cincvad was second only to the nearby Karle Buddhist caves as an *en route* tourist attraction for those who ascended the Bhor *ghāṭ* (pass), from Bombay to catch a glimpse of the last Peshva. The popular travel writer Lord Valentia made his observations on the 'reigning deity' at Cincvad.[3] Maria Graham (later Callcott), world traveler and very much a Regency lady of letters, passed by Cincvad and left her incisive impressions.[4] Her London acquaintance Sir James Mackintosh – jurist, philosopher, savant, friend of Malthus and many other luminaries, rival of Coleridge – similarly found the Devs of sufficient note to deserve a visit.[5] William Henry Sykes, known for his statistical and descriptive accounts of the Deccan

---

[3] *Voyages and Travels to India*, 3 vols. (London, 1809), pp. 151–9. For biographical details on George Annesley Mountnorris, Lord Valentia (1770–1844) see C. E. Buckland, *Dictionary of Indian Biography* (London, 1906), pp. 433–44.

[4] *Journal of a Residence in India* (Edinburgh, 1813), pp. 70–3. For Maria Graham (1785–1842) see *Dictionary of National Biography*, III, 710 (listed under Callcott). She was the author of the enduring children's classic *Little Arthur's History of England* (1835).

[5] See his diary entries quoted in Robert James Mackintosh, *Memoirs of the Life of Sir James Mackintosh*, 2 vols. (London, 1835), I, 275–6, 456–7, 465. For a slightly less sanctifying biography of Mackintosh (1765–1832) see *Dictionary of National Biography*, XII, 617–21.

and later a director and chairman of the East India Company, made inquiries into the lineage's semi-mythological origins.[6]

After a cursory inspection of Cincvad's main temple, with its shrines to the *samādhis* ('death and sanctification') of Moroba Gosavi and subsequent Devs of Cincvad, most visitors sought out the then current Dev of Cincvad for an interview.[7] Somewhat hidden in a maze of streets was the Dev's *vāḍā* (mansion). Moor describes this building as 'an extensive walled enclosure' with 'a fortified gateway.'[8] Maria Graham saw it as simply 'an enormous pile of buildings, without any kind of elegance,' furthermore, it was 'dirty, and every window was crowded with sleek well-fed Bramins, who doubtless take great care of the Deo's revenues.'[9] With its tall, blank, brick walls, the military-like descriptions of the vada are particularly apt. So also is Maria Graham's impression of the vada as a center of administration. The mansion was the Devs' headquarters; from there they administered their extensive landed estates and other revenues. The great vadas of Maharashtra are still today a conspicuous feature of the country's villages and towns. Interesting as a form of domestic architecture, the vada also vividly and concretely expresses the importance of the landed lineage in Maharashtrian society. Although the early nineteenth-century British travelers visited the Dev because he was a religious curiosity, in effect they were encountering a powerful representative of the landholding elite in preconquest Indian society.[10]

All the early British tourists made their visits to Cincvad in the last phase of independent Maratha rule. The two- or three-day journey from Bombay to Pune, followed by a pleasurable stay with the British resident to the Peshva's court, would be rewarded with some exciting tales of a formerly great empire. Since at least 1803 and the Treaty of Bassein the Peshva had been a helpless ally of the British. A dynasty that had rivaled the imperialists for the empire of India then slid into a 15-year decadence, characterized by unceasing political intrigue, that ended in military débâcle in 1817–18.[11] With the conquest of the Marathas,

---

[6] 'An Account of the Origin of the Living God at the Village of Chinchore, near Poona,' *Transactions of the Literary Society of Bombay*, 3 (1823, rpt. 1877), 69–78. For the life of Sykes (1790–1872) see *Dictionary of National Biography*, IX, 258. His observations on Cincvad date between 1817 and 1818.

[7] Graham, *Journal of a Residence*, p. 72 for a description of the temple and its ceremonies.

[8] Moor, 'Hereditary Living Deity', p. 394.

[9] Graham, *Journal of a Residence*, p. 71.

[10] See also the comments of Frank Perlin, 'Of White Whale and Countrymen in the Eighteenth-century Maratha Deccan,' *Journal of Peasant Studies*, 5 (1978), 183.

[11] The most reliable history of the Marathas is Govind Sakharam Sardesai, *New History of the Marathas*, 3 vols. (Bombay, 1946–8), which is written from published Marathi

British control of India was at last undisputed, and their rule entered a new era where imperial administration largely replaced imperial conquest.

Mundane matters of administration, the work of the new government, also replaced the orientalist fascination for the traditional society.[12] Being just one of the many landed lineages now subject to the British, and not one that was a political or military threat, the Devs were left to adapt to the changed circumstances as best they could. At first they were almost ignored, even by the tourists. Slowly, however, the British became very much involved with their privileged subjects at Cincvad, though less for the supposed divinity of the Dev than for his immunity to government's revenue demands. This culminated in the 1850s when the Inam Commission was established to determine the validity of all rent-free tenures. This detailed scrutiny was short-lived. It ended with the demise of the East India Company following the Indian Mutiny (1857–9) when the British became convinced they should not further test the loyalty of what was considered India's 'native aristocracy.'

The Inam Commission, which became the focus of a sustained criticism during and after the Mutiny, was accused of reneging on guarantees of security given at the conquest to the landholders of western India. Thus, or so the arguments went, the British had antagonized and threatened those within Indian society who were most likely to have acceded wholeheartedly to the new security of Company rule. Such critics of the Inam Commission and the East India Company pointed to the views of several past luminaries of the Company's administration, notably Sir John Malcolm, to prove that the Inam Commission's policies were simultaneously destroying the fabric of Indian society and the basis of British conquest in India.[13]

Within the general British self-criticism on the nature of their rule in

documents though without citation. This work does not completely replace the dry elegance of James Grant Duff, *A History of the Mahrattas*, 3 vols. (London, 1826), which has the strength of being written by a contemporary participant in the overthrow of the Peshva. For a competent narrative of British penetration of the Marathas, see R. D. Choksey, *A History of British Diplomacy at the Court of the Peshwas* (Pune, 1951).

[12] For the Bombay Presidency, 1817–60, see Kenneth Ballhatchet, *Social Policy and Social Change in Western India, 1817–30* (London, 1957); Ravinder Kumar, *Western India in the Nineteenth Century* (London, 1972); for certain aspects of the latter part of the pre-Mutiny period see Christine Dobbin, *Urban Leadership in Western India* (London, 1972). Perhaps surprisingly, no satisfactory history of the Bombay Presidency's civil administration has yet been written.

[13] See, for example, Robert Knight, *The Inam Commission Unmasked* (London, 1859). Knight was the crusading editor of the *Bombay Times*. Typical views of Sir John Malcolm can be found in John Malcolm, *Government of India* (London, 1833).

An inamdar lineage in Indian history

India in the aftermath of the Mutiny, a lively pamphlet and newspaper debate arose that either tried to link the Inam Commission with the Mutiny or, conversely, show that there was no connection whatsoever. This 'paper war' ranged wide and furious in both India and England; eventually, debates about the activities of the commission, especially the alleged resumptions of 'freehold' property, reached even Parliament.[14] These after-the-fact controversies, though important as indicative of the changing ideologies of foreign rule in India, do rather less to explain the impact of British pre-Mutiny policies on the *ināmdārs* of the Deccan. While occasionally noting the accusations of the Inam Commission's later critics, this study therefore concentrates on the effect of British alienated revenue policy as it impinged on those people who were the object of East India Company legislation.

The years between the conquest of the Deccan and the end of the Company's administration can be characterized as a time when imperial rule gradually replaced a more traditional and Indian style of government. Throughout this period the British sought to understand the nature and authority of preconquest dynasties. Even in the 1850s the Company's officers grappled with the facts of the old order as they attempted to comprehened the rights and immunities held by lineages such as the Devs. The last generation of Company officers instituted, through the Inam Commission, a social and economic policy that perhaps paradoxically attempted to derive its justification from the traditional Indian state's paramount authority over its landed feudatories.[15] Reversing their initial policy of noninterference in the affairs of landed lineages, the British then sought to control the social, economic and legal lives of India's privileged landholding elite. Very soon, however, the policy of the new rulers became arbitrary and high-handed. When exercising the state's authority within the Indian cultural milieu, the British were under fewer, and different, social and political restraints than their Indian predecessors. But this could not last, and it is no coincidence that the transitional period of British rule in India ended climactically: violent revolt and murmurs of rebellion produced the first political movements directed against the presumptions of the imperialists.

It was a time of great change, and the overriding theme of this book is to see how one Indian lineage fared in the transition from indigenous to

[14] Especially in the 'Reports of the Select Committee...Colonisation and Settlement of India,' *Parliamentary Papers* 1857–8. VII (pt. 1); VII (pt. 2).
[15] Laurence W. Preston, 'The Authority of the State in Western India, 1818–1857,' in *City, Countryside and Society in Maharashtra*, ed. D. W. Attwood, Milton Israel and N. K. Wagle (Toronto, 1987).

foreign rule. To develop this theme the following chapters are organized around the conquest. Part One concerns the Devs under the Marathas; Part Two describes their dealings with the new government. It is not my intention merely to assess the influence of the British on the traditional world. Nor is the Maratha period used simply as an introductory backdrop for the doings of the British. Here I want to explore the issues that most concerned the lineage in the eighteenth and nineteenth centuries, and further, how these issues affected its relations with both the old and new governments.

From such a perspective many of what have been considered the important historical themes of the period are passed over. The politics and wars of the Marathas are only peripherally mentioned. Politics were never far from the affairs and interests of the Devs; but clearly the lineage was not a major actor in the convoluted political history of the Marathas. British land policies, to cite a postconquest example, are perhaps given surprisingly little attention. The Devs had their own system for obtaining the land revenue of their inam villages that was quite independent of British modes of revenue assessment and collection. Consider an even more direct postconquest case. The Bombay–Pune railway, the first through-line in western India, was opened in 1858 during the height of the inam inquiries. This was surely one of the most significant events of the time; what is more, the railway ran right through Cincvad village. Apart from the possibility of negotiations for right of way, a tantalizing topic for which I have no sources, the new technology had little impact on the Devs. Perhaps they could go more quickly to Pune or Bombay to argue with the Inam Commissioners. But notwithstanding the effect of improved communications on state decision making, the issues that were being fought over in Pune and Bombay were not new.

It is my contention that within the lineage there existed certain constant considerations and problems that ordered its social and economic activities. This 'internal history' of the Devs – primarily involving questions of inheritance and status – necessitated strategies to deal with any governing power that sought to exert influence over the lineage's affairs. Of course, political change required adaptation to many differing circumstances. This the Devs successfully did. New solutions and strategies were produced for often old problems. Therefore, I seek to explore the continuities of Indian society that adapt to and transcend periods of political change. Perhaps, too, the present work starts to explore the roots of Indian social conservatism. There can be few better examples of the conservative ethos in India than a brahman, rural-based lineage whose social renown and economic status derived from its religiosity. But such a conservatism is squarely based on what is constant, yet manifoldly adaptive in Indian history: the family and the lineage.

Such essential social structures remain relatively neglected topics in the historiography of early modern and modern India. Recently, one caste has been examined in terms of the bilateral kinship relations of its constituent families with a view to exploring the interrelations between caste and social change.[16] A history of one village in the British period has been written largely from the perspective of its landholding lineages.[17] A landed and political caste grouping, the Rajputs, has been analyzed in a broad kind of evolutionist historicism.[18] Even with the lead of these varied and valuable studies, few if any major works on individual Indian lineages have been produced. Moreover, examples are completely wanting in Indian history where one lineage is used as a vehicle to explore aspects of its contemporary history. Thus, a history of the Devs of Cincvad not only points to the importance of lineage as an institution, but a new perspective on little-examined areas of the Indian past necessarily follows.

Outside of South Asia many useful histories have been written that use one family or one lineage as an instrument for a deeper understanding of a past society. Economic history especially has been concerned with the all pervading institution of the family. Thus, the study of the great landed families of England has emerged from a purely antiquarian interest in manorial records and such to produce economic histories of much worth. Characteristically, these are attended with much diligent and original work in difficult primary sources.[19] In a completely different context, though with many similarities of approach, method and sources, one Mexican family and its estate has been convincingly used to study the transition from colonial rule to independence.[20] Chinese history, to cite an Asian example, has been enriched with a monograph detailing two centuries of one lineage's economic and cultural activities on the frontier of Chinese civilization, in Taiwan in the eighteenth and nineteenth centuries.[21] The present work seeks to contribute to the growing literature that sees family and lineage as fundamental institutions of the past.

[16] Karen Isaksen Leonard, *Social History of an Indian Caste* (Berkeley, 1978).
[17] Tom G. Kessinger, *Vilyatpur, 1848–1968* (Berkeley, 1974).
[18] Richard G. Fox, *Kin, Clan, Raja and Rule* (Berkeley, 1974).
[19] For example, J. M. W. Bean, *The Estates of the Percy Family, 1416–1537* (London, 1958); and Eric Richards, *The Leviathan of Wealth* (London, 1973) for a nineteenth-century case.
[20] Charles H. Harris, *A Mexican Family Empire* (Austin, 1975).
[21] Johanna Menzel Meskill, *A Chinese Pioneer Family* (Princeton, 1977).

This assumption on the worth of lineage history has, however, not been without its critics. Writing of Leonard's *Social History of an Indian Caste*, one reviewer has questioned the fusion of the a-historical 'structural-functionalism' of social anthropology with historical research of high empirical content but far too restricted a focus. In consequence, 'the family study may not be the best place from which to develop an understanding [of the general social process]. While it may indeed provide a valuable testing ground for existing theories of change, it is difficult to see how it can generate new hypotheses.'[22] In short, the social history of India should not, and cannot, be written from methodologically questionable case studies.

Such an argument would be persuasive if Indian social history were not so sorely lacking in detailed studies that use vernacular sources together with the more well-known imperial documentation. As will become clear in the following chapters, the organization and subject matter of much of the neglected archival material in India concerns place and person (whether individual, lineage or caste). The land, revenue, rights and inheritance – these were the things that occupied Indians and their rulers. These can be traced through much of the archival material, especially the vernacular but also to an extent in the English sources, by simply concentrating on selected places and people. Indian social history, unlike European or American history, does not have a corpus of local and case studies on the basic concerns of the people and the state upon which to draw for comparative and analytic purposes.[23] The underlying themes of Indian history are to be found in studying essential units of Indian society; the virgin sources for such an undertaking dictate the use of the case study. We need not further debate whether theory or empiricism comes first in social history. But surely one cannot be had without the other.

One further reservation about imposing any theory of 'social process' on early modern India needs to be voiced. Far too often, theory has been distilled from the observations, sometimes brilliant and sometimes misplaced, of British civil servants. The latter were, in the main, practical men. Often, therefore, observations and theory became mixed with and part of official policy. By relying overly much on imperial sources, Indian social history can become a history of nineteenth-century ideas on how to rule India. The historian who tackles Indian social institutions often lives in the shadows of the British administra-

---

[22] David Washbrook, *Pacific Affairs*, 52 (1979–80), 736.
[23] A fundamental work of social history, such as George C. Homans, *English Villagers of the Thirteenth Century* (Cambridge, Mass., 1941), could not be written for eighteenth- and nineteenth-century India so limited is the work in the relevant primary sources.

tion; however, efforts must be made to understand the indigenous categories of social organization.[24]

I therefore base this study squarely on the belief that Indian society itself recognizes the enduring social significance of the lineage. This has been particularly so in Maratha society. The great political families of Maharashtra were the subject of traditional biographies and histories. These *kaiphiyat*s were further developed after the conquest when the British desired information on their landed feudatories.[25] Apparently, these narrative accounts, which often cover more than a century and are accompanied by genealogies, were compiled from both oral tradition and documentary sources. However done, the British had no difficulty in obtaining the information. The great families of Maharashtra knew their own history. Similarly, in this century certain brahman lineages (or at least those who share the same surname) have produced family histories, *kulvṛttānta*, which are notable for their extreme detail on divisions within the lineage, connections between lines of descent (real or imagined), and the identity and personal details of all known kin.[26] These modern products, meant for the lineages' own self-congratulation, have been seen as deriving from the Maratha historical tradition and also as caste response to contemporary socio-economic threats.[27] While such explanations are not without relevance, uni-lineal descent, the means by which lineages are structured, ensures a strong sense of genealogy. The kulvrttanta form is a reflection of the corporate unity of the kin; for the lineage no other motivation is needed to record its pedigree.

Several important topics in Indian history emerge from exploring the history of the Devs of Cincvad. Perhaps the most prominent, developed

---

[24] Cf. Burton Stein, 'Idiom and Ideology in Early Nineteenth Century South India,' in *Rural India: Land, Power and Society Under British Rule*, ed. Peter Robb (London, 1983), pp. 23–58.

[25] For the Maratha historical tradition see Shankar Gopal Tulpule, *Classical Marathi Literature* (Wiesbaden, 1979), pp. 442–8. For examples of kaiphiyats produced in the early British period see Ganesh Chimnaji Vad, Purshotam Vishram Mawjee and D. B. Parasins, *Kaifiyats, Yadis, & c.* (Pune, 1908); and Khanderav Anandrav Gaykvad, ed., *Karvir sardaramcya kaiphiyati (Kolhapur, 1971).* G. S. Sardesai, *Historical Genealogies* (Bombay, 1957) contains details (in Marathi) of most of the important lineages of Maharashtra plus references to published documentary sources that are often produced in the form of collections from family archives.

[26] Maureen L. P. Patterson, 'Chitpavan Brahman Family Histories: Sources for a Study of Social Structure and Social Change in Maharashtra,' in *Structure and Change in Indian Society*, ed. Milton Singer and Bernard S. Cohn (Chicago, 1968), pp. 397–411. A more scholarly type of family history also exists in contemporary Maharashtra: see, for example, Vasudev Vaman Khare, *Himmatbahaddar Cavhan gharanyaca itihas* (Kolhapur, 1967).

[27] Patterson 'Family Histories', pp. 401–2, 409–10.

in varying ways in the following chapters, is an analysis of alienated – that is, 'rent-free' – tenures. Such Anglicisms are used to gloss the vernacular term inam. Coming into Indian languages from Arabic through Persian, this word can have many varying technical usages. However, the basic concept is straightforward: any right could be held in inam, that is, the state alienated an item of potential revenue to the holder of a right. Land, of course, was the most common right held in inam.[28] A field in a village could be granted to a cultivator or anyone else and thereafter its revenue and produce were not subject to the state's fiscal demands. Generally, such 'village land inams' (as I refer to them) were deducted from the total assessment before the net revenue of a village was forwarded to government. An entire village could also be held in inam (here called a 'whole village inam'). In such instances the inamdar (holder of inam), simply took the place of the state and collected village revenues for his own purposes. Although land was the most coveted rent-free grant, nearly any state revenues could be similarly alienated. The Devs of Cincvad, for example, held in inam the internal transit duties of the region encompassing their villages.

While inam was most usually a way of characterising the conditions upon which a land tenure was held, it was also used to designate a specific type of tenure. In this technical sense inam was a personal grant made through the favor of the state and without any obvious, contractual conditions placed upon the holding of the revenue so alienated. Various village tenures were considered to be subcategories of inam.[29] Perhaps the most notable in the lives of the Devs was *devasthān*, that is, inam granted to a deity (in a juridical sense) and used for the support of a temple and its proprietors. Whatever the technical designation and character of an alienated tenure – and these were subjects of near-constant litigation – the effect of a grant in inam was the same. Village lands or whole villages were held outside the state's central revenue administration and thus largely, though never wholly outside of government control.

[28] Recent scholarship on alienated tenures includes Eric Stokes, 'Privileged Land Tenure in Village India in the Early Nineteenth Century,' in his *The Peasant and the Raj* (Cambridge, 1978), pp. 46–62 concerning village land inams throughout India; for South India see Robert Eric Frykenberg, 'The Silent Settlement in South India, 1793–1853: An Analysis of the Role of Inams in the Rise of the Indian Imperial System,' in *Land Tenure and Peasant in South Asia* (New Delhi, 1977), pp. 37–53; Burton Stein, '"Privileged Landholding": The Concept Stretched to Cover the Case,' in ibid., pp. 67–77. All three articles concentrate almost solely on the technical aspects of inam as recorded in British sources.
[29] H. H. Wilson, *A Glossary of Judicial and Revenue Terms* (1855, rpt. Delhi, 1968), pp. 217–18 for a partial list of village inam tenures.

Other land tenures sharing the same basic features of inam, however, were not enumerated as personal grants. *Jāgīr*, for example, referred to a political tenure.[30] Generally, *jāgīrdār*s held entire districts rent free. They became the true landed feudatories of the Maratha state, in the sense that their continued existence depended upon their active political support of the existing state order. After the conquest many jagirdars assumed a type of internal sovereignty and became the minor princely rulers of imperial India. *Saranjām*, to cite another example, was a purely military allowance where a village was granted to an officer supposedly only on the basis of immediate and limited need.[31] Such political and military assignments of land will be only briefly noted in the following chapters. A study of the Devs of Cincvad will show how artificial such technical distinctions sometimes were. In many ways, the Devs assumed a sovereignty over their estates more characteristic of holders of jagir than of other ordinary inamdars.

In fact, this book shows that the Devs were, in their own particular ways, one of the leading feudatory families of preconquest Maharashtra. With some 22 whole villages held in inam, in addition to numerous other lands and shares, the Devs were perforce a significant economic institution in their own right. But beyond the mere facts of their income (probably in excess of Rs. 50,000 in any year), we must also consider the close and enduring relationship the Devs had with the leading powers of the Maratha state. Moreover, the religious aspect of the lineage and its place in Maratha society necessarily adds a special dimension to the status of the Cincvad Devs. Thus, apart from the facts and figures that may be adduced to place the Devs in their contemporary society, eventually we must fall back on some subjective description of their place in the history and society of Maharashtra. The Devs were, I believe, an important and powerful lineage. But they could never be in the first rank of state feudatories. The very factors that gave the lineage some long-term stability in Maratha society – religion, and, in the broadest sense, the lineage as a cultural symbol – precluded the Devs from assuming a place in the ranks of the political elite of Maharashtra. The exercise of pure power – controlling the lives of millions, leading armies in the often militaristic Maratha state, or guiding an Indian state in the face of the incursions of the British imperialists – likely could never have been real possibilities for the Devs. Instead, the lineage occupied a somewhat paradoxical status: a local landed power dealing in village affairs, but, at the same time, able to function in the highest corridors of power of the Maratha state. In some way this apparent

---

[30] Ibid., p. 224.   [31] Ibid., p. 465.

paradox sets the type of history that must be written about the Devs. The following chapters will attempt to meld the local affairs of lineage and village with the perspective of state dealings with its privileged subjects.

While the Devs were recipients of a fairly broad sample of the more prominent alienated tenures, particularly those granted from personal or religious favor, here the effects issuing from the possession of this type of revenue are emphasized, not the mere fact of the tenures. I have not, therefore, attempted a comprehensive catalog of all the technical designations of inam and such. Inam is here used as a vehicle for the study of the lineage. Some problems associated with this approach soon become manifest. Individual Devs can easily become shadows, 'landlords under seige, tied to the offices of their lawyers and accountants.'[32] My use of revenue documentation makes this inevitable; the historian stands or falls upon his sources. But beyond such a plea, we must focus upon the cultural context about which this history is being written. The affairs of the lineage, especially in the way it presented a mask of solidarity to the world, dominated the lives of all its members. Sometimes, when lineage solidarity was sorely tested (as will be fully described here), an individual Dev emerges as almost a complete and living personality. But such is exceptional; and for the lineage, such was undesirable in the extreme. More usually, the sources used in this study present the lineage in the way it wanted to be seen: as a corporate entity.

The acquisition and preservation of rent-free lands were critical concerns for the historic lineages of Maharashtra. I believe, therefore, that my focus on the Devs' inams is no accident of the extant sources. Moreover, the importance of alienated tenures in the social and economic history of western India can fairly be assessed through a cursory examination of the extent of rent-free lands and villages in the preconquest society.[33] Table 1 is a survey from published sources of the number of alienated villages in the collectorates of the Deccan compiled soon after the conquest. The figures vary between the sources used because it is not evident that identical administrative units have been enumerated. Furthermore, this table combines all types of alienated tenures, making no distinction, for example, between personal and political holdings. An accurate accounting of rent-free villages in the Deccan could perhaps be obtained from further archival research in both pre- and postconquest sources. Nevertheless, it is apparent, even from such restricted evidence, that alienated villages were major facts in the revenue history of Maharashtra. Upwards of 20 percent of villages in

---

[32] This phrase belongs to Professor Milton Israel, University of Toronto.
[33] Stokes, 'Privileged Land Tenure,' pp. 51–3 considers the problem of the extent of inam in Bombay.

Table 1. *Extent of alienated villages in the Deccan*

| Collectorates | Sources | Nos. of villages | | | Alienated % of total |
		Government	Alienated	Total	
Pune	DC 1822[a]	885.5	317.5	1203	26.4
	Sykes[b]	899.5	268.5	1168	23.0
(including Solapur)	Sykes	1473.5	423.5	1897	22.3
Ahmednagar	DC 1822	1963.5	683.5	2647	25.8
	Sykes	1878.5	586.5	2465	23.8
Khandesh	DC 1822	2249.0	540.0	2789	19.4
	Sykes	2697.5	314.5	3012	10.4
Southern Maratha	DC 1822	2544.0	711.0	3255	28.0
country	Sykes	2279.0	367.0	2646	16.1
Subtotals	DC 1822	7641.5	2252.0	9893.5	22.8
(excluding Satara)	Sykes	9802.0	2115.0	11917	17.7
	Chaplin[c]	7229.0	2252.0	9481	23.8
Average	DC 1822				24.9
	Sykes				18.2
Satara	DC 1822	1211.0	494.0	1705	29.0
	Sykes n/a				
Totals	DC 1822	8852.5	2746.0	11598.5	23.7

Sources: [a]D[eccan] C[ommission] collectors' reports to W. Chaplin, Commissioner in the Deccan, various dates, accompaniments to Chaplin's report to Government, 20 August 1822 in *Selections of Papers from the Records at the East-India House*, 4 vols. (London, 1820–6), IV, 453–864.
[b]W. H. Sykes, 'Special Report on the Statistics of the Four Collectorates of Dukhun,' *British Association for the Advancement of Science, Report*, 6 (1838), 267–9.
[c]Independent calculation of Chaplin in report of 20 August 1822.

the Deccan were held under some form of rent-free tenure. In Pune district, to consider the Devs' home territory, perhaps one-quarter of the villages were not subject to government's revenue demands. By studying an inam holding lineage this study therefore seeks to examine, from one particular perspective, an important factor in the complexities of Indian rural history.

The primary sources for a study of inam, and thus for the Devs, are housed in the Pune Archives, an extraordinary collection of approximately 40,000,000 Marathi documents written in the cursive *moḍī* script. Substantial numbers of nineteenth-century English files that have direct reference to the vernacular documents are also found in the archives.[34]

[34] See G. S. Sardesai, *Hand Book to the Records in the Alienation Office Poona* (Bombay, 1933) being a summary of the superior 'Note on the Alienation office, Poona, compiled

These are perhaps the most underused sources for all aspects of Indian history from the early seventeenth to mid-nineteenth centuries. Social and economic history from these documents is almost wholly wanting.

The Marathi documents in Pune are more than just a passive repository of data for lineages such as the Devs. The very existence and organization of the Pune Archives can largely be ascribed to British concern for alienated tenures.[35] The Inam Commission came into being because of the unparalleled richness of the archival sources either inherited from the Peshva's government or rescued (the critics of the commission said stolen) from the countryside.[36] The documents in turn molded the Inam Commission's policies and decisions, which thereupon took on a lustre of authoritativeness and arrogance not seen elsewhere in British revenue settlements in India.

The presence of such a rich archival source for inam is central to the history of the Devs in both the Maratha and British periods. The documents were the lineage's charter for rights that could only be protected if proved to exist. In the Maratha period the physical written word confirmed all social and economic relations, especially between state and privileged subject. Chapter 1 examines this issue by document-ing the process by which Cincvad's inam was acquired. For the British the proofs of tenure that could be derived from the records of the Maratha state became critical. Because of the Pune Archives (often inaccurately called the Peshva *daphtar* (archive)), the Inam Commission would seek a degree of factual evidence that ironically clogged its administration with too many documents. But here were the facts of the old order that had to be understood. How the documents were interpreted was vital to both the British and the inamdar lineages. The Devs and the Inam Commission alike put ultimate faith in the records. Therefore, in the second part of this study the Devs' internal history is often set in the context of debates between government and claimant over the meaning of the archival sources for inam.

The Devs' history is also a story of villages, their landed estate as it

for the Committee appointed by Government Resolution No. 6099, dated the 27th July 1905,' by A. C. Logan, Acting Commissioner Central Division, printed pamphlet, 48pp. in PA: Printed Index, vol. 1, pp. 165–212.

[35] See 'Correspondence exhibiting the Nature and Use of the Poona Duftur, and Measures adopted for its Preservation and Arrangement since the Introduction of British Rule,' *Selections from the Records of the Bombay Government*, n.s. 30 (Bombay, 1856). A considerable amount of material exists in the Pune Archives on the creation of the collection. This fascinating story deserves a separate study.

[36] See 'Correspondence regarding the Concealment by the Hereditary Officers and Others of the Revenue Records of the Former Government and the remedial measures in progress,' *Selections from the Records of the Bombay Government*, n.s. 29 (Bombay, 1856).

were, and as such the present work necessarily discusses aspects of
Indian rural history. Yet, some important topics in this context, in which
the lineage undoubtably had a significant influence, are not given much
prominence. Agriculture, village administration, rural social history and
such have been introduced only briefly in Chapter 2 and some indication
given of the sources for further research. In this study the lineage is
primarily seen operating in the rural setting in an institutional framework. The Devs, through their control of inam and certain popular
Ganesh temples, created the Cincvad Samsthan, an autonomous entity
that in its own sphere was almost a parallel state in the villages around
Pune.[37] Revenue rights over widespread and often noncontiguous lands
linked villages in one set of interconnections not much noticed in
modern scholarship.[38] From their landed base the lineage extended its
influence over the countryside through means such as the imposition of
transit duties on trade. Chapter 5 examines the role the Devs played in
the commerce of their domains. In summary, the Devs had an important
part in the organization of rural Maharashtra, a role as vital in the
British period as it was under the Peshvas, and this theme underlies
much of this study.

Because the Devs' villages were located in a restricted area, not many
being outside modern Pune district, I necessarily write from a regional
and subregional (or local) perspective. Regional studies, for example of
a British district administration, are not new to Indian history.[39] In the
general sense, region is here equated with the British revenue district,
which corresponds tolerably well to the Maratha *prānt*. Subregions may
be considered as being the district's constituent *tālukā*s, often called
*tarph*s in the Maratha period. Chapter 1, when concentrating on
Cincvad's inam heartland in Haveli taluka, is in effect describing a
subregion. However, I make no attempt to confine the Devs to any
preconceived notion of region based either on administrative or physical
boundaries. At any particular time in the past a region's boundaries are,

[37] The word Samsthan is not amenable to a simple translation. The standard
Marathi – English dictionary, a valuable contemporary source for the early
nineteenth-century language, defines Samsthan as either a royal capital or a place
favored by or dedicated to a deity; see J. T. Molesworth, *A Dictionary, Marathi and
English* (1857 rpt. Pune, 1975), p. 836.
 The religious connotation of Samsthan is appropriate to Cincvad village. In a sense
too, Cincvad was a capital, though for a distinctive type of religious royalty. However,
in the case of Cincvad, Samsthan had wider connotations than just one place. It
encompassed all the Devs' inam and hence became a way of describing the institutional
aspect of the lineage. Hence, I prefer to leave the word untranslated or to refer
obliquely to the Cincvad Samsthan as the 'Devs' domain.'
[38] Perlin, 'Of White Whale and Countrymen,' pp. 172–237 is perhaps an exception.
[39] For example, Robert Eric Frykenberg, *Guntur District, 1788–1848* (Oxford, 1965).

of course, important. But regions are in constant flux, being defined by the specific varieties of human activity we choose to study.[40]

For the Devs the Pune region (perhaps it might even be called the Cincvad region) was simply the place where their temples and inams were located. It was their theater of operations in which the lineage's holdings were acquired and expanded. Inam acquisition in this regional context was therefore a spatial process. The growth of the Devs' revenue rights and the formation of the Cincvad Samsthan can be well illustrated by certain simple cartographic techniques that are employed in Chapter 1.

As the Devs operated in and expanded through the Pune region, the lineage helped to define the area's rather distinctive character. Matters of religion is one very obvious example. Starting with the presence of locally popular Ganesh sacred sites that ring Pune city, the Devs ordered their Samsthan on a type of religious geography that they in turn promoted. Today, a visit to all eight Ganesh villages. the *aṣṭavināyak*, in or near Pune district, is a popular pilgrimage. In many ways the astavinayak help to define the regional identity of Pune, and in this the Devs have had an important role.[41] Ultimately, the Devs' renown, wealth, all their consequent activities in Maratha society start with Ganesh and the lineage's religious associations. Hence, the following chapters do describe the social and economic manifestations of one part of the religious life of Maharashtra. In Chapter 2 some specific consideration is given to the lineage's religious activities in the preconquest society. Chapter 4 concentrates on the postconquest transformation of the Dev's pilgrimage to Morgav village, one of the premier events in his ritual calendar. Much on the religious life of the lineage remains to be explored, especially the part the Devs played in the day-to-day social life of Pune region. What, for example, was the popular perception of the Dev of Cincvad and his supposed divinity?

[40] Carl O. Sauer, the noted American historical geographer, has provided the best description of the part the regional concept can play in historical studies. What he calls 'economic areas' and 'culture areas,' 'may experience shifts of centers, peripheries, and changes of structure. They have the quality of gaining or losing territory and often of mobility of their centers of dominance. They are fields of energy, within which changes in dynamism may show characteristic directional shifts.' See 'Foreword to Historical Geography,' in *Land and Life*, ed. John Leighly (Berkeley, 1963), p. 364.

[41] See Laurence W. Preston, 'Subregional Religious Centres in the History of Maharashtra: The Sites Sacred to Ganesh,' in *Images of Maharashtra*, ed. N. K. Wagle (London 1980), pp. 102–28. Bus tours are currently organized by private operators in Pune, and even by the Maharashtra State Tourist Office, which has published a handsome and informative booklet on the subject (in Marathi), *Astavinayak* (Bombay, n.d.). A type of popular devotional literature, available in bazaar stalls specializing in such works, has also arisen on the eight Ganesh centers, see *Shriastavinayak stotra va mahatmya* (Bombay, n.d.).

How did this affect relations with the residents and tenants of Cincvad's inam villages? What part did the lineage play in local festivals and ritual occasions? The connections Cincvad may have had with nearby religious centers, such as Dehu and Alandi, also located within the Pune region, are certainly worth investigation. The historical sources so far examined give only slight hints about these and many other important religious issues.

The Pune region is also of particular note because of Pune city, the capital of the Maratha state of the Peshvas and the only significant urban concentration in the preconquest society. Since the early eighteenth century the city has been the cultural capital of Maharashtra. After the conquest, when the city ceased to be a political capital, Pune continued to have a distinctive place in the life of Maharashtra. The city's cultural identity engendered a brand of right-wing nationalist politics that would often frustrate the imperialists. For the Raj, Pune was a source of sedition and treachery. B. G. ('Lokmanya') Tilak's use of Ganesh in his political strategies speaks strongly of the special character of the city and its regional hinterland.[42] Although it appears that the Devs were not especially active in promoting Tilak's use of the annual Pune Ganesh festival for political ends, nevertheless it is clear that the Lokmanya utilized cultural factors preexisting in Pune district. The present study will show that the Devs had, throughout the seventeenth, eighteenth and nineteenth centuries, a continuing close contact with Pune city and all the social, economic and political activities of that city.

Since the early Maratha period the Pune region has been perhaps the foremost economic area of upland Maharashtra. Pune city's prominence made it an important market, which the Devs' villages in part served. The land around the city, particularly to the north-west, is rich, being well watered by several rivers and a monsoon usually more substantial than in districts to the east. Today, the pull of Pune, with its good road and rail connections with Bombay, has transformed the region into one of India's fastest growing and most modern industrial areas. Cincvad and many of the Devs' villages have been incorporated into a separate local government, the Pimpri-Cincvad Municipal Corporation, the industrial twin to Pune. Many factories have been erected on the Devs' inam, a development that causes the lineage (now in the guise of a temple trust) some difficulty with the legal definition of its land tenures. The Devs' interest in and influence on the growth of this

---

[42] Richard I. Cashman, *The Myth of the Lokamanya* (Berkeley, 1975), pp. 75–97. Tilak's promotion of Ganesh caturthi, now the great annual festival in Pune, has been documented with details on its performance in various places year by year in J. S. Karandikar, *Shriganesotsavaci sath varse* (Pune, 1953).

and many other modern expressions of the Pune region can be traced to the historic structures of the Cincvad Samsthan.

Before concluding this introduction, some mention should be made of two assumptions and one intention operating in this history of the Dev lineage. Firstly, by design, I have not written a caste history like several recent Indian social histories. These appear to be most useful when studying small groups that have developed some internal organization, whether formal and institutional or informal kinship networks, which can be applied to some particular social, economic or political activity.[43] Some evidence suggests that the Devs were active in *deśastha* (upland) brahman affairs, particularly regarding questions of pollution, excommunication, expiation and caste readmission.[44] Undoubtably, kinship connections between lineages were also important. Arranging advantageous marriages created one more source of influence as well as a further set of obligations. However, the historical sources for these inter-lineage relations are at present somewhat limited. For a historical study the deshasthas were far too dispersed throughout the society of upland Maharashtra to allow a sustained analysis of their institutional and kinship organization.

In fact, perhaps it can be said that, with certain important restrictions, the deshastha brahmans are really only a collection of exogamous lineages that are together endogamous. When adopting this perspective, caste is seldom discussed in this study because, although important in itself and for many ritual reasons, it was not a major activating factor in the Devs' affairs. It had no part in the internal history of the lineage except in the sense that brahman lineages had certain customary modes of inheritance that were usually, though not invariably, followed. Caste rules, when so defined, were the context from which other considerations emerged. Of course, the Devs' ritual superiority, their religious renown, and hence their wealth, derived in part from their elite brahman status. But such were obvious facts to the Devs' contemporaries, something well understood but little mentioned,[45] and I likewise assume at the outset the elevated social position of the Devs.

[43] For example, Frank F. Conlon, *A Caste in a Changing World* (Berkeley, 1977).

[44] For example, in the case of Shripat Sesadri Parlikar who in 1844 was denied reentry into the caste after having associated with missionaries in Bombay. This was something of a *cause célèbre* for the progressives in Maratha society. Documents referring incidentally to the Devs' part in this case have been printed in Rajaram Vinayak Oturkar, *Peshavekalin samajik va arthik patravyavahar* (Pune, 1950), pp. 141–50.

[45] By way of support for this statement, among hundreds of documents I have examined that refer to the Devs, almost none refer to the lineage's caste. The recipient of a document was usually carefully identified by name and place of residence, and also, on occasion, by technical designations such as *gotra*. Caste was just too obvious to mention.

The first of my two basic assumptions in this work concerns the use of chronology when writing lineage history. A long time-scale is a necessity. One could conceive of examining the Devs at one period, and thus developing a cross-section that would in some way be a portrait of the times as seen by one lineage. But such a cross-section would not be able to discern the dynamics within the lineage that issued from problems of inheritance and such. I have, therefore, ranged quite freely over 200 years of history. Although the narrative in the following chapter follows a generally straightforward chronology – I start at the beginning – my intent has not been to write a chronicle of the Devs. The history of a lineage must rather be thought of in terms of generations: two centuries of Dev history amount to only eight or nine generations in descent from the saint Moroba Gosavi. Only when a group of kin with common descent reach this genealogical depth does the internal structure of a complex lineage become clear.

Lastly, I make no claim to describe a 'typical', Indian family or lineage. Certain problems and developments in the Devs' history are here considered in the context of Indian legal theory. These issues would bear comparison with other cases in Maharashtra and throughout India. At times social anthropology has provided valuable tools for analysis. Their use suggests the presence of sociological themes within India that place this one culture in a world perspective. Nevertheless, the Devs were probably not truly representative of even their elite peers. This assumption, of course, needs to be probed and qualified by further research. But for the present, like Captain Moor and his fellow tourists journeying to Cincvad, I have searched out this one family because their history is in many ways extraordinary.

PART ONE
The inamdar under the Marathas

1

The acquisition of inam

Surveying the administration of the countryside, William H. Tone, perhaps the first European to be a serious observer of the Maratha polity, noted almost in exasperation how 'everything respecting this extraordinary people becomes an object of curiosity'; in particular, 'their principles of government excite our attention, as they discover a mode of thinking and acting totally different from the regular system of European policy. The very local arrangements of empire are peculiar, the territory of the different chiefs being blended and interspersed with each other.'[1] The Peshva and his political feudatories had detached territories all over the subcontinent. At the local level, a subdistrict or even a single village would be shared between different 'chiefs'; even the sometime archrivals, the Nizam of Hyderabad and the Peshva, held villages in common. For 'a disposition so chequered' Tone could find little explanation, not even to discover whether it was 'the effect of policy or accident.'[2] Although Tone confused several levels of Maratha political and economic administration, from that of imperial conquest down to very local revenue collections, his remarks strike a responsive chord in the historian attempting to understand the complexities of the Maratha government. Moreover, the situation was apparently even more chaotic than even Tone imagined. Within individual villages, for example, there existed a similar pattern of overlapping and shared control of land and revenue.

Inam was one factor creating this patchwork of revenue rights in rural Maharashtra. While not in itself supporting the great independent feudatories of the Maratha state (who ruled whole districts as jagir), the Maratha concept of inam was not confined to the arena of village fields, their produce and revenue. Grants of fields were often converted into inams that encompassed the net revenue of a village. From one village inam rights could be gained in neighbouring lands and villages. Behind the very real complexities of the Maratha system of revenue adminis-

---

[1] William Henry Tone, *A Letter to an Officer on the Madras Establishment: Being an Attempt to Illustrate Some Particular Institutions of the Maratta People...* (1796, rpt. London, 1799), pp. 12–13.
[2] Ibid.

tration, there can thus be discerned a historical process of inam acquisition.

This was preeminently a spatial process. As an inamdar lineage acquired successive grants of lands and villages in one locality, creating its own domain of activity, its sway gradually expanded over the countryside. For the Devs of Cincvad, a century of inam acquisition created the Cincvad Samsthan, a dispersed collection of villages around Pune but nonetheless a recognizable landed entity with a definite spatial structure. This chapter therefore describes the stages by which the Devs expanded their landed influence in Pune district. Particular and detailed attention is given to the Samsthan's villages in north-west Haveli taluka (tarph of the Maratha period) surrounding Cincvad village. This subregion was the lineage's inam heartland.

The apparent chaos of revenue rights within villages and over villages, creating many different levels of political control, was in fact a well-regulated phenomenon. The Maratha state knew with great precision who held what and where. All transactions and grants were recorded, filed away, periodically examined, renewed, and reentered in the archives. Quite simply, it was the state's revenue being sacrificed and government wanted to know why. For the inamdar lineages, their *sanad*s, the title deeds to their inam, were the proof of the privileged status accorded by the state. These were papers that had to be guarded. When combined with the records of the inamdars' own administration of their villages, these sanads (and every other bit of correspondence, official or otherwise) form the family papers so prevalent in the historiography of Maharashtra.[3]

The inamdar's title deeds were the visible proof of his almost contractual relationship with the state. As such, when the inamdar was favored with further grants of fields and villages, this contract was continually being redefined. For the Devs of Cincvad, their inam was

---

[3] Many of these collections have been deposited in the Bharat Itihas Samshodhak Mandal, Pune. Notices of these family daphtars have appeared irregularly in the *Proceedings, Indian History Congress* (mostly reports by G. H. Khare). The Mandal has also published selections of these papers, which have been utilized throughout this study. Early in this century certain early Marathi and Persian documents from Cincvad were deposited in the Mandal, and selections have been published by Datto Vaman Potdar, 'Moraya Dev samsthan Cincvad sambandhi kahi junat assal kagad,' *Bharat Itihas Samshodhak Mandal Quarterly*, 2 (June 1922), 52–69. In addition, certain miscellaneous documents from this collection have appeared in the Mandal's various publications. However, I have not attempted to comprehensively use this valuable but chaotic manuscript source in this study. The collection appears to be generally early documents, and also contains an emphasis on the Samsthan's internal administration. In passing, it should be remarked that a comprehensive listing of all such collections of family papers held in institutions such as the Mandal, with some description of contents, is urgently needed.

held under the cumulative authority of all rights the state had previously granted. After analyzing the formation of the Cincvad Samsthan, this chapter thus describes the Devs' formal relations with the successive political overlords to which the lineage deferred. In part this is seen in the context of the elaborate state bureaucracy needed to administer inam. In this strictly defined sphere the Devs played out their own landed interests.

I. The places of the saint

A history of the Devs of Cincvad must begin with the life of Moroba Gosavi, saint of Cincvad and progenitor of the Dev lineage.[4] (For an abbreviated genealogy of the Devs see Figure 2.[5]) This *bhakta* ('devotee' of Ganesh) who died *circa* 1655, belongs to an era of Maratha history where historical fact merges with hagiography.[6] Moroba was a con-

---

[4] Often called Moraya, perhaps a more formal rendering of his name, which is derived from Moreshvar (one of the names of Ganesh and particularly that of the deity of Morgav after which Moroba was apparently named). The earliest documents always use the more familiar Moroba, and I have used this form throughout the book. The Devs' family name was originally Shaligram, being desastha brahmans, their gotra is *harit*, their *sutra* ('line of descent') *ashvalayana*, see sanad of 21 October 1694 from Rajaram re Cikhli village in Ganesh Chimnaji Vad, Purshotam Vishtram Mawjee and D. B. Parasnis, *Sanads & Letters* (Pune, 1913), p. 174.

[5] Based on manuscript genealogies to *circa* 1860 in PA: IC rumal 11 (Marathi/modi) and PA: xIV; 28/322, fol. 195 (English). A printed genealogy to *circa* 1900 is in PA: Printed Index, vol. 11, p. 366 foldout. The abbreviated genealogy given here records only the names of those Devs mentioned in this study.

[6] The date of Moroba's death is inferred from an inscription recording the building (27 November 1659–13 June 1659) of the temple in Cincvad dedicated to his samadhi, see D. V. Potdar, 'Cincvad-Moraya Gosavi-devalay kadhi bandhale?,' *Bharat Itihas Samshodhak Mandal Quarterly*, 21, 3 (January 1941) 78–9. A document of 6 May 1655, confirming Moroba's inams, appears to be the last available contemporary reference to the saint: *Selections from the Peshwa Daftar*, xxxi, 19–20. While this document may, in fact, be a confirmation following Moroba's death, the presence of later documents still referring to the saint, when he was surely dead, make this assumption problematic. Nineteenth-century tradition had Moroba living for 150 years: Ganesh Chimnaji Vad, Purshotam Vishram Mawjee and D. B. Parasnis, *Kaifiyats, Yadis & c.* (Pune, 1908), p. 218. Similarly, present tradition has him living nearly 200 years from the thirteenth to fifteenth centuries. Ramcandra Cintaman Dhere, *Mangalmurti Moraya* (Bombay, 1958), p. 16 also concludes that Moroba died *circa* 1655. Dhere's small and popular book is perhaps the best general study of Cincvad containing many logical conclusions based on slight evidence.

The seventeenth-century poets and bhakta saints of Maharashtra have not been well served in modern secondary scholarship. The nationalist view of Ranade and others had them as sort of the Indian equivalent of the Protestant Reformation reacting against foreign, Muslim rule, see M. G. Ranade, *Rise of Maratha Power* (Bombay, 1900), pp. 143–72. Recently, these religious personalities have often been seen as a kind of supra-caste and sometimes nationalist movement, see for example Ravinder Kumar, *Western India in the Nineteenth Century* (London, 1968), pp. 6–12. These related interpretations seem to me to be somewhat exaggerated. A study of the social history of

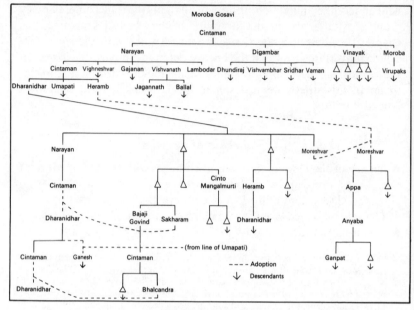

Figure 2. The Dev lineage

temporary of Tukaram and Ramdas, and like his more illustrious rivals, the saint's life and poetry have become objects of devotion for his followers.[7] Although a reasonable number of contemporary documents mention Moroba, these matter-of-fact references do not always sit happily with traditions that have descended over three centuries. A conceptual gap exists between the hagiography of Moroba and the historical record. The former should not be discounted as a historical

seventeenth-century Maharashtra, combining the plentiful documentary sources already published with an analysis of the structures behind the poetry and biographies of these saints, is much needed.

[7] See *Cincvadksetrastha Shri Moraya Gosavi caritra* (Cincvad, n.d.). Although produced in an antique fashion, this appears to be a modern work. For the devotional poetry of Moroba and his immediate descendants, see *Sadguru Shri Moraya Gosavi, Shri Cintamani Maharaj, Shri Narayan Maharaj, Shri Dharanidhar Maharaj yamcya padamca gatha* (Cincvad, 1977). The published versions of this poetry apparently do not date before 1896; these works were brought to light by one Krsnaji Babaji Subhedar (who also contributed a verse to the most recent edition), see Shankar Ganesh Date, *Marathi grantha suci* (Pune, 1943), I, 585, 612. The authenticity of these poetical works cannot be verified; at best, even if seventeenth-century works, they are minor verses.

The popular traditions on Moroba are recorded in W. H. Sykes, "An Account of the Origin of the Living God at the Village of Chinchore, near Poona," *Transactions of the Literary Society of Bombay*, 3 (1823, rpt. 1877), 69–72; and Dhere, *Mangalmurti Moraya*, pp. 9–16.

source. A type of structure exists in the biographies of the saints, particularly in terms of relations with persons of ritual or political authority, which could be very illustrative for the social history of seventeenth-century Maharashtra. Here, however, the narrow historical view is taken. Within the documentary sources on Moroba can be found the seeds of the Cincvad Samsthan.

In one fundamental way Moroba's biographies are critical for the subsequent development of the Samsthan. The places of the saint and the sacred Ganesh sites were the anchors around which the Devs' inam was acquired. Not until the late Maratha period did the Devs' interest reach far outside an area circumscribed by two places essential to all versions of the saint's life. The first was Morgav, to the south-east of Pune, the most ancient site of the Ganesh cult in the Pune region.[8] The other, Cincvad village itself, was Moroba's place, supposedly his own creation, and a village that represented the new expression of Ganesh devotion in the Pune region.

At Morgav Moroba underwent his rigorous devotions to Ganesh. There, too, he received his enlightenment. His sainthood was affirmed by the appearance of a *svayambhū* ('self-existent or created') image of Ganesh discovered while Moroba was taking a ritual bath. The stone, the *mangalmūrti*, became the symbol of the Dev lineage and the proof of their intimate association with the deity.[9] While Moroba was closely associated with Morgav, it was not really his place. The legends refer to the established presiding brahmans of the temple who were foolish enough not to immediately recognize Moroba's saintliness. Published documents too clearly delineate an entrenched brahmanical hierarchy in Morgav during and after Moroba's time.[10] In fact, Moroba was only a pious pilgrim visiting Morgav in the course of his austerities. His parents had apparently settled in a village north-west of Pune after

---

[8] For the background to Morgav and the Ganesh cult in the Pune region see Laurence W. Preston, "Subregional Religious Centres in the History of Maharashtra: The Sites Sacred to Ganesh," in *Images of Maharashtra*, ed. N. K. Wagle (London, 1980), pp. 104–10, 116.

[9] This mangalmurti image was established in a temple within the Devs' vada, distinct from the main Cincvad temple dedicated to Moroba's samadhi. In Maratha times the mangalmurti apparently accompanied the Dev of Cincvad wherever he went. The family temple dates, from inscriptional evidence, to 1675/6, see D. V. Potdar, 'Cincvad yethil don shilalekh,' in *Shiva-caritra-sahitya*, vol. 5, pp. 61–2 (in *Bharat Itihas Samshodhak Mandal Quarterly*, 18, 4 (April 1938)).

[10] See documents dated 1610–1711, re lineage of Krsnabhat, in Vishvanath Kashinath Rajvade, *Shivakalin gharani* (Pune, 1915), pp. 341–61; documents of 1631–1776, re lineage of Moreshvar Gosavi (definitely not Moroba), in *Shiva-caritra-sahitya*, 3 (Pune, 1930), pp. 509–75; see also documents of 1615–1711, in *Shiva-caritra-sahitya* 2 (Pune, 1930), pp. 176–90.

migrating to the area from the Marathi-speaking region of northern Karnataka. Like a *sanyāsin* (recluse), Moroba is said to have established himself in the unsettled forest that became the future Cincvad village, and from there he undertook his frequent pilgrimages to Morgav to act out his devotions.

In the nineteenth century the Devs recorded, at the behest of the British, a kaiphiyat, that put the story in the simplest possible terms:

Cincvad was a forest. Tamarind (*cinc*) and fig (*vaḍ*) trees were there. There [Moroba] served Ganpati; and as the fourth [of the bright and dark halves of the lunar month] is the day of Ganpati, and as on these days Ganpati is in Morgav, [Moroba] went there for a glimpse [of the deity and] always performed the *pujā* [of the image]. Continuing in this way for many years, one day [when] the Morgav Ganpati was propitiated, one moment with Ganpati was given to the *gosāvī*; and Ganpati said: 'I am with you; from today you are not to come for the fourth of each month in Morgav. You should come once a year on the fourth of the bright half of Bhadrapad.'[11]

The yearly visit to Morgav for the most sacred Ganesh festival day represented the continuing deference the Devs paid to Morgav. This Morgav pilgrimage is further described in Chapter 4.

But Moroba had in effect established his own sacred site. Cincvad was the home of the mangalmurti, and later, a similar svayambhu Ganesh image miraculously appeared on the site of Moroba's samadhi (that is, his death). This sign of the deity's favor continued upon the deaths of the saint's lineal descendants, forming subshrines to the main Cincvad temple. Therefore, like all the sacred Ganesh sites in the Pune region, Cincvad also possessed the requisite self-created images, which in the Ganesh cult must be the actual, physical objects of devotion. However, at Cincvad the bhakta transferred his devotions to the person of saint, and subsequently to his eldest descendants. The Dev of Cincvad personified, in a sense, a new Morgav. It was an ambiguous situation. Because Cincvad had all the trappings of the sacred Ganesh centers but without their supposed antiquity, the Devs could only base their claim to inam on the reputation of the saint and ultimately his connection with the Morgav Ganesh.

Although the legends, as briefly related in the above-quoted kaiphiyat, have Cincvad's sanctity emerging fully formed from the words of Ganesh, clearly this must symbolize a process taking several decades. The earliest available document mentioning Moroba apparently does not even refer to Cincvad. Instead, Moroba was granted land in Cincoli village, where he was then (in 1618) resident.[12] (For the location of

---

[11] Vad, *Kaifiyats,* pp. 217–18.
[12] Sanad of 30 September 1618 in Potdar, "Moraya Dev," pp. 55–6.

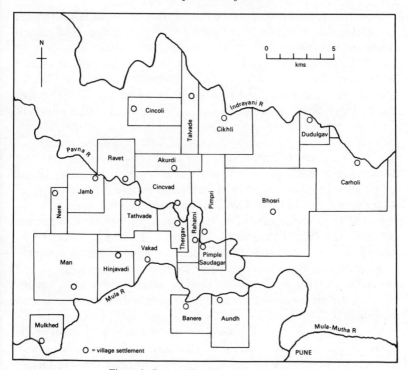

Figure 3. Devs' villages in north-west Haveli

Cincoli and other villages in north-west Haveli see Figure 3.[13]) This document raises several, as yet unanswerable, questions on the origin of Cincvad village.

Perhaps Moroba did in fact live in Cincoli, not Cincvad, and this reference predates the foundation of the latter village. In support of this literal interpretation of the document, it should be noted that the Devs did later possess a land grant in Cincoli, which apparently was the lineal descendant of this 1618 inam. Or, without referring to the original source, it might be supposed that the editor of this published document misread Cincoli for Cincvad, quite a possible error when interpreting seventeenth-century modi. It seems unlikely that D. V. Potdar, surely one of the best modi scholars, would not have been alive to the importance of this distinction.

[13] Based on 1:126,720 topographic maps reduced 25% with village areas taken from *Gazetteer of Bombay State*, Poona District (Bombay, 1954). While the area of the villages is to scale and their general shape and contiguities are accurate, some schematization has been effected.

Possibly the authority granting this village land inam in Cincoli did
not at that date recognize the existence of Cincvad village. The general
tenor of seventeenth-century documents, particularly in respect to
transit duties, indicates that Cincoli was then much more important and
larger than the later, rather small village would suggest.[14] Perhaps
Cincoli encompassed all the land between the Pavna and Indrayani
rivers. Since the eighteenth century Cincoli has been due north of
Cincvad, which suggests the latter village was carved out of land
originally part of the revenue division of Cincoli. Hence, though the
evidence is rather tenuous and subject to interpretation, it seems that
Moroba 'colonized' part of Cincoli, creating a new official village
designation based in the first instance on a grant of rent-free land. Later,
as the boundaries of Cincoli assumed their more restricted dimensions,
this land inam remained within the village territory because that was
where it was technically granted. In general, this interpretation corresponds well with the legends that have Moroba founding Cincvad.
Whether it was all forest, completely unpopulated and uncultivated is
uncertain – likely not – but in any case, the saint was probably responsible for the creation of Cincvad as a separate and state-recognized
revenue unit.

The earliest history of Cincvad belongs to a time when land in the
Pune region was still being brought into cultivation and village
boundaries for revenue collection purposes were not fixed. The turn of
the seventeenth century is almost the earliest limit of Marathi documents on land-revenue administration. As for Cincvad, the information
these early sources yield is often hazy, needing considerable interpretation of language and contents. Yet, this was a formative period in the
rural history of upland western Maharashtra. At this time, for example,
land revenues were being fixed in the almost legendary settlements of
Malik Ambar, minister to the then-reigning Nizam Shahi sultanate.[15]
Perhaps in few other cases will we be able to see the apparent creation of
a village. Moroba's part in the origin of Cincvad, whether seen in
legends or contemporary documents, has therefore special interests for
the rural historian. But, in essence, this particularity was only one aspect
in the formation of the present shape of the countryside of the Pune
region.

At this earliest period it appears Moroba was not even formally
granted inam in his own name. Instead, the land in Cincoli is described as

[14] See pp. 136–9.
[15] For Malik Ambar and his land settlements of 1605–26 see *Gazetteer of the Bombay
Presidency*, Poona District (Bombay, 1885), 18, 2, pp. 317–25 for a summary based on
Deccan Commission correspondence.

being given to Moroba for service to the Morgav deity.[16] Apparently, at
this time the granting authorities did not acknowledge Moroba's
connection with any other place except Morgav. This is, however, the
first and last time the available documentation makes reference to the
saint's temporal subservience to Morgav. Even in the 1620s, two grants
of land near Morgav, recorded in the same formulaic language as the
Cincoli inam, are significantly silent on this point.[17] The next of these
early documents dates to 1649, and then Moroba is explicitly identified
with Cincvad.[18] Like the legends, the historical record, such as it exists,
clearly indicates that the saint established Cincvad as his own place
independent of, though never superseding, the sanctity of Morgav.

By 1649 the available documentation records numerous land inams to
Moroba in villages near Cincvad in north-west Haveli.[19] This document
is essentially a list of all the saint's lands recording the particular rights
held in specific villages. A similar accounting of inam for 1663, five years
before the death of Moroba's son Cintaman, may be taken with the 1649
document.[20] Cintaman obtained few new inams, though certain cash
allowances from the government revenues of Cincvad and neighbouring
Ravet village allowed to the *desmukh* (hereditary district officer) of
Pune were given over to the Dev.[21]

A few brief observations should be made on the nature of the land
inams as shown in these early accountings. Firstly, land is recorded in a
variety of measures: generally in *cāvar*s (approximately 80 to 90 acres),
but also in denominations such as *rukā*s and *ṭakā*s, which perhaps refer
to productivity of land rather than physical measure. Sometimes, the
revenue measure of village land is expressed in nominal monetary
amounts, which apparently indicated fractional degrees of assessment,
not cash realizations. The vexed question of the relation between land
areas and value will be taken up in the next chapter when a consideration
of the worth of the Devs' inam assumes a particular importance in the
history of the lineage.[22]

16 'Apanasi inambadal khijmati devasthan Mordev mauje Morgav.'
17 Documents of 24 February 1623 (one cavar in kasba (town, market center), Supe) and
   20 July 1627 (one cavar in Kumbharvalan village) in Potdar, 'Moraya Dev,' pp. 57–9.
18 Document of 7 September 1649 in ibid., pp. 59–60.
19 Ibid. This summary is given in connection with a *farman* (i.e., sanad) issued from the
   Adilshahi dynasty who succeeded the Nizam Shahis as the local political power in the
   Pune region. In the village list read the often confused Mulkhed for 'Morkhal
   (Markal)' as printed. Also, read Bopegav for 'Popangav' as printed.
20 Ibid., pp. 63–5. Mulkhed is here printed as 'Kuddel', a further confusion originating in
   the reading of the modi original.
21 Sanad of May–June 1663/4 from Krsnaji Kalbhor, deshmukh of Pune to Cintaman
   Gosavi Dev in *Shiva-caritra-sahitya*, vol. 4, pp. 20–1 (in *Bharat Itihas Samsodhak
   Mandal Quarterly*, 11, 4 (1931)).
22 See pp. 77–9.

A further difficulty is peculiar to seventeenth-century village accounts. Apparently, if taken at face value, these summaries of the Devs' inam indicate that in certain villages the saint and his son received part of their inams in kind. But it is quite possible that even the accounting of measures of grain and such could have been just another way of recording land for revenue purposes. At the same time, there does exist substantial documentation to indicate that Cincvad was supplied with food for the charitable feedings of brahmans and mendicants, the *annasatra*, which later is always declared one of the primary functions of the Samsthan.[23] Cintaman also seems to have been granted a right to a substantial amount of fodder, though for what purposes is not clear.[24] While it is tempting to identify such grants in kind with the recorded measures of grain in village summaries, such an association is yet without foundation. Furthermore, while the precise measures of land inams recur in later documentation, mention of these apparent grants in kind have not so far surfaced for the eighteenth and nineteenth centuries, though it is certain that institutions such as the annasatra still functioned and probably became more elaborate.

Like the meaning of land measures in Marathi documents, mention of inams in kind and many other features of the internal administration of villages are recorded in particular modes of expression and systems of accounting requiring a very detailed and specialized type of textual analysis. While surveying the broad features of the Devs' inam, this study can only touch on some aspects of these problems. Cincvad's internal administration of its inam villages enters an area of historical research for which there are few precedents or guides to assist in deciphering the cryptic language of the abundant but neglected primary sources.

Taken as a whole, the earliest sources for the Devs present a cumulative picture of all land acquisitions prior to 1668, but with very little evidence for the chronology of these grants. Figure 4 displays the original core of the Cincvad Samsthan in north-west Haveli. Essentially,

---

[23] The annasatra (or *annachatra*) is referred to in early sanads, see example from 22 January 1683 in Vad, *Sanad*s, p. 162. For documents of the Shivaji period (22, 23 June 1676) referring to grants of food see *Shiva-caritra-sahitya*, vol. 4, pp. 12–13, 15–17.

[24] See document of 29 November 1658 recording a grant of 50,000 (units?) of grass from villages near Cincvad in V. S. Bendre, *Maharastretihasaci sadhane*, 3 vols. (Bombay, 1966–7), II, 96. The original published source for this document has not been seen. These '50,000 grasses' (?) are also listed in the village summary of 25 October 1663, Potdar, 'Moraya Dev,' pp. 63–5. Similarly, this grant is specifically renewed in a document of 28 June 1699(?) issued by Balaji Vishvanath (future Peshwa), see *Sammelanvrtta*, 3 (1915), pp. 151–2.

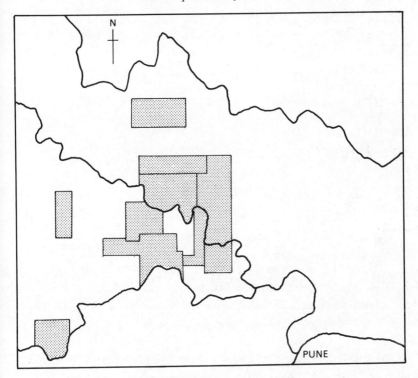

Figure 4. Village land inams to 1668

inams were obtained in a small knot of villages around Cincvad. Many of these places are said to have some specific association with Moroba and figure in his later biographies.[25] Perhaps inams were acquired in these villages because they too were places of the saint, though there is no contemporary evidence for this appealing inference. The physical contiguity of the villages to Cincvad is probably explanation enough for the location of these early inams.

Apart from the inams recorded in Figure 4, Moroba and Cintaman also possessed two grants in the Morgav subregion, which have been noticed above as dating to at least the 1620s. Before 1668, however, the Devs had no direct interest in Morgav village itself. The two grants in Purandhar taluka (tarph Karhepathar of the Maratha period) were the seed from which later Dev acquisitions in this local area, eventually including Morgav, originated. Never as important as north-west Haveli,

---

[25] For example, Tathvade village in *Cincvadksetrastha Shri Moraya Gosavi caritra*, pp. 24–5; see also Sykes, pp. 69–70 (as 'Tatoor').

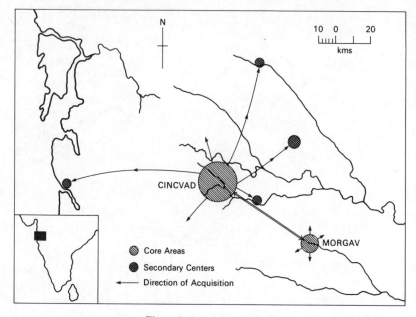

Figure 5. Acquisition of inam

nevertheless the Morgav area would become a significant field of activity for the Devs' inam acquisition.

Cincvad and Morgav would henceforth set the spatial framework for the Devs' inam. Between these two ritual poles the lineage would, in the pattern set by the life and devotions of Moroba, for long confine their landed interests. Only in the mid-eighteenth century would the first tentative moves be made to significantly expand out of this locality. Figure 5 diagrammatically portrays the spatial relationship between Cincvad and Morgav. These were the two 'core areas' of the Cincvad Samsthan. From these, the Devs would later expand into 'secondary centers,' often outlying Ganesh centers, some of which will be further noticed in subsequent chapters.[26]

In summary, the Devs' inam was acquired within a definite sacred geography of the Pune region. Cincvad and Morgav were both religious centers, though of different characters. Morgav was the place of the deity; it was, even in the seventeenth century, the 'ancient' sacred site. Cincvad was the place of the saint. The village would become the center of the Devs' landed interests. The vast majority of the lineage's inam was located within easy reach of Cincvad. But Cincvad's renown and wealth

[26] See pp. 82–3 and 181–2.

The acquisition of inam

could not exist separately from the sanctity of Morgav. Thus, the two
core areas of the Devs' inam would always form parts of a whole – the
Cincvad Samsthan. The next section of this chapter will again return to
the Cincvad core area to explore the process by which inam was acquired
in one locality.

II. The acquisition of inam, to circa 1750

Seen now on a map, the Devs' inams seem to encircle Pune city. In the
seventeenth century, however, Pune was merely a regional market center
(*kasba*) and not a place of special preeminence in the Deccan.[27] Pune's
growth and fame would come when it became the imperial capital of the
Peshvas. Then it was indeed fortuitous that the Devs' lands were so close
to the city. Proximity to the seat of power had many material advantages
for the inamdar. But at the turn of the eighteenth century, the Devs
looked outside their immediate locality for patronage.

King Shahu of Satara was the great patron of the Devs. Between his
accession and death (1707/8 – 1749/50), the Devs acquired most of their
inam. The Samsthan grew quickly, and the pattern of the lineage's
landholding was in great measure fixed by 1750. By this time, too, after a
slow transformation taking decades, the Peshva's political power was
unrivaled. Originally the chief ministers to Shahu, the hereditary
Peshvas had in part appropriated and in part been granted the
stewardship of the Maratha state and empire.[28] By making Pune their
seat of power, the city's hinterland came into particular prominence in
the Deccan. The rise of Pune and the growth of the Cincvad Samsthan
were thus contemporary and parallel events. There was no direct causal
relationship between the two. Like the Peshvas, the Devs were at first
dependent on the patronage of Shahu. Later the Devs would attach
themselves to the Peshvas, but this was after much of their wealth had
been obtained. In many ways, therefore, the development of the Cincvad
Samsthan through the acquisition of inam just outside Pune city only
mirrors the ascent of the Peshvas.

Analyzing the chronology of the Devs' village grants requires an
examination of the plenitude of sanads preserved in the Pune Archives.
Here, over 200 such documents have been seen in manuscript.[29] In

---

[27] *Gazetteer of the Bombay Presidency*, 18, 3, pp. 272, 276.
[28] Govind Sakharam Sardesai, *New History of the Marathas*, 3 vols. (Bombay, 1946–8),
II, 24–5.
[29] Preserved in Inam Commission copies in PA: IC rumal 11, manuscript volume,
pp. 125–528. See modi index to collection, pp. 89–123. In referring to this source I will
cite the document number as registered in this index.

addition, published documents not available in manuscript have been utilized. Some gaps in the Marathi documentation have been filled through nineteenth-century British summaries of eighteenth-century archival material.[30] This has especially been the case with the acquisitions of Vinayak Dev, younger brother of the third Dev Narayan. The relevant documentation for Vinayak's villages was not found in an initial survey of the Marathi archival material.

Sources are available to detail each stage of the Devs' acquisition of inam. When each village was obtained could be stated to the exact year, month and day. Lists could be compiled giving a very elaborate chronology of inam acquisition. However, to cite each document individually would be, I believe, unnecessary, if not pedantic. Instead, here the spatial process of inam acquisition is shown graphically using the same base village map for north-west Haveli previously employed in Figures 3 and 4. At a glance one can then see the remarkable growth of the Cincvad Samsthan in the first half of the eighteenth century.

Figure 6 shows the Devs' inam acquisitions to about 1700. Basically, this figure records the state of the Samsthan prior to the accession of Shahu. If this figure is compared with that displaying village land inams obtained by 1668, several important changes can be seen. While the land inams remain, the revenue of several whole villages has also been acquired. Cincvad village itself is a case in point. Probably, however, the Devs enjoyed the revenue of Cincvad from the creation of the village. Between 1668 and 1700 it appears the Maratha state officially recognized this reality. At least, the first sanads concerning Cincvad appear during these years.[31] In 1694 Cincvad also acquired Cikhli and Man villages in inam.[32] Vinayak Dev began the somewhat separate career of his branch of the Dev lineage by obtaining Hinjavadi and Jamb villages in the decade before 1700.[33] Finally, outside the area of Figure 6, acquisitions in the same decade of the sacred sites of Morgav and Theur should be noted. All these whole village inams of the 1690s were the gift of Rajaram, son of Shivaji. Politically this was a most confused time.[34] The Mughals were almost continually campaigning in

[30] Inam Commission decisions summarized in Laurence Wade Preston, 'Land, Lineage and the State in Maharashtra: The Devs of Cincvad under the Marathas and the British' (Ph.D. disertation, University of Toronto, 1984), Appendix B, pp. 400–04.

[31] For example, the sanad of 1683 referred to above (note 23). See also Vad, *Sanads*, p. 172 for a similar sanad dated 6 March 1692.

[32] Sanads of 17 February 1694 (Man) and 21 October 1694 (Cikhli) are printed in ibid., pp. 173–4.

[33] See Sanskrit sanad of 2 June 1691 re Hinjavadi in ibid., pp. 214–17 (with Marathi translation).

[34] Sardesai, I, 330–54.

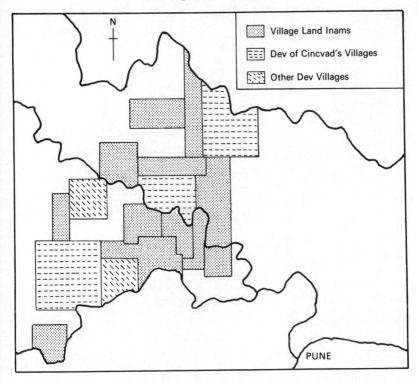

Figure 6. Inam acquisitions to *circa* 1700

the Deccan. Aurangzeb's armies had chased the *chatrapati* ('king') to Jinji in the far south. Yet, even under these circumstances the Maratha king exercised enough control over the villages of the Pune region to be able to order the granting of inams.

Between 1668 and 1700 the Cincvad Devs also received various new village land inams in the villages to the north-west of Pune, for example at Ravet in 1700.[35] These grants tended to tie together the Samsthan's landed interests. Nearly every village in which the Devs had some landed right was then contiguous with another. Of course, as Figure 6 shows, there were gaps in the Samsthan's acquisitions. Some villages very near Cincvad were never, at any time and in any way, part of the Devs' lands. Furthermore, the 'shape' of the Samsthan in 1700 was very irregular with the Devs' villages stretching north-east and south-west from Cincvad. Comparing Figures 4 and 6, however, it becomes apparent

[35] See sanad of 21 January 1700 in *Sammelanvrtta*, 3, p. 152.

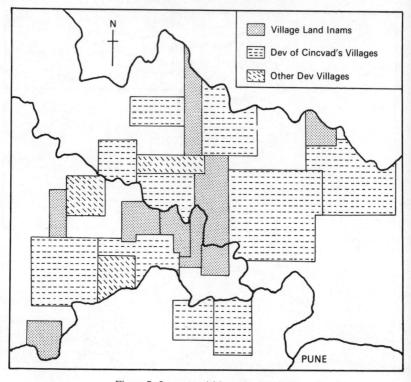

Figure 7. Inam acquisitions to *circa* 1750

that the Devs' sway over the countryside of north-west Haveli tended to expand from Cincvad.

Cincvad thus became the node of inam acquisition in this area. Figure 7 further illustrates this process. This figure shows all the Devs' inams acquired by the time of Shahu's death. Now villages in which only lands had previously been granted, such as Vakad, Cincoli and Akurdi, were converted into inams of the entire village revenues. Moreover, new whole villages were acquired, especially towards the east and south from Cincvad and closer to Pune city. Figure 7 thus displays an elaboration of the pattern set by 1700. But now a considerable amount of inam had been acquired. Eight entire villages were added to the Samsthan by 1750. In making these additions, the Devs and the granting authorities were careful to preserve and reinforce the contiguity of the Samsthan's villages. In essence, Figure 7 represents the consolidation of the Devs' landed interests in north-west Haveli.

Only in one case, Banere, did the Devs apparently ever lose an inam once it had been granted. This village was acquired sometime around 1699/1700,[36] and there is sufficient evidence to indicate that Banere was held up to about 1720.[37] Thereafter, the Devs temporarily lost control of the village's revenue, apparently because of the prior claims of another inamdar.[38] Banere has nevertheless been included in Figure 7 because in the 1760s the Peshva again granted this village to the Samsthan. The Devs' previously unclear title to this inam was, it appears, finally regularized.[39]

Between 1700 and 1750 the Devs also expanded their landed interests outside of Haveli. In the Morgav core area, for example, the villages of Saste and Ambi Budruk were obtained during this period.

Although Figure 7 includes acquisitions up to 1750, in fact most of the Devs' inams were granted before 1720. The third Dev Narayan, for reasons yet to be explained, was apparently a great favorite of both Rajaram and Shahu. The list of villages bestowed on Narayan between Shahu's accession (1707/8) and the Dev's death (1719/20)[40] is truly remarkable: Aundh, Bhosri, Carholi, Cincoli, Ravet and Vakad (all in 1709/10); part of Siddhatek (1711/12) and Ambi Budruk (not later than 1713/14). In addition, Shahu granted certain separate acquisitions to Vinayak (Narayan's brother) and even to the third Dev's son, Vighneshvar. Although the piety of Shahu is well known,[41] the generosity of this endowment must still be acknowledged.

Throughout their history under the Marathas the Devs would strive to acquire new inams wherever they could be had. Thus, the lineage had holdings even as distant as coastal Ceul (Chaul).[42] Despite this apparent diversity in its acquisitions, the Cincvad Samsthan did try to localize its inams in the core areas of Cincvad and Morgav. Within these localities the Devs acquired new villages as close to each other as possible. Most desirable was the situation where inams were contiguous. Particularly around Cincvad village, the Samsthan attempted to create a compact and unified administrative unit. Only through this spatial solidity of their holdings, as if the Samsthan were a political entity, could the Devs' control of landed revenue rights be clearly impressed upon the countryside of north-west Haveli.

[36] Documents of 6 February 1699, 10 December 1700 in Shankar Laksman Vaidya, *Vaidya daphtaramtun nivadalele kagas*, 4 vols. (Pune, 1944–9), II, 44–5.
[37] Ibid., II, 45–8.
[38] Sanad of 29 September 1735 in Bendre, II, 437–9.
[39] PA: IC rumal 11, nos. 71–80.
[40] *Mestak* (chronological notations) of 1818 in G. S. Sardesai, Y. M. Kale and V. S. Vakaskar, *Aitihasik patre yadi vagaire lekh* (Pune, 1930).
[41] Sardesai, II, 275–6, quoting contemporary opinions.
[42] Re transit duties, see p. 137, n. 65.

III. The inam granting process

Previously, this chapter has considered the history of the Devs' inam in broad terms by describing the overall pattern of acquisition. In this present section the focus will shift to one village and its revenue history between the time it was first granted in inam and 1750. Vakad has been chosen for this case study. If not a completely typical example, this one village nonetheless shares many of the documentary features typical to many of the Devs' inams. The main concern of this section is the process by which inam was granted. This will first be a study of the administrative structure of the Maratha state's revenue administration. Emerging from such a consideration will be an appreciation of how important it was for both the state and the inamdar that proper title to an inam village be maintained. The available documentation on Vakad clearly illustrates how the right to collect the state's land revenue was a privilege that had to be continually reinforced. Further, this was a right that the state recorded with great precision whenever an occasion arose requiring another statement of an inamdar's rights.

Shahu granted Vakad to the Dev of Cincvad on 1 November 1709. The following is a translation of the sanad issued to the village headman (*mokadam* or *pāṭīl*) of Vakad concerning the grant:[43]

Greetings, in the coronation year 36 [of Shivaji], called *virodhī* of the [60 year] cycle, Tuesday, the tenth day of the bright half of Kartik, an order was made by the blessed king Shahu chatrapati *svāmī* to the village headman of Vakad village in Haveli division of Pune district, thus:

Out of devotion for the saint who stays at Cincvad, that very venerable image of the supreme being, inam has been willingly given to the saint by Shivaji. New inam was given by Sambhaji. Later, inam was given to the saint by Rajaram. Having done this, the saint's blessing is [bestowed] for the well-being of the king and the king's government. Knowing this, [there is] new inam in the previously mentioned village [allowed] by the king for the saint's food distribution (*annachatra*). The inam, which is recognized as heritable, was granted to the saint, and having been removed from government revenues, now the revenues and assessments are for the saint [in particular, the following:] the plough tax, the coming years' taxes, the *sardeśmukhī*, the *sāhotrā*, the *sarpatilkī*, the *sargaudkī*, together with water, trees, plants, thickets and buried treasure according to established village boundaries. The village taxes and such, having been admitted by you, [therefore] the revenue and assessments under the control of the saint should continue to be regularly given. A new grant document should not be issued each year.

---

[43] Sanad of 1 November 1709 in D. B. Parasnis, *Itihasasamgraha* 7 (August–September 1915), 237; PA: IC rumal 11, no. 38.

The form of this sanad fairly represents the many similar documents issued in connection with all of the Devs' villages. Of course, the details of date, recipient, village and such differ in each example. So, too, do the specific revenue rights granted change in specific villages. Nevertheless, basically each sanad shares enough features to be considered a type of form letter. Because sanads were issued in such profusion when inam was granted, this regularity of form and language had obvious benefits for the king's central bureaucracy.

Shahu not only informed the village headman of his grant of Vakad, but nearly identical documents of almost the same date were sent to the inamdar, the district revenue officers, officers in the district military establishment, and other district officials.[44] At the same time, Shahu informed the Peshva, Balaji Vishvanath, of Vakad's grant in inam.[45] Consequently, the Peshva issued his own orders to the village headman of Vakad and various military officials.[46] Because the Pant Saciv of Bhor had an interest in Vakad as collector of the sahotra portion of the village assessment, he too issued orders to the village headman, and also to his own district subordinates, concerning the grant.[47] Unlike the royal sanads of Shahu, the orders of the Pesva and the Pant Saciv were merely recorded as *ajñāpatra*s (orders). The sanad form was the sole prerogative of the chatrapatis of Satara and Kolhapur. The Peshvas, at least until 1750, never preempted the kings' right to issue a sanad. The ajnapatra indicates the technically subsidiary nature of the Peshva's status. He was, in theory, only one of Shahu's many ministers. Consequently, the ajnapatra form of grant was always dated in Muslim style rather than a sanad's Hindu dating in the era of Shivaji.

Each time an inam was granted and reconfirmed to the Devs, the above dual or triple sets of documentation were produced. Figure 8 is a flow chart illustrating this inam granting process. This figure combines all available documentation for Vakad, shown in solid lines, to show the issuers and recipients of granting documents. Those channels of administration not found in the Vakad documents, but attested to in other villages, are illustrated with broken lines.

Although Figure 8 appears to include most possibilities whereby sanads and orders passed from the central administration down to the

---

[44] PA: IC rumal 11, nos. 39–41, 188. In IC rumal 11 sanads directly issued to the inamdar are generally lacking. This reflects the origin of these copies of the original documents. The Inam Commission generally copied the central and district sanads. The inamdar's copies presumably remain at Cincvad or are preserved in other archival collections.

[45] PA: IC rumal 11, no. 196.

[46] PA: IC rumal 11, nos. 43, 192.

[47] PA: IC rumal 11, nos. 190–1. The sahotra equaled 6% of revenues.

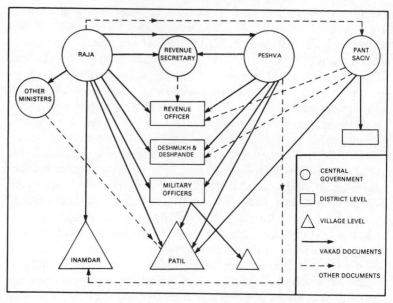

Figure 8. Inam granting process, Vakad village

district officers and the village level administration, some possible channels of communication are not found included in any of the documents so far examined. Thus, I can find no examples of orders between the district revenue officers and village headman. Shahu, the Peshva, the Pant Saciv apparently communicated directly with the village headman. That the district revenue officers would not also have been in close contact with the village authorities seems unlikely. Orders between district military officers and their local village representatives and the village headman, for example, are not wanting.[48] The sources also lack much in the way of orders issued directly to the inamdar. An example of an ajnapatra directly from the Peshva to the Dev of Cincvad, for example, cannot be found for Vakad, though such is available for other villages. Figure 8 moreover only displays the downward issuance of sanads and orders. Any communications that back up the bureaucratic hierarchy, say from the village headman to the Peshva, have not been included in the archival collections so far examined.

Between 1707/8 and 1719/20 the Peshva, like any other minister, appears to have received his orders concerning inam directly from Shahu. After the latter date, however, subsequent Peshvas were

---

[48] For example in 1709/10, PA: IC rumal 11, nos. 42, 44.

exercising increasingly independent powers. With the accession of Bajirav Ballal Peshva (1720/1), the system of dual government displayed in Figure 8 became an administrative reality. Until at least 1750 two sets of orders (if not more) were issued for each inam. Between 1720 and 1750 Shahu appears to have infrequently communicated with his Peshva. Instead, both Shahu and the Peshva, in addition to issuing sanads and orders to the district and village officials, dealt with a common central revenue 'secretary' (*karbhāri*). This revenue secretariat official appears to have coordinated the dual system of inam granting. Evidence from some villages suggests that this official had his own avenues of communication with the district officials and perhaps even the village level administration. During the period under consideration the central revenue official who appears again and again in the documentation is one Bapuji Shripat Citrav.[49] Later his son, Shripat Bapuji Citrav, undertook this function.[50]

Not only was the process by which the Maratha state granted inam very complex, as Figure 8 amply illustrates, but this entire procedure needed to be repeated on numerous occasions. Of course, it first occurred when Vakad was first granted in 1709/10. With the death of a grantee the procedure was duplicated. So, on 16 and 17 December 1719 Shahu issued sanads for Vakad and other villages allowing the succession of Cintaman II to the inams of his father Narayan Dev. Often such succession documents were omnibus sanads encompassing several inams.[51] The form of the document nonetheless remained constant. At the same time, the Peshva again issued his own orders, as did the Pant Saciv.[52]

In 1726 and 1727 the entire granting process was again repeated for Vakad and other villages in north-west Haveli. Now the *moglaī* portion of the village assessment (that share nominally due to the Mughals of Delhi) was formally granted to the Dev.[53] During this period the Marathas and the technical representative of the Mughals, the Nizam of Hyderabad, were very much at odds. Pune district had previously been in that part of the Deccan where revenue was meant to be shared between the two powers. However, it appears with the rise of Bajirav Ballal Peshva and with his military conquests, the Marathas took the opportunity to exercise complete control over the revenues of villages

---

[49] See sanad of Shahu, 21 August 1726, PA: IC rumal 11, pp. 125–6 (not numbered).
[50] PA: IC rumal 11, no. 224.
[51] PA: IC rumal 11, nos. 203, 206.
[52] PA: IC rumal 11, nos. 189, 200, 204 (Pant Saciv); the Peshva's orders for Vakad are lacking though they are available for other villages.
[53] PA: IC rumal 11, nos. 45, 207–9 (Peshva); 212 (Pant Saciv); pp. 125–6 (not numbered), 46, 213 (Shahu sanad of 21 August 1726).

The inamdar under the Marathas

around Pune.[54] With the growth of Pune as the capital of an expanding empire, it is perhaps not surprising that the Peshvas would have wanted to fully control villages almost within sight of the city.

Nevertheless, the revenue division of Vakad and other villages could not be ignored. Some formal grant of the moglai was apparently necessary. However, it is not clear that before this time the Devs had *not* received the full revenue of Vakad and other villages. Later divisions of the Devs' inam, as recorded in settlement documents, would seem to indicate that the grant of the moglai was, here at least, simply an administrative technicality.[55] In districts north of Pune, on the other hand, where the claims of the Nizam were more firmly entrenched – and supported by military force through both Muslim and Hindu families in the service of Hyderabad – this distinction between the moglai and the Maratha share of villages (the *svarājya*) apparently had more force. So for example, Sudumbare village in Cakan subdistrict (north of the Indrayani river) was granted in stages to a scion of the Dev lineage. Not until 1753/4 was the moglai included in the inam.[56] In fact, the Devs' interests north of the Indrayani river were until 1750 severely restricted. Inam was acquired south of this river and eastwards towards Pune. Apparently, it was not politically expedient for either Shahu or the Peshvas to grant inam in areas where the Nizam claimed some control over village revenues.

The intrusion of political and military events in the inam granting process can again be traced in 1727 and 1728. At this time the Nizam had enlisted the chaptrapati of Kolhapur, Sambhaji (Shambhu), as his ally against the Kolhapur chatrapati's kinsman Shahu and his Peshva. Sambhaji campaigned with the Nizam throughout the Deccan. He even 'toured through the district of Poona as the defacto ruler receiving homage from and granting sanads to the local officials.'[57] Vakad's headman consequently received a sanad from the Kolhapur chatrapati reconfirming the village's inam status.[58] The temporary conquests of

---

[54] *Gazetteer of the Bombay Presidency*, 18, 2, p. 324 for divided revenue system in Pune district. For the general complexities of the system see M. A. Nayeem, 'The Working of the *Chauth* and *Sardesmukhi* System in the Mughal Provinces of the Deccan (1707–1803 A.D.),' *Indian Economic and Social History Review*, 14 (1977), 153–206.

[55] See p. 80 no. 76.

[56] Document of 29 January 1754 in *Selections from the Satara Rajas' and Peshwas' Diaries*, part 2, vol. 2, p. 103.

[57] Sardesai, II, 94.

[58] PA: IC rumal 11 no. 47, dated 29 February 1728, curiously the day after the Peshva decisively defeated the Nizam at the Battle of Palkhed. A treaty of 6 March 1728 then prohibited Sambhaji from claiming any rights over Pune district, see Sardesai, II, 94–99. Sambhaji, however, did later reconfirm his own, apparently valueless sanads, see PA: IC rumal 11, no. 219.

Sambhaji were thus seen as a change of political authority in north-west Haveli. As such, the possession of an inam could not be taken for granted. A new set of documents had to be issued.

With the death of the fourth Dev of Cincvad new sanads were again sent to the various district and village officers in 1741/2.[59] Here the reconfirmation of inam on the succession of a 'new' grantee exactly parallels that which occurred in 1719/20. In 1750/1 another succession required even further renewals of the Devs' titles to their inams. On this occasion the Peshva allowed the continuance of the Vakad and other grants following the death of Shahu and the succession of Ramraja.[60] The change of any formal granting authority, whether by usurpation as with Sambhaji of Kolhapur or a legitimate succession as that of Ramraja, necessitated a complete regranting of title to all inams. Surely this was a formality; but it was still a prerequisite for the possession of inam that its title be maintained in good order.

With the accession of Ramraja the available sources give no indication that the new chatrapati also issued the usual documents on Vakad or the other Dev villages. From the start of his reign Ramraja was a virtual prisoner of the Peshva. Perhaps the Peshva did not consider it even necessary to obtain the chatrapati's assent when inams needed to be reconfirmed.[61] However, apparently the King's sanad was, even after 1750, still needed to formally grant new inams.[62] Some evidence exists to suggest that after 1750 the inam granting process, as detailed above, underwent considerable alteration with the ajnapatras of the Peshvas taking on the virtual force of a royal sanad. Without an examination of the documentation still to be found in the archives, the exact details of the inam granting process in the later eighteenth century can only be surmised.

By 1750, however, the Devs of Cincvad had acquired most of their inam. The creation of the Cincvad Samsthan was largely complete. The Devs now turned their attention to the preservation of their inam. Acquisitions so carefully accumulated over a century had to be retained intact to support the ever-expanding Dev lineage. How the inamdar kept what he already had is the subject of the next chapter.

[59] PA: IC rumal 11, nos. 48, 219–21. The Peshva's ajnapatras on this are lacking.
[60] PA: IC rumal 11, nos. 49, 223–4 (orders of 7 April 1750).
[61] The Peshva was in fact in Satara with the new chatrapati when the Vakad inam was reconfirmed, Sardesai II, 289. For Ramraja's confinement see ibid., II, 294–6.
[62] PA: IC rumal 11, pp. 648–9, 659, 665–71 re village land inam in Bhosri village alienated on behalf of Dev of Cincvad. Perhaps these documents were necessary because the chatrapati had granted the village in the first place.

2

The preservation of inam, 1720–1818

After 1719/20 and the death of the third Dev Narayan, a gradual transformation overtook the Devs' relations with the inam granting powers. Seemingly less intent on expanding their holdings, to judge from available sources, the lineage now sought to establish itself in the ritual, social and economic hierarchies of the Peshvas' Maharashtra. Although the Devs' position in the fabric of eighteenth-century society was secure – a more solidly placed lineage is difficult to find – still, revenue received from the state and held at its pleasure had to be jealously guarded. Acquisitions were still important, and this chapter shows why an expanding inamdar lineage always needed more inam. Specific grants received after King Shahu's death in 1750 are therefore noted in passing in this and subsequent chapters. However, throughout the ascendancy of the Peshvas (and thereafter under the British) inam became an inheritance to be preserved from all possible encroachments. This prime duty of the inamdar both ordered the internal affairs of the lineage and animated its external relations with state and society. These twin and related aspects of the Devs' history are now examined in detail.

Because of the vicissitudes of the Maratha polity, even apparently secure alienated tenures were not immune from the ruler's financial demands. Periodic surveys of alienated tenures were ordered to determine which were improperly held.[1] Political tenures, jagir and saranjam, were notoriously insecure, especially when government revenues were short. Changes of political climate, disloyalty or treason in the broadest sense, or even the personal pique of the sovereign, were all satisfactory reasons for the state to resume what it had granted. It is not difficult to find cases of political resumptions in the history of the Marathas. In 1822, for example, the Deccan Commission supplied Sir Thomas Munro with a list of over 500 instances in the 50 years before the conquest.[2]

---

[1] See *Selections from the Satara Rajas' and Peshwas' Diaries*, ed. Ganesh Chimnaji Vad (Bombay and Pune, 1906–11), part 8, vol. 3, pp. 205–7 for two examples from the time of Savai Madhavrav. Note particularly the wide range of tenures to be investigated for proper sanads (p. 245).

[2] Minute of Sir Thomas Munro on altamgha inam, 15 March 1822, in G. R. Gleig, *The Life of Major-General Sir Thomas Munro*, 3 vols. (London, 1830), II, 337; see also

Grants held under a sanad were usually respected by the Peshva; and such inams allowed religious institutions and personages, whether personal and hereditary holdings or devasthans juridically the property of a deity, were deemed nearly untouchable in the normal course of affairs. A vigorously Hindu power such as the Marathas, and especially the brahman Peshvas, naturally protected the religious heritage of the Deccan. Texts on Maratha political theory commend this to the enlightened ruler. Ramcandrapant Amatya in his *Ajnapatra*, while condemning most revenue alienations, emphasizes the permanence of religious grants:

after the grant is made there should not be any desire to retake whatever may be the times of difficulty and even in cases of danger to life; on the contrary after remembering that worldly happiness is momentary and considering the fear of the other world, even a sipful of water from what is given should not be coveted even as a joke.[3]

The sternness of the warning perhaps hints at a rather different reality. Munro for one, with his wide knowledge of the traditional administration, was adamant that even

[g]rants for religious and charitable purposes to individuals or bodies of men though often granted for ever or while the sun and moon endure were frequently resumed at short intervals. Grants of Jageers and Enam lands from favor or affection or as rewards for service were scarcely ever perpetual.[4]

Even where reasonably secure under one ruler or dynasty, religious endowments might suffer with political change. Hence, rights were continually reconfirmed with new sanads. This feature of Marathi inam documentation is particularly apparent for Cincvad's acquisitions, a point developed in the previous chapter.[5] In an analysis of vernacular deeds, Munro, too, alluded to the transitory nature of inam: 'the injunction with which they usually conclude – "Let them not require a fresh sunnud every year," indicates plainly enough the opinion that such

Alexander J. Arbuthnot, *Major-General Sir Thomas Munro: Selections from his Minutes and Other Official Writings*, 2 vols. (London, 1881), I, 154 (here dated 1 February 1822).
[3] Shrikrishna Venkatesh Puntambekar, trans., *A Royal Edict on Principles of State Policy... Ramachandrapant Amatya's Rajaniti, dated A.D. 1716* (Madras, 1929), pp. 37–8.
[4] Minute of Sir Thomas Munro, 16 December 1823, accompaniment to Government of India to Government of Bombay, 1 October 1838, PA: XII; 21/743, fol. 14. See also Alfred Thomas Etheridge, 'Narrative of the Bombay Inam Commission and Supplementary Settlements,' *Selections from the Records of the Bombay Government*, n.s. 132 (Bombay, 1874), pp. 16–17, here dated 16 January 1823. This minute is based in large part on the minute on altamgha inams of 15 March 1822 cited above.
[5] See pp. 41–5.

grants were not secure from revocation.'[6] Examples of wholesale resumptions of revenue alienations are not wanting in the eighteenth century. In Kanara, for example, Hyder Ali abolished most minor disbursements and halved inams to brahmans and temples. His son Tipu Sultan resumed all inams to effect a substantial increase in the land revenue.[7] Admittedly, these were acts of a Muslim government. But in the final analysis Hyder and Tipu were only cxcrcising the state's ultimate authority over its grants.

How then did a lineage forestall the possibility of incursions into its revenue? The short answer is that it had to remain in the state's favor and be on the winning side in any political upheaval. This much is obvious. But depending on his position and role in society, every inamdar had a different strategy to achieve this end. To take an illustration far removed from the concerns of the Devs of Cincvad: a *sardār* holding a large saranjam in exchange for supplying the Peshva's armies would want to win battles if his holding was to be preserved and perhaps converted into a heritable estate. However, behind any social role, from the military to the religious, there existed in all lineages a common concern in the quest for security: internal harmony between the kin had to be maintained. Primarily this was achieved through the arrangement of some means for the uncontested descent of any patrimony, be it inam or the most commonplace of village land rights. For inamdars such as the Devs the point was critical. The state could not allow its grants to become the subject of internecine disputes and would intervene in 'family affairs' to preserve the decorous management of inam. In extreme instances, if the kin's differences were irreconcilable, grants might even be resumed. For the lineage to be a successful social entity it had to settle its internal affairs and present at least a mask of solidarity to the public world.

This chapter first explores the Devs' special place in eighteenth-century Maratha society. Based on scattered sources, this section can only give a general survey of the wide variety of activities in which the lineage was involved. The bulk of the chapter analyzes the Peshva's settlement of the Devs' inam. By its decisive intervention the Maratha state ordered the manner by which its grants would descend in the lineage. While maintaining the peace of the lineage and thus preserving its inam, this settlement also had far-reaching consequences for the structure of the lineage.

[6] Minute of 15 March 1822, Gleig, II, 315.
[7] Report of Principal Collector of Canara, 31 May 1800, in *The Fifth Report from the Select Committee of the House of Commons on the Affairs of the East India Company, dated 28th July, 1812*, ed. Walter Kelly Firminger, 3 vols. (Calcutta, 1918), III, 305–6.

The preservation of inam, 1720–1818

I. The Devs under the Peshvas

If never complacent, the Dev of Cincvad could feel reasonably confident that the Peshva would never resume his inam. The Cincvad family had extensive personal religious connections with the Peshvas and their relatives, as well as with other state dignitaries. Ganpati was the *kuldaivat* (family deity), of the Peshvas, and the Devs as the near-divine descendants of the most renowned *ganpatya bhakta* Moroba Gosavi would as a matter of course be revered. The Peshva regularly visited the sacred Ganesh temples.[8] He even regulated their ceremonies.[9] 'Shri Dev Cincvad' appears on lists of those worthies to be honored with token gifts on auspicious occasions.[10]

Mentions of even more personal connections abound in the sources. After Madhavrav Peshva's death (18 November 1772) his wife, prior to her *sati*, distributed her possessions to her favorites: the Dev received two necklaces, each with eight diamonds, five rubies and one emerald; the wife of Jagannath Dev was given pearl earrings.[11] In 1736 the Dev was entertained in Pune on the occasion of the thread ceremony of the Peshva's nephew, Sadashivrav ('Bhausaheb'), the future tragic hero of the Battle of Panipat.[12] That the Dev would find it advantageous to deign to attend the ceremony of a *konkanastha* (coastal) brahman, his ritual inferior in the view of the deshasthas, is especially revealing. Similarly, in 1777 Nana Phadnis took time out from his diplomatic intrigues with the French to travel from Purandhar to Cincvad to solemnize one of his nine marriages.[13] Again the Dev ministered to the konkanasthas, which lends some credence to a popular tradition (circa 1900) that he was responsible for raising the politically powerful coastal *citpāvan*s brahmans to ritual equality with the deshasthas.[14] Such examples could be multiplied – albeit in a somewhat disconnected manner – by a careful reading of those sources that touch upon the

[8] Laurence W. Preston, 'Subregional Religious Centres in the History of Maharashtra: The Sites Sacred to Ganesh,' in *Images of Maharashtra: A Regional Profile of India*, ed. N. K. Wagle (London, 1980), pp. 120–2 for an analysis of the Peshvas' visits to Ganesh sites.
[9] For example, at Siddhatek in documents of 11 January 1765 and 10 December 1768 in *Selections from the Peshwa Daftar*, XXXII, 100, 103.
[10] List of 1739 (?) in *Selections from the Peshwa Daftar*, XVII, 65–6.
[11] List of 10 August 1773 in *Selections from the Peshwa Daftar*, XXXII, 107–12.
[12] Entry in Peshva's diaries for 12 February 1736 in *Selections from the Peshwa Daftar*, XXII, 171.
[13] *Akhbār* (newspaper) of 17 February 1777 in *Poona Akhbars*, 3 vols. (Hyderabad, 1952–6), I, 26. The marriage was to occur on 24 February 1777. Nana (d. 1800, for many years the real power in the Maratha State), being very much at odds with the British, was awaiting the arranged visit of the French adventurer St. Lubin.
[14] R. E. Enthoven, *Folklore of the Konkan* (1915, rpt. Delhi, 1976), p. 45.

The inamdar under the Marathas

social life of eighteenth-century Maharashtra. Many of the historical personalities of the Maratha state held the Dev in great reverence, and he in turn cultivated their patronage.

The Dev was also an important participant in state religious celebrations. Being more than just the usual round of Hindu festivals, these ceremonies expressed both the structure of the state and also the political aspirations of government. Considering briefly the former, each year when the Dev was on pilgrimage to Morgav, a very stylized meeting took place just outside Pune between him and the Peshva. Greetings were made, homage paid, and gifts given – all in a prescribed and closely regulated manner. Temporal and ritual superiors reaffirmed each other's domain of precedence. This ceremony, in many ways symbolic of the relations between the state and Cincvad, is of considerable interest, particularly in its postconquest transformation, and is fully described in Chapter 4.

Turning now to the aspirations and policies of government, the Devs were conspicuously enlisted to ensure success of an enterprise. Such is particularly apt, given the popular notion of Ganesh as the deity to be worshiped at the start of an undertaking. In February 1777, for example, Vishvambhar Dev (apparently the grandson of Cintaman I, and then very old and venerable to judge from his appellation *vedamurti rajashri*) was asked to perform as *anusthān* (propitiation ceremony) 'on account of a commencement' (*ārambāvisaī*).[15] Exactly what was being started that attracted the notice of the political correspondent who made this notation is not stated. Perhaps it referred to the imminent initiation of Nana Phadnis' French policy, but equally it could have been anything the state thought important enough to require the sanctification of the Cincvad Devs. In a similar case, when various vows were made at religious centers in the Deccan to ensure victory in north India against the Afghans (ending in disaster at Panipat), Ganesh shrines are prominent among the famous temples to be visited. The Dev of Cincvad was particularly to be approached.[16] One of the most striking instances

---

[15] On 27 February 1777 in akhbar of 1 March 1777, *Poona Akhbars*, I, 37.
[16] *Yādī* (memorandum) of 1 April 1760 in *Selections from the Peshwa Daftar*, XL, 127–33: 'Cincvadi devakade jave.' Note that this entry is under the section for the command (*pāgā*) of Sadashivrav, 'Bhausaheb.' This document, an excellent summary of the major religious centres of Maharashtra, has also been printed in *Aitihasik sankirna sahitya*, VI, 14–17 (*Bharat Itihas Samshodhan Mandal Quarterly*, 16, 1–3 (July 1945–January 1946). Substantial textual differences indicate a different manuscript source.

For similar documents on the performance of an anusthan, see *Aitihasik sankirna sahitya*, VI, 63 (dating to the 1760s but incomplete) and *Selections from the Satara Rajas' and Peshwas' Diaries*, pt. 2, vol. 2, p. 205 (document of 6 November 1753). In both cases instructions for ceremonies at Ganesh shrines were issued through the intermediacy of the Dev.

of this kind occurred just after the British were forced to sign the 'Convention' of Vadgav (17 January 1779), which followed their humiliating defeat at the Battle of Talegav. When on 18 January British hostages arrived at the Maratha camp and the defeated army was to be escorted back to Bombay, the blessing (*prasād*) of the Dev was first taken in nearby Cincvad.[17]

The Devs were not content, however, to be mere ritual functionaries of the state, or to rest under the passive protection of the Peshva and his entourage. Only with a visible and active presence in society and at court could their ritual status be further enhanced. Finance was one avenue through which the Samsthan could exert its influence. Of course, with its inams and other endowments Cincvad was wealthy and thus demanded respect. The Devs were accustomed to operating within the financial infrastructure of the period. This is particularly so with the operation of the Cincvad mint, which dates from the later eighteenth century. Chapter 5 examines this institution in more detail. Because of its financial activities, the lineage appears to have had warm relations with traditional banking families such as the Vaidyas of Satara and Vai.[18] Perhaps, then, it is not surprising that on one occasion the Peshva asked the Dev to use his influence to stop creditors from hounding (*tagādā*) the household of one of his courtiers.[19] The Dev's unique combination of sanctity and financial acumen made him a good choice for the task.

Moneylending was another way to be indispensable. On one notable occasion, recorded in a document much reprinted, the mother of Shahu asked the Dev for a loan of Rs. 7,000 to repay borrowings so that she could obtain further credit. At this time (1705), near the confused end of Aurangzeb's reign, Shahu and his mother were the emperor's hostages and, together with the entire Mughal court, had been reduced to dire straits.[20] Cincvad also had the ready money the state needed to meet

---

[17] Letter of 19 January 1779 in *Aitihasik sankirna sahitya*, III, 28–9 (*Bharat Itihas Samshodhan Mandal Quarterly*, 16,4 (March 1946)).

[18] Shankar Laksman Vaidya, *Vaidya daphtaramtun nivadalele kagad*, 4 vols. (Pune, 1944–9). For example, condolences were sent on the death of the Dev of Cincvad in 1740 (II, 49); the Devs sent a turban on the death of Raghunath Vaidya in 1743 (IV, pt. 2, 2–4). Apparently the Vaidyas acted as Cincvad's financial agents at Shahu's court, see letter of 19 May 1742 (IV, pt. 1, 12–13) concerning the granting of an inam (Dhoraj village, however, has not yet been identified as one of the Devs' inams).

[19] Bajirav Ballal Peshva to Dev of Cincvad, 26 November 1736 (?) in *Selections from the Peshwa Daftar*, XXX, 139.

[20] Letter of 19 April 1705 in V. S. Bendre, *Maharastretihasaci sadhane*, 3 vols. (Bombay, 1966–7), II, 280–1 being reprinted from a source I have not seen. It is also reprinted in R. V. Oturkar, *Maharastraca patrarup itihas* (Pune, 1941), pp. 13–15. G. S. Sardesai, *New History of the Marathas*, 3 vols. (Bombay, 1946–8), I, 367–8 has a more or less full translation.

extraordinary expenses. Rs. 10,000 were lent for the prosecution of the Bassein (Vasai) campaign, which ended in 1739 with the capture of that Portuguese fortress. The Dev received a bond (*khat*) for his loan, but as for repayment, 'the rupees should be realized by imposing a tax on village revenue assignments.'[21] In short, the Dev traded cash for permission to exact more revenue from his inam. This arrangement, though advantageous to both parties and having the salutary effect of cementing state–inamdar relations, later created unrest within the lineage, a development which is discussed below.

By acting as an intermediary, as an arbiter of disputes or as an advocate for just causes, the Dev further capitalized on his peculiar social standing. The financial intervention on behalf of one of the Peshva's retinue has already been noted. Equally, the affairs of the common inhabitants of his inam villages were the Dev's concern, especially when the villagers came into contact with the state. The Dev routinely received copies of legal decisions on local disputes – concerning vatan rights, order of precedence, or whatever – if *his* villagers were involved.[22] Or he might initiate proceedings with the Peshva to redress grievances. One time he had a *pāṭilkī* (patil's rights) restored to its former owner after it had been partially sold (and perhaps also renounced).[23] The Povla family in Pirangut village held an ancient half share of the patilki, but because of a sexual indiscretion by one of their women, the holder of the office fled the village in anticipation of certain public shame. While in exile he was forced, or so he said, to alienate a portion of his inheritance. The Dev prevailed upon the Peshva to have the sale canceled, buy up the patil's half share, and hold the rights in trust. Employment in the Peshva's retinue was also found for one of the Povlas, who was subsequently killed at Panipat. Thereupon the family petitioned for the restoration of

---

[21] Madhavrav Peshva to Umapati Dev (undated) in *Aitihasik sankirna sahitya*, VI, 61–2: 'gavavarati pati ghalun rupaye ugaun dhyave.' The Dev's moneylending activities in support of the state are similar to those of the contemporary divine Brahmendrasvami, see D. V. Divekar, 'The Emergence of an Indigenous Business Class in Maharashtra in the Eighteenth Century,' *Modern Asian Studies*, 16 (1982), 439–40.

[22] *Nivadpatra* of 17 June 1723 (Banere village mokadam rights), PA: SD, 11474–476; document courtesy of N. K. Wagle.

[23] Document of 1 June 1784 re patilki of Cimaji Povla (deceased, case presented by his wife Janaki), PA: ghadni daphtar rumal 375; document courtesy of N. K. Wagle.

    The Devs served as kulkarni of Pirangut (in rotation among the five sons of Narayan and their descendants after 1744/5), which is apparently the reason this document is in the ghadni daphtar. For an old kulkarni account of this village, copied from the Cincvad records in the Bharat Itihas Samshodhan Mandal, see P. N. Patvardhan, 'Pirangut yethil kulkarnyacya haklajimyaca kagad,' *Sammelan-vrtta*, 3 (1915), 133–41.

    Incidentally, a considerable amount of documentation on the Devs exists in the ghadni, particularly rumals 400–3, 498, 502. All remain to be examined.

their patilki. Granting the request out of favor for the family's sacrifice, the Peshva waived the repayment of his costs (Rs. 400), but at the same time demanded a substantial *najar* (Rs. 1001). For some reason only the right to a *kuran* (a meadow for fodder) was withheld.[24] All these developments came out of the Dev's advocacy. In the normal course of affairs he received notice of the final disposition of the Povla case.

Combining sanctity with his wide range of temporal concerns, the Dev made the Cincvad Samsthan politically neutral, an island of peace in the often uncertain world of eighteenth-century Maharashtra. This is not to say he was immune from the daily hazards of life. In one curious incident, while taking a ritual bath in the Ghod river, the sixth Dev Narayan had his Ganesh idol stolen.[25] Two or three days later the idol was found thrown in the water, but now lacking its (presumably jewelled) eyes and navel. Unfortunately we are not told if the impious thieves were ever apprehended. This incident must have been of extraordinary significance to deserve mention in a source otherwise concerned with recording weighty historical facts. On a more memorable occasion, just prior to the 1779 Battle of Talegav, the Marathas had plans to burn Cincvad in the face of the invading British, but the danger passed before this became necessary.[26]

Mostly, however, the armies that occasionally ravaged the environs of Pune left Cincvad alone. The failure of the Mughals to plunder the Samsthan (circa 1700–2) is, in the traditions, always ascribed to divine intervention.[27] A more verifiable example occurred with Yashvantrav Holkar's 1803 looting campaign around Pune. Contemporary English

24 The kuran was then granted to one of the Peshva's military commanders, after whose death it was appropriated by the Dev. The Pant Saciv (Pirangut was in his territory) resumed the kuran in 1840/41 after an inquiry into all inams. In the mid-nineteenth century the descendants of the Povlas appealed to the British for the return of the kuran claiming the Devs had subjected them to intimidation because of the claim. The Inam Commissioners thought the British government had the right to this minor item of revenue, see PA: xiii; 58/76 for correspondence and abstract of Marathi documents.
25 *Mestak* of 1818 in G. S. Sardesai, Y. M. Kale and V. S. Vakaskar, *Aitihasik patre yadi vagaire lekh* (Pune, 1930), p. 464 reprinted from Kashinath Narayan Sane, *Aitihasik patre yadi vagaire* (Pune, 1889).
26 Sardesai, *New History*, iii, 81 citing *Calendar of Persian Documents*, V. See also A. Macdonald, *Memoir of the Life of the late Nana Farnavis* (rpt. London, 1927), p. 40).
27 Edward Moor, 'Account of an Hereditary Living Deity to whom devotion is paid by the bramins of Poona and its neighbourhood,' *Asiatick Researches*, 7 (1801), 386 for a factual account; W. H. Sykes, 'An Account of the Origin of the Living God at the Village of Chinchore, near Poona,' *Transactions of the Literary Society of Bombay*, 3 (rpt. 1877), 75–6 for the legends, particularly the often repeated and illustrated story of the Dev turning an offering of beef into flowers.
  The Mughal involved was perhaps the general Zulfikar Khan Nusrat Jang who camped at Cincvad in the monsoon of 1702, see Sir Jadunath Sarkar, trans. 'Nuskha-I-Dilkasha' by Bhimsen in *Sir Jadunath Sarkar Birth Centenary Volume* (Bombay, 1972), p. 235.

sources particularly noted that the Dev's villages were spared; moreover, he 'not only protected from plunder the extensive estates of his own pagoda, but afforded a secure shelter to the fugitives from the neighbourhood.'[28] Not five years afterwards, local brahmans attributed this variously to a guard of supernatural horses or acute bowel pains that struck down marauding troops as they approached the village.[29]

Cincvad's neutrality became of particular note in the late Maratha period. Because the village is located on the route to Pune from Bombay and was only a day's march out of the Maratha capital, the Peshvas used it as a convenient way-station in their diplomatic relations with the British. In 1782, while still at odds with Bombay, Nana Phadnis prevented British envoys from moving beyond Cincvad before he had arranged a guard to meet them.[30] When, in 1803, Bajirav Peshva was proceeding to Pune to reclaim his throne after signing the Treaty of Bassein, he unaccountably halted at Cincvad. For a week he would not move. According to one report, apparently sent to one of the Peshva's supporters, Bajirav was residing incommunicado (*gapcūp*) in the Cincvad vada and was delaying his departure from day to day (*ājudyā*).[31] Perhaps his reasons were religious, or maybe the Peshva only wanted to thoroughly prepare his ceremonial entry into Pune. Cincvad was also an ideal haven, given that Bajirav's enemies were still at large near Pune.

But by no coincidence, at the same time General Wellesley was also camped at Cincvad. He at least was apprised of the Peshva's plans and knew the exact date he would enter Pune.[32] Though the future Duke of Wellington did not actually meet the Peshva – Bajirav claimed not to have adequate quarters for an interview – the two were in close contact through an intermediary.[33] The Dev seems to have assumed this role. The surrender of Karnala fort, held by a recalcitrant commandant, is a case in point. The Dev wrote to this officer asking him to surrender to Bajirav; Wellesley did likewise and particularly pointed out the Dev's wishes.[34] Though the Dev made the request in the name of his legitimate

[28] Robert James Mackintosh, *Memoirs of the Life of Sir James Mackintosh*, 2 vols. (London, 1835), I, 456; and also I, 275 for similar comments in 1805.
[29] Lord Valentia, *Voyages and Travels to India*, 3 vols. (London, 1809), II, 159.
[30] *Akhbar*s of 12 – 14 January 1782, *Poona Akhbars*, III, 25–6, 30–1.
[31] Letter of 10 May 1803 in Krsnaji Vasudev Purandare, *Purandare daphtar*, 2 vols. (Pune, 1929), II, 170–1. Bajirav stayed in Cincvad from 7 to 13 May 1803, see B. Close, Resident at Pune to Court of Directors, 15 May 1803, in John Gurwood, ed., *The Dispatches of Field Marshall the Duke of Wellington*, 13 vols. (London, 1834–8), I, 167.
[32] A. Wellesley to Lord Hobart, Secretary of State, 10 May 1803, in Gurwood, III, 116. 'Chinsura' is a reasonable phonetic rendering of Cincvad.
[33] Wellesley to Commander-in-chief, 12 May 1803, in Gurwood, III, 120–1.
[34] Wellesley to Col. Murray, 7 May 1803; to *killedār* (commandant) of Karnala fort (Kolaba district), 8 May 1803, in Gurwood, III, 108–9, 111–12.

sovereign and with his approval, clearly he acted at the behest of the British who were at that moment preparing to take the fort by force. Cincvad was never unmindful of a change in the political order.

A very clear picture of the Devs in eighteenth-century Maratha society emerges from a number of incidental references. Only the number of sources yet to be examined limits a full descriptive analysis of the social role of the lineage. The main point is not in doubt. The Devs used their ritual status and the reverence it inspired, as well as their wealth, to further lineage welfare. Ceremonial specialist, financier, advocate, intermediary – all were activities that would promote the Devs as a vital force in society and valued subjects of the Maratha state. All this would come to naught if the kin were embroiled in dispute over the possession of their inam.

II. The Peshva's settlement of the Dev lineage

The settlement of the Devs' internal affairs was a carefully thoughtout process. Nothing was left to chance. Custom and traditional law were blended with pragmatic considerations to produce a distribution of wealth that is remarkable not only for its detail, but for the farsighted principles on which it is based. How was this achieved and what was its effect on the lineage in the later Maratha state?

On 6 December 1744 in the village of Dongargav-Mhase, tarph Karde (now Shirur taluka of Pune district), Balaji Bajirav Peshva called together most of the Dev kinsmen and issued a *tahanāmā*, a comprehensive treaty of settlement.[35] One simple rule, which would henceforth regulate the descent of Cincvad's inam was agreed to: one-half of all prior acquisitions belonged to the Samsthan, one-half was the personal inheritance of the kin. The Samsthan's moiety was an indivisible institutional endowment, whereas the personal share would be subject to equal partition among heirs, the customary mode of inheritance in Maharashtra. While providing for the maintenance of an expanding lineage and satisfying the kin's desire for a share of their patrimony, this settlement also sought to safeguard the sacred functions of the Samsthan and the ritual position of the Dev.

A tahanama is most often a political treaty, but one which contains elements of a lineage settlement. So, the treaty between the Kolhapur and Satara chatrapatis, which set out the 1731 territorial settlement

---

[35] For a Marathi edition and English translation see Laurence Wade Preston, 'Land, Lineage and the State in Maharashtra; The Devs of Cincvad under the Marathas and the British' (Ph.D. dissertation, University of Toronto, 1984), Appendix *A,* pp. 371–99.

between these close relatives, was a tahanama.[36] By extension the term implies the enumeration of detailed particulars, which distinguishes it from a simple *taha*, a settlement of contending opinions or a 'peace' in the broadest sense.[37]

Although not a political feudatory of the state in the way jagirdars or saranjamdars clearly were, the Dev had nevertheless assumed a type of sovereignty over his domain. His kingship was religious and perhaps social in its most extended manifestations. The state recognized this and mediated between contending parties to the wealth of a Samsthan, an institution that was more than just a landholder or a revenue collector. The settlement of the Dev's inheritance, at least some part of which was impartible as befitted his sovereignty, demanded the gravity of a tahanama. The political connotations of the term were thus entirely appropriate to what the Peshva undertook.

In its structure the tahanama in many respects resembles a partition of wealth within one family.[38] However, any Marathi equivalent for 'partition' as it might be understood in modern terminology (such as *dāyā-(vi)bhāg*) is conspicuously absent in the document. In part, with its provision of personal shares, the tahanama might reasonably be considered a lineage partition. But the separation of institutional and personal shares was a settlement of a different order. The second and third Devs had acquired a great quantity of inam. By 1744/5 there existed possible heirs down to the fifth Dev's generation in addition to the institutional claim of the Samsthan. When the Peshva asked the fifth Dev Dharanidhar about the disputes among the kin, he replied to the effect that three generations were involved. In other words, the succession of heirs had proceeded to the third generation from when the inam was first acquired. Under this circumstance there could be no regular partition of the joint property of brothers and their immediate collaterals. The impartible element in the patrimony further complicated such an unexceptional division of wealth.

The efforts to find a settlement for the lineage's internal affairs began shortly after the fifth Dev succeeded the fourth.[39] It is not clear, however, whether the new Dev instigated the proceedings that led to the

[36] Ganesh Chimnaji Vad, Purshotam Vishram Mawjee and D. B. Parasnis, *Treaties, Agreements and Sanads* (Pune, 1914), p. 44 for the Treaty of Varna of 13 April 1731. See also ibid., pp. 43–4 for a proposed but unsuccessful treaty of 1725, also a tahanama.
[37] Appasaheb Pavar, *Tarabai kalin kagadpatre*, 3 vols. (Kolhapur, 1969–72), III, 33–6 for a taha of 1751 between Tarabai and Balaji Bajirav. Note also that the word is used in the introduction to the Devs' tahanama, but only in the general sense of 'agreement.'
[38] Pavar, II, 21–35 for a partition dated 25 May 1723 by the three sons of Ramcandrapant Amatya, though this is simply called a *hish(e)b*, 'list'.
[39] Cintaman II died 18 November 1740, see *Vaidya daphtar*, II, 49.

tahanama either through a genuine desire to fix his new inheritance or because he antagonized his relations to such an extent that they demanded a settlement. When Dharanidhar assumed the sainthood all the Cincvad inam was apparently under his personal control. Only when the junior kin had their own separate holdings would they not be dependent on his generosity for their support. The consequent squabbles have left no record in the documentary sources so far discovered. The tahanama states only that a dispute had 'continually arisen over the ancestral wealth (*pitṛdhan*),' and the implication is that the protests of the disinherited were bitter.

In 1741 Dharanidhar attempted to resolve the situation by referring the problem to Shahu in Satara.[40] Not being represented in this *ex parte* settlement attempt, the kin petitioned the Peshva to intervene with the Dev. Although completely superseded by the document of 1744/5, Shahu produced a tahanama based on the same principles the Peshva would later adopt. It perhaps served as the latter's model. Shahu, however, reserved the inam of sacred sites (Morgav, Theur and a portion of Siddhatek) for the Samsthan before the equal division of personal and institutional shares was made. This the kin could not accept. The Peshva therefore included all acquisitions in the divisible inheritance, though the sacred sites would remain in the share assigned to the Samsthan.

The Peshva's tahanama succeeded as a lasting settlement only because all involved would agree to it. Even given Shahu's prior patronage of the Devs and his venerable position as titular head of the Maratha state, his will could not be imposed on the lineage. Perhaps he received biased advice from the Dev, and this seems to be the reason the kin approached the Peshva. Perhaps too, the politics of the time caused them to reject the chatrapati's arbitration – by the 1740s Shahu had almost completely abdicated real power to the Peshva. In any case, the state could only successfully intervene in a lineage when all concerned parties were ready to abide by the decision rendered. When the Peshva accepted such a commission he gave his judgment as arbiter of the known facts; he did not act as a medium for negotiations, nor did he preside over adversary proceedings. The introduction to the tahanama makes this clear. Only when all the contending parties had given the Peshva their assent would he consider the Cincvad inam.

First the Peshva turned his attention to the inams of the second Dev Cintaman, or at least those held at his death. As Cintaman was Moroba Gosavi's sole heir, the exact chronology of the seventeenth-century

---

[40] PA: SD 13186 (?); see *Chintaman Bajaji Dev* v. *Dhondo Ganesh Dev, Indian Law Reports*, 15 Bom. (1891), 619–20 for summary.

grants (briefly considered in the previous chapter) was irrelevant to the settlement. Here, Cincvad was the only whole village inam considered. The rest of the holdings were mainly village land inams, widely spread throughout Haveli, plus a few miscellaneous cash allowances. Being the sacred legacy of the saint, Cincvad was assigned to the Samsthan and would always remain an impartible inheritance. Perhaps the village should be considered a devasthan (a religious endowment) though the term is never used in the tahanama. But equally, because the Dev of Cincvad was the ritual and administrative head of the Samsthan, Cincvad might be seen as his own impartible inheritance. And in this latter way, what the Peshva allowed 'for the Samsthan' (as it is always designated) is analagous to the descent of a political sovereignty, which is always indivisible in the Hindu tradition.[41] In the eighteenth century the equivalence of the institution of the Samsthan with the Dev of Cincvad was so close, if not identical, that the Peshva had no need to elaborate on the precise nature of the impartible inheritance he created. A century later, however, the British would have much cause to speculate on the point.

All Cintaman's acquisitions additional to Cincvad village were divided between his four sons in equal shares. Here the ritual precedence of the Dev of Cincvad, through which he had until 1744/5 controlled all the Samsthan's endowments, was of no consequence. He and his descendants would in future receive only their quarter share of what was deemed Cintaman's personal legacy. In this respect the tahanama's partition completely conforms to the *Mitākṣarā* tradition of inheritance prevalent in Maharashtra.[42]

The resulting shares were relatively small amounts of cash and land. The descendants of the four brothers received Rs. 61/3/- in cash, carefully apportioned out of a plethora of minor casses and such. For example, Cintaman had the right to Rs. 4 out of the government revenues of Bopegav village (Purandhar taluka). Four shares, two as small as 3 annas, were created from the very minor revenue alienation. How the descent of such minute divisions of revenue was managed among the numerous descendants of the four brothers is not readily apparent. Some later evidence suggests that the strict partition of such small shares became somewhat obscured. Not all inams were subjected to such fracturing. No doubt for convenience in administration of revenue collections, each brother was given a major land holding in one

[41] Pandurang Vaman Kane, *History of Dharmashastra*, 5 vols. (Pune, 1930–62), II, 631 for an uncharacteristically brief discussion of this point.
[42] Kane, III, chapter 27, pp. 543 ff., especially pp. 560–1, 591–6.

village. The spatial consolidation of shares become especially important when larger holdings were divided. Still, if necessary to create precisely equal shares, minute divisions such as that for Bopegav were made throughout the tahanama. Equality of interests among brothers is the first and overriding principle in the descent of the personal portion of the Cincvad inam.

Notwithstanding the above description of the tahanama as an equal separation of Samsthan and personal inam, it is doubtful that the combined shares of Cintaman's four sons would ever have approached the worth of Cincvad village. This apparent inequality was due to the uncontested desire to retain Cincvad as the Samsthan's endowment. In attempting to estimate the relative worth of the division of Cintaman's inam certain real difficulties are encountered. Specifically, eighteenth-century values for certain items of revenue, especially village land inams, are difficult to determine. More generally, a brief consideration of monetary realizations from inam will show that the tahanama was based on a type of nominal accounting, not on actual revenues. Inam was divided in terms of fixed units of account: village land inams in areal measures, whole village inams in set *tankhā* valuations. The former made no explicit reference to real value, the latter, to be explained in detail below, only approximated what an inamdar could expect from his holdings. Furthermore, the two units of account were never compared with each other.

The tankha of Cincvad village is recorded as Rs. 1721/12-; against this the kin could only divide Rs. 244/12/- plus $9\frac{1}{2}$ cavars of land. The cash portion of the personal shares was invariable as it came from whatever government actually received from certain villages or other revenue divisions. However, the value of the land is problematic. In the mid-nineteenth century 4 of the $9\frac{1}{2}$ cavars, the only ones for which figures are readily available, realized Rs. 313/8/-, at which rate all the land would have returned about Rs. 745.[43] The personal share of the four brothers would then total on the order of Rs. 1000. The figures given here admittedly come from much after the date of the tahanama, so without a detailed exploration of eighteenth-century village accounts (not attempted in this study), the amounts are little more than loose estimates. Nevertheless, the definite impression remains that the personal shares bestowed on Cintaman's sons could not equal the nominal valuation of Cincvad village.

---

[43] The descent of shares detailed in the tahanama is traced in the accompaniment to Inam Commissioner, Northern Division to Revenue Commissioner for Alienations, 8 February 1861, PA: xiv; 28/322, fols. 316–17 (hereafter cited as 'Inam Commission's summary').

In fact, the tahanama makes no claim to precisely divide Cintaman's acquisitions in half. Perhaps the actual result was not grossly disparate, at least as equitable as the types of revenue involved would allow. But to compare land inams with whole villages does no justice to the tahanama's intentions. Valuations are never put on land because equal measures could not be guaranteed to produce the same revenue in different villages. Wetland (*bāgāīt*) would usually produce more revenue than dryland (*jirāīt*). Climatic conditions would affect the productivity of land from year to year and from village to village. Furthermore, the inamdar might make different arrangements with his various tenant farmers, for instance lightening revenue demands to encourage cultivation. A further difficulty is peculiar to any attempt to determine the value of a land measure: there is no certainty that the measures refer to the same area. They apparently varied from village to village with even some suggestion that they represented the value, that is the productivity of land.[44] In general, a cavar consisted of 120 *bighā*s each measuring in the range 0.7 to 0.81 of an acre.[45]

As previously mentioned, the tahanama's recorded values for whole village inams are expressed in tankha amounts. These nominal valuations, which are said to derive from pre-Maratha Muslim land settlements, are beset with difficulties of interpretation. The system of revenue accounting was not a precise measure of what an inamdar could or would expect from a village, his revenue demands rather being negotiated yearly with the rural authorities.[46] By the eighteenth century the tankha was little more than a loose guide to village revenues. It was, in short, a device for those clerks who prepared annual estimates of the

[44] G. Wingate, Superintendent Revenue Survey and Assessment, Southern Maratha Country to W. Hart, Inam Commissioner, 21 August 1847, PA: II; 1/8, fols. 83-91 makes these points. See also W. H. Sykes, 'Special Report on the Statistics of the Four Collectorates of Dukhun, under the British Government,' *Report of the Seventh Meeting of the British Association for the Advancement of Science*, 6 (1838), 310-11. Bighas, usually uniform, were defined in terms of measures such as takas, rukas, *paisā*, etc., which were apparently areal measures of productivity.

[45] Cincvad's one cavar at Pimple Saudagar measured 84 acres (0.7 acre per bigha), see Harold H. Mann, *Land and Labour in a Deccan Village* (Study No. 1) (Bombay, 1917), pp. 35-7. Sykes, 'Special Report,' uses the constant factor of 0.75 acre per bigha; H. D. Robertson in 1820 calculated the standard bigha dating from pre-Maratha Muslim dynasties as 0.81 acre per bigha, see *Gazetteer of the Bombay Presidency*, Poona District (Bombay, 1885), 18, 2, p. 320.

[46] This system of revenue administration continued throughout the Maratha and British periods, completely apart from the Peshva's *kamal* (highest realizations) survey and the many innovations of British revenue policy. This is the essential point for any contemplated study of an inamdar's revenue administration. For the kamal and tankha see *Gazetteer*, 18, 2, pp. 317-25.

state's revenues.[47] When numerous whole village inams are partitioned, as in Narayan's acquisitions to be considered below, the result is thus a formal exercise with no intention of apportioning precise amounts of money. In this way similar to the division of measures of land, nonetheless, tankha valuations are never set against cavars of land. The two could not be combined and then equitably partitioned.

The sources exist to precisely determine actual eighteenth-century realizations from land and villages.[48] Conceivably the tahanama could be checked to see if it was in fact financially equitable in the first instance, and further, to see how the settlement held up over time. So huge is the collection of documents, and so obscure their import, that the task of reconstructing all the variations in the yearly settlements – and what is more, the reasons why such occurred – would be difficult in the extreme.

But such precision of values was not the real purpose of the tahanama, nor was it what the Dev kin expected. The settlement was firstly concerned with certain principles of inheritance, not the actual ledger of Cincvad's inam. At the same time, the settlement must have satisfied the kin as being reasonably fair in its practical workings. Presumably no one sharer received all the poor land or less productive villages. Being located on some of the finest land in Pune district, Cincvad's villages probably did not have great discrepancies in their productive capacities. Nevertheless, those with less river frontage, being dependent on dryland farming, and subject to drought would be much poorer speculations, whatever their nominal rating.

The tahanama's tankha values should therefore be used with caution as being at best what inam may have realized in the eighteenth century. Unlike economic history, which more often deals in precise real values, the study of inheritance attempted in this chapter is well served with the system of nominal accounting adopted in the tahanama.

Turning now to the division of the third Dev's inam, the tahanama again strives for financial equity though tempering this with provision for the more numerous claims against revenues. The money involved is

[47] Perhaps, though, it was still a more reasonable indication of actual revenue performance than surveys based on the supposed productivity of the soil and such, if British experiences in Indapur taluka in the 1820s are taken as a guide, see Ravinder Kumar, *Western India in the Nineteenth Century* (London, 1968), pp. 93, 101.
[48] For example, in part from the annual revenue correspondence for Cincvad's inam villages directed to the hereditary district officers; for Haveli in PA: jamav daphtar rumals 1 (Akurdi), 78 (Cincvad), 79 (Cincoli), 80–83 (Cikhli), 84 (Carholi), 92 (Jamb), 184–85 (Banere), 196–99 (Bhosri), 203–06 (Man), 221 (Ravet), 242 (Vakad). Yearly abstracts of Cincvad's revenues and expenditures probably also exist, but their location is not at present known to me.

far greater than for Cintaman's acquisitions: cash receipts alone total nearly Rs. 23,000 made up of the income of several whole villages, shares of whole villages, and miscellaneous allowances. Included in the third Dev's patrimony was his personal share of his father's acquisitions.

Narayan's nearly 7 cavars of land were first divided equally between the Samsthan and the kin. Then his portion of Cintaman's land was added to the moiety apportioned among his five sons. Apparently the personal inheritance obtained from the second Dev was considered to belong to the descendants of the third Dev and not subject to the claim of the Samsthan.[49] Because Cintaman's land amounted to more than each of Narayan's five sons would obtain after partition, the old holdings could not remain the personal share of the eldest Dev, and consequently they were distributed rather widely among the brothers. Curiously, in the final disposition of land the Dev of Cincvad received half a bigha less than his brothers. A precise division would have produced unwanted fractions of bighas; the Dev could afford to take the loss.

The initial partition of Narayan's whole village inams was not quite equal, but into 'more or less' (*kamajvād*) half shares. The Samsthan received only 49.85 percent of the total. It is not obvious why the kin should have been allowed an additional Rs. 67. Generally, the Samsthan was assigned only major division of revenue, and perhaps the appropriate sums could not be so manipulated. On the other hand, it received 1 rupee 6 annas out of Aundh village, which shows that the Peshva was not adverse to making fine division of the revenue.

Special provisions made out of both the institutional and personal shares show the Peshva's desire to accommodate the claims of all possible heirs. Four widows were given allowances from the Samsthan's moiety.[50] But this was a short-term measure as the money reverted to the Samsthan after their deaths. From the kin's share allowance was made for collateral lines. Before Narayan's five sons received their equal shares, two of his three brothers were given legacies of Rs. 1000 each. These two had 'behaved like sons' to Narayan and so had been 'afforded support like sons,' hence their descendants deserved to have some part in his good fortune. In part, his inam was treated like the joint acquisition of brothers prior to partition. But the two younger brothers did not

[49] For some inexplicable reason, Narayan's share of his father's cash was enumerated among the acquisitions subject to division between the kin and the Samsthan. However, in practice it was included in the Dev's personal inheritance and thus not subject to the claim of the Samsthan. The amount involved (Rs. 61/3/-) was very trivial, and perhaps for that reason it was treated differently from the more substantial land inams.

[50] At least, I presume the 'respected ladies' who were given Rs. 726 for their personal maintenance were widows.

receive shares equal to those of Narayan's five sons (Rs. 1898 each). To this extent the inheritance of the collaterals was a gratuity; they could not claim an equal right with the Dev's direct descendants.

In practical terms the inheritance Narayan's brothers obtained from their father would have been insufficient to maintain their expanding families. An equal partition of Rs. 61 would have amounted to very little after two generations. The further endowment of the collaterals was simply a way of forestalling future claims against the Samsthan for their support. The characteristic sharing of inam among brothers was noticed in 1821 by William Chaplin, Commissioner in the Deccan. In general,

no uniform rule appears ever to have been observed in dividing amongst the brothers the estates of great Enamdars or Jageerdars or Zumeendars. The mode of sharing such property seems to have everywhere varied being neither regulated strictly by rules of Hindoo Law nor by any standard of established custom.[51]

Less fortunate brothers were usually provided for, especially when the recipient of an inam had used a joint patrimony as a member of an unseparated family to obtain his wealth. But even without this special case,

the indulgent and human precepts of Hindoo ethics prescribe that the more fortunate brother shall make an adequate provision for the sustenance of the others and the allotment of such a provision seems to have become part of the Common Law.[52]

Chaplin might have added that lineage harmony demanded such a concession.

Vinayak Dev, Cintaman's third son, had no need for a share of his elder brother's acquisitions. Apparently popularly revered in his own right, to judge by his honorific 'Kakamaharaj', Vinayak had been granted his own inam. His three villages, previously noticed in connection with the formation of the Samsthan, yielded his descendants revenues in excess of Rs. 3800.[53] The tahanama takes no notice of this substantial sum. Vinayak's brothers and their descendants could not claim against his inam in the manner they shared anything granted to the Dev of Cincvad (whether person or institution). Separate acquisitions descended only to the heirs of the original grantee, a principle invariable in the history of the lineage.[54]

---

[51] Chaplin to Government, 27 April 1821, PA: DC 381/123–47.
[52] Ibid.
[53] See p. 36. Tankha values are from Collector of Pune to Government, 9 September 1852, PA: xiii; 55/740, pp. 9–11.
[54] Günther-Dietz Sontheimer, *The Joint Hindu Family* (New Delhi, 1977), p. 75 for comments on 'self-acquisitions,' their exemption from partition and role in preserving family jointness.

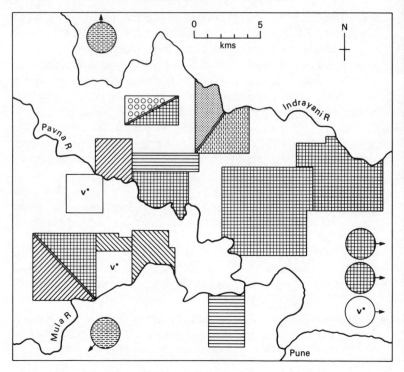

Figure 9(a). Distribution of Dev village inams, 1744/5

One further anomaly in the settlement deserves mention. Cincvad possessed a *dastak* (pass for the movement of trade without taxation) for 150 bullocks on four trips (600 'bullock-trips'). The Samsthan, which probably had the most immediate need for this right, was assigned all the bullock-trips except for 96 shared by several of Narayan's collaterals and descendants. Again Vinayak was excluded. But also the Dev of Cincvad himself was not allowed a personal allotment of bullock-trips. Perhaps his control of the Samsthan made this concession unnecessary. Although really a minor item of potential revenue, the irregular partition of the bullock-trips required a detailed explanation. Moreover, after imploring the kin to behave themselves and act according to their *dharma* (duty), almost as an afterthought the tahanama again describes the arrangement in its final sentences. Such a departure from the principles of juridical and financial equity required additional emphasis.

Although Cintaman's village land inams had been distributed so that each of his four sons would have a major holding in one village, no such consideration influenced the partition of Narayan's lands. The amount

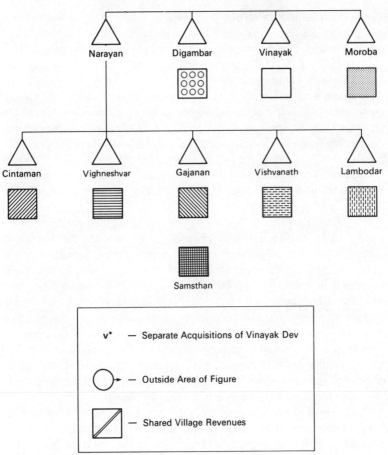

Figure 9(b). Genealogical key to Figure 9(a)

each son received was small, with almost every village land inam being split five ways if practicable. No intentional pattern in the distribution of shares can be discerned.

Instead, the Peshva concentrated on the spatial distribution of whole village inams, which in any case accounted for by far the bulk of Narayan's acquisitions. A genealogical map (again, as in Chapter 1, using a schematized rendering of villages by area in riverine north-west Haveli as a base) shows the way the tahanama assigned these villages.[55] (See Figure 9 (a) and (b).) The map records as closely as possible the

[55] I owe the concept of a genealogical map to Paul and Laura Bohannan, *Tiv Economy* (London, 1968), Chapter 3, especially figures 8 and 9, pp. 35, 37.

Devs' inam as it was settled in 1744/5 by including the Samsthan's villages and also Vinayak's separate acquisitions. Only major holdings can be portrayed: either where one sharer held nearly the entire village revenue (within about 10 percent); or where two sharers held a village in approximately equal portions.

Narayan's direct and collateral descendants became so closely associated with their assigned villages that later sources often refer to the Devs by village name plus the territorial affix *kar*. So far example, the descendants of Gajanan became 'Dev Vakadkar.' This territoriality became the hallmark of the lineage in the later eighteenth century. Only in one case, when Lambodar died heirless and the Samsthan took over his portion (61.9 percent) of Cikhli village, did a share lose its separate identity.[56]

While the tahanama consolidated the kins' shares, whenever possible brothers were not assigned adjoining villages. Never did they share one village. Those few joint holdings were held with the Samsthan or, in Cikhli, between collaterals. The Samsthan's inams were in part fixed because it had to hold Cincvad and the other sacred sites (Theur and Morgav). Even then, the Peshva was able to intersperse the feuding kin's villages with Samsthan territory, though in one case (Vishvanath, son of Narayan) this meant creating a share from miscellaneous revenues outside Haveli. Though Cincvad's inam was quite concentrated in one locality, and given the limited number of territorial units with which to create equal revenues, the tahanama's seven consolidated but separate personal domains must be one of its notable features.

A glance at the tahanama reveals small portions of revenue distributed rather freely among the kin. These raise again the problems connected with the inamdar's internal administration of his estate, particularly questions of revenue assessment and collection. In several villages the sardeshmukhi, the 10 percent on top of the tankha, is assigned to someone different from the village's major revenue receiver. This impost was apparently not considered as part of the nominal village rating and was used as a convenient unit to make up the required total of another share. Whether the recipient of the sardeshmukhi received a fixed allowance from a village's gross receipts, or perhaps took a 10 percent share, are points that remain to be elucidated. The extreme instance of a minor share in a village in the Samsthan's 1 rupee 6 annas from Aundh, which amounted to only 0.072 percent of the total village

[56] Inam Commission's summary, 8 February 1861. In a related case the fifth Dev apparently renounced his one-third personal share of Ravet, which was bestowed on his two younger brothers. However, this did not affect the descent of the share as it was still held by the heirs of Narayan's eldest son.

revenue (tankha and sardeshmukhi). Probably this was never taken as a percentage of gross receipts. At least in the mid-nineteenth century the Samsthan received a fixed cash payment from the descendants of Vighneshvar, second son of Narayan.[57] Of more consequence was the revenue from transit duties (*jakāt*) shared by four of Narayan's sons. The Samsthan managed this profitable commercial enterprise, which, as Chapter 5 shows, likely produced at least six times the annual revenue recorded in the tahanama. It is at best a guess, but most probably the Samsthan paid only fixed allowances to the descendants of the sharers, not a quarter of actual realizations.

Lacking the Samsthan's administrative resources, the kin's minute shares in farflung villages tended to disappear over time. So, the 8 rupees 1 anna (0.31 percent) from Cikhli assigned to Digambar's sons were apparently abandoned by their descendants.[58] Often the Samsthan, and sometimes the major sharer in a village, simply appropriated the most minor of these miscellaneous assignments of revenue. Such only tended to reinforce the territorial consolidation of personal sharers in specific villages. What happened was that the technical niceties of the tahanama yielded to the realities of administration.

With village land inams the situation became even more confused. Often these were exchanged (in whole or part), reassigned or, on occasion, resumed. Because many of these holdings were very obscure, depending on the annual village settlements for their valuation and payment, there are no convincing sources at present available to show whether they underwent the same process of consolidation as whole village inams. Even in the mid-nineteenth century the British could only list without comment the fact of these inams as recorded in the tahanama and other summaries.[59] A full explication of such minor revenue alienations must wait for a close study of village records.

III. The descent of a partible inheritance

Not being a once-only settlement among contending parties alive at a particular time, the tahanama instead sought to regulate the Dev inheritance for future generations. To be a success, to preserve lineage harmony, the document's provisions had to be workable while preserving financial equity in an expanding lineage. In general the tahanama served the Devs well, but as the number of heirs multiplied, the potential of the Cincvad inam to support everyone concurrently declined. After 75 years and the succession of about four generations, which was roughly

[57] Ibid.   [58] Ibid.   [59] Ibid.

the time of the British conquest, the tahanama's utility was definitely on the wane. The senior branches of the lineage obtained new grants that altered the settlement in important particulars. With their increasingly fractured inheritances, the junior kin lost their relative importance within the totality of the lineage.

Although thus a charter for the lineage's patrimony, the tahanama did not explicitly state how its provisions would apply to future Dev generations. Once it had established partible and impartible inheritances, and delineated the details of each, the manner of their descent was left to the operation of custom and law. The Samsthan's endowment would, of course, always remain intact. It would also always come under the direct management of the Dev of Cincvad. It was not the Dev's personal property at all, but in the subsequent history of the Samsthan this strict distinction between management and possession was often obscured. The point is taken up again in Chapter 7 when describing the Devs under the British. In the eighteenth century, the equal partition of the partible inheritance had a more immediate effect on the mass of the Dev kin. Thus, we must now examine the relation between inheritance and lineage structure. In particular, the concept of lineage segmentation and its effect on the Devs will be analyzed.

Social anthropology speaks of two basic forms of lineage organization, both of which have relevance for the Devs. Sometimes a lineage is organized around a kingship. Here 'there is a dominant line associated with the property. It is continually "sloughing off" collateral lineages.'[60] In this basically political structure the kin are seen in terms of their relations to those who control an impartible inheritance. If we consider a political model of the Cincvad Samsthan, then the Dev lineage could be seen as organized in terms of relative genealogical distance from the Dev of Cincvad, the manager of the tahanama's impartible inheritance. While everyone was descended from the saint and his son, fewer could claim descent from the third Dev, fewer from the fourth and so on. This became of critical importance when, in the nineteenth century, adoptions became necessary to fill the sacred office. This issue is explored at length in Chapter 7. One further practical effect of being closely related to the Dev of Cincvad should be borne in mind. While he controlled the

---

[60] Paul Bohannan, *Social Anthropology* (New York, 1963), p. 138; see Meyer Fortes, 'The Structure of Unilineal Descent Groups,' *American Anthropologist*, 55 (1953), 26 on lineages in centralized societies. Early in the development of lineage theory, lineages tended to be defined only on the basis of segmental organization (to be considered below), see M. Fortes and E. E. Evans-Pritchard, 'Introduction' to *African Political Systems* (London, 1940), p. 6. I believe Bohannan's views are important in understanding the relations between kingship and unilineal descent.

Samsthan through his ritual primacy, his near agnates could expect to play an important part in the disposition of Cincvad's resources. These were the relatives who advised the Dev and became his 'ministers,' to use the political analogy. In this sense the Dev's immediate kin did tend to form a 'dominant line' as described above.

In common with lost Indian cases, the Devs are a patrilineage whose corporate identity is based on unilineal descent. All males have a claim to the legacy of common ancestors. Every line of descent from a progenitor is of equal theoretical significance; hence, all kin at the same genealogical level are equal in terms of each other. Such patrilineages have a strong sense of genealogy with all members knowing their line of descent and, by the use of pivotal ancestors, the relations between lines. At times in certain societies (the Nuer and Tiv being classic cases) genealogies are putative, adjusted so that the actual state of lines of descent can conveniently be included in an oral reckoning.[61]

A lineage with such characteristics can only occur when property is in some respect shared. A. R. Radcliffe-Brown put this fundamental into what has become almost an anthropological axiom: '[a] corporation can only form itself on the basis of a common interest.'[62] Without a collective inheritance (their 'interest') a body of kin (the 'corporation') with only the most distant connections – ancestors several generations removed – could not preserve their corporate identity. While anyone can construct his biological genealogy (given, of course, adequate historical records or traditions), only with a shared descent of property does this have a social relevance.

Such lineages form themselves into sublineages or segments. Here

the general rule is that every segment is, in form, a replica of every other segment and of the whole lineage. But the segments are, as a rule, hierarchically organized by fixed steps of greater and greater inclusiveness, each step being defined by genealogical reference.[63]

Each segment has a common ancestor who in turn has apical ancestors shared with other segments and so on back to the lineage founder. Often this lineage progenitor is mythological, but equally, as for the Devs, it can be a historical personality. In either case the formal structure of the segmentary lineage is the same. Being firstly a description of the

[61] Fortes, 'Unilineal Descent Groups,' 27–8; E. E. Evans-Pritchard, *The Nuer* (Oxford, 1940), p. 199: 'in those lines that persist names drop out of the steps in ascent to the founder of the clan, so that the distance in generations from the founder of a clan to the present day remains fairly constant.'
[62] 'Patrilineal and Matrilineal Succession,' in *Structure and Function in Primitive Society* (London, 1952), p. 45.
[63] Fortes, 'Unilineal Descent Groups,' 31.

characteristic genealogical pyramid, only by extension does the segmentary structure have any functional importance for the operation of the lineage itself. Again in Meyer Fortes' words: 'it is perhaps hardly necessary to mention again that when we talk of lineage structure we are really concerned, from a particular analytical angle, with the organization of jural, economic, and ritual activities.'[64] For segmentation to be a useful historical tool, and not merely a neat conceptualization, it must be asked in what contexts a lineage member would describe himself as descended from x (being the segmental apical ancestor) while also being a descendant of y (the lineage progenitor).

In Africa, starting with Evans-Pritchard's studies of the Nuer, the segmentary lineage is often a description of a type of acephalous polity, one lacking in centralized political power.[65] Here society is organized in terms of 'segmental opposition,' the relations between equivalent segments of the same genealogical order. In principle, a lineage member finds his social allies in his own 'minimal' segment, then in segments of greater inclusiveness ('maximal') and so on until all possess a kind of national identity as descendants of an eponymous founder. The genealogical hierarchy is often imprinted on the organization of terrestrial space.[66] An extreme view has, in fact, seen the segmentary lineage as solely a kind of device for cultural expansion in certain ecological contexts.[67]

Passing over the many controversies that have surrounded such a structural analysis of very particular societies, and wary of describing complex historical Indian polities as 'segmenatry states,' nevertheless the concept of the segment has particular value when analyzing the inheritance of inam and other alienated revenues. The basic proposition is straightforward: the grantee of an inam became the apical ancestor of a segment, all members of which received some portion of the original grant as their patrimony. If the growth of the segment was perfectly geometrical – x had two sons, both of whom had two sons, and so on – then the shares at any genealogical level would be identical. Of course, nothing of the sort ever happened, and in any generation numerous fractions of the original sum would coexist. A corollary to the concept of segment creation through inam acquisition is that when any

[64] Ibid., see also M. G. Smith, 'On Segmentary Lineage Systems,' *Journal of the Royal Anthropological Institute*, 86, 2 (1956), 57.
[65] *The Nuer*, pp. 192–248 for the first extended description of the segmentary lineage in such societies. See also the discussion in Smith, pp. 43–5.
[66] Paul and Laura Bohannan, pp. 13–38 for an excellent description.
[67] Marshall D. Sahlins, 'The Segmentary Lineage: An Organization of Predatory Expansion,' *American Anthropologist*, 63 (1961), 322–45; see the comments of Meyer Fortes, *Kinship and the Social Order* (London, 1969), pp. 289–90.

heir obtained his own source of revenue, a grant shared with no other kin, then a further segment was born. The new grantee retained his patrimony and created another, both of which were passed on to his descendants. Because inams were often shared between brothers living jointly, regardless of the titular recipient, lineage segments in this sense may have multiple apical ancestors, a feature that only affected the rate at which shares divided.

In certain circumstances it is useful to think in terms of a 'subsegment,' though such is formally equivalent to the major division. So, when a Dev kinsman obtained a village land inam, this acquisition did produce a new line of descent within the totality of the lineage. But because this subsegment was still in receipt of shares of whole village inams, it was always identified with the major segment created in the tahanama. Only with a substantial new grant – a whole village or especially a temple site – did any individual stand as head of a new segment that would have been identified within the lineage as an independent line of descent.

The genealogical depth of any segment is of no consequence as a fundamental of lineage organization when considering the descent of inam. As corporate units each segment was equal. Having the inheritance pass through many successions produced no precedence in itself. Perhaps, even, a hoary genealogy was a decided disadvantage. More heirs meant smaller shares of the original patrimony, and also that the segment was far removed from the state's favor and new grants.

As an economic analysis of the effect of lineage segmentation on inheritance the above description is not peculiar to inam. Any partible estate once gained creates such segments. With inam, however, the major heritable property is relatively fixed. Firstly, the time of acquisition and identity of the grantee can be precisely known from historical sources. Secondly, through the use of tankha values for whole village inams, a set of standard figures can be used to follow through the division of shares within a segment. Though the tankha is not without serious difficulties, as indicated previously and which will be further discussed below,[68] the following analysis illustrating the principles of descent in a partible inheritance gives at least some idea what an heir actually received.

Two Dev lineage segments will serve as examples. The first, that of Gajanan son of Narayan (see Figure 10 (a)) is one of the simplest. The other, of greater genealogical depth and complexity, traces the descent of Vinayak's separate acquisitions plus his share of Cintaman's inam (Figure 10 (b)). Both have features common to all segments issuing from

[68] See pp. 78–9.

The inamdar under the Marathas

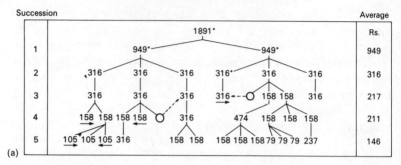

○ Adopted out
--→ Adopted to
⟶ Share (underlined) to collaterals
* Died before the introduction of British rule

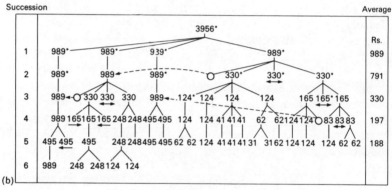

Figure 10. Shares of a partible inheritance
(a) Segment of Gajanan
(b) Segment of Vinayak

the tahanama excepting that of the Dev of Cincvad, a consideration of which will be the subject of a separate analysis in this chapter. After the Peshva's settlement none, apart from the senior line, was granted a whole village inam that affected the descent of shares within their segment. Two post-tahanama inams require explanation. Vishvanath's eldest son obtained the moglai of Sudumbare village where his family already held the svarajya. The grantee shared the inam with his brother thus not altering how the segment's patrimony was apportioned. Just after the tahanama was drawn up, Vighneshvar gained a minor portion of a whole village inam, but this was simply added to the inheritance distributed among his sons.

The situation with village land inams was much different. Many instances of post-tahanama grants to junior Dev kin can be deduced from the sources. Often, however, the identities of specific grantees cannot be accurately determined. Hence, the subsegments that issue from these inams are still obscure. All but a few representative examples of village land inams must therefore be excluded from the present analysis.

Both of the illustrated examples of tahanama lineage segments show how quickly a share of a partible inheritance declines in worth. In both cases, three successions produce shares as little as 8.3 percent of the original inheritance. In other segments the low values for the third succession are comparable, ranging from 3.1 percent to 11.1 percent of the original inheritance.

Yet it is a commonplace that always dividing inheritances will rapidly dwindle them to nearly nothing. Each segment had means to resist precisely this effect of partition. In the first instance, brothers would often hold shares jointly, in effect pooling their resources. The actual revenue any domestic group had at its disposal would thus depend on prevailing family and kinship patterns in the Dev lineage. Lacking much detailed information on the individual Dev families (in the domestic sense), the frequency of joint shares cannot be portrayed in the purely mechanical divisions of Figure 10 (a) and (b). Probably such joint arrangements were frequent. There were good financial reasons to maintain some form of extended family with shared domestic arrangements.

Related to questions of kinship and family structure is the means by which shares were distributed within a segment. Its senior member may have apportioned the actual yearly realizations of the inam to his brethren so as to better husband a relatively fixed patrimony. In support of this inference we find, at the time of the Inam Commission, the eldest living descendant of Gajanan claiming to control the revenue of Vakad village.[69] Whether this 'segment head,' if he may be so called, assigned portions strictly according to the principle of equal division through each succession, or perhaps made a more pragmatic and equitable settlement, is not yet clear. When more than one village was held by a segment, specific inams were given to separate lines of descent, in effect creating subsegments. Thus, three of Vinayak's four sons were assigned villages that remained in the control of their descendants until the mid-nineteenth century.[70] The fourth son apparently managed the village land inams. Within segments possessing relatively large amounts of inam, some form of partition was necessary to forestall discord similar

[69] Inam Commission's summary, 8 February 1861.
[70] Inam Commission decisions on Urali, Jamb and Hinjavadi, see PA: xiii; 55/740, pp. 264–79, 325–43; PA: xiii; 1/6.

to that affecting the lineage as a whole. Whether this was a formal, written arrangement remains to be discovered.

Joint inheritances and segment partitions may have better utilized available resources, but they could not halt the relentless diminution of shares in a partible inheritance. Certain demographic characteristics of the lineage did, on the other hand, noticeably reduce the number of sharers in a segment. Always, as Figure 10 (a) and (b) shows, some heirs retain relatively large shares. Out of the 23 Devs in the fifth succession of Vinayak's segment, one held 25 percent of the original inheritance. A nearly identical case occurs in Digambar's segment. These are extremes, but nevertheless the uneven distribution of shares is apparent. Sometimes this appears to be merely fortuitous, as when a line of descent will have nothing but sole heirs. But given that little is known of the demography of historical India, the line between happenstance and design is difficult to draw. A study of the Dev genealogy leads to the conclusion that some strategies were at work to reduce the number of possible heirs.

Dev sons were firstly never very numerous; the maximum was five, particularly in the early period. An equal number of daughters makes domestic groups of ten children, perhaps still not excessive in the premodern context.[71] This is especially so considering that polygyny was apparently common in the lineage.[72] Generally, two or three sons was the norm; one, often adopted, was not unusual. The Dev genealogy seems to record only those sons who reached a certain age, which might have been that of the thread ceremony (*upanāyana*). On this assumption, recorded heirs would have been of a marriageable age. But it is clear some sons died young, predeceasing their fathers, and before marrying and procreating.[73] But I doubt that the relative paucity of recorded heirs can be solely attributed to infant or child mortality. Many times where there are at least two (and more often three or more) brothers, one has no heirs and in consequence his share of the segment patrimony would

[71] By way of comparison, in an English example of the sixteenth to seventeenth centuries, more than half the women married before age 30 and surviving to 45 had six or more children: see E. A. Wrigley, *Population and History* (London, 1969), pp. 86–7. Reproduction rate is subject to any number of variables, and I do not wish to dwell on this aspect of historical demography, especially as I have little standard of comparison for the Devs in premodern India. Further, the number of potential and actual heirs is something quite different from family, 'household', size as analyzed in Peter Laslett, ed., *Household and Family in Past Time* (Cambridge, 1972). Clearly, I am here not concerned with the domestic units within the Dev lineage. However, the following analysis provides some support to the general thesis of Laslett's book that the family has never been as large as supposed for premodern societies.

[72] For example, the eighth Dev Dharanidhar had three wives.

[73] The manuscript genealogies in PA: IC rumal 11 (Marathi) and PA: XIV; 28/322, fol. 195 give *phaslī* era dates for those who died after the introduction of British rule.

have reverted to his immediate agnates and their descendants. Although unusual in the Indian social environment, perhaps some brothers chose to remain unmarried, thus letting their inheritances be put at the disposal of their collateral descendants for the ultimate benefit of the entire segment.

This inference is supported by the fact that only sons were almost never without an heir. It is therefore not a question of the simple failure of issue. Adoptions were commonly made to continue sole lines of descent. Even child-widows could adopt for their late husbands. There was no lack of opportunity to have a son. Those Devs who remained childless, thus reducing the potential number of heirs, must have done so either through choice or other unexplained and extraordinary circumstances.

Adoption had a dual significance in the lineage. In the first place, it was a religious ceremony, with the provision of male progeny having theological implications. At the same time, a secular heir was provided. Thus, a single line of descent – that is, when a man had no paternal cousins – would always be continued regardless of the negative effects on the division of the segment's patrimony. But adoption was as important for the family giving the son as that receiving. Not only did the adopted son renounce a divided share of his own patrimony, which helped his natal brothers, but he obtained an unpartitioned inheritance in his own right. Often this was in a generation senior to his birth (for example, if adopted by his father's brother), which was even more advantageous because likely his inheritance would be even less divided. Because adoption was almost always made from within the lineage, and further, between close collaterals, it was one very intentional strategy to prevent an excessive fracturing of the inheritance. The various motivations and effects of adoption are considered again when the issue comes to the fore in the British period.

Using average shares per heir in each succession, the relative performance of the lineage segments in preserving their per capita worth can be measured. The question to be asked is how effective, especially over the long term, was the seemingly conscious effort to limit the number of heirs. A graph plotting amounts (on a logarithmic scale) against successions shows each segment performing significantly better than the theoretical norm of genealogical expansion (see Figure 11). On this graph the straight diagonals indicate a perfect geometric progression of heirs, with a steeper angle of descent for higher multiples (times two and three are illustrated and labeled $\times/2$ and $\times/3$ respectively). Only in one instance (Digambar) did a segment, after five successions, approach the rate where each heir had two heirs and so on.

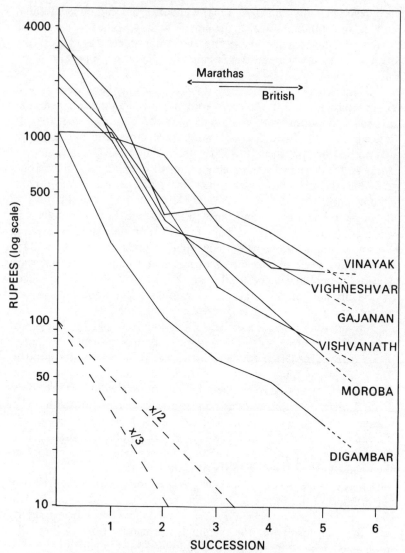

Figure 11. Descent of Dev inam shares

In the first two successions, where large amounts were divided into halves, thirds and quarters, the rate of division was correspondingly high. Thereafter, the decline was somewhat arrested, and each segment's share partitioned at a rate close to 1.5 heirs per heir. In a premodern society placing great emphasis on male progeny – certainly a *sine qua non* for a patrilineage – this must be seen as a definite achievement for the corporate financial interests of the Dev lineage.

During the Maratha period, which approximately included the first three to four successions, while the rate of decline in per capita share value was high, most heirs still received a relatively large amount of money. The exception was Digambar's segment. With only a relatively small original share (Rs. 1061), Digambar's many descendants saw their incomes dwindle into near-trivial amounts. Perhaps in compensation for its prolificacy this segment would later be granted several village land inams.[74] In general terms, through the first three successions most Devs could expect an average share not much below Rs. 300. These were still substantial amounts, even more so when held jointly. Incomes were certainly declining with the passage of the eighteenth century, but this was not drastic enough to cause dissension among the Devs. Nevertheless, however delayed, the collapse of the supportive capacity of the junior segments' inam was always imminent.

Moving into the British period (nearly all heirs in the fourth succession died after the conquest), while the rate of decline in per capita share value continued to decrease, real amounts contracted further. By the mid-nineteenth century (fifth to sixth successions) no individual could expect much more than Rs. 200 per annum, with many well below Rs. 100. Given that the original patrimonies ranged from Rs. 1000 to Rs. 4000, the ultimate spread of values is remarkably close. Increasingly in the nineteenth century the Dev lineage presents a picture of a large body of kin being only partially successful in preserving the worth of their inam. Still the shares were not quite inconsequential; but the fate of the junior Dev lineage segments was to be mean pensioners dependent on the inam and reputation of their forefathers. Combined with the intrusive British inam settlements, this situation provided the necessary conditions for the discord between the Dev kin that will be described in Part Two.

Three factors may have alleviated the plight of the junior kin by causing their average incomes to rise over time. The first, revenue expectations and (in a loose sense) land values, is common to all the Devs' inam and indeed is a problem in the general economic history of India. The other two – village land inams and separate acquisitions – are more peculiar to inamdar lineages.

[74] Cavars were granted in Takli village (now Dhaund taluka), 1738/9, and Supe town, 1730/1, see Inam Commissioner's summary, 1 February 1861. Though these lands date from before the tahanama, as separate acquisitions they were not included in the settlement. Furthermore, because these inams were granted to Digambar's sons, it appears that the pattern of descent in the segments predates the settlement. That is, the Peshva was already dealing with multiple lines of descent when he assigned a share to Digambar and his descendants.

Turning now to the question of village receipts, it may be supposed that after averaging out particularly good and bad years, land revenues showed a steady general increase. While land in Maharashtra was not usually a saleable commodity – we are not therefore considering marketplace pressures – constantly rising revenue might indicate a village's increased productivity and hence its relative worth as inam. Such might be caused by the extension of cultivation (due to population pressures), more fruitful or valuable crops (perhaps indicating better markets, especially in politically stable situations), or in some cases decreased deductions (village expenses, inams and such) from gross village revenues. A general rise in land assessment rates had the potential of producing more revenue, but without expansion and improvement in market and crops it is unlikely the inamdar could realize his expectations. The very few studies that have examined village accounts in both the eighteenth and nineteenth centuries do not lend much support to the thesis of rising values, even on a straight comparison of the Maratha and British periods.[75] Revenues in the first 30–40 years of the nineteenth century, a time of political instability and then drought, were depressed. At least, less revenue found its way to government and inamdar overlords. Although comparisons of British land settlements and their modes of assessment with traditional methods of collection should only be made with caution, the general impression is that periods of peace, Maratha or British, produced similarly favorable revenues.

Some idea of the rise of revenue expectations in good times can be had by comparing tankha village valuations, used as a base, with the figures for the Devs' inam submitted to the British in 1861. The former amounts are subject to the cautions noted earlier, the latter are for one year of uncertain typicality. Table 2 records a 43.2 percent general rise over the tankha, being an average increase of 37.0 percent per village (excluding Saste as not significant). If, as I have suggested, the late eighteenth century was comparable to the British peace, then the lineage segments would have been able to offset their growth by demanding higher revenues from their villages. Increases of one-third or even one-half would not, however, have been nearly sufficient. At the same time, conditions in the unstable decades before and after the conquest must have been even worse than the rates of decline in Figure 11 would indicate.

Table 2 also shows that certain villages, particularly large ones

---

[75] Mann, *Land and Labour*, pp. 42–3; see also Harold H. Mann, 'A Deccan Village under the Peshwas,' in *The Social Framework of Agriculture*, ed. Daniel Thorner (New York, 1967), p. 128. The gross village revenues of Jategav Budruk here being extremely variable, though note the exceptional years at the end of the eighteenth century.

Table 2. *Change in revenues of Devs' inam villages*

Village	Revenue (nearest rupee)		
	Tankha	1861	% change
Akurdi	837	949	13.4
Ambi	701	1,064	51.8
Aundh	1,918	1,938	1.0
Banere	1,630	2,214	35.8
Bhosri	2,667	5,260	97.2
Carholi	3,422	5,980	74.8
Cikhli	2,648	4,580	73.0
Cincoli	765	1,671	18.4
Cincvad	1,722	2,418	40.4
Hinjavadi	939	1,308	39.3
Jamb	639	950	48.7
Man	2,351	2,334	(− 0.7)
Morgav	1,381	2,320	68.0
Ravet	1,402	1,849	31.9
Saste	128	241	88.3
Sudumbare	797	1,281	60.7
Theur	1,663	1,449	(− 12.9)
Urali	2,318	2,935	26.2
Vakad	1,712	1,701	(− 0.6)
Totals	29,640	42,442	43.2
Average (w/o Saste)			37.0

Sources: Peshva's tahanama of 1744/5; Collector of Pune to Government, 9 September 1852; Inam Commission's summary, 8 February 1861.

(Carholi, Cikhli, Morgav and Bhosri) with high tankhas, performed much better than the average. Perhaps this was due to the greater area available for the expansion of cultivation. Lineage segments that held these villages were in a clearly advantageous position in good times. By coincidence or not, the Samsthan controlled three of these larger villages. Another factor that may have influenced the revenue performance of some villages was their relative proximity to Pune and its fluctuating market for grain and high value produce, such as vegetables and dairy products. Without access to village records, this and many other variables in determining historical trends in land revenue can only be noted in passing.

Village land inams may have helped to mitigate the effects of genealogical growth. Although there is no present way of assessing these as items of inheritance, presumably the right to collect revenue directly from villagers, apart from the total village assessment, was of value if there were not too many intermediaries between cultivator and inamdar. If one was prepared to work the soil (or had a right to), a piece of rent-free land would have been a lucrative source of family support. That the Devs ever farmed their land is unlikely; probably they always had tenant sharecroppers.

When the ever-multiplying members of a lineage segment could not expect adequate support from their inam and they would not or could not become ordinary (if privileged) cultivators, then other sources of income would have to be found. Until the conquest new inams could possibly be obtained. This was the course the Dev of Cincvad's near agnates took. For the junior kin new grants were unlikely. Any other type of income would have had the effect of distancing the kin from a lineage based on the possession of inam. Such separate acquisitions would have created new lineage segments that were only remotely connected with the sacred functions of the Samsthan. For the Devs – and this is a feature of a brahman lineage – occupations such as government service, business speculations and private ritual activities were the only remunerative avenues open in the traditional society. Later, teaching became an acceptable profession, if never very profitable. Ultimately, those Devs in segments distant from the senior line of the Dev of Cincvad would have been forced to take up outside occupations. They remained Devs in name, lineal descendants of the saint and still inamdars with some share of a common inheritance, but only much later, under the peculiar circumstances of the late nineteenth century, would they be able to assert a claim on the Cincvad Samsthan.

IV. The dominant lineage segment

Until now the personal inam of the Dev of Cincvad has been excluded from the analysis of the descent of a partible inheritance. To recapitulate: the Peshva assigned equal shares to the third Dev's five sons; by implication the fourth Dev's allotment was divided between his three sons. Hence a lineage segment, as the term has been here defined by inam acquisition, issues from the fourth Dev Cintaman (II). But even at the time of the tahanama this partition was out of date. The Peshva considered only revenue obtained before 1719 and the death of the third Dev. By 1744/5 and the tenure of the fifth Dev, Cincvad held considerably more inam. New revenues included the remaining portions of villages already partly alienated to the Dev (for example, the moglai of Man obtained by the fourth Dev).[76] In other instances the tahanama

[76] Concerning the moglai of nine villages granted in 1725/6 (see pp. 43–4), it should be noted that this does not enter the tahanama, all these villages being considered to have been completely granted before 1719. This perhaps reinforces my earlier suggestion that the grants of moglai were technical procedures meant to make the actual situation conform to political reality.

had ignored villages that were not completely in the Devs' possession by 1719 (for example Ambi), or were in dispute as to inam rights at the time of the settlement (notably Banere).[77] Of course, grants continued to be made to 'Shri Dev Cincvad' after the Peshva's settlement. Part of Siddhatek, for example, was acquired in 1763/4 when Gangadhar Yashvant (Gangoba Tatya) Candracud (d. 1774) granted from his jagir all of the village not previously held by Cincvad.[78] All inams either left out of the tahanama or acquired since 1744/5 became in effect the personal holdings of the Dev.

In the senior line of the lineage the post-tahanama situation was thus in many points identical to that which prevailed before the settlement. Again there was a body of unpartitioned inam. The many heirs did not have their rights delineated: the fourth Dev's descendants had a claim on his acquisitions; likewise, the fifth Dev's sons would share in their father's inam plus his still undefined inheritance. With the fifth Dev's death (16 December 1772[79]), the disruptive disputes among his sons and collaterals necessitated a formal division of all inam acquired since 1719 or excluded from the tahanama.

A reflection of this renewed factionalism can be gathered from Madhavrav Peshva's previously noticed letter concerning the Rs. 10,000 lent by Cincvad for the Bassein campaign of 1739.[80] Umapati Dev, brother of the fifth Dev, was unhappy with the final disposition of the bond given for the loan. Negotiations for its return to government had been conducted by Umapati's younger brother Heramb (Bunyaba) and the fifth Dev had assented to the agreed arrangement. But so dissatisfied was Umapati about what had transpired that 'concerning his share, the *svāmī* [Umapati] undertakes a fast being camped in the house of the *śrī* [Dev].'[81] Madhavrav attempted to mediate, but Umapati would not appear in Pune, preferring instead to fast. Negotiations were conducted at Morgav with the courtier Apaji Tulshibagvale (d. 1775), apparently related to the Devs by marriage, acting as intermediary. All this was to no avail. The Peshva beseeched Umapati to halt the fast, stop ignoring his personal messages, and agree to come to Pune. 'Is this proper! Now you should not fast . . . you should not create a dispute.'[82] The trouble was deeper than a disagreement over Rs. 10,000, and the Peshva recognized this: it was 'a dispute between

---

[77] Banere had originally been granted to Narayan, for its subsequent history see p. 39.
[78] Inam Commission decision of 22 March 1859. For the Candracud lineage, see D. V. Apte, *Candracud daphtar* (Pune, 1920).
[79] *Mestak* of 1818, *Aitihasik patre yadi vagaire lekh*, p. 463.
[80] *Aitihasik sankirna sahitya*, VI, 61–2.
[81] Ibid.: 'tyace vighagavisi svami shri-ce ghari baison uposane karitat.'
[82] Ibid.: 'he ucit ki kaye atahpar. . . uposane na karavi kalaha na karava.'

brothers' (*bhāūpāncā...kalaha*). Umapati should 'come [to Pune] for talks on the shares of the brethren, the discussions will be according to the proper customs as before.'[83]

Both Madhavrav and the fifth Dev Dharanidhar died before the matter could be resolved, and it was left to the Pune ministers (probably Nana Phadnis) to effect a new settlement in 1775/6.[84] Although the document is not at present available, and so it is impossible to describe its form, nevertheless its provisions and effects are clear enough. Again the inam was equally divided between those kin descended from its grantees and the Samsthan. In effect, five new lineage segments were created, each with a share of the new acquisitions plus one-fifth of the previous personal inheritance of the Dev of Cincvad. The fifth Dev's two brothers received a share as did the sixth Dev (Narayan II) and two of his three brothers. Because Narayan's youngest brother Moreshvar had previously been adopted by the fifth Dev's heirless brother Heramb (Moreshvar and Narayan's paternal uncle), Moreshvar did not head a new line of descent for a partible inheritance.

The state had once again put its hand into the lineage's internal affairs. Preserving the Samsthan and the ritual position of the Dev of Cincvad, important institutions of Maratha society, required an equitable settlement with all who could claim a personal share of the state's grants. What had previously been done for the whole lineage was now reproduced in the senior segment. If grants continued to be made to the Dev of Cincvad, the same type of settlements causing a realignment of inheritance within the lineage's senior lines would again be needed. But by the time this was required the Peshva had long since departed; the British felt no obligation for such constructive interventions in the Dev lineage.

The sixth Dev and his three brothers introduced some innovations into the structure of lineage segments that had the potential of changing the normal pattern of inheritance for the personal inam of the Dev's immediate collaterals. Each brother became associated with a temple village sacred to Ganesh and dedicated inam to a religious institution. The Dev himself, of course, continued to be the senior partner; his ritual precedence was never challenged. The fourth brother Moreshvar, after being adopted by his uncle, was granted a portion of Ranjangav. This Ganesh center, sacred to Mahaganpati, was added to a half share of Ravet village obtained through his adoption. At the turn of the

---

[83] Ibid.: 'yethe yeun badhutvace vighagace bolane assel te bolave yevisi hone te vajvic purvavat calipramane hoil.'

[84] Petition of Laksmibai to Collector of Pune, 23 June 1860, PA: xiv; 28/322, fols. 304–7 refers to the *shaka era* year 1697; *Chintaman* v. *Dhondo*, p. 615 has 1774 *and* 1775.

nineteenth century Moreshvar attempted, through suspicious means, to gain all of Ranjangav to consolidate his new segment's holdings.[85] In 1797 the third brother's son, who was already a co-sharer in Ambi village, was granted Ojhar village with its temple of Vighneshvar-ganpati.[86] Both Ranjangav and Ojhar were popularly accorded the dignity of being Samsthans with the segment heads being styled the Devs of their respective temple-villages. Finally, through the provisions of the partition of 1775/6, the second brother was assigned the new acquisition at Siddhatek, a sacred site (of Siddhivinayak) his descendants quickly made their own. The Siddhatek Devs would, in the nineteenth century, supply an adopted Dev of Cincvad and later contend for the leadership of the Cincvad Samsthan.

Because the three younger brothers of Narayan II made a sacred site the centerpiece of their segment's inam, they were in effect recreating the structure of the whole Dev lineage in their own restricted spheres. In this the state helped by granting the appropriate temple-villages. Moreover, examples are not wanting where village land inams were bestowed on these lately created Samsthans.[87] The process of inam acquisition began again. As these segments grew, then presumably the same type of internecine disputes would arise as dominated the history of their parent lineage. Settlements based on the same principles as the tahanama – half for the Samsthan, half for the kin – would become necessary. But a reconstruction of the full cycle would be speculation. These mimics of the Cincvad Samsthan were products of the last years of Maratha rule, and before they could mature the British assumed the government of the Deccan.

V. Conclusion

The Dev lineage sought to preserve its inam, the patrimony of the Cincvad saints and the inheritance of all the kin, by assuming a multifaceted role in Maratha society that, while based on the sacred character of the Samsthan, transcended the solely religious. To be able to act out these social functions lineage peace had to be established and maintained. Some way had to be found to satisfy both institutional and personal claims on the inam. Because the state granted inam, it had a

---

[85] The case of Ranjangav is fully detailed in Chapter 6.
[86] Inam Commission decision of 11 December 1857, see PA: XIII; 7/132, pp. 1–6.
[87] Ranjangav: 42 bighas in Babhulsar Khurd (now in Shirur taluka of Pune district, village adjacent to Ranjangav; Ojhar: 11 acres in Dhalevadi Haveli (now in Junnar taluka of Pune district, village across river from Ojhar) plus 10 bighas in Ojhar village itself, see Inam Commission's summary, 8 February 1861.

duty to order the Devs' affairs. The lineage was, in the broadest sense, a public institution. In particular, an impartible endowment for the Samsthan had to be safeguarded. But to create this institutional inam necessarily meant the delineation of private partible inheritances. Once created, the personal inam ceased to be of immediate concern to the state. Provided the Devs did not in some way fall foul of the Peshva – a most unlikely eventuality – then these partible inheritances would simply descend in the lineage in a manner usual for brahman society as a whole. However, if the Devs continued to receive inam, further state intervention in the lineage's internal affairs was inevitable. The public *and* private intent of the state's grants had to be maintained.

Under the Marathas the inamdar lineage was very much the vassal of the state. We have seen how the acquisition of inam depended entirely on the pleasure of the granting power. The elaborate documentation necessarily meant the delineation of private partible inheritances. Once emphasized the ultimate authority of the state. Inam was a precarious right. Resumption was always possible. Like the Devs, a lineage may have been the most perfect supporter of the state's cultural ideology and political objectives. Also, an inamdar might assume a type of sovereignty in his own restricted domain. But no inamdar, no matter how much in favor or sovereign in his own right, could ignore the state's interests in his affairs without jeopardizing the preservation of inam. For the Devs this simply meant that they depended on the state to structure the lineage's affairs so that their endowments and inheritances could be enjoyed in an orderly fashion. It was this close relationship with the state that the Devs brought to the British after the conquest. Clearly, the overthrow of the Peshva and the traditional order would change much in state – inamdar relations. The Devs were prepared either to conciliate the new rulers or challenge and deflect their presumptions. But as the following chapters will show, many of the issues at stake were not new.

The inamdar under the British

3

Introduction to Part Two

Only slowly did the British become interested in their privileged inamdar subjects. Between the conquest of the Deccan in 1817–18 (Pune was occupied on 7 November 1817 after the Battle of Khadki[1]) and 1860 (marking the aftermath of the Mutiny and the end of the East India Company's government), three phases of state–inamdar relations can be discerned. Until 1826 all the affairs of the Maratha state's feudatories were solely in the hands of the provisional government of the Deccan Commission.[2] Between 1826 and 1852 the Company's district revenue officers shared this duty with the Agent for Sardars, an officer charged with overseeing political and judicial affairs.[3] After 1852 the Inam Commission assumed formal responsibility for most matters that affected inamdars and other holders of alienated revenue. The four chapters in this section examine postconquest state–inamdar relations through these three periods by concentrating on the actual administration of British alienated revenue policy and its effect on the Devs of Cincvad.

The policy of the Deccan Commission in all its dealings in the 'new conquests' was political conciliation. Mountstuart Elphinstone, the first Commissioner in the Deccan, his successor William Chaplin, and the subordinate district officers knew the old order at first hand as political residents or army officers.[4] They had no illusions about their often

---

[1] For the political and military history of the conquest see G. S. Sardesai, *New History of the Marathas*, 3 vols. (Bombay, 1946–8), III, 469–500; G. S. Sardesai, ed., *Poona Affairs, (Elphinstone's Embassy) (Part II, 1816–1818)* (Bombay, 1958) for documents.

[2] For the Deccan Commission generally, see Kenneth Ballhatchet, *Social Policy and Social Change in Western India, 1817–1830* (London, 1957); for the correspondence of the Deccan Commission (PA: DC), see bibliography for compilations of R. D. Choksey.

[3] The files of the Agent for Sardars, housed in the Pune Archives (PA: IX), are arranged subject-wise by individual inamdar or jagirdar lineage. Each file crosses the strictly delineated revenue, political and judicial categories of the corresponding records in the Bombay Archives. The agent's correspondence is thus an ideal and convenient source for family and lineage studies in western India. Apart from passing references in Ballhatchet and other sources, the agent's rather distinctive position in the district administration has not yet been much considered in modern scholarship.

[4] It is instructive to consult the standard nineteenth-century biography of Elphinstone to appreciate the depth of his and his subordinates' realistic understanding and sympathy

generous treatment of the privileged subjects of the Maratha state. But a
kind of benevolent pragmatism tempered a sometimes cynical political
realism. The Deccan Commission largely ignored inamdars such as the
Dev of Cincvad. It was known they were important personalities in the
traditional society; and further, the state's accounts showed the
inamdars holding a considerable amount of alienated revenue.[5] However, more pressing to the new administration was the presence of
landed jagirdars, political powers in their own right who could still
possibly raise armies in support of the deposed Peshva.[6] Generally
inamdars were no such military threat. They could be appeased, if that
was considered politic, by simply not disturbing their revenues and
social position. Immediately after the conquest the inamdars thus rested
easily under the benign protection of the new rulers.

Between 1826 and 1852 changes were in the air. The Deccan was
formally incorporated into the Bombay Presidency. Now the revenue
and judicial officers ruled the countryside directly under the guidance of
their departmental superiors in Bombay. The settlement of the land
revenue was the main business of the district officers. Schemes to
accurately measure land productivity and levels of assessment were
propounded to fix government's revenues.[7] At the same time, the East
India Company was possessed of a new vigor in attempting to institute
fundamental changes in India. The commercial infrastructure of the

for the preconquest society and polity. See T. E. Colebrooke, *Life of the Honourable
Mountstuart Elphinstone*, 2 vols. (London. 1884); R. D. Choksey, *Mountstuart
Elphinstone, The Indian Years 1796–1827* (Bombay, 1971) adds more detail.

Elphinstone's subordinates – H. D. Robertson, John Briggs, Henry Pottinger, and
James Grant – though not deserving of individual biographical study, had similarly
fascinating Indian careers. William Chaplin, really a Madras civil servant and protege
of Sir Thomas Munro, has been the most neglected of the Deccan Commission officers.
He was not a historian like Briggs and Grant, nor was his later career of note like
Pottinger (Governor of Hong Kong during the Opium War). Upon examination, it
seems his biography can be almost entirely equated with the history of the Deccan
Commission.
[5] For the question of the extent of inam and other alienated revenues in the preconquest
Deccan, see pp. 12–13.
[6] While the Peshva was still alive and in exile in north India this fear appears to have
animated a great part of the economic, social and political policies of the British in the
Deccan. This insecurity of the foreign conqueror is especially apparent immediately
after the conquest. For example, Elphinstone reported to the Governor-General (18
June 1818) on those jagirdars who held land for the support of troops, that while it was
'politic and humane to allow a liberal maintenance even to those who have obstinately
resisted us,' it was 'neither required by humanity nor policy to give such persons the
command of troops paid from revenues which have fallen into our hands.' See R. D.
Choksey, *The Aftermath* (Bombay, 1950), p. 162.
[7] This has therefore been the subject of much of the modern scholarship on the period:
for example, Eric Stokes, *The English Utilitarians and India* (Oxford, 1959); Ravinder
Kumar, *Western India in the Nineteenth Century* (London, 1968).

country was reformed; transportation developed; industrialization slowly began.[8] But behind all these visible changes, which parallel developments in Europe, the Company was undergoing a basic change of heart about the nature of its own rule. Seeing themselves less as Indian sovereigns, the heirs to native dynasties, the British adopted a more self-conscious role as imperial administrators.

This change in the ideological basis of British rule has often been described.[9] But perhaps surprisingly, in the 1830s and 1840s this change in the imperial mentality little affected the inamdars of the Deccan. Inam and such, rights which were viewed as some sort of real property, remained sacrosanct. The district officers had neither the authority or inclination to enquire too deeply into the inamdars' rights in land, the cornerstone of their privileged position. Neither had the Agent for Sardars. The holders of this office inherited many of Elphinstone's attitudes about the conciliation of native political powers. Also, although the agent held the records of the Maratha state, he lacked the means or desire to closely examine the actual record of the inamdars' rights.[10] However, between 1826 and 1852 the close, almost cozy relations between state and inamdar were slowly changing. The British would now challenge some old and established rights and perquisites if they conflicted with the broad outlines of imperial policy.

In the last decade of the Company's government (from 1852), the Inam Commission at last seized the changing temper of the times and confronted the inamdars' privileges inherited from the old order. The commission attempted, in the face of considerable opposition, to redefine from the Marathi records the notion of inam as property. A general discussion of the Inam Commission need not be started here; a consideration of the specific features of the commission's settlements and view of inam follows in Chapters 6 and 7. Here, however, the

[8] The extent to which the Company played an active role in the development of India has received little detailed attention. Propagandists for the Company maintained that much had been achieved, for example [John Stuart Mill], *Memorandum of the Improvements in the Administration of India* (1858; rpt. Farnsborough, 1969). Parliamentary critics of the Company, however, were adamant that, particularly in public works, the Company was notoriously deficient. For a summary regarding cotton development and the consequent public works required, see Peter Harnetty, *Imperialism and Free Trade: Lancashire and India in the Mid-nineteenth Century* (Vancouver, 1972), pp. 59–61; see also R. J. Moore, *Sir Charles Wood's Indian Policy, 1853–66* (Manchester, 1966), pp. 124–35 summarizing late Company developments.
[9] Most notably by Stokes, *The English Utilitarians and India*; see also Stokes, 'The First Century of British Colonial Rule in India; Social Revolution or Social Stagnation?' in *The Peasant and the Raj* (Cambridge, 1978), pp. 19–45 discussing the place of ideology in historical studies of British India.
[10] On the history of the Pune daphtar, see pp. 13–14.

chronological sequence of the inam settlements should be emphasized. A generation had passed between the conquest and the Inam Commission. By 1852 the inamdars were prepared to challenge the British, in the new rulers' legal and bureaucratic terms, when ancient privileges were thought to be under threat.

In each of the four following chapters the evolution of British policy towards inamdars is taken from the time of the conquest through to the Inam Commission. Also, each chapter is based on the settlement of some form of alienated revenue. Without doubt, money was the catalyst in all dealings inamdars such as the Devs had with the British between 1818 and 1860. But it is hoped that the following chapters will be more than a catalog of British revenue settlements and will instead suggest some basic themes in postconquest state–inamdar relations.

Chapters 4 and 5 concentrate on the period up to 1852 when nonlanded revenues were the points of contention between Bombay and Cincvad. Because of the thematic approach here adopted, the narrative will be taken into the time of the Inam Commission. The settlements were resolved finally after 1852, but the revenues involved were actually peripheral to landed inam as conceived by the commission.

Firstly, the changing British perception of their privileged subjects is seen through the settlement of *varṣāsan*s, Maratha state allowances to the leading personalities of the country. One such grant paid to the Dev of Cincvad, on the occasion of his annual pilgrimage to Morgav, forced the British to reappraise their responsibilities as ritual successors to the Peshvas. This was done in the context of the India-wide policy of distancing government from the support of idolatry. The second case study will consider the Devs' revenue from the local commerce of Pune, in particular their long-established mint and transit duties. In the 1830s and 1840s, in line with a general policy of commercial reform, the Bombay government attempted to buy up these 'impediments' to trade by offering generous compensation. The inamdar strongly resisted this challenge to his revenues. Although the British did not see it, these commercial rights were closely tied to landed inam and a concept of the inamdar's 'domain.' For the British, commercial reform was seen as so clearly for the common good, and profitable for the inamdars too, but for the Devs it was the first threat to the landed estate of the lineage and the Samsthan. Hence the lineage developed arguments and strategies to deflect the inquiring energies of the new rulers. These would be of particular use after 1852.

Chapters 6 and 7 thus concern the Inam Commission's settlement of the Devs' inam. Firstly, the growth of the Inam Commission as a revenue settlement is emphasized. The nature of the commission's operations is illustrated through one example of a resumption of part of the Ranjangav Devs' holdings. While examining the commission as an official instrument for the implementation of policy, we will also see the threat the alienation settlements posed to inamdars. Chapter 7 returns to the concerns of the senior lines of descent in the Dev lineage. While settling the bulk of Cincvad's inam, the commission became inextricably entwined in the same disputes over the lineage patrimony that the Peshva had seen fit to mediate. The results were disastrous. The traditional issues in the descent of an inheritance came into full conflict with British policy. Finally the real impact of the conquest was felt.

4

From ritual grandee to state pensioner: varsasans and the Morgav pilgrimage

Varsasans were annual cash allowances from the Maratha state to its subjects. With this largess the state particularly favored priests and other divines, astrologers, magicians, and scholars; hence the varsasan was largely, though not completely, a brahman allowance. It sustained the high culture of the country, and the incomes were often a sort of social welfare for the indigent but ritually superior members of society. But the recipients of allowances rendered a valuable service to the state: by accepting an allowance they acknowledged the legitimacy of the Peshva's government. The allegiance of what were considered the influential members of society was assured. Supported for reasons in equal measure political and cultural, the presence of numerous recipients of small cash allowances was a characteristic feature of the Hindu state.

After the conquest the British, as successors to the Marathas, assumed the support of the ritual elite and took the place of the Peshva in the relations of subject and state. However, seeing varsasans as either indiscriminate charity or the cash equivalent of landed inam, the Company's officers sought to bring order to a mass of trifling payments through the formulation of fixed rules. Most of the miscellaneous varsasans held by the Dev of Cincvad, the Samsthan, or members of junior lineage segments were settled as a matter of course under the general regulations to be here considered.[1] But the Dev's allowance for his annual Morgav pilgrimage had many distinctive features that caused the British problems. Hence, a considerable volume of correspondence was generated over relatively trivial amounts of cash. Despite certain peculiarities, the history of this allowance well illustrates how varsasans were transformed from a perquisite of the ritual elite and an expression of Maratha state policy to a perplexing collection of gratuitous pensions from the Bombay government.

---

[1] Table to Cincvad's holdings, prepared by Assistant Inam Commissioner, accompaniment to C. J. Griffith, Inam Commissioner Northern Division to T. A. Cowper, Revenue Commissioner for Alienations, 8 February 1861, PA; XIV; 28/322, fols. 316–38 for some of these. See also note 24 below.

I. The pilgrimage and the varsasan

In the biographies of Moroba Gosavi a prominent place is given to his frequent, even monthly or daily, pilgrimages from Cincvad to Morgav. Later, the poetry of the early Devs extolled the virtues of visiting the Mayureshvar deity of the village.[2] Despite the growing economic and social predominance of Cincvad in the eighteenth century, Morgav remained the spiritual center of the Ganpati cult in western India. Eventually the village became Cincvad's inam, but still religious considerations brought the Dev to Morgav. To reassert their spiritual connection with the sacred shrine, the later Devs in a way reenacted the almost legendary pilgrimages of Moroba Gosavi. To my knowledge this interpretation is nowhere explicitly stated in contemporary sources. But the intimate connection of Moroba with Morgav, the Cincvad Samsthan's clear desire to control the most sacred of Ganpati centers as its inam, and the formalized character of the pilgrimage as described below, all lead to the conclusion that ritual was the motivating factor. In the eighteenth century the receipt of a varsasan from the Peshva became part of the pilgrimage ceremony. The Dev was far too wealthy to depend on this revenue for his livelihood, which in part distinguishes this allowance from many others. Rather, the manner in which the money was received was the significant point for the Dev. The ceremony of presentation placed Cincvad's formal relations with the Peshva's government on a ritual footing.

Whether the pilgrimage in all its ritual aspects dates to the seventeenth century and the early Devs or was an eighteenth-century institution is not clear from available sources. The ceremony the British encountered in 1818 appears to have continued more or less unchanged since 1750. A very detailed description of the eighteenth-century pilgrimage in the 1801 article of Edward Moor, with other stray references, gives an unusually full picture of one of the relatively minor ritual occasions of the Maratha state.[3]

Moor had visited Cincvad on 10 January 1800 and was apparently in Pune when he encountered the Dev's pilgrimage later the same month.[4] He says the Dev undertook the pilgrimage three times a year, but the actual number of occurrences per year is not so certain. More important was that, as Moor says, the pilgrimage occurred on 'fixed days,' usually

---

[2] For the poetical reference to Morgav see *Sadguru Srimoraya Gosavi...gatha* (Cincvad, 1959), *padas* 28, 56, 57, pp. 28–9, 50–2.

[3] 'Account of an Hereditary Living Deity to whom devotion is paid by the bramins of Poona and its neighbourhood,' *Asiatick Researches* 7(1801), 390–2.

[4] Ibid., p. 393.

shortly before the fourth of the bright half of the Hindu lunar month, all of which days are sacred to Ganpati.[5] Although Moor describes a pilgrimage that occurred in the month of Magh, his account could equally apply to Bhadrapad, the fourth of the bright half of this month (Ganesh *caturthī*) being one of the most sacred days in the calendar of Ganpati's devotees. As this was also the occasion of the Ganpati festival in the Peshva's palace, Bhadrapad appears to have been the preferred time for the Morgav pilgrimage. In 1800, however, the Dev left Cincvad on the second of Magh (*śuddha*).[6] In Pune, Moor records, 'the *Peshwa*, and Court, apprized of his approach, go forth to meet him, generally about halfway between a hill called *Gunniskunda* [Ganeshkhind], two miles off, and the city.'[7] The meeting of the Dev's procession was a regular event in court life. In August 1781, for example, the Nizam's representative in Pune reported to Hyderabad:

29 Shaban, Monday [20 August, 1 Bhadrapad shuddha] – The Dev of Cincvad went to Morgav for the fourth [of Bhadrapad]. The Shrimant [the Peshva], Nana [Phadnis] and others went out of Pune for a view (*darśan*) of him. Having taken a view they came back into town.[8]

After this meeting the combined procession of the Dev and the Peshva with their retinues entered Pune. Only then did the Peshva's personal Ganpati festival commence in his palace.[9]

The ritual of the actual meeting was not described by the writer of the above-quoted newsletter (*akhbār*). As an outsider Moor found it of sufficient interest to give a detailed, apparently eyewitness account:

The Deo rides in his palkee [*pālkhī*], attended (I speak now of the present Deo) by a suwaree [*savārī = svārī*, 'state'] elephant given him by the late Peshwa

---

[5] Yasvant Vinayak Shaligram, *Shriganpati-atharvashirsa-rahasya* (Pune, n.d.), pp. 155–60 lists these days. The fourth of the dark half of the lunar month is also sacred, but does not appear important for the pilgrimage.

[6] Moor, p. 390 has the second of Magh as 31 January, 'this year.' In 1800, however, the second of Magh shuddha was 27 January. In 1801 the second of Magh krsna (or *vadya*), the dark half of the lunar month, was in fact 31 January and perhaps Moor became confused with the intricacies of the Hindu lunar calandar.

[7] Ibid. Ganeshkhind, the site of the monsoon Government House of the Bombay Presidency and now the University of Pune, had some importance for the Devs. The break between two hills (*khind*), it was the gateway to Pune from the west. On the side of one hill is a small temple of Ganpati, which like the astavinayak is supposed to have a svayambhu, 'self-existent or self-created,' image of Ganpati. The appearance of this image supposedly dates to the time of Bajirav II; see Edward Moor, *Oriental Fragments* (London, 1834), p. 375.

[8] Akhbar of 22 August 1781, *Poona Akhbars* (Hyderabad, 1952–6), I, 281. Note that the term darsan has strong religious overtones, in the sense of being in the presence of a deity.

[9] Akhbar of 27 August 1781 (for 23–27 August, 4–9 Bhadrapad shuddha), ibid., p. 287.

Madhoo Row [Madhavrav], a few, perhaps a dozen, of his own domestic horsemen, and about a hundred servants on foot. As he approaches the Peshwa, his palkee is put down, and he seats himself on a carpet with the sacred stone [the mangalmurti], which he never quits, in a box beside him. The *Peshwa* alights from his palkee or elephant, advances towards the Deo with folded hands, the posture of a supplicant, prostrates himself, and kisses his feet. The Deo neither rises, nor makes a salaam but with his hand raised a little, with palms downward, makes a benedictory gesticulation, accompanied by a motion, signifying his desire that his visitor may be seated. The *Peshwa*, and a few distinguished persons... sit, but at some distance, on the carpet. Two or three questions and answers of supplication and blessing are exchanged, and the Deo bestows on the *Peshwa*, and others, a quantity of rice and dal, and perhaps a coca nut, or such trifle. The *Peshwa* receives them, makes a humble obeisance, and takes leave. The Deo enters his palkee, and proceeds, followed by the *Peshwa*, &c. by the wooden bridge to the city. The *Peshwa* quits him near the palace, which the Deo never enters, nor the house of any mortal, but always finds his tents pitched at fixed stations.[10]

The Peshva thus acknowledged his ritual superior. The Dev in return bestowed his blessing on the supplicant with a gift of a *prasād*, a favor from a deity or ritual superior. Moor's description of the ceremony lends some credence to nineteenth-century traditions that the Dev was one of 'only two individuals the Peshwas regarded as their Superiors.'[11] Such devotion, if the traditions can be believed, resulted from the Devs' favor in raising the Peshvas 'to a position of social equality among the Deccan Brahmins.'[12] At any rate, on the occasion of the Morgav pilgrimage the Peshva, on a personal level, yielded precedence to the Dev.

Curiously, Moor fails to mention the Peshva's gifts to the Dev, a necessary part of the ritual exchange between supplicant and superior. His offering was usually 5 gold *mohar*s (a coin nominally worth Rs. 16[13]) and a pair of shawls. In addition, the government gave food, fodder, draught animals, and tentage for the Dev's statelike retinue of horsemen and servants. British officers afterwards researched the Pune daphtar to determine the history of the payments to the Dev; the results of this inquiry are given in Table 3.[14] Although these researches provide only a

---

[10] Moor, 'Account of an Hereditary Living Deity,' pp. 390–1.

[11] P. Dods, Inam Commissioner Northern Division to Revenue Commissioner for Alienations, 30 June 1860, PA: xiii; 55/740, pp. 490–504.

[12] R. E. Enthoven, *Folklore of the Konkan* (1915, rpt. Delhi, 1976), p. 45, that is, the Peshvas had been raised to equality with the desastha brahmans.

[13] H. H. Wilson, *A Glossary of Judicial and Revenue Terms* (1855, rpt. Delhi, 1968), p. 350; William Henry Tone, *A Letter to an Officer on the Madras Establishment* (1796, rpt. London, 1799), p. 15 says the common mohar struck at Pune was worth Rs. 13.

[14] Report of J. Anding, Sub-Assistant Settlement Officer to Settlement Officer Deccan and Satara, 25 September 1861, PA xiii; 55/740; pp. 518–44.

Table 3. *Morgav pilgrimage allowance (values in rupees)*

Date debited in accounts		Mohars		Shawls		Remarks
		No.	Value	value	Total	
21 August 1750	1 Bhadrapad shuddha	0	0	232.74	272.74	Rs. 40 in addition for garment (*dhotar*)
8 September 1755	2 Bhadrapad shuddha	11	162.25	0	162	
11 September 1760	2 Bhadrapad shuddha	n/a	n/a	n/a	n/a	
22 April 1763	9 Vaishakh shuddha	1	15.5	0	15.5	Peshva not in Pune
17 August 1765	1 Bhadrapad shuddha	2	31.5	0	31.5	
21 August 1770	1 Bhadrapad shuddha	2	30.5	152	182.5	
9 October 1777	7 Bhadrapad shuddha	5	67.5	300	367.5	
8 September 1782	1 Bhadrapad shuddha	5	66.25	354.5	420.75	
11 September 1787	30 Shravan *krsna*	5	70	370	440	Day before 1 Bhadrapad shuddha
18 August 1792	1 Bhadrapad Shuddha	5	67.5	400	467.5	Day before 1 Bhadrapad shuddha
22 August 1797	30 Shravan krsna	7	94.5	400	494.5	5 mohars from Peshva, 2 from his brother

17 October 1802	1 Kartik shuddha	7	86.75	484	570.75	5 mohars from Peshva
13 September 1806	1 Bhadrapad shuddha	5	n/a	n/a	n/a	From Samsthan's accounts
4 September 1807	2 Bhadrapad shuddha	5	70	200	270	Only month given; designated as dakṣiṇā
September 1812	Bhadrapad	5	67	200	267	
25 December 1813	3 Paus shuddha	5	67.5	200	267.5	For provisions see below
24 August 1816	1 Bhadrapad shuddha	5	67	200	267	For provisions see below
1818	Bhadrapad	5	86.25	175	261.25	For provisions see below
1819	Bhadrapad	5	67.5	100	167.5	For provisions see below
1820	Bhadrapad	5	67.5	100	167.5	For provisions see below

Details of provisions (expenses in rupees)

Date	Food	Bearers	Animals	Food for 400 men for two days
1813	170.5	–	–	(150 going, 250 coming)
1818	268[a]	40[b]	100	For 10 bearers and 30 animals
1820	170.5	40	100	For 10 bearers and 12 animals

n/a = not available.

[a] 183 according to Samsthan's accounts.

[b] 25 according to Samsthan's accounts.

representative sample of information provided in the daphtar, it is clear
that the precise of offerings of the Peshva – the number of mohars and
their rupee value, and the value of the shawls – varied from year to year
with particular circumstances. In 1763, for example, only 1 mohar was
given as the Peshva was not in Pune. Hence, while the gifts were entered
in the accounts as government expenses because the Peshva gave mohars
and shawls on behalf of the state, the extent of the expense depended on
the nature of the ritual exchange between two individual leaders. There
was indeed a certain regularity of offerings, which appears to have
become increasingly fixed after 1800, and although an average gift could
be determined, never was the Dev's varsasan conceived of as an exact
and immutable payment. In the case of provisions, these were supplied
from government stores; their value would depend on yearly requirements and prevailing market rates.[15]

After meeting the Peshva, the Dev proceeded to the Ganpati temple in
his inam village of Theur, some 19 kilometers east of Pune, where he
made his first camp. The next day he halted at the village of Rajvadi, and
finally, on the fourth of the lunar month, proceeded into Morgav.[16]
Known as the Jejuri or Miraj road, this was the usual route to the south
from Pune. Sir James Mackintosh, for example, in 1808 passed this way
on his tour of the Deccan. He notices the stage from Rajvadi to Morgav,
which passed through Cincvad's inam village of Ambi, as taking only
three hours.[17] Clearly, the Dev's pilgrimage was a carefully timed event.
His ceremonial entry into Morgav was planned to coincide with the start
of the holy day.

Returning after religious ceremonies in Morgav, the Dev occasionally
took the opportunity of the pilgrimage to receive other offerings. An
account paper from the daphtar of one of the Peshva's sardars records
that at Theur on 10 September 1772 (14 Bhadrapad shuddha) Trimbakrav Pethe gave an offering (*dharmadāy*) to the Dev of shawls worth
Rs. 332.[18] At this time, shortly before his death, Madhavrav Peshva had
established his court in Theur, his favorite religious center.[19]

The Morgav pilgrimage was an important religious occasion for the

[15] Ibid., the Sub-Assistant Settlement Officer could find few reliable accounts of these
expenses.
[16] Moor, 'Account of an Hereditary Living Deity,' p. 391.
[17] Robert James Mackintosh, *Memoirs of the Life of Sir James Mackintosh* (London,
1835), I, 463–5. Sir James notes that the Dev of Cincvad came to Morgav four times a
year.
[18] Visnu Sitaram Citale, *Pethe Daphtar* (Pune, 1950), I, 68.
[19] For Madhavrav and Theur see *Peshavyamci bakhar*, ed. V. M. Kulkarni, A. R.
Kulkarni and A. N. Deshpande (Pune, 1963), p. 62. The Peshva died on 18 November
1772.

Dev of Cincvad. It recalled the life of the saint and the sacred connections with Morgav. In addition, it gave the Dev the opportunity to visit some of his more important inam villages. Moreover, it was an occasion to reaffirm the Dev lineage's relations, religious and political, with the Peshva, his government and the principals of the Maratha state. The Pune ceremonies were primarily an exchange between ritual superior and supplicant cemented through the not-insignificant offering of the Peshva and the Dev's return prasad. Although in real political and economic terms the Dev was very much the dependent party, the Maratha state acknowledged his assumption of spiritual authority. At the same time, by accepting the gift of the state, its varsasan, the Dev recognized the temporal precedence of the Peshva. So also, the Dev accepted the provisions and such, which in fact financed his pilgrimage.

II. The settlement of varsasans

On 11 February 1818 Mountstuart Elphinstone issued the Proclamation of Satara in which he described the treachery of Bajirav Peshva, thus justifying the annexation of the Deccan. At the same time, Elphinstone went some way to conciliate popular feeling in the new conquests by promising to respect the institutions and religion of the country. The British would, for example, continue all the Peshva's annual cash allowances. The Marathi version of the proclamation specified these as varsasans, devasthans ('grants to temples'), *kharc* ('expenses in general'), and *khairāt* ('Muslim allowances').[20] In his instructions to H. D. Robertson, the Collector of Pune, soon after the proclamation was issued but before its purport was widely known, Elphinstone requested the collector to 'pay scrupulous attention to all the promises contained in it.' Varsasans and other allowances, the 'great and partial charities of the Brahmin Government,' were to be continued. But the guarantees were not to extend to the Peshva's 'personal charities,' without any definition of what these constituted, or to 'Bajee Row's establishment for performing magical ceremonies.'[21]

Elphinstone's decision to confirm most of the cash allowances of the Maratha state was in line with the opinions of Sir Thomas Munro in

---

[20] Proclamation of Satara, 11 February 1818 in G. S. Sardesai, *Poona Affairs* (*Elphinstone's Embassy*) (*Part II, 1816–1818*) (Bombay, 1958), pp. 299–302. Marathi original in Kashinath Narayan Sane, *Aitihasik patre yadi vagaire* (Pune, 1889), pp. 517–19 (in mestak of 1818); 2nd edn, G. S. Sardesai, Y. M. Kale and V. S. Vakskar, eds. (Pune, 1930), pp. 468–70.

[21] Elphinstone to Robertson, 26 February 1818 in R. D. Choksey, *The Last Phase* (Bombay, 1948), p. 214.

Madras. Writing to Elphinstone, he recommended that 'all charities and religious expenses' should be maintained, but only 'for the present.' Such grants were probably relatively old, and Munro did not consider it judicious in the then unsettled situation to investigate them. But many would be found to be 'frauds'; and in accordance with native precedent, these grants 'should be carefully investigated' after peace had been restored. Those which were relatively recent or not legitimately granted by the former government should be stopped.[22] Elphinstone, too, perhaps following Munro's lead, had his doubts about the great extent of cash grants. In a long despatch to the Governor–General describing the measures taken for the settlement of the recently conquered territories, he noted that 'charities and other religious expenses' amounted to Rs. 15,00,000. It was necessary to continue these expenses to appease the 'temporal power' of the brahmans. And although it was 'absurd to imitate this prodigality,' Elphinstone's own public pronouncements guaranteed much of the expenditure.[23]

The general tenor of Elphinstone's decisions, consonant with his Proclamation of Satara, was to give the most generous benefit of any doubts that arose about individual allowances. Most were confirmed if it appeared a competent authority of the Maratha state or its feudatories had made the grant. However, occasional questions as to the authenticity or appropriateness of particular cases did occur. Of course, the British had a continuing and keen interest in the various types of cash alienations that together accounted for a significant annual expenditure. A selection of miscellaneous cases from the correspondence of the Collector of Pune under the Deccan Commission both illustrates the wide variety of annual allowances common under Maratha rule and traces the somewhat fitful development of initial British policy towards these 'charities.'

Perhaps the most prevalent example, the devasthan of the Proclamation of Satara, was for the funding of temples. The payment of such well accommodated Elphinstone's often-stated intention to support the religious institutions of the country; hence, devasthans at first received rather favorable consideration. In one of the earliest examples (April 1818) Robertson approved grants to some of the most notable temples dependent on the Pune Collectorate treasury: Parvati and Tulsi Bag in Pune city; Morgav, Siddhatek and Theur (these three controlled by the

---

[22] Sir Thomas Munro to Elphinstone, 8 March 1818 in G. R. Gleig, *The Life of Major-General Sir Thomas Munro*, 3 vols. (London, 1830), III, 240.
[23] Elphinstone to Lord Hastings, 18 June 1818 in Saredesai, *Poona Affairs*, p. 402; Choksey, *Last Phase*, p. 163.

Dev of Cincvad[24]); Jejuri and others. Robertson was careful to clearly
associate the introduction of British rule with the reinstatement of
devasthans to such sacred institutions. Displaying a perceptive astrological sense for obviously political reasons, he organized a type of
commencement ceremony and delayed the grants' payment because 'of
the general notion of the excellence of beginning so good a work on so
good a day as Parva.' The expense of this good and politic work
amounted to Rs. 27,000, which Robertson tried to reduce to Rs. 20,000,
however, as he explained to Elphinstone:

when I saw the operation of the reductions in detail I was convinced that for the
sake of a few thousand rupees, I would engender, or rather not eradicate, any
lurking wish for Bajee Rao's re-accession to the Musnud [throne]. I therefore,
ordered everything carried on as before.[25]

Very soon though, Robertson became conscious of a need for a more
thorough examination of devasthans. Within a year of the conquest the
authenticity of claims was being verified in the Pune daphtar. So for
example, devasthans in Sasvad (for Rs. 1030 claimed by Trimbakrav
Purandhare on behalf of the temple of Laksmi-Narayan) and in Satara
were in 1819 routinely submitted to the test of the daphtar.[26] In the case
of the notable temples dependent on the Pune treasury, by December
1819 the necessary documentation had been found 'to place these
institutions on the footing they were in during the last years of Bajee
Row's reign.'[27] Robertson was then able to make the reductions
contemplated the previous year because he found that in 1812/13 the
Peshva had ordered the recorded nominal allowances of certain temples
(including Theur, Siddhatek and Morgav) cut by approximately 35
percent.

In the later years of the Deccan Commission requests for the
continuance of devasthans were treated with more suspicion. In 1825
brahmans from 18 temples in forts around Pune submitted claims for
allowances totaling Rs. 436. Though supported by entries in the
daphtar, 'the delay of referring these claims casts some doubt on their

[24] The grants to Morgav were later fixed at Rs. 936; for Theur Rs. 885, see PA: 'List of
Cash Alienations in the Poona Collectorate as they stood on 1st July 1877,'
printed lists.
[25] Robertson to Elphinstone, 8 April 1818, PA: DC 89/8; in Choksey, *Last Phase*,
pp. 219–24, *parva* being either an astrological conjunction or certain important days
in the lunar month.
[26] Sasvad: Robertson to Elphinstone, 6 August 1819, PA: DC 95/406; Satara: Robertson
to Elphinstone, 9 April 1819, PA: DC 94/294. The claim was referred to Pune by James
Grant in Satara.
[27] Robertson to William Chaplin, Deccan Commissioner, 3 December 1819, PA: DC
96/524.

having been enjoyed up to the War.' Perhaps the brahmans had been hesitant because of the location of their temples – the British spent some time reducing recalcitrant forts after the conquest – but the delay was 'the only reason why [the claims] should not be immediately admitted.'[28] In another case, R. K. Pringle, Assistant Collector of Pune, reported from Junnar that temples in neighborhood of the town were due Rs. 532, which in 1824 had remained unpaid since 1819. Although the allowances appeared genuine and to have been paid by the Peshva's district officers, Pringle appealed to Robertson to have their authenticity checked in the daphtar. Some of the temples in question had 'a high reputation for sanctity,' and the allowances' 'renewal at the expense of Government would be highly gratifying for the feelings of the people.'[29]

Not all devasthans came directly from the government treasury; payments from village revenues supported the great majority of the lesser temples of the Deccan. These village expenses, the kharc of the Proclamation of Satara, were rather thoroughly investigated. Robertson found that such cash devasthan expenses amounted to some Rs. 11,000 in the Pune Collectorate. This figure, taken from the records of the village accountants (*kulkarṇīs*) was considered a 'very moderate' expense. Indeed, 'if the villagers had been more on their guard in respect to the consequences of their honesty they would probably have rated their charges for religious institutions much higher.'[30] Generally, Robertson was suspicious of any Maratha accounts of allowances, particularly the village devasthan expenses, except those obtained under his direct supervision. Hence, he had been very 'scrupulous' in making payments that 'if given without due consideration entail a greater annual expense on our Government than is at all requisite,' nevertheless

it ought perhaps to be laid down as a maxim that however correct the Dufters of the late Government may be in other respects they will exhibit an expenditure for the support of pagodas & for charitable donations which never reached its assigned destination.

The district accounts could possibly be used as a check, but even then 'wherever they agree with the [Pune] Dufters we may rest assured perhaps that there has been some collusion.'[31]

In attempting to reconcile village accounts of temple allowances with the Pune records, the British were seeking to control and limit the

---

[28] Robertson to Chaplin, 24 February 1825, PA: DC 117/2259.

[29] R. K. Pringle, Assistant Collector of Pune to Robertson, 29 December 1824 enclosure to Robertson to Chaplin, 24 February 1825, PA: DC 117/2260.

[30] Robertson to Elphinstone, 31 October 1818, PA: DC 91/155 enclosure, in R. D. Choksey, *Early British Administration* (Pune, 1964), pp. 40–2.

[31] Ibid.

deductions from the gross revenue of a village made before its receipts reached government. Robertson, for one, was always ready to question the veracity of village accounts. To take but one example, he believed that the stated expenses of a temple in Sasvad were incorrect. Inquiries through the Indian revenue officer (*māmlatdār*) confirmed the outlay, but still Robertson requested a search of the daphtar to see if the truth of the matter could be found.[32] The collectors were suspicious of annual allowances they did not directly pay, over which they thought they had no power, and which were, in effect, hidden charges on the land revenue.

Considerable control could be exercised over varsasans paid to individuals as few were given at the village level. Most of the perquisites of the village officers and servants were calculated in terms of land assignments or granted in kind. In all of Pune district Robertson found only Rs. 858 of cash village varsasans not credited to temples or in trust with their ministrants (the distinctions were not always easy to make).[33] Even these could not be paid without the annual approval of government.[34] Because the British had a much greater part in the management of the several varieties of personal allowances, some general rules could be soon formulated for their payment.

In the Marathi sources allowances to individuals are given numerous, apparently imprecise designations that appear to refer to a grant's purpose and mode of payment.[35] Varsasan is the general term, but clearly this was meant as a sum to be paid yearly (*varṣa*, 'year'). Whether the money was disbursed once a year or in instalments is not now easy to determine. A *dharmadān* (less properly but more commonly, *–dāy*, *–dāv*), though also an annual charge in the accounts, was always distinguished because of its religious and pious connotations. Occasionally, however, this term was used to designate inam land or gifts in kind; here the constant factor was the grant's intention of rewarding particularly brahman divines. A *nemṇūk*, in practise identical to a varsasan, was meant as a reward for specific past services to the state (by

[32] Robertson to Elphinstone, 13 April 1819, PA: DC 94/298.
[33] Robertson to Elphinstone, 31 October 1818, PA: DC 91/155 enclosure.
[34] Robertson to Elphinstone, November 1818 in R. D. Choksey, *The Aftermath* (Bombay, 1950), p. 185.
[35] The varieties of allowances are well described in J. Macleod's report to Elphinstone, 31 August 1819. This report can be found in an appendix to Forrest's edition of Elphinstone's 'Report on the Territories Conquered from the Peshwa [Paishwa]' in George W. Forrest, *Selections from the Minutes and Other Official Writings of the Honourable Mountstuart Elphinstone, Governor of Bombay* (London, 1884), pp. 407–10. This appendix, however, refers to a section of the report not reproduced by Forrest. For the section on alienated revenue see Report of Elphinstone to Governor-General 25 October 1819 in *Selections of Papers from the Records at East-India House* (London, 1826), IV, 170–1.

the grantee or his ancestors) and was paid from a designated revenue source such as a specified field or the transit duties of a certain area. *Rojinā*, as the term implies (*roj*, 'day'), apparently referred to allowances paid originally on a per diem basis. *Khairāt* (when referring to cash allowances) and rojina were almost always initially granted by Muslim rulers. In addition, there were other minor cash allowances, including the *dakṣiṇā* to be considered below. However, a minute analysis of the Maratha terminology would not be very useful. The effect of all such varsasans, to revert to the general usage, was the same: to produce a large number of individuals wholly or partially dependent on government for their livelihood, and so creating a complex network of relations between subject and state. To the British, all these allowances were merely the 'indiscriminate charities' or 'alms-giving' of a brahman government.[36]

The annual daksina distribution in the month of Shravan, discussed by Ballhatchet and Kumar, is perhaps the best-known annual allowance.[37] It differed, the British believed, from other 'alms to Brahmins,' which 'were almost indiscriminate, and were regulated rather by caprice and interest than any principle,' in that it 'was professedly for the encouragement of learning... It was doubtless subject to abuse, but was upon the whole fairly applied, and certainly had the effect of encouraging the studies of the learned men of the Mahratta country.'[38] Elphinstone had authorized Rs. 50,000, and Robertson in Pune devised a ranking to determine the allowances to the numerous recipients.[39] By reducing the total amount of the distribution and the number of recipients – in 1806 60,000 brahmans had received Rs. 1,94,560[40] – and also by rewarding brahmans on the basis of their achievements, it was hoped to emphasize the educational rather than charitable aspects of the daksina. Robertson further attempted to distinguish it from the Peshva's 'indiscriminate charity' by not altering the time of the distribution. 'I was in no hurry to close the list [of recipients] in order that the idea of the donation being received in Shrawan Mas [Shravan *mās*] might render it less liable to misinterpretation.'[41] The daksina, given in conjunction with the establishment of a

[36] These descriptions are from John Adam, Secretary to the Governor-General to Elphinstone, 26 September 1818 in Sardesai, *Poona Affairs*, p. 472.
[37] Kenneth Ballhatchet, *Social Policy and Social Change in Western India, 1817–1830* (London, 1957), p. 86. Ravinder Kumar, *Western India in the Nineteenth Century* (London, 1968), pp. 48–50.
[38] Chaplin to Government, 15 April 1820 in Choksey, *Early British Administration*, p. 53.
[39] Robertson to Elphinstone, 24 May 1819, PA: DC 95/377.
[40] *Selections from the Peshwa Daftar* XXXII, 94.
[41] Robertson to Elphinstone, 24 May 1819.

Hindu college teaching nontraditional subjects, seemed an ideal expenditure to organize for the public good.

The benefits of other forms of cash allowances were less obvious. On one occasion Robertson reported that an astrologer (*josī*) came to Pune on the occasion of solar or lunar eclipses and certain Hindu holidays and claimed Rs. 5 'for reading & explaining the good & evil which he pretends to foretell on such occasions.'[42] Evidently the demand was based on precedent, and Robertson had paid the astrologer on previous occasions. But was such a claim to be honored in the future? Often varsasans were paid for ceremonies previously performed for the Peshva. Robertson, as Collector of Pune, received petitions for these allowances as if he had inherited the ritual position of the Peshva. One brahman, for example, claimed Rs. 300 to perform an *anuṣṭhān* ('propitiatory ceremony') for the image of Visnu of the former Peshva Narayanrav. However, this brahman had been on a pilgrimage to Banaras during the war with the British and returning to Pune, in the natural order of things, called upon Robertson to reinstate his allowance.[43]

Many times unusual and unique claims were presented. The Peshva had given 65 brahmans funds to erect houses in Pune, but only 45 houses had been built by the time of the war. The claimants, 'some... are respectable Shastrees & some are poor Bramins,' asserted it had been the intention of the Peshva to grant varsasans for their support after the houses had been completed. Robertson thought only those who had built houses might have a claim to an allowance. Anything they received would be 'an act of grace,' and furthermore, 'if they be presented with a sum of money they should consider themselves well of it if it subsists them for a few years till they can acquire the means of living by their own professional industry.'[44]

The reasons why the Maratha state created varsasans concerned the British somewhat less than the problem of whether to continue paying them. No investigation took place to discover why respectable *śāstrīs* (scholars) and poor brahmans should receive funds to erect houses. Nor were the services of the astrologer or the brahman returned from

[42] Robertson to Elphinstone, 2 October 1819, PA: DC 95/453. Allowances to brahmans, interestingly called *daksanā* (sic), paid at the time of a solar eclipse are noted in a document of 26 March 1763, *Selections from the Peshwa Daftar* XXXII, 95–6.
[43] Robertson to Elphinstone, 6 October 1819, PA: DC 95/455. An allowance for an anusthan of Ganpati is, however, designated a daksina in a document of 2 December 1768. This may perhaps refer to an occasional grant or indicate the not very distinct use of terms to designate such grants; see *Selections from the Peshwa Daftar*, XXXII, 102–3.
[44] Robertson to Elphinstone, 19 March 1819, PA: DC 93/276.

Banaras considered relevant or important reasons for continuing their allowances. With the possible exception of the daksina, the British did not seriously consider that allowances represented a bond between subject and state based on either substantive or ritual service. Robertson occasionally wondered about obsolete service allowances, as when he inquired whether he should continue to support *agnihotrīs* ('keepers of the sacrificial fire'), whose utility to the British government was questionable.[45] But this was not really an important point. For the British, the prodigious number and variety of allowances was seen as a political problem – at its most basic, how to keep the brahmans happy. The first task was therefore to establish criteria for the assessment of claims for the continuance of allowances.

As early as November 1818 Robertson requested a definite list of those individuals entitled to receive varsasans. Many people were presenting petitions or preferring sanads, but there was no means of determining which cases were legitimate. It was difficult to distinguish what was intended as an 'occasional charity' from an annual allowance:

Bajee Row's charitable donations from his own treasury were regulated by no fixed rules and he gave to the Wurshasuns of the Wurshasundars of the time of his predecessors with as much irregularity as the new donations conferred during his own Government.[46]

Possessors of a sanad might be given preference, but Robertson believed claimants would come forward who, though in receipt of long-standing allowances, had not been favored with a sanad (probably the majority of the cases). The only way to prepare a register of varsasan recipients was, he believed, to examine the accounts for all payments in the previous 12 years – quite a formidable job. In addition to the question of legitimacy, the collectors were ignorant of some of the most basic facts about the grants. Robertson, for example, questioned whether varsasans were hereditary (in practise they were) or could be received by widows of recipients (it was possible). These crucial points would obviously influence future government policy. Varsasans were thus being settled without their number or nature being known. There was no real long-term policy. A state of affairs so uncertain was bound to adversely affect both recipients and the new government. Hence, it was critical to have some plan, any plan, for the payment of varsasans, because whether the course adopted 'be precisely that of the old

---

[45] Robertson to Elphinstone, 30 September 1819, PA: DC 95/447.
[46] Robertson to Elphinstone, 11 November 1818, PA: DC 91/160.

Government or not [it] will be looked upon as that which is to hold good in the future.'[47]

The first step, compiling a list of all recipients, was undertaken in late 1818 and early 1819 when instructions on the matter were issued to the collectors and the commissioner's assistant in charge of the Pune daphtar.[48] The resulting registers were, Elphinstone believed, merely a tentative measure. The collated daphtar and district accounts were probably not correct in all items, but the recorded amounts would give some idea of the relative importance of individual allowances.[49] The next problem was to prepare rules that could be used in adjudicating all types of cash grants. Conciliation and expedience, the twin foundations of Elphinstone's settlement of the Deccan, meant that claims to varsasans could not be lightly denied. His policy on all alienated revenue was the same: 'the Enams, Wurshasuns, Khyrauts and religious establishments are secured to the holders by the proclamation of Sattara; and it would be obviously impolitic, as well as unjust, to resume them if not so secured.'[50] And the collectors were warned against an overzealous interpretation of his formal written rules, which

show clearly, that any saving which can be made to Government... must be effected not by resumptions either now or hereafter but by vigilance in preventing the advantages of the grants being enjoyed by imposters after the extinction of the individuals or families for whose benefit they were intended, and still more in guarding against the renewal of grants... which have been virtually resumed long before the expiration of the Government of the Paishwa.[51]

Elphinstone first divided varsasans into those paid from the government treasury and those received from village or district revenues.[52] With respect to the former, they were to be continued if entered in the public accounts. When not recorded in the Pune records, they would be paid if held under a sanad from the Peshva or certain of his designated

[47] Robertson to Elphinstone, 1 February 1819, PA: DC 93/233.
[48] W. Chaplin, Collector of Dharvad, 'Instructions to Amlitdars [amanatdar] regarding Wurshasun [varsasan] Pensions, Pagoda and Mosque Allowances and Russooms [*rasūm*, 'fees'],' n.d., accompaniment to Elphinstone's circular to collectors, 13 October 1818; Elphinstone to A. E. R. McDonnell, Assistant in charge of Pune daphtar, 9 April 1819 (circular to collectors, 6 May 1819), PA: XIV; 1/1.
[49] Elphinstone, circular to collectors, 21 July 1819, PA: DC 405/1448–49. A copy of this circular is found in the Inam Commission's files, PA: XIV; 1/1.
[50] Ibid.
[51] Ibid.
[52] All of the following discussion of Elphinstone's rules is based on 'Rules for the Decision of Claims to Wurshasuns, and for the payment of such as are proved to be due;' Elphinstone, circular to collectors, 19 July 1819, PA: DC 405/1430–31; in Inam Commission's files, PA: XIV; 1/5.

officers. In both cases the allowance must have been regularly paid since the accession of Bajirav; there must be no suspicion that the rights had for any reason lapsed before the end of Maratha rule. Claims on the Pune treasury could therefore be reasonably regulated on the authority of the daphtar records supplemented by the sanads of the recipients.

The real problem lay in varsasans paid in the districts and villages, and the rules were necessarily complex. Sanads from the Peshva or other sovereigns whenever issued were to be honored without exception provided, of course, regular payments had been made. The same applied to sanads from the Peshva's great feudatories if they 'exercised independent authority in their Districts for 30 or 40 years.' The deeds of lesser sardars and revenue officers were valid only if they dated before 1803 – Bajirav's return to Pune after the Treaty of Bassein. This choice as the dividing line for determining granting competency reflects British opinion on Bajirav's deteriorating control of his government's servants after the second Anglo-Maratha war. Therefore, allowances granted by the more important district officers after 1803 would only be continued if regular payments had been made in the ten years prior to 1817/18, and the right would cease on the death of the recipient. Those paid only occasionally during these ten years were to be immediately halved and were also limited to the life of the recipient.

Generous provisions allowed the reinstatement of 'old' district and village varsasans, that is, those granted before 1803. These would be continued on the basis of a single entry in the village accounts 'confirmed by other satisfactory proof of uninterrupted enjoyment.' If old village grants had 'been occasionally stopped, and occasionally paid during the last 10 years, without any authority of Government for their discontinuance,' then an annual allowance would be renewed. Even in cases where no payments had been made in the ten-year period, the collectors were to reinstate the allowances provided their resumption had been inadvertent or capricious, 'not implying a design on the part of Government.'

Further general rules regulated how the collectors would pay allowances. Recipients were required to 'muster' in person 'at least once a year' in front of a British officer. Presumably, this was to prevent money being paid to deceased grantees. Finally, the question of a varsasan's heritability was left entirely to the recommendation of the collector.

In the districts Elphinstone's rules did not meet with the entire approval of the collectors. Henry Pottinger from Ahmednagar, in particular, felt 'considerable regret... that it is utterly impossible, consistently with your benevolent views and liberal policy, either to conform to your orders, or to frame any general system for the examination of these alleged rights.'[53] The records of the Maratha government for the ten years before the war were in such disarray that most claimants would not be able to fulfill Elphinstone's liberal expectations. Even sanad holders would be prevented from receiving their due allowances because these documents had not been 'attended to for the last eight or ten years.'[54] Sanads had apparently not been reconfirmed to the heirs of deceased recipients. A test of Elphinstone's rules for allowances paid from village and district revenues had, Pottinger reported,

defeated your wishes of people receiving what they were justly entitled to... [the rules] would have led to our renewing grants which from their nature, and the long cessation in their being paid, it can only be fairly inferred were known to the late Government to have been discontinued.[55]

Hence, old varsasans would be renewed to the neglect of newer grants, which could not be confirmed because of the poor state of recent accounts. In the same way, to place too much emphasis on sanads would be a mistake, as old documents were not recalled after a grant had been resumed, 'a fact which greatly adds to the perplexity of this subject.'[56]

In fact, the disarray of recent accounts did not mean that more cash allowances had been taken from village and district revenues. Pottinger believed it would only make proving claims a near impossible task. Moreover, 'Bajee Row himself made very few... donations of any kind, and he appears to have rather encouraged than otherwise the resumption, by his ministers and mamlutdars, of the grants of his predecessors,' and as the revenue farmers under Bajirav had no contractual obligation to pay village and district allowances, 'this was in fact virtually abolishing them.'[57] Under these circumstances, any recent varsasans were probably perfectly valid.

Pottinger suggested that the Marathi accounts on which Elphinstone heavily relied could not be trusted. For instance, an authentic record of the devasthan expenses of Ahmednagar city could not be obtained. 'There was nothing regularly paid,' and in reality, 'the trifling sums bestowed seem to have been mere extortions from the Government officers by the incessant clamours and reproaches of the bramins and

[53] H. Pottinger, Collector of Ahmednagar to Elphinstone, 20 September 1819 in Choksey, *Aftermath*, p. 247.
[54] Ibid.
[55] Ibid.
[56] Ibid., pp. 248–9.
[57] Ibid., p. 249.

attendants about the Pagodas.'[58] Such devasthans should therefore be all fixed anew on the basis of the fame of the temples judged against former accounts. This could only increase the popularity of British rule, as Bajirav had paid little or nothing to any but the most famous institutions. Such an undertaking, Pottinger conceded, would be difficult, but it would settle devasthans with a precision not possible in any other way.[59]

In his long letter to Elphinstone, Pottinger took the opportunity to present his own, simplified rules for annual allowances.[60] In general, varsasans should be proved to have been paid for only the five years preceding British rule. No differentiation should be made with regard to the granting authority, except that allowances specifically approved by Bajirav or his nominated ministers required only three years' proof of payment. However, grants dating before 1803 were to be continued only if entered in the Pune daphtar. The overall intention of Pottinger's plan was to confirm those varsasans paid just before the conquest, and turn Bajirav's last recipients into British pensioners. This would have had the dual advantages of political continuity and creating a reasonably well-defined base for calculating future payments; furthermore, the collectors would not be put into the position of second-guessing the actions or intentions of the Peshva. What was therefore needed from grantees was proof of actual payment, not occasional entries in accounts or the presentation of sanads. 'These proofs,' presumably in the form of receipts, would 'be easily obtained if [the allowances] were really paid.'[61] Pottinger's premise was that under Bajirav allowances had been closely regulated, if not always their registration. He was thus moving close to a view that saw Maratha varsasans as based more on changing and particular circumstances – the ritual and political bonds between subject and state – than on the unquestioned continuance of a charity.

Pottinger's closely argued letter was answered by a point-by-point refutation in which the new Commissioner in the Deccan declined to alter Elphinstone's rules for varsasans. Like most of his proposals, Pottinger's suggestions for devasthans were found 'perhaps a little too

---

[58] Ibid., p. 248. Perhaps Pottinger did not look closely enough for the accounts. A document of 13 March 1811, for example, has been published that gives in great detail the gifts, called daksana, to the deities in Pune city and environs on the occasion of the birth of a son of the Peshva (Babasaheb?) on 17 October 1810. The Morgav shrine was given one mohar worth Rs. 13.25, see *Selections from the Satara Rajas' and Peshwas' Diaries*, v, 285–309.
[59] Pottinger to Elphinstone, 20 September 1819 in Choksey, *Aftermath*, pp. 250–1.
[60] Ibid., pp. 251–4.
[61] Ibid., p. 253.

comprehensive.'[62] Just such a thorough investigation was later con-templated by Sir John Malcolm when he was Governor of Bombay. The aims of this inquiry would be as much to confirm the rights of legitimate recipients as to detect frauds. But the proposal was never taken up because of difficulties in obtaining the necessary documents from the collectors.[63]

Elphinstone's settlement of varsasans therefore remained in force for more than two decades after his really quite temporary and tentative rules were introduced. When formal regulations, to be described below,[64] were finally adopted, the imprint of inam settlements on government policy came to the fore. But because allowances as a group were never subjected to such intensive scrutiny as landed inams, the Deccan Commission's lists of recipients and amounts payable remained essentially current until the end of the British rule after being in-corporated into the Government of India's Pension Act (XXIII of 1871).[65] If individual payments were small, as was often the case, later legislation often assumed that the initial decisions of Elphinstone and his collectors were correct. Most allowances, in fact, were not worth anything more than a *pro forma* inquiry and confirmation. Some special cases, which for whatever reasons received some special attention and were settled under the regulations then in force, tended to raise again, however belatedly, questions about the purpose of this charity.

III. A varsasan resumed

In 1818 Robertson requested and received Elphinstone's private sanction to pay Rs. 669/4/- on account of the Dev of Cincvad's pilgrimage to Morgav. The following year Elphinstone gave his official approval to the expenditure, but the collector now wanted the legitimacy of the allowance and the correctness of the charges checked in the daphtar.[66] The Maratha accounts indicated that the Dev had previously

---

[62] Chaplin to Pottinger, 20 October 1819, PA: XIV; 1/5.
[63] Sir John Malcolm, minute on leaving India, 30 November 1830 in Sir John Malcolm, *Government of India* (London, 1830), Appendix A, p. 61.
[64] See pp. 115–16.
[65] See R. N. Joglekar, *Alienation Manual* (Pune, 1921), Appendix, pp. 17–33, 228 (for form of sanad issued); Govindlal D. Patel, *The Indian Land Problem and Legislation* (Bombay, 1954), p. 59.
[66] Robertson to Elphinstone, 11 August 1819, PA: DC 95/415. The amounts of the various allowances (see Table 3) were documented in a Marathi memorandum not found in the Deccan Commission files. This memorandum is abstracted in the Report of the Sub-Assistant Settlement Officer, 25 September 1861, PA: XIII, 55/740, pp. 518–44.

been overpaid. Retrospectively sanctioning the apparent error, Elphinstone now allowed a payment of Rs. 338: the cost of the pair of shawls was reduced; the five gold mohars were valued more closely to their market rather than nominal exchange rate (from Rs. 17/4/- to 13/8/- per mohar); and the credit allowed for provisioning the Dev and his entourage was slashed.[67] In 1818 the expenses had been excessive because, as Robertson explained, the Dev had requested bearers and transport, and 'the old Government having large establishments of Hamals [*hamāl*, 'bearer'] and beasts of burden unemployed, could furnish them without expenses and as I had none to give him I hired them.'[68] Again approving the allowance in 1820, the commissioner (now William Chaplin) set the values of the shawls, mohars and provisions as found in the accounts and confirmed by Elphinstone. But now the expense of draught animals (ten horses and two bullocks) and ten bearers was acknowledged.[69] The Dev's varsasan was fixed at Rs. 478.

Although Chaplin, in 1820, approved the 'usual expenses' of the Dev and saw the varsasan as generally conforming to Elphinstone's rules, Robertson had some doubts about the permanence of the expenditure. To the collector it seemed to 'depend on the pleasure of Government.' However, the matter was not pursued; rather, the first concern was to determine an exact amount for the allowance. Part, of course, could be calculated from the accounts at hand, but part had to be estimated by converting grants in kind (provisions and animals), very variable expenses, to precise cash amounts.[70] Presumably Rs. 478, really quite an arbitrary figure, represented a fair average of the Dev's former receipts. No doubt the collector also preferred having a constant sum on his books rather than instituting a yearly inquiry into the actual expenses of the pilgrimage. However, for all the liberal intentions of the Deccan Commission, the very act of fixing the Dev's varsasan as an unchanging pension altered the nature and purpose of the grant.

Though with somewhat less pomp, the Morgav pilgrimage continued in its accustomed way until 1840. Of course, the Peshva no longer received the Dev in Pune, but correct form was observed when, as the Dev's *vakīl* ('advocate') later reminded the Agent for Sardars: 'the Dufterdar [*daphtardār*, 'record keeper'] accompanied by the Mamlutdar

---

[67] Elphinstone to Robertson, 14 August 1819, PA: DC 405/1521.

[68] Robertson to Elphinstone, 17 August 1819, PA: DC 95/421.

[69] Robertson to Chaplin, 6 August 1820; Chaplin to Robertson 7 September 1820 in Report of Sub-Assistant Settlement Officer, 25 September 1861.

[70] A problem often encountered was whether to convert former grain allowances to annual cash payments. For example, the cases of Ambadas Pujari and Hardas Gosavi in Robertson to Chaplin, 23 December 1819, PA: DC 96/548.

and a party of police sepoys used to come out to escort the Dev, who thus received the respect to which he had hitherto been accustomed.'[71] Increasingly this became a mere recital of a moribund tradition. Apart from the expense of an annual pension, the ritual of the Maratha state had no relevance for the British. In fact, the continued acting out of the ceremonials would direct official attention to the payment of the Dev's varsasan.

In April 1841 Bombay ordered the Dev's pilgrimage allowance stopped.[72] Bombay saw the presentation of shawls as an official offering to a Hindu deity or institution and hence a clear violation of despatches from the Court of Directors ordering the removal of all official connections with 'idolatry.'[73] These orders evolved out of evangelical pressure on the Company, and they mainly concerned the pilgrim tax in Puri in Orissa and other places in the Bengal Presidency.[74] The direct government administration of temple revenues, the collection of the pilgrim tax, and other official connections with religion were minor matters in Bombay. A total of only Rs. 9520, distinct from indirect connections through revenue alienations, was paid in such cases.[75] The collectorate accounts had been scoured to find all offending examples, including the presentation to the Dev, which were duly reported to Calcutta.[76] In the general context of the Company's relations with Indian religion, one of the most acute concerns of the 1830s and 1840s, the case of the Dev's varsasan illustrates the difficulties encountered by local governments in implementing the Court's instructions while preserving the longstanding political policy of respecting religious endowments. How could the direct administration of religion be separated from inams, devasthans and varsasans, all of which ultimately came from government revenue?[77]

---

[71] Memorandum of Moro Udhav, vakil of Cincvad to Agent for Sardars (translation), 29 July 1842, PA: IX; 4/59, pp. 66–70.

[72] Government to Collector of Pune, 22 April 1841 in Report of Sub-Assistant Settlement Officer, 25 September 1861.

[73] Despatches of Court of Directors to Governor-General, 20 February 1833 in *Parliamentary Papers* 1837, XLIII, 190–9; 8 August 1838 in ibid., 1839, XXXIX, 189–90.

[74] Nancy Gardner Cassels, 'The 'Pilgrim Tax': A Case Study in the Development of East India Company Social Policy' (Ph.D. dissertation, University of Toronto, 1976), pp. 189–202 for the background of these despatches; pp. 202–06 for the case of Bombay.

[75] Government circular to collectors, 10 August 1837, PA: XIV; 9/128, fols. 1–7, statement no. 1.

[76] Government of Bombay to Government of India, 27 February 1841, *Parliamentary Papers* 1845, XXXIV, 330–4.

[77] The problem is discussed in a contemporary (1838) minute by Henry St. George Tucker, Director of the East India Company, 'Religious ceremonies and endow-

In 1841 the Dev as usual sent a memorandum (*yādī*) to the Collector
of Pune requesting the normal advance payments for transport and
provisions for his upcoming pilgrimage.[78] But inexplicably, as the
Cincvad vakil recalled,

the Collector, who through an oversight, has misrepresented the nature of this
outlay which is really a 'Deowusthan expenditure' to be a 'Bucksees' [*bakhšīs*,
'alms to inferior'] or gift – induced Government to suspend the continuance of
the ... offerings to the Deo.[79]

Describing the various components of the allowance to the Agent for
Sardars, the Dev requested the payments be immediately reinstated in
their customary manner.[80] Because of this representation, Bombay was
prompted to have the Collector of Pune make a detailed investigation of
the allowance. Apparently, all parts of the varsasan had been discontinued because 'the whole expenditure is entered under one head in the
accounts of this collectorate.'[81] The collector proposed to separate the
gift of shawls and mohars, which would be discontinued, from the grant
of provisions and carriage. Maintaining only the latter as a devasthan
would effectively remove any direct contact with idolatry. This suggestion concerning the components of the Dev's allowance surprised
Bombay. Only the presentation of shawls had previously been at issue.[82]
Having received further amplification of the case, government concluded that the collector had gone beyond its policy not 'to
reduce the amount of grants for religious purposes, but only to
withdraw from any objectionable forms in the payment of them.'[83] The
entire allowance was to be reinstated, but the 'accustomed honours'
could not be paid the Dev on his visit to Pune. These 'he received, under
the Murata Government, in his religious character, and their continuance would be inconsistent with the principles which regulate the

ments,' in *Memorials of Indian Government: Being a Selection from the Papers of Henry
St. George Tucker*, ed. John William Kaye (London, 1853), pp. 353–69. This minute
was written in conjunction with the despatch of 18 August 1838 from the Court of
Directors, see Cassels, pp. 229–31.
[78] Moro Udhav, vakil of Cincvad to Agent for Sardars (Agent's translation), 5 August
1841, PA: ix; 4/59, pp. 57–62. The fourth of Bhadrapad shuddha was 20 August in
1841.
[79] Cincvad to Agent for Sardars, 29 July 1842.
[80] Cincvad to Agent for Sardars, 5 August 1841, referred to Government 16 August
1841, PA: ix; 4/59, p. 63.
[81] The correspondence of 1841 is cited from P. Dods, Inam Commissioner Northern
Division to Revenue Commissioner for Alienations, 30 June 1860, PA: xiii; 55/740,
pp. 490–504.
[82] Government to Collector of Pune, 21 October 1841.
[83] Collector of Pune to Government, 24 December 1841; Government to Collector of
Pune, 30 December 1841.

connexion of the British Government with the religious institutions of the country.'[84] By 1842 all ceremony in the presentation of the allowance had been eliminated.

Rather than being particularly grateful for the indulgence shown him, the Dev complained about the lack of ceremony. He had received an order reinstating his varsasan; 'the cash was accordingly paid'; however, because he was not now received by the daphtardar with an escort of sepoys,

the ancient Honor & dignity of the Suwusthawn [Samsthan] have been affected – that it is the wish of the British Government to maintain & preserve unimpaired all the ancient rights & institutions existing in this country – and that the uninterrupted continuance of the privileges which the Deo of Chinchwud has enjoyed from time immemorial will not only shew the greatness of the British Government; but also preserve the ancient dignity of the 'Deity' [the Dev].[85]

The 1842 pilgrimage was coming. The collector had to be told to make the necessary arrangements, which 'should be speedily effected.'[86] However, rhetoric about the meaning of ceremony, the benevolence of the state, or the 'ancient dignity' of the Dev failed to move Bombay. Henceforth, the varsasan would be paid as just another charitable pension, without context or purpose.

In the same year that Bombay settled the question of participation in the Morgav pilgrimage, new rules for varsasans were formulated. By 1852 these had been slightly modified and reissued as the Amended Rules of 1842.[87] These rules were never formal regulations of government, but were merely issued in a circular to collectors. Although anticipating legislation regulating landed inam, these rules soon became supplementary to the main settlements of alienated land revenue. Hence, a discussion of the background, principles and intentions of legislation on alienated revenues will be deferred until the origins of the Inam Commission are examined in Chapter 6. Briefly here, however, the varsasan rules first required the presence of sanads issued by a competent granting authority of the former government. Or in the case of uninterrupted possession, varsasans received at the conquest for 60 years and two successions (to the grandson of the original grantee) were deemed to be held by a prescriptive right and were hereditary to the male

---

[84] Government to Agent for Sardars, 27 August 1842, PA: IX; 4/59, pp. 71–2.
[85] Cincvad to Agent for Sardars, 29 July 1842.
[86] Ibid.
[87] Joglekar, *Alienation Manual*, Appendix, pp. 1–6; see also Alfred Thomas Etheridge, 'Narrative of the Bombay Inam Commission,' *Selections from the Records of the Bombay government*, n.s. 132 (Bombay, 1874), pp. 35–6.

descendants of the recipient. Those allowances claimed under a prescriptive title of 40 years' possession before the conquest and one succession were to be continued to the death of the last surviving son of the recipient in 1818. Varsasans and devasthans held by religious institutions (but not individuals on their behalf), when supported by a valid title or continuous possession, were to be considered permanent endowments juridically the property of a deity.

Even though these rules were essentially in force in 1842 and were finalized in 1852, many years would pass before the Morgav pilgrimage allowance was subjected to their test. After 1852 the Inam Commission was completely occupied with landed inams. Varsasans were just not significant items of revenue and would have to wait. Because the rules for cash and land alienations were so similar, if investigated varsasans tended to be treated as identical to inam. Under these circumstances many of the points of debate that arose in the final settlement of the Dev's varsasan introduce some of the general issues in the inamdar's relations with the Inam Commission. These themes are developed at more length in Chapters 6 and 7.

Perhaps the most fundamental point of contention after 1852 concerned the tenure of the Devs' holdings. Were they endowments to a religious institution or personal grants? If the former, which might at first glance seem logical in view of the religious associations of the Dev lineage and the Cincvad Samsthan, then all revenues would have to be declared permanent endowments to Cincvad with the Devs being only the hereditary managers of a religious institution. But the Inam Commission, from its reading of the Marathi documentation, concluded that all Cincvad's inam had been granted to a person, not an institution. The Devs would dispute this. Firstly, it conflicted with their own perception of the lineage's place in Maratha society – as the Dev and the deity were one then obviously, in their view, all Cincvad's revenues were devasthans. But in addition, because of statutory provisions, personal holdings could only be inherited under certain conditions and in a particular manner whereas devasthans had few such restrictions placed upon them. When the eighth Dev Dharanidhar died in 1852 without an obvious heir, the implementation of the commission's set rules for the descent of personal inam produced much resistance from certain sections of the lineage. The consequences of this are a major topic of Chapter 7.

The disputes over the identity of the heir to the Cincvad estate eventually caused the Collector of Pune to become uncertain about who should receive the Morgav pilgrimage allowance. Until 1859 he had paid it to Laksmibai, Dharanidhar's widow and, in the commission's view, his provisional heir. The widow's position was challenged in 1859, and as a result the collector stopped the allowance and called upon the Inam Commission to investigate all aspects of the claim.[88]

Reviewing all previous correspondence on the pilgrimage allowance, the Inam Commissioner conceded that if the grant was in fact a devasthan, as the Dev had asserted in 1842, then it probably had been held long enough before the conquest to qualify as a permanent religious endowment under the Amended Rules of 1842. But he did not believe it a devasthan 'in the usual acceptation of the term.' Elphinstone's sanctions in the first years after the conquest could not be construed as authorizing a 'perpetual payment.' Government had apparently been completely misinformed about the nature of the expenditure: 'had not the Collector of Poona erroneously reported in 1841 that Government continued the allowance at the conquest as a "Deosthan,"' then surely all payments would have ceased.[89] Raising again the specter of official connections with Hinduism, the Inam Commissioner offered the following perhaps accurate characterization of the allowance:

the shawls & Mohurs given to the Chinchore Deo on his approaching Poona can only be looked upon in the light of a Nuzzerana [*najaṟṇā*, 'present to a superior'] presented by a Hindoo Prince in his religious character to his Superior a Hindoo God.[90]

That the ceremonies had in fact long since ceased was unimportant. If allowances had once derived from objectionable sources, they were outside the protection of the rules, and government should exercise its right to withdraw such a pension.

After this decidedly negative opinion, Captain Cowper, the Revenue Commissioner for Alienations, received advice that threatened to redefine the tenure of the Dev's varsasan. In correspondence unconnected with the Morgav pilgrimage, Cowper had wondered whether an entry in the Peshva's tahanama, '*yātrā* Morgav [Rs.] 562½', referred to pilgrim taxes or offerings from the fair (yatra) at Morgav. The Inam Commissioner, a new officer in that post and seemingly unaware of his predecessor's researches, guessed that it concerned revenue derived from the Dev's pilgrimage, and it 'included the payment made by the state for humuls, food, clothing & carriage, and also the value of the offerings of

---

[88] G. Inverarity, Collector of Pune to P. Dods, Inam Commissioner Northern Division, 28 December 1859, PA: XIII; 55/740, pp. 480–1.

[89] Dods to Revenue Commissioner for Alienations, 30 June 1860, PA: XIII; 55/740, pp. 490–504.

[90] Ibid.

The inamdar under the British

the Pilgrims.'[91] Cowper pressed for the grounds upon which this conclusion was drawn.[92] However, apart from the similarity in amounts of revenue, there was no real evidence to link the Morgav fair with the pilgrimage allowance. The commissioner conceded that the accounts never debited the various components of the varsasan under the head 'yatra Morgav,' though perhaps the tahanama could have used such a general notation for diverse revenues. At any rate, the commissioner maintained there was no way of knowing which interpretation of the entry in the tahanama was correct. (It may be mentioned here that some evidence now suggests that 'yatra Morgav' was a collection division of the internal transit duties.[93]) Furthermore, the commissioner could not see why it was so important because the settlement of a varsasan presumably did not depend on the interpretation of such a minor point.[94] Cowper recognized, however, that if the Peshva acknowledged the allowance in the tahanama, then it would probably have to be continued as a permanent devasthan. The revenue was explicitly included in that moiety of the Dev inheritance set aside for the Samsthan.[95]

When William Hart succeeded Cowper as head of the Alienation Department the various doubts about the allowance had still not been resolved and a fresh examination of the case was ordered.[96] This included calling upon the widow Laksmibai to make a deposition on behalf of the Samsthan. She was apparently prepared to plead that the Peshva's tahanama did indeed guarantee the varsasan, a position in keeping with her desire to have all Cincvad's holdings declared permanent devasthans with herself as manager. But a lengthy report on the matter from the Sub-Assistant Settlement Officer concluded that the allusion to 'yatra Morgav' referred only to offerings made during the Morgav fair.[97] This assessment was based on an examination of the

[91] T. A. Cowper, Revenue Commissioner for Alienations to C. J. Griffith, Inam Commissioner Northern Division, 9 January 1861; Griffith to Cowper, 24 January 1861, PA: XIII; 55/740, pp. 505–7.
[92] Cowper to Griffith, 30 January 1861, PA: XIII; 55/740, p. 507.
[93] M. D. Apte, 'The Nature and Scope of the Records from the Peshwa Daftar with Reference to Zakat System,' *Indian Economic and Social History Review*, 6 (1969), 374 citing evidence from jakat rumals in the daphtar names it as a duty subdivision near Pune city. Conceivably, it may have referred to a transit duty on people, that is, a toll or kind of pilgrim tax.
[94] Griffith to Cowper, 4 February 1861, PA: XIII; 55/740, pp. 508–9.
[95] The effect of the tahanama on the tenure of Cincvad's inam is considered on pp. 223–6.
[96] W. Hart, Officiating Revenue Commissioner Southern Division to Settlement Officer Deccan and Satara, 18 September 1861, PA: XIII; 55/740, pp. 510–11.
[97] Report of Sub-Assistant Settlement Officer, 25 September 1861, PA: XIII; 55/740, pp. 518–44.

118

Peshva's diaries (*rojkīrd*s), which indicated that no varsasan disbursements were made on account of the yatra in the years immediately
preceding or in the year of the tahanama's issue. In addition, the
accounts of the *deśpāṇḍe* of Pune included Rs. 562½ from the yatra in the
nominal valuation of Morgav, which could only be a way of accounting
for pilgrim offerings. Therefore, no connection could be made between
the tahanama and the pilgrimage allowance. The Devs had asserted
otherwise only because the commission itself had first put forward the
suggestion. The lineage had quickly endorsed something favorable to its
interests. Elphinstone and Chaplin had not contemplated giving
hereditary or permanent rights. If they had, Robertson would not have
requested their annual approval for the expenditure. The allowance
could only be considered the personal offering of a Hindu prince, in
which the British government should have no part. Through some
oversight, what was in effect a political gratuity of the Deccan
Commission (requiring approval each time it was paid) had been
converted into a varsasan.

Considering the issues on the basis of recommendations from Hart,
Bombay agreed that the only claim the Dev had was for Rs. 167½ for two
shawls and five mohars. Although this was a religious offering, it was not
so different from many similar cases, and it did have a sufficiently long
history under the Peshvas to make it a type of personal varsasan. The
payments for food, animals and such were simply contingency expenses
approved by the Deccan Commission and never meant as either a
devasthan or varsasan.[98] Government thus confirmed a hereditary
allowance held under a prescriptive title. But lacking a sanad, it could
only be claimed by direct male heirs, 'of the body,' of the recipient at the
time of the conquest. Because government recognized no such living
heir, the allowance was not resumed.[99]

So ended the last vestiges of the ritual relations between the Maratha
state and the Dev of Cincvad that the British assumed by the payment of
a varsasan for the Morgav pilgrimage. From the beginning the British
had attempted to distance themselves from the implications of the
expenditure and see it as but one more charitable pension. The Deccan
Commission had deputed one of their Indian subordinates to play the
part of the Peshva in the presentation ceremony; in 1841-2 Bombay
stopped even this. Nevertheless, the district officers and junior members

[98] Government to Hart, 18 January 1862 referring to Hart's letter of 19 December 1861
(lacking in PA), PA: XIII; 55/740, p. 545.
[99] J. Dracup, Assistant Settlement Officer to Collector of Pune, 5 March 1862, PA: XIII;
55/740, pp. 522-3.

of the Inam Commission thought even continued payment violated the principles upon which the British should govern.

This general line of thinking on religious grants was also the unequivocal position of the Bombay Missionary Conference in an 1858 petition to the Court of Directors. Perhaps not unreasonably describing all allowances as 'patronage,' the missionaries demanded the abolition of this hidden connection with idolatry. Befitting the rule of a Christian government, the money should be better employed for the general welfare of the Indian people.[100]

Bombay resisted such pressure and declined to sever, indeed refused to acknowledge, the remaining tenuous ritual relations with pensioners such as the Dev. Minuting on the missionaries' proposals, the Governor, Lord Elphinstone, could not discern any such idolatrous connections from the payment of legitimate grants. He recalled, near the end of the Company's rule, the political considerations that had motivated his uncle's decisions at the conquest:

> it was the obvious policy of the East India Company when it assumed the Government, to endeavour to conciliate the Hindoos, the great bulk of their subjects ... That this policy was pushed to an extreme, and that it led us to make some lamentable mistakes, I have no wish to deny.[101]

The possible excesses of this policy had been corrected when objectionable forms of administration had been stopped. Now, the cash allowances of former rulers were paid in a completely impartial manner: '[government] treats them exactly as it treats all other property, inams, or assignments of revenue.'[102] It was, another member of council declared, only 'under a civil obligation that Government continues these alienations.' All grants were property of some sort, and as such

> there can be no doubt that former sovereigns were fully competent to assign the revenues of the country in cash or in land for the maintenance of their religion, and although the property so acquired cannot be disposed of or inherited in the same manner as private property, it is evident that a formal grant by a competent authority, supported by uninterrupted enjoyment for a series of years, conveys a title to continuance which ought to be allowed all the validity of a chartered right.[103]

In short, varsasans from whatever source and granted for whatever

---

[100] Memorial of Bombay Missionary Conference, 22 February 1858 in *Parliamentary Papers* 1857–58, XLII, 329–31.
[101] Minute of Lord Elphinstone, 3 April 1858, ibid., p. 332.
[102] Ibid.
[103] Minute of H. W. Reeves, 7 April 1858, ibid., pp. 334–5.

purpose had become cash pensions indistinguishable from minor land inams. When an allowance needed to be settled it became part of the alienation inquiries of the 1850s and was subjected to the Inam Commission's rules. And such, really, was the fate the Dev's varsasan suffered.

5

An inamdar's domain: Cincvad and the commerce of Pune-Haveli

Under the Marathas the Dev of Cincvad had an important part in the control of commerce in Pune-Haveli. He could coin rupees, levy fees from artisans (*mohtarphā*), operate caravans under special passes (*dastak*), and collect internal transit duties (jakat). All these state prerogatives were given over to the Dev, alienated in a way analogous to inam land. A territorial base, either inam or jagir was usually necessary for the independent possession of these rights: mints had to be located, at least in name, in a sardar's village; the mohtarpha was collected in his bazaars; the holder of a dastak ran caravans to and from his own villages; collection posts for the jakat were established on roads passing through a right-holder's territory. For the inamdar or jagirdar, revenues derived from the control of commerce were simply one more income allowed a landed feudatory of the Maratha state.

Seeing the traditional commercial infrastructure of India as a hindrance to trade, in the 1830s the East India Company standardized coinage and abolished transit duties. Viewed from the long perspective, these reforms were perhaps the logical extension of the Company's mercantile origins. In the general and international economic sphere, the creation of a measure of commercial uniformity in British conquests was part of a process that would ultimately lead India into the wider Victorian 'imperialism of free trade.'[1] How could the empire's trade prosper if a merchant was continually hindered by uncertain rates of exchange and his goods subject to any number of vexing duties? In the specific context of British rule in India, the reform of commerce is best seen as indicative of the growing confidence of the Company's government in the 1830s and 1840s. Desirable changes in India, if they were to be achieved at all, required a more intrusive policy towards indigenous institutions. An inamdar possessing claims on the internal commerce of the country was just one particular impediment to trade among many. The amounts of money involved were not large. With

---

[1] John Gallagher and Ronald Robinson, 'The Imperialism of Free Trade,' *Economic History Review*, 2nd series, 6 (1953), 1–15.

adequate compensation surely these minor rights could be easily eliminated.

The inamdar, however, was not interested in the common good as the British saw it. The Company wanted to abolish ancient rights. In the Deccan the generation of the conquest saw the first example of a concerted and general policy aimed at altering Elphinstone's settlement. Compensation, however generous, offered no assurances. The state was now intervening in the affairs of the inamdar's domain. His inam was threatened: Hence, strategies and tactics had to be developed to meet this intrusion.

I. The Cincvad mint

In February 1819 H. D. Robertson informed Mountstuart Elphinstone that the Dev of Cincvad possessed the right to coin money. Since the establishment of the British government in Pune, the Dev had been requested not to exercise this privilege. By his act of 'good will' in voluntarily and 'without hesitation' closing his mint he had apparently lost an annual revenue of Rs. 1800. But subsequently, the Dev had petitioned for permission to reestablish the mint to recover lost revenue. Robertson wondered whether it would be 'politic to buy up his right of coining money at Chinchore'; if so, the collector would 'enter into an enquiry of what [the Dev] actually gained by his mint and endeavour to persuade him to accept of [sic] an annual allowance from Government to give it up.'[2] Elphinstone routinely approved the suggestion.[3] After some negotiations with Robertson's assistants, the Dev accepted Rs. 1300 annual compensation for his minting rights.[4] According to the Dev's vakil, the Samsthan had once minted *ankuśī* ('elephant goad' mint mark) rupees in Cincvad village, but when the Peshva ordered the operation transferred to Pune, the Dev received Rs. 1500 'more or less' (*kampeś*, 'approximately') from the manager of the mint. But the *kārkūn* ('clerk') of Cincvad estimated the amount was approximately Rs. 1300, and this lower figure was accepted by the Collector of Pune. Compensation was calculated retroactively to 17 November 1817, soon after the occupation of Pune.[5]

The collector's accounts recorded the payment as Cincvad's *inām*

[2] Robertson to Elphinstone, 27 February 1819, PA: DC 93/257.
[3] Elphinstone to Robertson, 28 February 1819, PA: DC 404/1295.
[4] Robertson to Elphinstone, 29 April 1819, PA: DC 94/302.
[5] Yadi of viva voce examination of Dev's agents (translation), 26 April 1819, enclosure to Collector of Pune to Revenue Commissioner, 29 June 1850, BA: RD 1850, 218/634, pp. 197–203.

amal: an alienated share of government revenue received from a specific source.[6] This is a land revenue term, but the compensation was more akin to a varsasan created by the British, which Robertson himself recognized when he asked for permission to grant an annual allowance for the mint. But none of the rules created for the settlement of varsasans could apply to the compensation; it was held entirely at the pleasure of the British government. Never previously had the Dev received a direct grant, the Peshva only allowing him to license a mint. With the approval of the Peshva, the Dev sold the license to the highest bidder, the 'farmer' or contractor, who actually coined the rupees. Each year the amount realized from this auction would vary slightly with the past performance and expected production of the mint. When a fixed annual compensation was granted, these distinctions in the source of the Dev's revenue were lost. Elphinstone was more immediately concerned with stopping the Cincvad mint.

Shortly after the conquest Elphinstone closed all mints in Pune city, but later agreed to resume coining silver after receiving representations from the city's leading merchants.[7] Really he had little choice as the technical facilities were not available in India for the introduction of a uniform coinage.[8] Until 1834 the Pune mint continued to produce rupees of 'dump' fabric (that is, coins that are relatively thick in proportion to their diameter) bearing Persian legends of the Mughal emperor. In this period machine-minted copper and silver in the different standards of the Presidency cities, traditional-style rupees from provincial mints, and issues from extinct governments were all legal coin throughout British India. A standard coinage in the name of the Company, introduced first in copper and gradually in silver, was an obvious commercial reform.[9] The ending of Cincvad's minting rights was merely one small part of this strongly felt need.

In the Deccan the British faced three main problems before coinage could be standardized. Firstly, debased or forged specie had to be

---

[6] List of alienations in Pune Collectorate for 1821/2, cited in Report of W. Turquand, Superintendent of Pune daphtar to Collector of Pune, 25 June 1850, BA: RD 1850; 218/634, pp. 205–15.

[7] R. D. Choksey, *Economic History of the Bombay Deccan and Karnatak* (Pune, 1945), p. 53; pp. 53–8 for a general summary of coinage under the Deccan Commission. See also W. Chaplin to Government, 20 August 1822 in *Selections of Papers from the Records at East India House* (hereafter *East India Records*), 4 vols. (London, 1820–6), IV, 488.

[8] Revenue letter from Bombay to Court of Directors, 5 November 1823 in *East India Records*, III, 812.

[9] See for example, minute of Lord Bentinck on a uniform currency for British India, 10 November 1829 in *The Correspondence of Lord William Bentinck, Governor-General of India, 1828–1835*, ed. C. H. Philips, 2 vols. (Oxford, 1977), I, 345–8.

eliminated. In 1820, for example, poor quality rupees of the Candvad mint (Nasik district) were found circulating in Khandesh.[10] It was suspected that an authentic die had been used to produce these debased coins. A close comparison of the counterfeit with true issues from Candvad proved this not to be the case. The suspect rupees were completely spurious. But much difficulty had been encountered in separating the forged from the authentic but debased: dies were often changed, each year or sooner, so a mint's numerous issues and specific runs all had to be scrutinized.

The second problem, closely related to the difficulties of a debased and spurious coinage, was the impossibility of properly supervising Maratha mints. Where they were farmed little control could be exercised over the quantity of coins produced. The farmer collected a fee on bullion brought for coining, which in Pune was Rs. 12/8/- per thousand coined. Government was supposed to receive Rs. 5/8/- of this fee, but as the farmer's contract was for a fixed sum based on estimated output at this rate (Rs. 1440 per month in Pune for 1819), there was every incentive to increase production.[11] If the contractor was simultaneously dealing in bullion, he would lower his minting charges to attract business. In such an instance, government had no real control over the number of rupees minted. Debasing the coinage was another easy way to increase profits and play havoc with any state monetary policy. Even when a mint was supposedly directly under government control, little real supervision was exercised. At Candvad, for example, while there was no farmer, still the day to day operations were 'entrusted to natives who pay a percentage to Government upon the number of rupees coined,' and

the only control exercised by the [government] mint master is that whenever the operation of coining takes place, one of the Carkoons of the Kumavisdar's establishment with a peon is present to take an account of the number of coins which are struck during the day and who, when the day's work is over locks up the dies and the keys are deposited with the Kumavisdar.[12]

There seemed thus to be every opportunity for peculation.

Finally, the British were seriously troubled by the lack of official

[10] W. Wiering, Sub-collector of Ahmednagar to Chaplin, 2 March 1820 in R. D. Choksey, *Period of Transition* (Pune, 1945), pp. 82–3.

[11] Robertson to Chaplin, 28 December 1819, PA: DC 96/555; see also G. H. Khare, 'A Report on the Maratha Mints of the Peshwa Period located at Poona, Chakan and Chinchavad, both near Poona,' *Journal of the Numismatic Society of India*, 38 (1976), 106–7. For mint fees and an interesting description of the traditional coining process, see John Malcolm, *A Memoir of Central India*, 2 vols. (3rd edn, London, 1832), II, 80–6.

[12] W. Wilkins, Sub-collector of Ahmednagar to H. Pottinger, Collector of Ahmednagar, 20 January 1820 in Choksey, *Period of Transition*, pp. 93–6.

exchange rates for the numerous freely circulating coins. The value of
the local coinage had to be standardized as well as its form. In the
bazaars this was not a problem; money was easily bought and sold by its
intrinsic worth. The payment of troops and the collection of the land
revenue, however, required some degree of precision in monetary values.
Officers in Solapur and the Southern Maratha Country were especially
perplexed by the near hundred varieties of current coin, including many
non-Maratha issues.[13]

Cincvad ankushi rupees were found in general circulation throughout
the Deccan and adjacent areas. Most of the land revenue in the southern
Konkan was received in this coin.[14] In 1820 bills for 2,00,000 Cincvad
rupees, exchanged at 0.92 per Company rupee, were sent from Dharvad
to Pune.[15] Stopping Cincvad's mint would therefore have the advantages of preventing possible suspect and spurious specie, bringing the
money supply under closer supervision, and also slowly removing one
common rupee from the marketplace.

Having regularly received the agreed compensation until July 1834,
the Dev was concerned when for two years he was not paid the annual
Rs. 1300. Government was sent two petitions demanding payment. At
the same time, the significance of the revenue was explained. The money
was needed to finance an annasatra, a ceremonial feeding of brahmans.[16] The British had a clear responsibility to support this ancient
institution:

the ruling power has always interested itself in the cause of the Sounsthan
[Samsthan], and the Company's Government has also hitherto maintained it, on
the same footing, and it will be an act of virtue on its part to continue to support
this charitable institution.[17]

[13] For correspondence on this issue and the rates of exchange established see Choksey,
Period of Transition, pp. 84–93, 180–90.
[14] J. A. Dunlop, Collector of Southern Konkan to Government, 13 June 1823 in R. D.
Choksey, *Ratnagiri Collectorate* (Pune, 1958), pp. 91–4, statement of revenue from
grain sale in 'Chinchore currency;' G. More, Collector of Southern Konkan, 'Coins in
circulation in the Southern Concun,' 19 December 1826 in ibid., pp. 164–5: 'The
greater part of the revenue received in this currency ['Chinchori rupee'].' For an
illustration of the ankushi rupee see Ganesh Hari Khare, *Mandalamtil nani* (Pune,
1933), plate 4, no. 20.
[15] St. John Thackeray, Collector of Dharvad to Chaplin, 20 March 1820 in Choksey,
Period of Transition, pp. 180–1. The discount rate here appears somewhat inflated, no
doubt the margin for the dealers of the bills of exchange. Considerable later evidence
had the exchange rate between Cincvad and Company rupees at 4.08% or 0.9592
Cincvad rupee per Company rupee, see for example, Collector of Pune to Revenue
Commissioner, 23 January 1846, BA: RD 1846; 199/674, pp. 153–7 on calculation of
transit duties.
[16] Dev of Cincvad to Government, 28 February 1837; Balkrsna Bhimaji Vagh, vakil of
Cincvad to Government, 1 March 1837 (translations), PA: IX; 4/59, pp. 23–5.
[17] Vakil of Cincvad to Government, 1 March 1837.

Before Bombay answered this plea, Cincvad enlarged upon the purpose of the revenue from the mint. The annasatra was 'open to the needy, Fakeer, Bramin, traveller and pilgrim, and on the fourth day of every month, 1000 Bramins are entertained.' The considerable expense involved could not now be met, and the consequences for the Samsthan were disastrous:

were I [the Dev] to curtail the expenses of the unnsutru news would immediately be spread throughout the world, that I discontinued an institution which had been maintained by my forefather[s] and thus I would be degraded in public estimation. For this reason I have upheld the institution by borrowing money from others.[18]

Furthermore, and this was perhaps the most telling point, the Dev asserted that it was government's duty to continue the compensation, as his right to license a mint was guaranteed by sanad.

When the district officers were asked to offer opinions on the Dev's petitions, the Collector of Pune reported that compensation had been stopped with the closure of the Pune mint.[19] For the collector the India-wide coinage reform of 1834 and 1835 unquestionably meant

that when sources of Revenue are abolished by Government . . . all perquisites, fees or rights derived from, or dependent on such sources should [be] abolished . . . the Deo of Chinchore should receive no indemnification on account of the loss which he had suffered, by the Political arrangement adopted by Government of abolishing all Mints.[20]

He doubted that the Dev had any real authority to license a mint. No sanad had been produced and it was probable the Dev 'like many of the chieftains usurped the Right of coining money.' The collector brought forward some contradictory historical evidence to support his contention: in 1773 the Peshva stopped all mints because of debased coinage, but he afterwards allowed Cincvad to defray the expenses of the annasatra by operating a mint. The first point was the important one. As a matter of state policy the Maratha government had not hesitated in closing the Cincvad mint, which was an authority the British could likewise exercise.

The Agent for Sardars was able to supply a translation of the

[18] Cincvad to Government (translation), yadi received 20 March 1838, PA: IX; 4/59, pp. 17–20.
[19] Government to Agent for Sardars, 21 April 1838; to Collector of Pune, 18 April 1838; R. Mills, Collector of Pune to Government, 16 May 1838, PA: IX; 4/59, pp. 20, 25–7, 38–9.
[20] Collector of Pune to Government, 16 May 1838. For the background of the coinage reforms of 1835, see S. Ambirajan, *Classical Political Economy and British Policy in India* (Cambridge, 1978), pp. 232–7.

document of 1773, which the Indian assistants (amanatdars) in the Pune daphtar had discovered when searching for the mint's sanad. What was found was an entry in the Peshva's diaries for the period 16 December 1773 to 29 January 1774, recording an agreement (*kaul*) to recommence coinage made on behalf of the Dev between the Peshva and Dulabshet Govindji, the mint contractor. Proper standards for silver rupees and gold mohars were specified, and as previously, the profits were to go to finance the Dev's annasatra. For executing the agreement, or perhaps as a fine for debased production, Dulabshet gave the Peshva a najar of Rs. 500.[21] The agent did not offer an opinion on the significance of this document. Certainly the mint had been in operation before the agreement, but under what authority was not apparent, and in 1773/4 the Peshva did give some form of official sanction to the mint. Even if this was equivalent to a sanad, the possibility of government offering further compensation for the lost right remained an open question.

A year passed and nothing happened. In May 1839 the Dev reminded the agent that five years' compensation remained unpaid.[22] In the meantime, Bombay had sent the whole matter to the Government of India for final decision as coinage was a matter affecting the whole of British India.[23] The eventual decision was not unlike the Collector of Pune's earlier opinion about the political authority of the state:

no compensation can be granted to the Chinchorekur as the Chinchore rupee is no longer the currency of the Hon'ble Company's territory; and that had his mint continued up to the period when the Chinchore was superseded by the Company's coin, his mint would necessarily have been unproductive, as its produce could not have entered into the circulation.[24]

Presumably this settled the matter.

[21] Memorandum of Ramcandra Pandurang Devdhar (Dhamdhere) and Narso Laksman (Malvankar) Daphtardar, amanatdars of Pune daphtar, 4 August 1838, accompaniment to Agent for Sardars to Government, 23 August 1838, PA: ix; 4/59, pp. 21–2, 29–33.

Ramcandra Pandurang Devdhar (Dhamdhere), the native judge of Pune, gives some biographical and family information and details of his family's traditional connection with the daphtar in a yadi prepared for the British in 1833, see Ganesh Chimnaji Vad, Pushotam Vishram Mawjee and D. B. Parasnis, *Kaifiyats, Yadis &c.* (Pune, 1908), pp. 108–10.

Dulabshet apparently held many different licenses to operate mints. He is found, for example, coining copper in the Konkan; see M. G. Ranade, 'Currencies and Mints under Mahratta Rule,' *Journal of the Bombay Branch of the Royal Asiatic Society,* 20 (1897–1900), 197.

[22] Yadi of Dev of Cincvad to Agent for Sardars (translation), 31 May 1839, PA: ix; 4/59, pp. 43–5.

[23] Resolution of Government, accompaniment to Government to Agent for Sardars, 6 July 1839, PA: ix; 4/59, pp. 46–7.

[24] Government to Agent for Sardars, 18 October 1839, PA: ix; 4/59, pp. 53–4.

Nearly a decade later the Dev again claimed compensation for the mint. The revenue had been 'discontinued irregularly.'[25] Obviously, 'such compensation must have been considered to be in perpetuity and your Memorialist continued to receive such for a period [of] sixteen or seventeen years.'[26] Whether the British established mints in Pune or Bombay, or changed the currency of the country, did not, the Dev maintained, affect the rights of the Samsthan. Although making indirect reference to government's earlier 'final' decision, the Dev's petitions were worded in such a way as to avoid discussing the earlier inquiries. Instead, a demand for Rs. 18,000 for 14 years' lost compensation was put forward. In 1850 the Dev again reminded government that compensation had not been paid since 1834.[27] He must have been encouraged with the effect of these petitions and believed the previous decisions were about to be changed (or had been forgotten) when he was required to present documentary evidence on the mint for a report being compiled by the Superintendent of the Pune daphtar.[28] The very number of relevant or marginally important facts that could be found about the history of the mint, and the Dev's persistence in pressing his claims, tended to obscure the matter before government: why no compensation had been paid since 1834. At this point, therefore, it would be useful to review the report from the daphtar to see how this new and largely unnecessary inquiry assessed both the historical evidence and the question of compensation.

Documenting the mint was the first task. Cincvad presented documents of 13 February 1767 and 1773/4. The former, apparently the earliest reference at present available, was found registered in the Peshva's diaries, but it only showed the mint to be then in operation.[29] The latter document was the same agreement recommencing production that the amanatdars of the daphtar had searched out in 1838.[30] The

---

[25] Memorandum of Cincvad to Agent for Sardars (English petition), transmitting petition to Government, 2 December 1848, PA: IX; 4/59, pp. 88–9.

[26] Petition of Dharanidhar Dev to Government (English petition), 2 December 1848, BA: RD 1850; 218/634, pp. 177–84.

[27] Petition of Dharanidhar Dev to Government (English petition), 15 August 1850, BA: RD 1850; 218/634, pp. 247–53.

[28] Report of W. Turquand, Superintendent of the Pune daphtar to Collector of Pune, 25 June 1850, BA: RD 1850; 218/634, pp. 205–15.

[29] Ranade, p. 197 also mentions that a license was issued to two *sonārs* ('goldsmith' caste) to open a mint at Cincvad in 1767/8. This appears to be a reference to the document of 13 February 1767. This document was later referred to by the vakil of Cincvad as an *abhayapatra* (letter of assurance) to Tukoji Sonar and Morarji Sonar, see yadi of vakil of Cincvad to Collector of Pune, 15 October 1851, PA: XIII; 55/740, pp. 91–4.

[30] Report of amanatdars of Pune daphtar, 4 August 1838.

superintendent called this a sanad, but it is clearly a *kaulnāmā*, a document of agreement and arrangement. Interpreting this evidence, the superintendent particularly drew attention to the apparent ease with which the Maratha government had abolished the mint. Notwithstanding the lack of documentation, it could be assumed to have happened between 1766/7 and 1773/4. He also believed the mint had been stopped in 1760/1 and reopened sometime before 1766/7. In the earlier year the Maratha government had closed many independent mints, particularly in the Southern Maratha Country.[31] The weight of evidence now suggests this was not the statewide measure inferred by the superintendent. Whatever the case, obviously under the Marathas, 'Government authority was requisite to establish the Mint and make the coin current, and that the former Government in the exercise of its undoubted right, abolished the Chinchore and other Mints at its pleasure.'[32]

Moving to the issue of compensation, the superintendent believed the Rs. 1300 had been obtained under false pretenses. A statement of alienations in the Pune Collectorate for 1821/2 recorded the then Cincvad vakil as stating how the mint had formerly been in Cincvad, was transferred to Pune by the Peshva, whereupon the Dev received 'from the superintendent of the Mint... the value in cash [of previous profits] according as it slightly exceeded or fell short [of the previous profits].'[33] This was, according to the superintendent, 'unquestionably a trick to mislead our Government,' meant to make the British believe they were 'bound to compensate the Deo on account of the profits, the Deo's right to which the Peishwah's Government had recognized.'[34] In other words, compensation had been granted when the Peshva abolished the mint and moved it to Pune. This was certainly not the case, nor was it what the Dev had stated in 1819. Furthermore, Elphinstone and Robertson were under no illusions about their compensation. They offered to pay the Dev only to stop the mint from producing; and as we can see from the early correspondence, they had no interest in the Peshva's supposed actions.

Central to the superintendent's interpretation was the assumption that moving a mint ended its independent existence. This he attempted to link to the Maratha government's policy of reducing damaging private competiton with its own mints in the period 1803–5. On

[31] For this document see *Selections from the Satara Rajas' and Peshwas' Diaries*, part 2, vol. 2, p. 164 translated in Surendranath Sen, *Administrative System of the Marathas* (Calcutta, 1925), pp. 319–21.
[32] Report of the Superintendent of the Pune daphtar, 25 June 1850.
[33] Quoted in ibid.
[34] Ibid.

12 March 1804, for example, the mint mark of the Cincvad ankushi rupee was slightly altered to distinguish it from the identical type of government rupee. This apparent attempt to isolate the Cincvad mint was not entirely effective as it was 'notorious in Poonah that when the Government mint had in some measure effected its object of putting down the Chinchore Mint the Deo attempted to recover himself by reducing his seignorage.'[35] Another document, a yadi dated only in 1805/6, while not part of the superintendent's evidence, continues the story of the Peshva's reforms. In order to eliminate ever-present debased coinage, a single mint for ankushi rupees was established in Pune.[36] Presumably the striking of rupees in Cincvad ceased after this order, but it appears the Dev's license for a mint was not withdrawn. At most, only the workshop (*kārkhānā*) was moved to Pune and consolidated with the government works. In support of this inference we find the Cincvad vakil later explaining how the government and Cincvad mint licenses were held by the same individual, and how an arrangement was effected to regulate the production of the two separate units.[37] At other times, too, the minting did not occur in Cincvad. In 1776, for example, while complaining about being cheated by his various contractors, the Dev appealed to the Peshva to order the mint works returned to Cincvad. This document is careful to distinguish the karkhana, the 'workshop', from the *ṭankśāl*, a more compreshensive term for a mint in both its physical and revenue senses.[38] The Dev no doubt possessed the revenue right, but he probably rightly felt he had greater control over the mint and its contractor if the coining took place in Cincvad.

In 1776 the Dev may have complained about the location of the mint workshop, but no specific restrictions on this point were contained in the kaulnama of 1773/4. It only stated that the revenue was to go to the Dev because Cincvad was his inam village. The superintendent took this as proving the mint had been abolished when moved to Pune. An alternative interpretation, linking the revenue right with landed inam, might have occurred to the British had not they so confounded the possession of a mint license with the actual production of rupees. Instead, the superintendent could only conclude it 'improbable' that the

---

[35] Ibid., see also Khare, 'A Report on Maratha Mints,' pp. 106–7.

[36] *Aitihasik sankirna sahitya*, III, 253–4 (in *Bharat Itihas Samshodhak Mandal Quarterly*, 21, 3 (January 1941)).

[37] Translation of replies of viva voce examination of Moro Udhav, vakil of Cincvad, n.d., accompaniment to Collector of Pune to Revenue Commissioner, 27 February 1852, PA: XIII; 55/740, pp. 86–9, 94–6.

[38] Letter of Dev of Cincvad, 7 December 1776 in *Selections from the Peshwa Daftar*, XLV, 149. (The published date of this document is incorrect.) Note: 'pharshi nane va rupaye Punyatac padile, srikade dakhla nahi. Hasilaca aivaj dilha nahi.'

Maratha government had ever granted compensation, and he even queried: 'why should we pay the Deo Rupees 1300 annually as compensation for an Enam umul? Does it not rather appear that our Government is entitled to recover from the Deo?'[39]

After reviewing the proceedings in the case, Bombay was confused by the Collector of Pune's recommendation not to give compensation to the Dev 'till his claim is established and recognized by Government.'[40] Had not the superintendent decisively rejected the Dev's demands? The senior district officer involved, the Revenue Commissioner, was asked to analyze the report to ascertain if the claim was in fact established.[41]

A marginal note on the collector's translation of the yadi of the vernacular proceedings in 1819 further perplexed government. The word *kampeś*, the amount 'approximately' received on account of the mint, had been thought 'by persons of experience' to mean compensation. Rightly doubting this interpretation, the anonymous writer of the note commented that while 'compensation' was good English in 1819, it was not likely used in the office of the Collector of Pune; Cincvad certainly did not use the term. Entering into a discursive etymology of the word, Bombay concluded it meant 'more or less' as translated. Yet the import of the note eluded government. In explanation the collector stated it merely indicated the Dev did not receive compensation, which only strengthened the superintendent's conclusions.[42]

According to the Revenue Commissioner, kampesh could not possibly mean compensation:

no one even slightly acquainted with Maratha usage will believe that the Peishwa's Government ever granted '*compensation*' for any of its acts[,] the word and practice were equally unknown till the British accession. Hence the word is often written by Natives 'Company-shaysun' it being supposed to be something quite peculiar to 'the Company's' Government.[43]

The commissioner wondered why the Dev had waited until 1848 to demand compensation for a right abolished in 1834. The Dev must have known his claim would not be accepted. If he had previously raised the

[39] Report of the Superintendent of the Pune daphtar, 25 June 1850.
[40] Collector of Pune to Revenue Commissioner, 29 June 1850, BA: RD 1850, 218/634, p. 189.
[41] E. H. Townsend, Revenue Commissioner to Government, 19 July 1850 with accompaniments; Government to Revenue Commissioner, 23 August 1850, BA: RD 1850; 218/634, pp. 197–9, 217–19.
[42] Yadi of 26 April 1819 (translation), BA: RD 1850; 218/634, pp. 201–3; H. P. Malet, Collector of Pune to Revenue Commissioner, 16 October 1850, PA: XIII; 55/740, pp. 68–9.
[43] Revenue Commissioner to Government, 28 December 1850, PA: XIII; 55/740, pp. 71–6.

matter, government must have already made some decision. The compensation granted in 1819 was, the commissioner concluded, 'a blunder or oversight by whomsoever committed.'[44] Government had since rectified the error, and the Dev had passively agreed with the decision. It remained, however, to discover whether any compensation had been granted or claimed since 1834.

The Collector of Pune 'inferred' none had been granted between 1834 and 1848.[45] This and further evasive answers brought the collector a rebuke for causing 'unnecessary trouble' by not giving straightforward replies to direct questions.[46] At length the answer was provided: no claim was made by the Dev and no compensation granted for the Cincvad mint between 1834 and 1848.[47] Why then did the Dev now press his demands? Bombay was still concerned that the Peshva may have formally granted compensation, a pledge the British were perhaps obliged to honor. Likewise, the 'superfluous' marginal note and the identity of the 'people of experience' who argued that kampesh meant compensation still occupied the mind of government.[48] There was no record of those who expressed this opinion, and the collector conceded that the note should not have reached government 'as it appears to have caused some useless trouble.'[49]

Bombay then moved to settle the whole matter of the Cincvad mint by having the Dev prove the correctness of statements allegedly made in 1819:

he [the Dev] should prove that portions of the proceeds of the Mint at Poona had been continuously paid to him by the Peishwa's Government in consideration of the business of the Chinchore Mint having been transferred there.[50]

His claims would 'be at once and finally rejected' if these proofs were not forthcoming within a month. Yet another interpretation of the settlement of 1819 was being put forward for proof. Previously, the district officers had only supposed the Dev had fraudulently claimed to have been paid a set allowance by the Peshva in lieu of abolished coinage

---

44 Ibid.
45 Collector of Pune to Revenue Commissioner, 8 January 1851, PA: XIII; 55/740, pp. 77–8.
46 Government to Collector of Pune, 26 February 1851, PA: XIII; 55/740, pp. 82–3.
47 Collector of Pune to Government, 26 March 1851, PA: XIII; 55/740, pp. 83–4. The collector was not strictly correct. Cincvad made claims until 1838.
48 Government to Revenue Commissioner, 14 January 1851, PA: XIII; 55/740, pp. 79–80.
49 Collector of Pune to Revenue Commissioner, 25 January 1851, PA: XIII; 55/740, pp. 81–2.
50 Government to E. G. Fawcett, Revenue Commissioner, 5 September 1851, PA: XIII; 55/740, pp. 84–6.

rights. Now government had evidently decided that the Dev had claimed to have received, and Elphinstone routinely continued to pay, a share from the revenue of the government mint at Pune. While moving closer to the truth of the matter, Bombay's really quite logical conclusion still assumed the Cincvad mint had been abolished as a separate entity.

Again the Dev undertook to claim his rights. The documents of 1766/7, 1773/4 and 1819, all previously examined, and extracts from the Samsthan's accounts for various years between 1809/10 and 1815/16 were produced to prove that the mint had not been abolished.[51] These were unsatisfactory to the Collector of Pune. In a subsequent verbal examination the Cincvad vakil stated that, in fact, the representation of 1819 did not mean the mint had been transferred to Pune; the same person bought the licenses for both the Cincvad and government mints; there was an arrangement determining the quantity of coins produced at each; and the Dev received 'more or less' than Rs. 1300 'because his share was not always properly paid.'[52] The vakil's statement suggests that the existence of the Cincvad mint as a revenue-producing entity at least, if not the actual workshop, had no connection with government's separate coining business. The Dev would therefore not attempt to prove he had received a portion of the proceeds from the government mint, and according to an exasperated Revenue Commissioner, 'he rather attempts to shift his ground and to deny that any statement of the kind he has been called upon to substantiate, was made by his Vakeel at all [in 1819].'[53]

Eventually the correspondence of 1838–9, denying on instructions from the Government of India any compensation for the Cincvad mint, was discovered in the records of the Agent for Sardars.[54] (The Collector of Pune had apparently lost the relevant files.[55]) Government therefore closed the matter and instituted no more belated inquiries.

All in government concerned with the Cincvad mint became obsessed with the issue of compensation and the likelihood of the Peshva having given something that the British were bound to continue. The purpose of the Rs. 1300 granted by the Deccan Commission – to stop one mint not under the control of government – was never considered. Hence, the

---

[51] Moro Udhav, vakil of Cincvad to Collector of Pune, 15 October 1851; E. C. Jones, Collector of Pune to W. Courtney, Revenue Commissioner, 22 March 1851, PA: xiii; 55/740, pp. 91–4, 98–101.
[52] Translation of replies of viva voce examination of Moro Udhav, accompaniment to Collector of Pune to Revenue Commissioner, 27 February 1852.
[53] Revenue Commissioner to Government, 30 March 1852, PA: xiii; 55/740, pp. 101–4.
[54] Government to Revenue Commissioner, 26 April 1852, PA: xiii; 55/740, pp. 104–6.
[55] Collector of Pune to Agent for Sardars, 6 May 1852; Agent to Collector, 11 May 1852; Collector to Revenue Commissioner, 9 June 1852, PA: xiii; 55/740, pp. 107–9.

Dev was called upon to prove positions neither he nor the British had originally asserted. Ever jealous of rights gained from the Peshva, the Dev would certainly attempt to prove what the British wanted, or at least vigorously advance his claim to lost rights. Bombay saw the matter in much the same way as the contemporary settlements of varsasans, and from 1848 to 1852 instituted a type of inquiry that was then being perfected for inam lands. Cincvad had to offer proof, a sanad or evidence of uninterrupted possession under the former government, if the state was to confirm a right to hold an item of alienated revenue.

The discovery of the decision of 1838–9 abruptly halted the normal course of such an inquiry. Still, however, by abandoning its preconceptions about the Peshva's supposed compensation, government was beginning to move towards an understanding of why the Deccan Commission had offered the Dev a cash allowance as an inam amal. The mint was a right the Dev held as inamdar of Cincvad village and as head of a samsthan possessing numerous inam villages. In reality, it was only this right he sold, as a license to the actual mint contractor, in order to turn a potential source of revenue into ready cash. The Dev preferred to have the mint workshop as close to hand as possible – there was always the possibility he would be defrauded of his agreed share of the minting charges – but where the coins were actually produced was not the important point.

II. Transit duties and related revenues

John Stuart Mill, when reviewing the achievements of the East India Company in his *Memorandum on the Improvements in the Administration of India* (1858), paid particular attention to the reform of the internal transit duties of India. 'There is no branch of taxation,' Mill asserted, in 'which the burthens of the people have been more conspicuously lightened by the British Government.'[56] He took pride in the fact that between 1836 and 1844 the internal transit duties were abolished in British territories throughout India. And in demonstration of the Company's liberality, this 'was not a small sacrifice of revenue.'[57] However, the acts ending transit duties did not extend to the native states or petty chiefdoms who continued to 'extort' the greatest possible revenues from trade passing through their territories. In cases where

duties levied by some particular chief have been an obstruction to important lines of mercantile communication, and in which it was not probable that the

---

[56] (London, 1858; rpt. Farnborough, 1968), p. 25; see also *Parliamentary Papers* 1857–58, XLIII, 1–38. This work was originally published anonymously.
[57] Ibid.

chief would be indemnified for their loss by the increase of his other revenue, our Government has even purchased his assent by pecuniary compensation.[58]

The Dev of Cincvad was one such 'chief' who held the right to levy transit duties on the important trade routes. Being closely linked to landed rights, these duties in a sense define the space of the Cincvad Samsthan along the main roads north and north-west of Pune city. This was the domain of the Samsthan, and the profitable duties collected on three major roads were the visible expression of the Dev's authority. When the Bombay government set about to eliminate this impediment to trade in the course of implementing the Company's reforms, the Dev's assent proved hard to purchase (to use Mill's expression). The difficult and protracted negotiations reveal much about the Dev's attitude to this important landed right and source of revenue.

The tahanama of 1744/5 records that Rs. 1031/4/- from the transit duties (jakat) of the Cincoli subdivision (*mahāl*) had been obtained by the third Dev, and this revenue was included in the moiety of Cincvad's holdings that was to descend as the personal shares of the Dev's sons. Land revenue terminology is used to describe the duties and divide them into the standard assessment, the tankha,[59] and the extra 10 percent of this total, the sardesh[mukhi]. Similar language for transit duty revenue can be found in published Marathi documents.[60] But because jakat accounts have not yet been studied in detail, it is uncertain whether these terms have any substantive connection with land assessments, or were simply account notations like those used in village land records to indicate nominal rates of revenue and the subsequent distribution of collections. The latter seems more likely. At least, all nineteenth-century references to Cincvad's total proceeds from the jakat record amounts considerably higher than that in the tahanama. Detailed early accounts are not at present available, however, and so the exact relation of the tankha of the transit duties to actual receipts, and further to the land revenue, cannot yet be precisely known.

King Shahu of Satara granted the transit duties of Cincoli mahal to Cincvad sometime before 1720 (that is, before the death of the third Dev). The original document (presumably a sanad) recording the gift is apparently not extant in the Shahu daphtar as preserved in the Pune Archives. However, in a sanad dated February 1728 Sambhaji II of

[58] Ibid.
[59] A variant reading has *yain* (read *ain*), which is more or less synonymous, see H. H. Wilson, *A Glossary of Judicial and Revenue Terms* (1855, rpt. Delhi, 1968), pp. 13–14.
[60] For example in a tahanama of 2 March 1711 for duties of prant Supe, in Appasaheb Pavar, *Tarabai kalin kagadpatre*, 3 vols. (Kolhapur, 1969–72), I, 347–50, note use of *yain*.

Kolhapur confirmed Shahu's grant made for the support of the Cincvad annasatra.[61] This is another example, previously noticed with inam, where the Kolhapur chatrapatis, with the support of the Nizam of Hyderabad, exercised their presumed prerogative of making and confirming grants in Pune district.[62] The British and the Cincvad Samsthan both took this sanad as the documentary basis of the right to levy the jakat, and presumably even in the nineteenth century the original sanad from Shahu had been lost. A special sanad was needed because, as Sir John Malcolm remarked, the transit duties were 'seldom included in the common grants, by which land is either temporarily or permanently alienated.'[63] Instead, possession of the jakat followed the granting of inam. Thus, Cincvad's landed interests of north-west Haveli had been largely consolidated when Shahu extended his munificence to the jakat. The control of the local trade of an inamdar's domain must therefore be seen as an extension of the process of inam acquisition described in Chapter 1.

Cincvad did, however, have interests in transit duties and the internal trade of the Deccan predating both its control of inam and the formal grant of the jakat. Documents from the seventeenth century refer to the grant of exemptions, dastaks, from the payment of duties: in the 1670s Aurangzeb remitted the grain duty, *dhānyajakāt*,[64] and Shivaji permitted salt to be brought from the Konkan free of imposts.[65] Such exemptions continued in the eighteenth century: in 1730/1 the Peshva allowed a dastak for 50 bullock loads of goods of any origin;[66] this concession had been increased to 150 loads by the time of the tahanama. These privileges were granted for the provision of the Samsthan. Such was also the case when the Deccan Commission waived all government duties on goods intended for the Cincvad annasatra, an indulgence

---

[61] Sanad of 11/12 February 1728, copy of original and translation in memorandum of Cincvad to Government, 3 June 1846; transition from records of Collector of Pune forwarded to Government, 3 June 1846, BA: RD 1847; 200/1128, pp. 199–207.

[62] See pp. 44–5.

[63] Malcolm, *Memoir of Central India*, II, 91.

[64] Datto Vaman Potdar, 'Moraya Dev Samsthan Cincvad sambandhi kamhi junat assal kagad,' *Bharat Itihas Samshodhak Mandal Quarterly*, 2 (1922), 53–4.

[65] *Shiva-caritra-sahitya*, IV, 17–18 (in *Bharat Itihas Samshodhak Mandal Quarterly*, 11 (1931)). This document of 22 June 1676, addressed to the *subedār* ('district officer' in charge of a *subā*) of suba tarph Kalyan by Shivaji, is not a dastak as such. The document informs the district officer that Shri Dev (Cincvad) could bring salt from three places in the Konkan, the implication being that it could be taken up the Bhor ghat without taxes or charges. Note also that in the tahanama of 1744/5 the third Dev is listed as obtaining a minor land inam, *āgar* Ceul, the Ceul (Chaul) 'saltpans,' which is perhaps connected with the right granted by Shivaji.

[66] Dastak of 3 November 1730 in *Selections from the Peshwa Daftar*, XXII, 36.

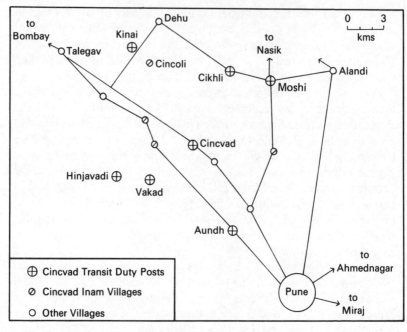

Figure 12. Pune-Haveli routes

confirmed from accounts found in the Pune daphtar.[67] A dastak thus was a longstanding right held by the Samsthan in its religious capacity, and so it differed from a general duty levied on all traders entering the Dev's domain. Yet even before Cincvad formally possessed the jakat, the Samsthan had a real and enduring interest in the trade of the Cincoli mahal, with itself as a major participant and beneficiary.

Although the Marathi sources consistently refer to Cincvad's right to levy the jakat in the Cincoli mahal, a transit duty post (*nākā*) was not located in Cincoli village itself. (The locations of Cincvad's nakas, as they existed at the end of the Maratha period, are shown in Figure 12.[68]) The mahal, a subdivision of tarph Haveli, was a loosely defined area surrounding Cincoli, a village which as early as the 1630s was associated

[67] Collector of Pune to Agent for Sardars, 17 August 1828; Agent to Collector, 27 August 1828; Government to Agent, 8 September 1828, PA: IX; 4/59, pp. 2–5. Similar exemptions were confirmed to the Devs of Ranjangav, see Collector to Agent, 17 July 1829; Agent to Collector, 30 July 1829, PA: IX: 4/59, pp. 2–3.

[68] Cincvad's transit duty posts are listed in J. N. Rose, Commissioner for Claims to Collector of Pune, 30 January 1850, BA: RD 1850; 218/634, pp. 163–70, tabular statement, column 18.

with the collection of transit duties.[69] The Mahal's extent cannot now be accurately portrayed because in the Maratha period Haveli and its subdivisions changed over time, and even were differently defined at any one time depending on the revenue or other criteria used. Therefore, any attempt to precisely define traditional Maratha administrative divisions or subjective regional designations is fraught with difficulties.[70] Generally, the Cincoli mahal would appear to refer to riverine north-west Haveli: bounded on the north by the Indrayani river; on the north-west by the Pavna river (running north-west to south-east); extending towards the *māvals*, valleys leading to the Western Ghats, on the west, and reaching southwards towards, but not including, Pune city.

The precise boundaries of a collection division were not a matter of critical concern. Through any duty area, only roads that could accommodate wheeled or pack animal traffic needed nakas placed somewhere along their route. Posts were not, in the manner of frontier customs, placed at fixed boundaries. Trade would keep to established routes, evading nakas only if cost effective. To estimate a caravan's profitability and to assure its security a merchant had to know how goods would move between two points and the time each stage would take. Transit duties were just one more expense of carriage. Consequently, the jakat could be successfully levied over any territory by a few carefully placed collection posts. Hence Cincvad could control the transit trade of the Cincoli mahal – between Pune city, the Konkan, and north India – with nakas placed in only three villages. With four additional posts, the area's local commerce was also subject to Cincvad's duties.

In the Maratha period trade between Pune and the Konkan (including Bombay) via the Bhor ghat usually crossed the Pavna river at Ravet and the Mula river at Aundh.[71] Cincvad placed its naka at the latter crossing. Both these villages were the Dev's inam, but his strategy appears to have been to locate a naka as close to Pune city as possible so as to be able to tax all goods, whatever their ultimate destination, that left or entered the city by the major river crossing at Aundh. An alternative route, via Cincvad over an 'indifferent road' along the north bank of the Pavna river, was somewhat shorter than the Aundh road

---

[69] See sanad of 28 December 1633 in *Selections from the Peshwa Daftar*, XXXI, 8; and yadi of 1630 including description (*hakīkat*) of routes in *Marathi rajavatimtil kamhi ghatmarg va caukya*, ed. S. N. Joshi (Pune, 1933), p. 3 (this volume is *Aitihasik sankirna sahitya*, IX).

[70] See for example, Ian Raeside, 'A Note on the 'Twelve Mavals' of Poona District,' *Modern Asian Studies*, 12 (1978), 393–417 attempting to define the traditional, subjective maval regions.

[71] John Clunes, *Itinerary and Directory for Western India* (Calcutta, 1826), p. 10.

and had the distinct advantage of one less river crossing. Shortly after the conquest the British saw these advantages and developed the route as a military road.[72] The Dev placed a naka in Cincvad village to collect tolls from merchants who chose to use what eventually became the main access to Pune from the west. The Pune–Bombay routes, and most particularly the new road north of the Pavna river, were the main lines of communication between the Presidency and the new Deccan conquests. By levying transit duties here, Cincvad in effect taxed the trade of Pune coming from Bombay and overseas, which in turn affected British trade in the greater part of their new conquests.

Prior to the conquest, trade between Pune and the north was probably more important than that with the coast. Caravans from Junnar, Nasik, Khandesh and most of the northern territories of the Marathas came via Cakan (the importance of which place can be seen by the dominating presence of a large fort) and crossed the Indrayani river into Pune district at the village of Moshi. Cincvad placed a naka here even though the Dev had no inam rights in the village. Perhaps the Moshi outpost was dependent on one located in the Dev's neighboring inam village of Cikhli. In a similar case, a naka in Kinai village, over which the Dev had no tenurial rights, was apparently connected with his neighboring inam village of Cincoli. Kinai controlled a road leading to the important religious center of Dehu, a village renowned both as the starting point of the pilgrimage of the Varkari sect and also in connection with the life of the seventeenth-century saint Tukaram. Early British officers noticed the curiosity of detached villages (*phuṭgāv*) situated on main roads to collect transit duties, but located at some distance from the parent village.[73] Cincvad may have established such phutgavs. Or perhaps nakas were merely placed in strategic villages. Whatever the case, some sort of state sanction was undoubtably needed. Whether the authority to establish nakas in villages where the Devs had no direct tenurial rights derived from the general permission to levy duties in the Cincoli mahal (issuing from Shahu's sanad) or had a more specific sanction (perhaps government orders to the village authorities) is not clear from the available sources.

The duty posts at Moshi, Cikhli and Kinai were also along what might have been an alternative east – west route to and from Pune that avoided the Aundh and Cincvad nakas. In this way, the multiplication

---

[72] Ibid., pp. 10–11. The military road, site of the present Bombay – Pune road and railway, ran somewhat to the north of the Maratha route.

[73] Pottinger to Chaplin, 24 August 1820, *East India Records*, IV, 733. Kinai itself was an inam of Dehu, see petition of Laksmibai to Government (Persian department translation), 2 July 1860, PA: XIV; 28/322, fols. 91–7.

of duty posts might have been, as the British often thought, 'considered requisite because merchants generally endeavour to avoid great towns or villages... if there were not chowkies [*caukī*, 'post'] in all directions, they might sometimes pass their goods through a district without paying anything.'[74] Equally, these posts taxed local trade. Moshi, Cikhli and Kinai controlled roads leading to Dehu and Alandi, both important religious centers that most likely attracted a lively local trade. A merchant coming from the west to Dehu or Alandi, from Pune to Dehu, or between Alandi and Dehu would have had difficulty avoiding Cincvad's duties. Two nakas were also located in the inam villages of Vakad and Hinjavadi. Although not on a main road, both are located on the Mula river and may have controlled local trade traveling the course of the river between Pune and the mavals.

Duties levied on trade passing through a district were called the *rahdārī*, or often *ubhāmārg* (literally 'highway'). They were levied at the first naka encountered in a district and were payable in every duty district through which goods passed. When levied by government, the rahdari was intended to pay for the protection of merchants, the cost of roads and bridges, and the revenue lost from land occupied by roads.[75] Goods purchased in one district and taken to another, and each similar transaction thereafter, were subject to an export duty, the *thaḷbharīt*. Goods in high demand were particularly affected by this duty; they initially attracted an enhanced levy, and with successive sales increased in price with the distance moved.[76] Trade into a district was subject to the *thaḷmoḍ*, import duties levied for the expenses and regulation of market places and recovered from the vendor of merchandise. As with the thalbharit, rates of duty were set by supply and demand; markets with brisker trade had the highest import duties.[77] In addition to the above three main divisions of the jakat, there were many other lesser imposts and local duties. In Khandesh, for example, trade entirely within a district was subject to the *aḍvāmārg*, literally 'cross road' or perhaps 'by-way' to be distinguished from the ubhamarg or 'highway.'[78] Patils of villages where caravans stopped and employees of nakas also collected small considerations for their services. Minor

[74] Pottinger to Chaplin, 24 August 1820, *East India Records*, IV, 770.
[75] Ibid.
[76] Ibid., p. 771.
[77] Ibid., p. 772.
[78] John Briggs to Chaplin, 31 October 1820 in R. D. Choksey, *Period of Transition* (Pune, 1945), p. 67 (as taken from PA: DC). For the Marathi words replaced by question marks, compare Briggs to Chaplin, n.d. (accompaniment to Chaplin's report to Government, 20 August 1822) in *East India Records*, IV, 713.

market-place fees such as the *śingotī*, a tax on the sale of livestock, were also considered part of the jakat.[79]

Another market fee was the mohtarpha, 'a tax on shop-keepers varying with their means: in fact, an income tax.'[80] These 'town duties' were always closely identified with the jakat, though the two were formally separate imposts. The mohtarpha was a very minor item of revenue. In Ahmednagar city in 1823, for example, it (here simply called a *paṭṭī*, 'tax') amounted to a mere Rs. 3000 per annum.[81] Nevertheless, the mohtarpha was often considered particularly vexatious: 'a tax on the industrious poor; the wealthy and the independent who are the main supporters of the credit, and the finance of European nations... are entirely exempt.'[82] Levied at varying rates on different groups of town merchants and artisans, it was either collected on a per head basis, or according to some sources, through a fixed sum charged to occupational castes.[83] Whether unfairly weighted against the poorer merchants or not, the mohtarpha was one of the few taxes to which artisans and small bazaar traders were directly subject.

The jakat was seldom directly collected by government. In a manner similar to that described for mints, the right to collect duties was put out to bid. Contractors eagerly sought the opportunity to collect the revenue in exchange for a fixed payment to government: 'the rent of the customs was a bold speculation that with good arrangement afforded a profitable return on the outlay of money.'[84] Partitioning the contractor's license among subcontractors, attracting business by lowering duty rates, or striking bargains with individual merchants would all increase the profitability of the speculation.[85] The last point was particularly important. Bankers and merchants in major market centers effected financial arrangements that allowed caravans along specified routes to pass without hindrance.[86] These *huṇḍīkarī*s, 'dealers in bills of exchange,'

---

[79] Pottinger to Chaplin, 24 August 1820 in *East India Records*, IV, 771–2. Pottinger notices the shingoti (often *śing-śingotī*) as the *nakās*.

[80] Mountstuart Elphinstone, 'Report on the Territories Conquered from the Peshwa,' in George W. Forrest, *Selections from the Minutes and other Official Writings of the Honourable Mountstuart Elphinstone* (London, 1884), p. 293.

[81] Pottinger to Chaplin, 5 May 1823 in Choksey, *Period of Transition*, pp. 60–2.

[82] Briggs to Elphinstone, 22 December 1818 in R. D. Choksey, *The Aftermath* (Bombay, 1950), p. 288.

[83] Sen, *Administrative System*, pp. 322–3; Ravinder Kumar, *Western India in the Nineteenth Century* (London, 1968), pp. 36–7.

[84] Briggs to Chaplin, 31 October 1820 in Choksey, *Period of Transition*, pp. 64–5.

[85] Ibid., p. 65.

[86] Pottinger to Chaplin, 24 August 1820 in *East India Records*, IV, 774. For banking under the Marathas, see G. T. Kulkarni, 'Banking in the 18th Century: A Case Study of a Poona Banker,' *Artha Vijnana*, 15 (1973), 180–200.

helped protect the investment of jakat contractors by directing trade of a predetermined volume and value through their nakas. Being thus able to demand advantageous duty rates, the brokers took their profits from the difference between the fee they charged small merchants and the duty negotiated with the contractors. In certain areas the hundikaris further increased their profits through collusion with government officers in the licensing of the transit duties.[87]

A jagirdar or inamdar granted the right to collect duties made similar arrangements for the actual management of the revenue, as for example Cincvad, which 'annually farmed the Custom Revenue' of the Cincoli mahal.[88] The inamdar simply took the place of government as licensor of the jakat.

The initial British impression of the Maratha jakat was unfavorable. It *must* be mismanaged and corrupt. Sir John Malcolm, for example, believed there was 'no branch of their revenue in which the Mahratta governments are more defrauded than that of customs. This arises chiefly from ministers, collectors, and renters, being almost without exception concerned in trade.'[89] Henry Pottinger, when considering the variety of rates, methods of assessment, and private arrangements between merchants, hindikaris and contractors, thought the Maratha jakat system 'never would answer under a regular Government like ours. Exclusive of the total confusion of accounts, if any such could be prepared,' the most serious fear was that

it would open a ready door to peculation and bribery; for as it would be utterly impossible for the Collector or his Assistants to give up their time to the minor details, much must necessarily be left in the hands of Camavisdars and other revenue officers, who, were nothing fixed, would assuredly avail themselves of the fact to turn the business to their own private emolument.[90]

The British did recognize the negative effects of the system on trade. Pottinger remarked that the duty posts had been 'augmented in a manner which would almost lead to a belief that they [the Marathas] studied how to destroy all inland trade.'[91] However, immediately after the conquest the partial or complete abolition of duties in the name of commercial efficiency was not a serious proposition. In the first instance attention was directed towards the reform of a system, which though

[87] Malcolm, *Memoir of Central India*, II, 95–6 here called *hundībharavālā*, 'those involved in bills of exchange.'
[88] Rose to Collector of Pune, 30 January 1850.
[89] Malcolm, *Memoir of Central India*, II, 92.
[90] Pottinger to Chaplin, 24 August 1820 in *East India Records*, IV, 774.
[91] Ibid., p. 773.

perhaps corrupt, did generate a substantial revenue for government. In 1818, for example, before any duty exemptions had been granted, Robertson sold the Pune jakat for Rs. 1,05,000.[92]

A recent study of some 6000 transit duty documents in the Pune daphtar found very few references to duty rates.[93] Similarly, the early British officers were unable to establish precise rates or any principles by which they were determined. Pottinger found the rahdari rates 'very fluctuating,' and he 'in vain attempted to trace any fixed principle by which [they] had been established.'[94] He attributed the diversity of rates to factors such as the length of road controlled by a naka and the private bargains made to attract trade along certain routes. Pottinger also inferred 'that the customs were originally calculated with reference to the goodness or otherwise of the soil which was included in the roads,' in a manner reminiscent of the land revenue.[95] In whatever way the duty rate was determined, it was applied at a fixed rate per bullock load of goods with only the most general distinctions as to the type of merchandise. One rate would apply to cloth, to grain and so on, whatever their market values. Consequently, 'the heaviest duties fall on the absolute necessaries of life, whilst its luxuries can hardly be said to pay at all.'[96] Opium, for example, paid a duty of only about 0.06 percent of its market value. A bullock load of the finest silks, worth Rs. 10,000–20,000, would pay the same duty as a load of the coarsest cloth, worth only Rs. 100. To Pottinger the obvious reform was to reconstruct duty rates on an *ad valorem* scale, taxing goods by their market value and not by mere quantity. He suggested luxuries could be assessed 6 percent duty, grain exported 4 percent, and grain imported 2 percent.[97]

But Pottinger's suggestion was considered to have more drawbacks than gains, particularly by Thackeray in the Southern Maratha Country. Not only would revenue be reduced, but the necessary inspections would in themselves impede trade, and the penalties for smuggling 'would give rise to much oppression and disgust.' Furthermore, it was in the interest of the jakat contractor 'to conciliate merchants not to oppress them, that the collection of an *ad valorem* duty would render it necessary to detain and inspect the whole trade of the

---

[92] Robertson to Elphinstone, 12 November 1818, PA: DC 91/162.
[93] M. D. Apte, 'The Nature and Scope of the Records from Peshwa Daftar with reference to Zakat System,' *Indian Economic and Social History Review*, 6 (1969), 373. See also S. V. Avalsakar and M. D. Apte, 'Pune shaharamtil jakat va vyapar,' *Artha Vijnana*, 6 (1964), 117–26.
[94] Pottinger to Chaplin, 24 August 1820 in *East India Records*, IV, 771.
[95] Ibid.
[96] Ibid., p. 773.
[97] Ibid., pp. 773–5.

country in order that the trifling proportion of it which is of superior value might be taxed with reference to its worth.'[98] These views were echoed in Bombay's report to the Court of Directors: not one bullock in a hundred carried luxury goods; an *ad valorem* duty would not be worth the trouble caused by inspections. In addition, if the duty was set at the suggested percentages, it would penalize local trade because in the existing system these rates were only reached when goods were transported great distances. Most importantly, the '*ad valorem* duty is not consistent with the mode of collecting the customs here.'[99] The system could not be implemented without the direct government administration of the transit duties.

In the first place, the contractors did not collect duties in a manner conducive for the strict account keeping demanded by the *ad valorem* duties:

the custom farmers never have been, either since the establishment of our authority in these provinces, or under the late Government, in the habit of keeping any returns of the value of grain, or indeed any other imports and exports. All they have looked to has been the collection of the duties in the cheapest possible terms, and in many hundred Nakahs or custom Chowkies there is no one station [for accounts?], but a common peon who can neither read nor write, and who simply takes the dues of the farmers and allows the goods to pass or accompanies the convoys to the Carkoon of which class there is one in each Purgunnah.[100]

This simple, though suspect, method of collection would have to be entirely changed if the proposed reforms were introduced. In addition, strict *ad valorem* rates could never be maintained as there was every incentive for contractors to adjust government-determined rates for their own purposes if jakat rights continued to be bought for a fixed sum.

But if government instead collected duties to overcome these problems, as had been attempted in Madras, 'it corrupts the whole mass of our revenue servants by the facility it gives to peculation.'[101] The contractors had better control over the naka employees, were unlikely to antagonize merchants by undue exactions, and generally ran a more efficient operation. The experiment in Madras, which was eventually abandoned, led most district officers in the Deccan to argue strongly

[98] Thackeray to Chaplin, 23 June 1822 in Choksey, *Period of Transition*, p. 157.
[99] Revenue letter to Court of Directors, 27 November 1822 in *East India Records*, III, 792.
[100] Pottinger to Chaplin, 9 December 1824 in Choksey, *Period of Transition*, p. 62.
[101] Minute of Sir Thomas Munro, 'On farming the land customs,' 28 December 1820 in Alexander J. Arbuthnot, *Major-General Sir Thomas Munro: Selections from his Minutes*, 2 vols. (London, 1881), I, 126.

against the innovation of directly collected duties.[102] Even in 1830 Elphinstone considered the licensing system the preferable mode of collection, 'because there is a competition among the farmers to give little vexation, to levy duties, so as to draw people on their roads.'[103] And on a purely financial level the existing system 'probably' brought more revenue than governnment could ever directly collect.

Most officers felt government should retain the sole power to grant licenses to collect the jakat. Pottinger suggested 'the first step' in any reform was

the immediate and positive abolition of the right of Jagheerdars, Enamdars, and Sirdars holding villages to levy customs. Very few of those who now do so can show any authority for such a procedure; but even where some court favourites or others have contrived to get the customs introduced into their sunnuds... they should be remunerated from the treasury.[104]

Sir Thomas Munro also recommended this course to Elphinstone for the Southern Maratha Country.[105] Here the duties levied by the many substantial jagirs contained within and dividing British territory were thought detrimental to the Company's trade.[106] But this was a political problem. Elphinstone would not casually deny the inherited rights of the powerful. Instead, the British first attempted to extend such minor reforms as were enacted to the duties of the sardars.

Regardless of the collectors' varied suggestions, jakat reform was first confined to exempting certain articles from assessment. When licensing the duties in 1819, Robertson made it known that 'Europe supplies' or 'shop goods' such as tea, bottled liquor and cloth were to pass free.[107] In 1822 grain and certain other agricultural produce (including cotton) were exempted as a partial relief to the high grain prices and near famine conditions in the first years of the Deccan Commission.[108] Chaplin, as Collector of Dharvad, had endorsed this move as early as 1819.[109] Later as commissioner he explained to Bombay the collectors' feelings on the abolition of the grain duties: even though they accounted for one-third

---

[102] Report of Chaplin to Government, 5 November 1821 in *East India Papers*, IV, 324; Robertson to Chaplin, 10 October 1821, ibid., p. 589.

[103] *Parliamentary Papers* 1830, VI, 152.

[104] Pottinger to Chaplin, 24 August 1820 in *East India Records*, IV, 772.

[105] Munro to Elphinstone, 28 August 1818 in G. R. Gleig, *The Life of Major-General Sir Thomas Munro*, 3 Vols. (London, 1830), III, 279.

[106] H. Oakes, Commercial Resident in Ceded Districts to St. John Thackeray, Collector of Dharvad, 28 October 1819, enclosure to Thackeray to Elphinstone, 30 October 1819 in Choksey, *Period of Transition,* pp. 152–3.

[107] Robertson to Elphinstone, 19 July 1819, ibid., pp. 63–4.

[108] Chaplin circular to collectors, 10 September 1822, ibid., p. 59.

[109] Chaplin to Elphinstone, 28 August 1819, ibid., p. 152.

of all jakat revenue, they

> must... be extremely prejudicial to the cultivating classes; for no Ryot can now carry the produce of his farm to a distant market without such an accumulation of road duties as must operate as a complete bar to the speculation; he is obliged therefore to sell on the spot, to carriers or grain merchants, instead of conveying his crops to market at a season of the year perhaps when he has no other employment for his carts and his bullocks.[110]

After the duties had been abolished there were some problems when a good crop caused falling prices for surplus grain. Without duties, cultivators in the immediate vicinity of major market centers were subjected to competition from distant producers. Also, government had been forced to reduce the cost of jakat licenses proportional to the amount contractors had received when grain was scarce and prices high. With low prices and little trade in the commodity, the contractors would regrettably receive a windfall. The cost of a jakat license would now be a much lower percentage of gross receipts, hence the relative level of net profits would be higher.[111]

These inequities could be worked out, but a more serious impediment to the grain trade was the continued levying of duties by jagirdars and inamdars, particularly those astride major trade routes and between detached parts of the Company's territory. Trade might avoid some of the minor jagirs. A few sardars, under the terms of their political arrangements with the British, might be forced to follow the Company's lead and exempt grain from duty. But major jagirdars, those with some claim to political independence, could easily continue to interrupt the commerce of the Company's territories. A threat of stiff frontier duties on the export of grain from the jagirs would surely 'render the continuance of [transit] duties so unpopular in the Jagheer and will affect their trade so seriously that... the Jagheerdars will all in time be sensible of the expediency of remitting the grain duties.'[112]

Inamdars were more or less ordered to discontinue grain duties. In the words of the proclamation Thackeray issued in the Southern Maratha Country:

> petty Jagheerdars and Enamdars will not think of taking duties upon grain when the neighbouring villages are freed from this impost; it has therefore been determined to allow grain imported from and exported to the village to pass free from [frontier] duty.[113]

[110] Chaplin to Government, 5 November 1821 in *East India Records*, IV, 323.
[111] Thackeray to Chaplin, 27 September 1822 in Choksey, *Period of Transition*, pp. 158–9.
[112] Thackeray to Chaplin, 5 December 1822, ibid., p. 160
[113] Ibid., p. 161.

Such an effective prohibition directly affected the Dev of Cincvad. He complained to government that he had lost Rs. 4500 of the total Rs. 6000 annual jakat of the Cincoli mahal.[114] The Collector of Pune calculated that the Dev in fact lost only Rs. 2000.[115] Rejecting the Dev's request for relief, the Deccan Commissioner simply commented: 'the right of reducing existing duties or to impose additional ones rests entirely with the Government.'[116]

Minor changes to the jakat continued to be made throughout the 1820s and 1830s. For example, in 1827 all miscellaneous goods imported by sea were exempted.[117] But almost all British officers, whether at Bombay or in the districts, were opposed to the total abolition of the jakat. In 1821 Chaplin succinctly put forward the reasons: abolition 'would occasion great pecuniary sacrifice,' and more particularly, 'as the tax is not loudly complained of as a grievance, the sacrifice is not immediately necessary.'[118] Likewise, Sir John Malcolm in 1830, while recognizing the possible impediments to trade, thought the duties

secure to government some recompense for its extensive police establishments, in the shape of a tax, which, sanctioned by immemorial usage common to all parts of India, and lightly distributed, is not generally unpopular, and is realized with much facility, and comparatively with so little dissatisfaction.[119]

The collectors had told Malcolm that the revenue was collected with little trouble, cost or opposition, and really, the jakat was not as confusing as it may have first appeared.

The impetus for ending transit duties thus came not from Bombay, but rather through the exertions of certain Bengal civil servants. Using the influence and authority of the Governor-General, their representations firstly affected only the local situations in Bengal and the short-lived Agra Presidency. Bombay and Madras perforce followed the lead of the senior Presidency. The details of the campaign for abolition are beyond the scope of this study and have been adequately described elsewhere.[120] Briefly, the Bengal officers linked their proposals to the

---

[114] Memorandum of Dev of Cincvad to Government (translation), 17 September 1825, enclosure to Government to Chaplin, 25 October 1825, PA: DC 82/4935. The Dev also complained about the exemptions on 'China articles,' perhaps tea, or more generally, imported goods.

[115] Robertson to Chaplin, 9 December 1825, PA: DC 121/2557.

[116] Chaplin to Government, 12 December 1825, PA: DC 398/4558.

[117] Regulation 20 of 1826, c. 6, *Parliamentary Papers* 1829, XXIII, 446.

[118] Chaplin to Government, 5 November 1821 in *East India Records*, IV, 323.

[119] Sir John Malcolm, minute on leaving India, 30 November 1830 in John Malcolm, *Government of India* (London, 1833), Appendix A, p. 52.

[120] Romesh Dutt, *The Economic History of British India* (London, 1902), pp. 303–10; recently by Ambirajan, *Classical Political Economy*, pp. 184–6.

expansion of India's foreign trade. Exports were declining, and even in 1825 Holt Mackenzie (Secretary to the Bengal government) demonstrated the need to do, 'in the present state of India, everything that can tend to bring its produce to the ports of export at a cheaper rate.'[121] He suggested replacing transit duties with a more comprehensive system of sea customs, which could be easily manipulated as part of an overall economic policy for India. It remained until 1835–6 before this policy came into effect. A report by Charles Trevelyan on the abuses and impediments of the transit duties caused Sir Charles Metcalfe, acting Governor-General, to confirm a course previously endorsed by Lord Bentinck and already carried out in the Agra Presidency.[122] The Court of Directors took a dim view of such a sacrifice of revenue, but acquiesced much after the fact.[123] The jakat remained in force in Bombay for two more years before (in 1838) being abolished and replaced with a uniform system of import and export customs.[124] In 1844 the Bombay mohtarpha and Madras jakat were finally ended.[125]

In line with these India-wide reforms, Bombay withdrew Cincvad's right to levy transit duties in the Cincoli mahal on 31 October 1837.[126] In December 1837 the Collector of Pune called upon the Dev to furnish duty accounts for the ten preceding years. No official reason was given for this sudden demand. When grain duties had been abolished the Deccan Commission curtly refused compensation. Now it was obvious that government intended to offer some sort of remuneration. This perhaps unexpected development offered the inamdar some chance of retaining his rights – or at least obtaining the best possible settlement.

---

[121] Holt Mackenzie, memorandum of 23 June 1825 in *Parliamentary Papers* 1831–2, XI, Appendix, p. 714.

[122] C. E. Trevelyan, *Report on the Inland Customs and Town-Duties of the Bengal Presidency* (Calcutta, 1834), see Eric Stokes, *The English Utilitarians and India* (Oxford, 1959), p. 239. For Trevelyan's comments on his report, see *Parliamentary Papers* 1840, VIII, 76–7. For Bentincks' opinions, see his minute on transit duties, 15 July 1834 in Philips, *Correspondence*, II, 1317–18.

[123] Act XIV of 1836, *Parliamentary Papers* 1840, VIII, 545–9; and 1852 X, 813–18. Despatches from Court of Directors, 1 February 1837 and 7 June 1837 in *Parliamentary Papers* 1852, X, 811–12, 819–22. Although the abolition of the transit duties may now seem like an obvious reform, it should be recalled that even in many parts of Europe (England being the notable exception) this came at a relatively late date. For example, France until the revolution still had a system of duties that provides an interesting comparison with India, see J. F. Bosher, *The Single Duty Project* (London, 1964).

[124] Act I of 1838, *Parliamentary Papers* 1840, VIII, 550–8; and 1852 X, 849–59.

[125] Mohtarpha: Act XIX of 1844, *Parliamentary Papers* 1845, XXXIV, 68; and 1852 X, 859. Madras transit duties: Act VI of 1844, *Parliamentary Papers* 1845, XXXIV, 52–66.

[126] Memorandum of Cincvad to Government (translation), 23 February 1846, BA: RD 1847; 200/1128, pp. 191–5.

Excluding revenue from grain duties abolished 15 years previously, the Dev's average annual collection was determined to be Rs. 6175.[127] This was remarkably similar to the Rs. 6000 (including grain duties) he had estimated as the total receipts in 1825.[128] The Dev was loath to surrender this revenue; his well-sited nakas and the British peace had proved profitable.

In March 1838, while complaining of the Samsthan's financial difficulties, the Dev petitioned the Agent for Sardars for Rs. 7000 in lieu of the abolished jakat. Neglecting to mention the Rs. 6175 average already determined, the Dev did admit that the Collector of Pune had required accounts for ten years. 'But how,' the Dev asked, 'am I to prepare and render them after the English manner? For my accounts are kept in the Maratha style of the Peshwa's government, in which the total receipts are only exhibited.'[129] The 'total receipts', that which the Dev annually sold the collection rights for, were not acceptable to the collector. The British wanted precision of accounts and amounts; the Dev professed not to know the details. These difficulties in procuring accurate accounts were, in the agent's opinion, 'unreasonable. If he expects remuneration in lieu of these Duties, he can easily procure the detailed accounts from his farmers and furnish them ... in the manner required.'[130] But these accounts were either hard to find or not willingly produced, and for 12 years the British would grope in the murky depths of Maratha accounting to find the facts of the Dev's revenue.

Following government's tentative moves towards compensation for the jakat, the Dev's immediate response was to demand an advance of Rs. 10,000 to ease his financial embarrassments. Although the agent lent his support, Bombay refused to authorize any payments before the details of compensation had been fixed.[131] The Dev renewed his request when he heard that another sardar, Caskar, had successfully petitioned for payment as a holder of a share (*amal*) of the jakat. Impressed by this precedent, the agent again favorably recommended the Dev's case to government, which again declined to authorize any advance. The case of Caskar was, government averred, quite different: his was a *hak*, 'perquisite,' or claim on the government transit duties, more like a *varsasan*, and one variety of many such claims on the government

[127] Ibid.
[128] Petition of Cincvad to Government (translation), 25 October 1825, PA: DC 82/4935.
[129] Memorandum of Cincvad to Agent for Sardars (translation), 20 March 1838, PA: IX; 4/59, pp. 17–20.
[130] Agent for Sardars to Government, 23 August 1838, PA: IX; 4/59, pp. 21–2.
[131] Memorandum of Cincvad to Agent for Sardars, 31 May 1839; Agent to Government, 11 June 1839; Resolution of Government, 6 July 1839, PA: IX; 4/59, pp. 41–7.

duties. These *hakdārs* would receive compensation immediately, but the question of the inamdars' duties had not been settled.[132]

By 1840 Bombay had formulated the following rules for the compensation of alienated jakat rights: firstly, hereditary district and transit duty officers holding haks for some real or nominal service would get life pensions; secondly, grants without service requirements and held by sanad, such as those to permanent institutions (mainly temples and including Cincvad), and also individuals holding hereditary rights, would receive a bond for ten times the net annual income from their duties. This bond was redeemable at the pleasure of government, but in the meantime would yield 10 percent interest to the bearer.[133] Compensation was costly. In the Southern Division of the Presidency it amounted to almost one-third of the annual revenue surrendered. A large backlog of compensation accumulated because of the collectors' slowness in fixing claims. In the Southern Division alone an estimated Rs. 9,72,595 was due by the end of 1844.[134] Eventually, a Commissioner for Claims had to be specially appointed to expedite the settlement, but his progress was little better: 'many difficulties and impediments occur in the course of my investigation, which it would not be easy to explain to one who had not personally engaged in them.'[135] Claimants would not respond to demands to appear before the commissioner; when they came they did not bring their accounts or sanads.

The Dev rejected outright the government's bond. In the first place, the arrangement was *'fraught with the most ruinous consequences to the maintenance of the Suwusthan expenses.'*[136] The Dev's vakil went on to explain how the Samsthan's reputation would suffer if the 'thousands'

[132] Memorandum of Cincvad to Agent for Sardars (translation), 4 October 1839; Agent to Government, 12 October 1839; Government to Agent, 9 November 1839, PA: IX; 4/59, pp. 48–52, 55–6. Haks on the transit duties were held by the deshmukhs and deshpandes, the hereditary government officers of the transit duties (*jakātdār*) and others. These haks are called *rasūms*, 'fees,' by W. Chaplin, Collector of Dharvad, 'Instructions to Amlitdars regarding Wurshasun Pensions, Pagoda and Mosque Allowances and Russooms,' n.d., accompaniment to Elphinstone's circular to collectors, 13 October 1818, PA: XIV; 1/1.
[133] Government of India to Government of Bombay, 23 May 1846, BA: RD 1847; 198/1145, pp. 111–23 approving and summarizing Bombay's mature plan.
[134] Revenue Commissioner Southern Division to Government, 8 August 1845, BA: RD 1845; 202/295, pp. 85–91.
[135] J. N. Rose, Commissioner for Claims to Government, 4 May 1848, BA: RD 1848; 256/94, pp. 167–70. The Commissioner for Claim's establishment has become known as the Hak Commission. For the records in PA see G. S. Sardesai, *Hand Book to the Records in the Alienation Office Poona* (Bombay, 1933). These Marathi records are "of no historical value" according to Sardesai (p. 32)!
[136] Memorandum of Cincvad, signed by Moro Udhav, vakil, to Government (English petition), 22 October 1841, BA: RD 1841; 56/218, pp. 271–5, emphasis in original.

who 'flocked' to Cincvad from all parts of India could not be fed in the annasatra. Much the same, of course, was said about the revenue from the Cincvad mint.[137] But now Cincvad offered the British an interpretation of the nature of the Dev's rights, not just their purpose. In offering compensation, 'Government seems not to have taken into consideration, the *nature* and *object* of the grants [of the jakat].'[138] The Dev's vakil therefore explained how the jakat was at once hereditary in the Dev's family – a copy of the sanad of 1728 was submitted as proof[139] – and also a religious endowment 'conferred in perpetuity.' In no sense, therefore, was the revenue the Dev's personal enjoyment. And offering the Dev compensation, as if he were any ordinary sardar, 'would altogether destroy the object of the grant, and cause the revenues of the Sowusthan to be *diverted into other channels* than their legitimate and proper source.'[140] Hence, in accord with the intent of Elphinstone's Proclamation of Satara guaranteeing the privileges of inamdars, and as all grants to Cincvad were obviously inam, the vakil proposed that the jakat revenues be granted in perpetuity to the Dev even if government saw fit to abolish the ultimate source of the revenue. The vakil here for the first time put forward an argument distinguishing between the purely personal rights of ordinary inamdars and the permanent endowment of the Samsthan, which was at the same time hereditary in the person of the Dev. We encounter this position again in this chapter, and it becomes even more elaborate in the 1850s with the inquiries into inam land. For the present such explanations were of little consequence because Bombay intended to treat all jakat rights, whether personal holdings or religious endowments, in exactly the same manner.

If a discourse on the relation between the Dev and the Samsthan would not appeal to the British, the vakil also pointed out some of the fundamental changes in the trade of India that were part of the abolition of the transit duties. 'It will be borne in mind,' government was informed,

that in abolishing the transit duties in the Districts that the loss is more than made up to Government by the Customs at the ports on articles passing thro[ugh] the Country where [the Dev's] rights and privileges on the customs extend, and also that this species of Revenue on the part of Government will tend in a great measure to increase their Land Revenue and prove beneficial to the general prosperity of the country, no possible ground therefore exists to suppose that Government are the sufferers by their abolition of the transit duties.[141]

[137] See above, pp. 126–7.
[138] Memorandum of Cincvad to Government, 22 October 1841, emphasis in original.
[139] Translation accompaniment to ibid., p. 277.
[140] Ibid.
[141] Ibid.

Holt Mackenzie and Charles Trevelyan would have agreed with the thrust of the vakil's analysis.

Such arguments were, however, irrelevant for the question at hand: what compensation to offer or accept. For his part the Dev demanded immediate payment of all outstanding revenues, which he now claimed to total precisely Rs. 20,000. Eventually he agreed to accept an offer of two-thirds of the due compensation pending a final settlement of his claim.[142] But the Collector of Pune was still not satisfied with either the previous estimates of the revenue or with additional accounts that had been supplied from Cincvad. The collector estimated the annual receipts at Rs. 6000, but proposed to advance only at the rate of Rs. 3500 prior to a more minute analysis of the evidence.[143]

Accounts for ten years, 1812/13–1816/17 and 1831/2–1835/6, five financial years before the end of Maratha rule and five before the abolition of all duties, were examined and averaged at Rs. 6300 per annum.[144] This amount included approximately Rs. 1000 of haks and varsasans, corresponding to such claims on the government jakat, which the Dev should presumably have paid each year to claimants out of his gross revenue. Certain deductions had also to be made from the proposed compensation. The thalmod and thalbharit on the imports and exports of Cincvad's inam villages had been collected for three years after the abolition of duties. Although difficult to evaluate, the daybooks of the contractor appeared to show that imports and exports, as distinct from the flourishing transit trade, usually amounted to only Rs. 200 per annum. After a complex balance sheet had been prepared, it was determined to pay the Dev Rs. 16,466 for four years' compensation of two-thirds of his net revenue lost to 30 September 1841. He attempted to have the two-thirds compensation turned into an annual payment by twice in 1842 petitioning for another year's advance. Further payments were refused.[145]

Not satisfied with direct refusals, in 1845 the Dev petitioned through the friendly offices of the Agent for Sardars for compensation due, or

---

[142] Memorandum of Cincvad, signed by Moro Udhav, vakil, to Government (English petition), 4 January 1842, BA: RD 1842; 103/139, p. 53.

[143] P. Stewart, Collector of Pune to Government, 5 February 1842, BA: RD 1842; 103/139, pp. 54–5.

[144] For calculations see receipt given by Moro Udhav, vakil of Cincvad, on receiving compensation (translation), 14 March 1842; Collector of Pune to Revenue Commissioner Southern Division, 23 January 1846, PA: IX; 4/59, pp. 105–8, 153–7.

[145] Memoranda from Cincvad to Government, 9 June 1842 and 26 December 1842; Government to Moro Udhav, 8 April 1844 (nos. 1085, 1099), BA: RD 1844; 138/578, pp. 209–19.

alternatively an advance of Rs. 10,000. By this time, however, Bombay had determined that the Dev was due no arrears at all.[146] From 1831/2 to 1835/6 the Dev had levied duties previously withdrawn: miscellaneous goods imported by sea, exempted in 1827, alone accounted for upwards of Rs. 2500 of his revenue. Deducting these items from gross revenues and reaveraging the net revenue produced the new and greatly reduced annual average of Rs. 1608.[147] By these calculations the Dev had been overpaid Rs. 893 on all compensation due to 1845.[148] Bombay supposed the excess would go towards further payments as they became due. But the Collector of Pune pointed out that with compensation having been only authorized for two-thirds of net revenue lost, then the Dev had in fact been overpaid Rs. 4110. Under these circumstances no further advances could be approved.[149]

On closer investigation of the accounts it appeared the Dev had deliberately frustrated all efforts at reforming transit duties. Revenues were collected on exempted goods; the jakat was levied after it had supposedly been abolished; and the Dev succeeded in obtaining more than his fair share of compensation. Further, it looked distinctly like he did not want any settlement of his rights. When in 1849 Cincvad's claims were transferred to the Commissioner for Claims, the Dev had been 'very urgent in his application for an advance, but he has displayed no desire for a speedy settlement of his claims.'[150] Repeated requests for advances were rejected because his reluctance to make a final settlement 'would increase if such advances... were generally made.'[151] The Dev was procrastinating, the commissioner believed, only to obtain more compensation than was properly due. The Cincvad vakil reinforced this impression by delaying the required appearance in the commissioner's office until the last possible day. In a related case, the vakil declined to present a claim for the Samsthan's rights to certain minor haks on the

[146] Memorandum of Cincvad to Agent for Sardars (translation), 26 September 1845; Government to Agent, 14 April 1846, PA: IX; 4/59, pp. 74–8.
[147] Collector of Pune to Revenue Commissioner Southern Division, 19 June 1845 and 23 January 1846, PA: IX; 4/59, pp. 82–7 for details of deductions and averaging.
[148] Collector of Pune to Government, 30 March 1846, BA: RD 1847; 200/1128, pp. 197–8.
[149] Government to Revenue Commissioner Southern Division, 21 August 1847; Collector of Pune to Revenue Commissioner, 7 September 1847; Revenue Commissioner to Government, 24 September 1847; Government to Revenue Commissioner, 12 November 1847, BA: RD 1847; 200/1128, pp. 213–21, 231.
[150] Commissioner for Claims to Collector of Pune, 26 January 1849, BA: RD 1850; 218/634, pp. 194–5.
[151] Ibid.

government duties of Haveli. These proceedings were consequently closed due to the nonappearance of the claimant.[152]

Certainly, the Dev attempted to put off a settlement that would see the end of further revenue. Although declining to enter into the details of a final payment, in eight petitions between 1846 and 1850 he was not slow to press his demands for what was already due. In 1848 this he calculated to be Rs. 58,000. (The Dev's figures were always based on the 1842 calculation of Rs. 6175; subsequent deductions were always ignored.) By 1848 too, he was claiming an annual loss of Rs. 1500 on account of the mohtarpha abolished in 1844.[153]

But the petitions of 1846–50 were more than just demands for payment. Again the Dev attempted to explain the nature of his jakat rights. While he now saw 'the object of Government in abolishing the transit duty as one of great benevolence,' this was only so 'where it does not interfere with the rights and immunities enjoyed therefrom.' Although he now did 'not claim the right to levy such duty,' if compensation was being paid it should be granted in perpetuity as the jakat was not a personal holding, 'but exclusively secured for the sacred use of the Temple by a Deed in perpetuity.'[154] Again Sambhaji's sanad of 1728 was submitted, but now it went to prove the permanence of the grant whereas in 1841 it had been used to demonstrate heritability.[155]

Between 1846 and 1850 Cincvad generally emphasized that its revenues were temple endowments, hence permanent devasthans. The Dev's role as hereditary recipient of the endowments was distinctly downplayed. At the same time, the jakat was equated with landed inam. In July 1847, for example, when presenting a petition to the Governor of Bombay (George Clerk) then staying at his monsoon residence in Dapodi (between Cincvad and Pune), the Cincvad vakil was quite explicit on this point: he 'earnestly prayed your Honor for an early Settlement of the claim of the Shree Dao, as his tenure of right to the

---

[152] Ibid., these minor haks, distinct from Cincvad's own transit duties, are mentioned in the tahanama of 1744/45.
[153] Petition of Dharanidhar Dev to Government (English petition), 2 December 1848, BA: RD 1850; 218/634, pp. 177–84.
[154] Petition of Dharanidhar Dev to Government (translation), 23 February 1846, BA: RD 1847; 200/1128, pp. 191–5.
[155] Memorandum of 3 June 1846 with accompanying copy and translation of sanad of 11–12 February 1728, BA: RD 1847; 200/1128, pp. 203–7. In fact, the translations of the sanad offered in 1841 (see above, note 138) and 1846 were quite different. In 1841 only the latter portion concerning inheritance was translated. In 1846 the first part of the sanad relating the purpose of the grant was emphasized.

Enam and its unalienable nature being a free grant to the Temple.'[156] Another petition identified the grant of the jakat with inam as guaranteed in the Proclamation of Satara. Elphinstone's promises on inam, varsasans and devasthans, which were to be continued if held at the accession of the British government, were cited as grounds for continuing some form of allowance to the Samsthan.[157] There was no reason, the Dev maintained, why government should, by granting a fixed compensation and so ending a permanent right, distinguish jakat rights from any other devasthan inam. In the mind of the inamdar the transit duties *were* landed rights; that they were also permanent rights, with all the advantages of tenure that designation implied, was at this point merely asserted and not pursued. The resolution of the question of permanent religious endowments versus personal hereditary inams would be delayed until the settlement of landed inam.

The Dev appears to have been reconciled to the fact that the justice of his arguments would not be appreciated. He therefore continued to demand a full payment of his compensation, which in 1850 he believed totaled Rs. 1,00,000. At the least, he assumed the Commissioner for Claims still calculated the Samsthan's revenue from the jakat at Rs. 6175, less the claims of the hakdars. The commissioner, 'satisfying himself as to the validity of the estimated amount of the proceeds in question sent in a report to Government,' but to the Dev's 'great astonishment' he had not received any money.[158]

A report had been prepared, but the conclusions were in no way favorable. The commissioner first undertook to recalculate the Dev's revenues. He firstly separated what was due the Dev from the claims of the Samsthan's hakdars, and 'for obvious reasons' proposed 'to make a separate settlement with the inferior Hukdars.'[159] Presumably, any compensation paid the Dev would not reach the minor claimants, and the commissioner noted that 'steps shall be taken to ascertain whether the sum [previously] advanced on their account has reached them or not, and whether or not they are entitled to any further payment.'[160] Next, the Dev's revenues were calculated afresh by examining accounts of 1818/19–1822/3 and 1828/9–1836/7. A deduction of 20 percent was made for five of these years because the daybooks of the contractor were

---

[156] Memorandum of Moro Udhav, vakil of Cincvad to Government (English petition), 26 November 1847, BA: RD 1847; 200/1128, pp. 233–5.

[157] Petition of Dharanidhar Dev to Government (English petition signed by Moro Udhav), 15 August 1850, BA: RD 1850; 218/634, pp. 247–53.

[158] Ibid.

[159] J. N. Rose, Commissioner for Claims to Collector of Pune, 30 January 1850, forwarded to Government, 7 February 1850, BA: RD 1850; 218/634, pp. 161–70.

[160] Ibid.

not submitted. The accounts of 1830/1 were 'irregularly kept, and are of a suspicious character,' and so also reduced by 20 percent. Deductions were also made for duties levied on exempted goods. However, 8 of the 13 years when these irregular duties were levied had to be estimated from the accounts of other years. A certain amount of guesswork was involved as 'the accounts entries have, in many instances, been so loosely and slovenly made, that it is impossible to ascertain from them whether the Merchandize upon which duty was levied was imported or exported.'[161] Certain deductions were also made on account of the mohtarpha collected after 1844, notwithstanding the Dev's earlier claims for compensation on that account.

Because the Dev was 'a large landholder,' the commissioner proposed to settle his claims as if he was a 'Holder of an Ultra Regulation Estate,' a jagirdar not bound by British regulations, whose duties government tried to end by example, persuasion, the promision of compensation, or the threat of stiff frontier duties. A regulation for the compensation of such estates decreed that a significant deduction could be made 'in consideration of the loss which would have been occasioned, had the transit duties been continued within their Estates, by the abolition of these duties in the Company's Territories.'[162] If no other duties existed, then the commissioner maintained that trade could have avoided Cincvad's nakas by resorting to a circuitous route north of Pune through Khed taluka. Moreover,

the whole of the country... is so level and free from impediments to the transport of merchandize... no trader would have paid transit duty to the Deo of Chinchore, had permission to levy it been continued to him, when it became known that Government had ceased to levy it.[163]

Even though the Dev was never offered the option of continuing to levy duties, he could still not 'claim compensation as a right.' But as an advance had already been paid, the commissioner took this as at least an admission of the claim. At any rate, it was perhaps not 'advisable to call on the Deo to refund any part of the sum advanced to him on 14th March 1842.'[164]

When asked to comment on the conclusions of the Commissioner for Claims, the Collector of Pune strenuously objected to the idea that compensation was not due as a matter of course. The Dev had been

[161] Ibid.
[162] Government to Collector of Pune, 2 October 1850, BA: RD 1850, 218/634, pp. 237–43.
[163] Report of Commissioner for Claims, 30 January 1850.
[164] Ibid.

deprived of his revenue through no act of his own; a loss had been suffered that should be made good. The impetus given to trade by the abolition of duties would only very indirectly benefit Cincvad. Nor could the collector accept the point about trade being able to avoid Cincvad's nakas. Would traders have had any economic incentive to prolong their journey? It was 'questionable,' for both financial and religious reasons, that trade would have 'diverted from its accustomed channel.' Considering the influence of tradition and religion, the collector noted:

it should also be remembered in considering the effect likely to have resulted, from the Deo's continuing to levy duties, that the Hoondekerrees or Brokers at Poona, the principal parties engaged in the trade are Hindoos, with whom the small sums levied from them by a person of so much sanctity as the Deo could scarcely be looked on, in the light of a vexatious impost, so much, as an offering to a religious object; they would therefore, it is not unreasonable to suppose, have hesitated to adopt an entirely new route, unsanctioned by the usage of their fore-fathers, merely to avoid payment of that which, in their eyes, tended to contribute to success in trade and good fortune in their speculations.[165]

The objection was perhaps pertinent as the merchants, through the person of the Dev, would have been making offerings to Ganpati, god of good fortune and success in enterprises, and a deity much favored by Pune merchants. But apart from supposition, it is now nearly impossible to determine whether such a consideration may have influenced commerce or in any way contributed to the Dev's jakat revenue. It seems unlikely if profits were at stake, but nevertheless the collector's point was original and worthy of attention.

Perhaps the collector's most telling argument was that the basis of settlement was being changed. The Dev had not been allowed to continue levying duties; whether his receipts would have decreased if he had was academic. 'It would be somewhat illiberal,' the collector thought, 'to turn round on him now, and tell him that he is entitled to no compensation, because, had Government made a different mode of settlement, he could have made nothing by his transit duties.'[166]

The collector's arguments were entirely rejected. Bombay instead preferred to accept in total the commissioner's opinions on the likely loss of revenue Cincvad would have experienced if it had continued to levy duties. The sanctity of the Dev was especially derided:

from inquiries that have been made the Governor in Council has learned that the character of the present claimant is bad; that he has been so debauched as to

---

[165] W. Courtney, Collector of Pune to Government, 11 April 1850, BA: RD 1850; 218/634, pp. 225–9.
[166] Ibid.

Cincvad and the commerce of Pune-Haveli

deprive himself of all respect in the estimation of the Natives, and is so deeply involved in debt as to render it improbable that any sum paid by Government would go in furtherance of the objects of his religion or the support of his religious character. He would therefore shew the Deo no greater consideration than would be shewn to an ordinary landholder.[167]

However, government would not completely deny the claim or attempt to recover money already paid. It was therefore decided to make a deduction of 50 percent from the commissioner's estimate of compensation due (Rs. 31,132, ten times the net annual revenue), less the amount previously advanced, with adjustments for the 10 percent interest due and already paid. To simplify the matter government decreed one final, slightly more generous payment of Rs. 10,000, 'and let all claim to compensation cease.'[168]

III. Conclusions

By 1852 the British had effectively stopped all Cincvad's claims on the commerce of Pune-Haveli. Taking upwards of 30 years, the laborious settlement process was repeated in many similar cases throughout the Bombay Presidency and India. The reform of the commercial infrastructure occupied the East India Company until the end of its rule and must stand as one of its lasting achievements. These were accomplishments often cited in support of the renewal of the Company's charter in 1852 and against the introduction of crown rule in 1858. These changes were seen as entirely benevolent; much more than the contemporary land settlements, they were thought to have no clear self-interest on the Company's part. In the first instance, the district officers, from whose impetus the measures were effected, saw only the increased prosperity of the country through greater trade. Their local reforms took more than a decade to be adopted as the Company's official policy and set into law. Higher levels of government could, of course, only respond to a felt need as information worked its way up through the administration. But also, there was revenue that had to be sacrificed, which was bound to create hesitancy for sweeping changes. Here the difference with land settlements, meant to enhance revenue, is obvious and important. In the end,

[167] Government to Collector of Pune, 2 October 1850. The origin of this information is not indicated in the sources, nor is the nature of the Dev's debauchery explained. This exchange between the collector and government appears to have become something of a watchword for the Inam Commission. The collector's observations on the Dev's religious nature (note 165) and government's response are found extracted in PA: XIII; 55/740, pp. 2–5 where they are prominently displayed.
[168] Ibid.

the elimination of the various impediments to trade would prove beneficial not only to local commerce, but also to the penetration of imperial capital into the economic life of India.

Clearly, the removal of 'private' interests in the control and taxation of trade was one of the foundations of the Company's commercial reforms. In this respect, the case of Cincvad examined in this chapter is in no way unique. It has its particular interests. The way the Samsthan exercised its control over all the main regulators of trade – mints, jakat, dastaks – in its domain is of special note. Here we get some glimpse of how the inamdar perceived all his revenues as part of his landed rights. In terms of general British policy, the settlement of the Dev's rights illustrates the Company's initial uncertainty in dealing with its landed feudatories. Perhaps the Deccan Commission had been less inhibited. Within its local sphere decisive reforms had been effected: mints had been stopped; grain duties were withdrawn and not compensated. Elphinstone knew his privileged subjects. He judged how far political conciliation could be tempered with practical reform. But in the 1830s, when relations with inamdars were directed from Bombay, the end objectives of a commercial policy seemed to get lost in the process of investigation and settlement.

Much hindered by the documentary basis of the Dev's rights, Bombay floundered on the issue of compensation. The amount had to be reduced – economy was uppermost – but eventually the Dev was paid when Elphinstone and Robertson would not have conceived of such a need for the exercise of the state's authority. In the case of the mint, compensation evolved from an unnecessary and misdirected interpretation of Maratha practices. If the Peshva had in fact granted compensation (he had not) then only the preconquest documents could supply the precise amount to be offered. The more the documents were examined, the more obscure the issue became. The actions of the Deccan Commission then had to fit preconceived interpretations. Elphinstone must have merely continued something already in existence. In a similar way, the documents became preeminent in the settlement of the transit duties. Accounts had to be examined and reexamined to discover what the Dev actually received for selling his jakat license. In both the mint and the jakat, government could ultimately only settle Cincvad's rights by decree. The Government of India's decision on the mint was finally enforced. The jakat compensation was reduced by the expedient of considering Cincvad an Ultra Regulation Estate, and the matter closed by offering one final sum quite different from any previously determined.

If the settlement of the Dev's rights was for Bombay just one more halting step towards commercial reform, for Cincvad the matter was of

utmost importance. Government's dilatory investigations were therefore to be encouraged. The mint inquiry was reopened at the Dev's
instigation. The Commissioner for Claims rightly suspected the Dev's
reluctance to settle his jakat claim. Perhaps government would increase
its offers; it was, after all, the Dev's revenue that would suffer most from
the proposed settlements. But the perspective of the inamdar was more
complex than a simple case of adversary negotiations over amounts of
money. While claims were pending rights were still held. If a settlement
was reached, all was lost.

Cincvad saw its interests in the control and taxation of commerce as
part of its inam, as part of the Dev's patrimony, and as an endowment to
the Samsthan, a devasthan. As inams, the mint and jakat were
inextricably bound to the control of land. The Dev would not willingly
surrender to the British the power to dominate the trade of his domain.
For the Company the reform of commerce had nothing to do with the
control of land – the connection was perhaps only dimly perceived – but
for the Dev, inam in the process of being lost was a threat that could not
be ignored.

When, in the 1850s, the British did consciously turn their attention to
landed rights, the inamdar was prepared. Because of the experience
gained in the settlements of varsasans and commercial rights, the Devs
knew what to expect from official inquiries, and now they had some
experience in deflecting the mechanisms of government. With the advent
of the Inam Commission the Devs faced a most serious challenge to their
rights, privileges and status. The following two chapters will examine the
various ways in which this crisis in the history of the inamdar lineage
developed and was overcome.

6

The genesis and operation of the Inam Commission

Notwithstanding the momentous political changes in India in the 1850s, nor even a military rebellion, the Inam Commission, whether under the East India Company or the Crown, labored to apply revenue policy to the multitude of individual cases that faced it. Policy was vigorously implemented without heed for considerable and vocal dissent. Having by the mid-1860s settled most of the major claims to inam lands in British districts, the commission accomplished what was intended. But it would be fallacious to assume that the day-to-day inquiries of the commission were purely mechanical settlements – claims considered and an act of government enforced. In many ways, each case was a vital struggle between the state and inamdar.

The commission believed the British to be the legitimate successors of the Marathas. The Company had therefore inherited the authority to regulate state grants as it saw fit. The commission asserted that the preconquest Marathi documents would show how inam was managed under the Marathas. Furthermore, the documents contained indisputable written evidence of the terms by which the state granted inam. In short, the commission was confident it could settle the rights of the state's privileged subjects solely by looking at the physical record. Much of the commission's evidence has here been described in the first part of this study. Inevitably, in examining the alienation inquiries of the 1850s, some retrospective analysis of the Marathi sources is necessary. These were the facts of the *ancien régime* about which the British and the representatives of the old order debated.

The inamdars for their part attempted by whatever means to maintain their traditional position in the state and combat the encroachments of overmighty government (in the person of the Inam Commissioners), which would deny their rights or confiscate their revenues. At first the claimants attempted to convince the British of the charitable and benevolent spirit behind the original grants of inam, and hence their absolute right to continue their tenures under the new government. Very soon, however, the inamdars realized that such arguments would not prevail, and they willingly debated the legal letter of old documents and its application in the context of government acts. In short, they adapted to the facts of the new regime and made the best of changed circumstances. It can be well argued that in this they were ultimately successful.

As vital as the settlement of tenure undoubtably was, the inamdars had a further and equally as important stake in the inam inquiries. When confirming tenures, the Inam Commissioners were in fact often regulating who could inherit an inam. It was not the commission's brief to do this; its only duty in this respect was to detect fraudulent successions that would affect tenurial decisions. Eventually the British realized that by recognizing a specific heir, they often revived the family disputes and rivalries which are so common a feature of the eighteenth-century sources. By their inquiries the commission, therefore, often brought the issues of the Maratha period into the nineteenth century. The commission, in a sense, assumed the position of the Peshva and claimed his authority over the inamdars. But it had no clear understanding of, or sympathy with, the spirit of inam grants. Perhaps worse, the commission was woefully ignorant of the internal affairs of the claimants, particularly questions of inheritance. Often, therefore, the issues at stake in its inquiries eluded the commission, even with its remarkable mastery of the Marathi sources.

Because the commission and its inamdar subjects were so often at cross-purposes, this and the following chapters examine their relations in three broad areas: procedure, interpretation and strategy. Procedure, the way the commission settled a claim when working in often contradictory and confusing Marathi documentation, occasioned many opportunities for conflict and made the inquiries lengthy and complex. The evidence of tenurial rights, once obtained, was then subject to interpretation of fact. As will be seen, even within the commission there was sometimes much debate as to the meaning of specific documents and their relation to established notions of Maratha revenue history. The claimants, of course, had still different interpretations of the facts of a case. Strategy – how the commission and claimant pursued their respective ends in an inam settlement – in some degree pervaded each case the British settled. The commission had ways of interpreting and enforcing the rules that would make its opinions prevail. The inamdars could manipulate the bureaucracy, points of fact, and a reading of the evidence for their own purposes. Even bribery was not beyond contemplation as a strategy to effect a favorable settlement. With so much scope for contention and controversy, even seemingly simple inam inquiries became a labyrinth of claims and counter-claims, new and unexpected documents, appeals and further appeals, all of which ultimately made the Inam Commission, in the words of the chief commissioner, 'an expensive failure.'[1]

The present chapter first gives some general background to the legislative foundations of the inam inquiries and their place in the revenue history of British India. While considering the development of legal criteria for evaluating the legitimacy of alienated tenures, this analysis also emphasizes the growth of the administrative machinery needed to institute a comprehensive alienation inquiry. This chapter, in fact, attempts to show that for the Inam Commission questions of procedure – how to physically handle all the cases – became of such importance that the legal aspects of the inam inquiries of the 1850s were, much to the commission's own misfortune, relatively neglected.

Most of the Inam Commission's settlements with small inamdars were concerned mainly with procedure and interpretation. Evidence of tenure had to be gathered, assessed and then a decision rendered under the terms of law. Within this closely managed context the small inamdar played out his relations with the Inam Commission and the state. When the British were possibly about to deny his revenue rights, the inamdar argued about procedure and interpretation. He had no other choice. To illustrate how state–inamdar relations were conducted in such a situation, this chapter includes a case study of the Devs of Ranjangav. Part of their inam was to be resumed. Naturally, the inamdar resisted this attack on his inheritance. We see how he attempted to convince the British of the unfairness of their actions and the inviolability of his inam.

The third member of the triad of state–inamdar relations in the 1850s – strategies of settlement – is a theme that could underly any Inam Commission settlement. However, apart from certain unique examples, small inamdars such as the Ranjangav Devs generally had little opportunity to manipulate an inam inquiry; for them, the issues were too clear and pressing to admit of much in the way of complex strategy. But when large holdings were at stake, such as the inam of the Cincvad Devs, and especially when the Inam Commission trespassed on questions of inheritance, the way was open to manifold and conflicting strategies to arise in an alienation inquiry. This third theme in state–inamdar relations is thus more fully developed in the following chapter.

I. The genesis of the Inam Commission

In 1852 the Bombay government passed into law Act XI of 1852 by

---

[1] T. A. Cowper, Revenue Commissioner for Alienations to Government, 30 April 1857 quoted in *Bombay Times*, 25 August 1859.

which most alienated land tenures, including inam, were henceforward to be regulated. Before this legislation could be enacted it had been forwarded to the supreme government in Calcutta for debate in council and the ultimate assent of the Governor-General, Lord Dalhousie. The then law member of the Calcutta council, Sir Charles Jackson, assures us that the legislation had a speedy passage. He personally had objected to the severity of some of its provisions, but not its underlying principles. However, Sir Charles was generally overruled in debate and he did not press the issue. Lord Dalhousie saw no difficulties with the act. The civilian members of council found Jackson's doubts, as they said, 'occidental rather than Oriental.'[2] As a trained lawyer and not a Company administrator, Jackson found the act's language 'very untechnical,' presumably being fraught with problems of interpretation and thus open to court challenge.[3]

The majority of the Calcutta council, however, being practical men with experience in the districts, apparently found the straightforward provisions of Act XI of 1852 admirably suited for the everyday work of revenue administration. Furthermore, the general nature of the act's provisions was familiar. In fact, though referring in its specifics to the Bombay Presidency, the background to the legislation is to be found in regulations enacted for Bengal. Furthermore, British awareness of the importance of alienated tenures and the necessity of their regulation stretches back to eighteenth-century Bengal and the earliest settlements of the Indian land revenue. In this context the Bombay law was, as the following paragraphs show, the culmination of East India Company legislation on alienated land tenures. It was not, apart from certain restricted innovations, even very original. Thus the Calcutta council merely assented to familiar rules for another jurisdiction.

The Bombay Inam Commission liked to trace its pedigree back to 1765 and Shah Alam's grant 'in inam' of the Diwani to Clive.[4] By this treaty, if it may be so-called, continuity with the pre-British past was established; and the Company thus succeeded to the absolute right to legislate for rent-free tenures. Be this as it may, several years would pass before the Company took much cognizance of alienated tenures. The Amini Commission of 1776–8, under Warren Hastings, while investigating the land revenue of Bengal, did, for example, notice what it called

---

[2] Sir Charles Jackson, *Vindication of the Marquis of Dalhousie's Indian Administration* (1865; rpt. Allahabad, 1975), p. 68.
[3] Ibid., p. 69.
[4] Alfred Thomas Etheridge, 'Narrative of the Bombay Inam Commission and Supplementary Settlements,' *Selections from the Records of the Bombay Government*, n.s. 132 (Bombay, 1874), pp. 7–8.

jagir, which was divided into various categories by the intention of the grant and the duration of its tenure.[5] Hereditary and personal grants, called in Bengal *āltamghā*, were so listed under jagir. These appear to have been equivalent to personal inam in Bombay. Thus, although the technical vocabulary varied, the types of land tenures described indicate that even at the early period of the Amini Commission the British were reasonably familiar with most of the varieties of revenue alienations the Bombay Inam Commission would later investigate.

Before 1793 the Bengal government did make some effort to legislate for rent-free tenures, but these first regulations apparently were ineffective.[6] In 1793, with the permanent settlement of Cornwallis, a further explicit effort was made to regulate rent-free tenures, called then altamgha or *lākhirāj*.[7] Regulations 19 and 37 assumed at the outset that government had the right to resume invalid alienations. Hence, some definition of validity had to be enacted. Basically the regulations categorized rent-free lands in terms of size (under 10 bighas, 10–100 bighas, over 100 bighas) and also the date of their grant in relation to Clive's assumption of the Diwani. Increasingly severe tests for larger units of land were imposed on recent grants. In effect, a large rent-free tract had to be proved to have been granted before the Diwani to be considered a legitimate alienation. Grants under 10 bighas, on the other hand, were allowed more latitude, provided, of course, they were seen to be held for their original charitable purposes.

Difficulties of administration arose because holders of alienated tenures would not likely admit to having obtained their grant after the Diwani. Even if proof of title was not produced, the claimant could claim that the relevant sanads had once existed. Or, spurious documents could be presented to government. There just was no advantage in not claiming an old title to a rent-free grant.

Perhaps as an indulgence to possessors of large holdings, or maybe as a way of circumventing the problems associated with the production of written titles, in 1805 the Governor-General, John Shore, allowed a title to be established through prescription. A lakhiraj then would be valid if held for 60 years.[8] This rather arbitrary period – perhaps meant to be two generations – becomes somewhat of a 'magic' figure in the history of British legislation on inam. The Bombay Inam Commission would

[5] Anil Chandra Banerjee, *The Agrarian System of Bengal*, 2 vols. (Calcutta, 1980–1), I, 14–15; for the report of the Amini Commission see R. B. Ramsbotham, *Studies in the Land Revenue History of Bengal, 1769–1787* (London, 1926), pp. 107ff.

[6] Banerjee, II, 71–2.

[7] The following discussion is generally taken from Banerjee, II, 72–5.

[8] Regulation 2 of 1805, see Banerjee, II, 75.

use the same period 50 years later to establish prescriptive rights. In many ways the entire concept of title by prescription, especially when so precisely defined, was a significant British innovation. Proof by title deed, the essence of preconquest tests of validity (as demonstrated in Part One) was supplemented by a more western concept of title. Henceforward these two legal definitions of proof would coexist, sometimes uneasily, in British legislation on alienated tenures.

The basic structure of the zamindari land settlements in Bengal hindered all attempts, before and after 1805, to discover invalid land alienations and assert the state's legitimate revenue demands. The permanent settlement effectively hid these tenures in the zamindar's estates, in which the British were not disposed to meddle. Shore, according to Banerjee,

realized the necessity of showing some 'indulgence' to the zamindars, for he knew that it was beyond the capacity of the Government to 'discover' the 'alienated lands' without their co-operation, or at least acquiescence. As resumptions would in many cases affect different kinds of rights which they had been enjoying for a long period by custom, fraud or force, it would be natural for them to oppose the official process of 'discovery' and conceal information of which they were practically the sole custodians.[9]

Quite simply, this explains why the alienation settlements, such as existed in Bengal, never assumed the importance for the Company as did the Bombay inquiries. The zamindars either hid those rent-free tenures in which they had some interest, or they would not themselves allow those that reduced their own revenue. In Bombay, where the British claimed to settle revenue directly with the landholder, this intervening level of administration was removed and the district administrators were exposed to the panoply of village land tenures. Of course, the situation was never so direct. As Part One has shown, village land inams were subsumed by whole village inams and so forth. And hence sometimes the British analogously referred to the Bombay inamdars as jamindars (zamindars), both because they controlled the land (jamin) and because they had under them numerous proprietors of petty inams, and below these the 'ordinary' villagers. In the basic organization of the countryside, however, Bengal and Bombay fundamentally differed; and it was this fact that explains much about the genesis of the Bombay Inam Commission.

In 1819 the Bengal government attempted to bring order to previous regulations concerning rent-free lands and to simultaneously enact means by which invalid tenures could be discovered. Regulation 2 of

[9] Banerjee, II, 76.

1819 provided that alienations outside zamindari estates were to be subjected to government scrutiny, and further, that the collectors could now try suits on rent-free lands. Previously, only civil courts had jurisdiction.[10] In 1825 the collectors' powers were extended to zamindari estates, and at the same time the definitions of rights by prescription and title deed were further refined.[11]

Despite these attempts to regularize proceedings, the enacted regulations failed as a basis for any protracted investigation of land alienations. Because both the civil courts and the collectors had concurrent authority to hear suits, litigants simply avoided any unfavorable decisions of collectors by launching civil suits.[12] Furthermore, the regulations failed because the collectors were not capable of exercising their assigned functions:

it is not to be wondered at that, when the Revenue officers were called upon to carry into effect a Regulation [2 of 1819], the detailed rules of which were essentially of a juridical nature, they were less ready and apt in the practical application of those rules to the cases which they investigated.[13]

To overcome this difficulty legislation was enacted in 1828 appointing revenue tribunals to investigate and hear all suits on land alienations.[14] The summary nature of these proceedings – the decision of the tribunal was final–alarmed the zamindars. Petitions to government, which were put in terms to be repeated in Bombay 30 years later, attacked the arbitrariness of the regulation.[15]

Eventually, after the intervention of the Court of Directors, Bengal established special commissioners as an avenue of appeal from the initial decisions of revenue officers. In somewhat enthusiastic terms Bengal described the superior qualities of the commissioners who would allay the fears of the propertied classes:

[these] individuals... should unite the qualities of extensive judicial experience and sound judgment, with a thorough knowledge of the principles of Revenue administration; individuals, in short, of that scope of talent and enlightened

[10] Banerjee, II, 76; A. F. Salahuddin Ahmed, *Social Ideas and Social Change in Bengal, 1818–1835* (Leiden, 1965), p. 103; Regulation 2 of 1819 in *Parliamentary Papers* 1821, XVIII, 201–10.
[11] Salahuddin Ahmed, p. 103; Regulation 9 of 1825 in *Parliamentary Papers* 1825, XXIII, 367–71; Regulation 14 of 1828 in ibid., 377–80.
[12] Revenue letter from Bengal to Court of Directors, 23 February 1830 in *Parliamentary Papers* 1831/2, XI, 336–51, paras. 18–21. This despatch is perhaps the best general survey of the official view of alienated revenue policy in Bengal.
[13] Revenue letter from Bengal, 23 February 1830.
[14] Regulation 3 of 1828 in *Parliamentary Papers* 1830, XXVIII, 642–54.
[15] Salahuddin Ahmed, pp. 104–8; petition, pp. 173–6; Revenue letter from Bengal, 23 February 1830, paras. 83ff.

views which would fit them to weigh calmly and without bias the conflicting claim of Government and its subjects, and to discriminate clearly between that ill-directed zeal which might lead Revenue officers with more limited views to aim at every petty opportunity of resuming land which presented itself, and the anxious desire of Government that nothing beyond the just rights of the State should be demanded.[16]

This idealized description of the officer charged with the investigation and settlement of revenue alienation is a model that was adopted, at least in spirit, in Bombay in the 1850s.

The role of alienated revenues in the patterns of landholding in Bengal and Bombay differed in many respects; really, these are two different histories in the development of British land revenue policies. But Bengal did provide Bombay with some of the basis concepts of validity of tenure – title deed and prescription – and also the idea of a settlement commission staffed by officers equally conversant in revenue and judicial administration.

Mountstuart Elphinstone, first as Commissioner in the Deccan and later as Governor of Bombay, must be charged with adapting the Bengal experience on alienated tenures to the Deccan after 1818. Initially, Elphinstone established the legislative basis by which inam and other tenures were to be regulated. At the same time, he set in motion the first limited inquiries into the estates of the state's privileged subjects. From 1818 to 1852 the legislative and administrative bases of alienation settlements in Bombay were elaborated and refined. The resulting shape of the Inam Commission was perhaps unlike anything Elphinstone ever contemplated.[17] But, in its essential nature, British alienated land policy in Bombay at the end of the Company's rule could rightly be seen as having its formative molding forces set soon after the conquest of the Deccan.

Elphinstone, sensing the importance of inam in the Deccan, identified its preservation with the establishment of the British administration at Pune in 1817/18. The Proclamation of Satara (11 February 1818), as it did for varsasans, specifically guaranteed inam as part of the 'property real or personal [which] will be secured.'[18]

However, the early correspondence of the Deccan Commission makes clear that Elphinstone never contemplated a blanket guarantee for the

[16] Revenue letter from Bengal, 23 February 1830, para. 70.
[17] Although Elphinstone (d. 1859) was still living in England during the course of the alienation inquiries of the 1850s, it appears that he never, in print, expressed his opinions on the matter.
[18] Proclamation of Satara, 11 February 1818 in G. S. Sardesai, ed. *Poona Affairs* (*Elphinstone's Embassy*) (*Part II, 1816–1818*) (Bombay, 1958), pp. 299–302.

security of every inam found at the conquest. Certainly, on the one hand, Elphinstone had no intention of restoring inams formerly resumed by the Peshvas: 'no right to possession is ever intended to be recognized that was not in force at the breaking out of the present war.'[19] The status quo, such as it was inherited from the native dynasty, would not be disturbed. But, on the other hand, the Commissioner in the Deccan emphasized to his subordinates that no inam was officially confirmed just because the British found it in place when they assumed the government. Hence, as Elphinstone explained to James Grant, any letters he issued to inamdars concerning their holdings were

merely to show you that the persons bringing them have submitted to our Government, and therefore eligible to hold Enams, provided they can prove their Right to them you will of course investigate the claims before putting them in possession, should you however not have time to do so to your satisfaction, you will inform them that an enquiry into the validity of their Titles will be made hereafter.[20]

Similarly, within a week of this pronouncement, Elphinstone informed Pottinger in Ahmednagar that all inams were to be continued 'unless there are strong and peculiar grounds of objection.'[21] Of course, Elphinstone again emphasized that this was not a 'formal confirmation' of tenure.

Such an official and permanent confirmation could only happen after the new administration had made a complete register of all inams and other alienated tenures. The initial pressure for this move came, not surprisingly, from Calcutta. In August 1818 the Chief Secretary to the Bengal government more or less ordered Elphinstone to turn his immediate attention to the matter. The importance of a complete register of rent-free lands had surely not, the commissioner was informed, escaped his attention. Only in the 'early period of the introduction of the British Authority' could the most 'useful' information be obtained. And this information would furthermore greatly affect 'the satisfactory establishment of a regular system of Revenue.'[22]

Although the district officers in the Deccan had already begun such a register of inams,[23] and Elphinstone did transmit Calcutta's explicit

[19] Mountstuart Elphinstone, Commissioner in the Deccan to James Grant, Resident at Satara, 27 June 1818, PA: DC 402/288; also in Inam Commission files, PA: XIV; 1/1.
[20] Ibid.
[21] Elphinstone to Henry Pottinger, Collector of Ahmednagar, 1 July 1818, PA: DC 402/298.
[22] Chief Secretary Adam to Elphinstone, 29 August 1818, accompaniment to Elphinstone's circular to collectors, 13 October 1818, PA: XIV; 1/1, fol. 12.
[23] James Grant, instructions to mamlatdars of Satara, 8 May 1818 (forwarded to Elphinstone) in R. D. Choksey, *Period of Transition* (Pune, 1945), pp. 108–10, para. 4.

wishes to the collectors,[24] still the new administration proceeded carefully when examining the rights of the Maratha state's privileged subjects. As for inam, although the required information could probably be obtained from village accounts, nevertheless 'it would probably create alarm at present to enter on a strict scrutiny.'[25] Early in 1819 Elphinstone pressed for all of the requisite data to be found in the Peshva's daphtar.[26] He recognized the immensity of his request. But before any scrutiny could begin, all sources of information on rent-free tenures had to be collated. As the new government settled into the administration of the Deccan, the matter became increasingly pressing. The chance to exactly record the state of the country at the conquest – Calcutta's hope – would be lost. Furthermore, the longer unauthorized grants were held under the British, the better would be their claim for title by prescription.

In 1818 Elphinstone had informed the collectors that correct registers of inams had to be compiled before he could specify 'the principles which are to be observed in determining the validity of grants.'[27] In the following year the first tentative rules were issued.[28] Eight tests were to be applied to determine the legitimacy of inams. All concerned the relative weight given to sanads issued by various authorities of the Maratha state. At this stage the idea of title through prescription had not been completely applied to grants in the Deccan. The exception was the case where alienations had been made by patils or 'other inferior functionaries,' which had to be held for at least 30 years to be considered valid. Basically, most of Elphinstone's rules centered on the year 1803 and the devolution of the Peshva's central control after the Treaty of Bassein. In this the inam rules and the contemporary first regulations for varsasans, examined in Chapter 4, share many similarities.[29] Most grants made after 1803, when clearly confirmed by inferior authority, were declared liable for resumption. However, inams that were without doubt issued under the Peshva's sole authority were to be continued without qualification. Inams meant for the support of temples

---

[24] Elphinstone circular to collectors, 13 October 1818, PA: DC 403/838; PA: xiv; 1/1, fol. 11.

[25] Ibid.

[26] Elphinstone to A. E. R. McDonell, in charge of Pune daphtar, 9 April 1819, PA: xiv; 1/1.

[27] Elphinstone circular to collectors, 13 October 1818.

[28] 'Rules for deciding on the validity of claims to Enams,' Elphinstone circular to collectors, 19 March 1819, PA: xiv; 1/5, fol. 7. This copy, signed by W. Chaplin, is found in the Inam Commission's files. It was apparently removed from the files of the collector and political agent in the Southern Maratha Country.

[29] See pp. 107–8.

were to be similarly treated, except when 'the institutions have other ample means of maintenance.'

Elphinstone's rules for inams were never considered anything more than a temporary expedient for the day-to-day use of collectors involved in the regularization of the revenue system in a conquered country. Because a particular inam had not been resumed after a test of the rules did not mean the British had officially confirmed the alienation. Many inams would, in the normal course of affairs, escape any notice from the collectors. Moreover, the rules did not attempt to draw out any specifications for judging pre-1803 grants. Nevertheless, in spite of Elphinstone's intentions, in the districts some sort of confirmation of alienated tenures was proceeding without any central control. John Briggs in Khandesh, for example, earned Elphinstone's censure:

I beg to be favored with an explanation of the manner in which the confirmation [of certain inams] has been conferred. It was my intention only to release Enams for the present & not to enter into any engagement that implied their being continued until there should be an opportunity of carefully examining [them].[30]

In Pune district Robertson found that Elphinstone's hopes were impossible to realize. A *de facto* inam settlement was in fact taking place through the revenue system. While not trying to enter 'on any general scrutiny of Enams,' Robertson remarked that

it will be abundantly evident ... that in the [revenue] settlement I am at present engaged in a very great number of unauthorized Enams must come to my knowledge. The effect of attaching these will probably in a great measure have the effect of a general scrutiny. The holders will naturally be discontented if ejected. But on the other hand they will naturally expect that, if the Enams be left in their possession ... they will not be resumed at a future date.[31]

In short, whether the British liked the fact or not, the longer the new administration consciously refrained from implementing an official criteria for the legitimacy of inams, and thereafter began some administrative mechanism for enforcing such rules, the more secure the inamdars would become in their holdings. Elphinstone's fear of any precipitate moves in settling alienated tenures was creating a situation where the real intentions of the British – to ultimately subject inams to a stringent scrutiny of their validity – had become obscured.

For both the British and the inamdars this situation was undesirable. Yet, until Act XI of 1852 and the Inam Commission, Elphinstone's rules

[30] Elphinstone to John Briggs, Collector of Khandesh, 14 June 1819, PA: DC 404/1333.
[31] H. D. Robertson, Collector of Pune to W. Chaplin, Commissioner in the Deccan, 24 November 1819, PA: DC 96/497.

on inams were the sole, semi-official means for settling alienations in the Deccan. The Bombay government did not neglect to legislate for rent-free tenures. Indeed, Elphinstone as Governor of Bombay was the activating force behind setting out the official regulations on the matter. First done in 1823 (Regulation 1 of 1823),[32] this legislation was incorporated into the consolidation of all regulations concerning revenue matters in 1827 (Regulation 17 of 1827).[33] In these regulations Elphinstone now introduced the concept of title by prescription in addition to that of title by deed. Where land had been exempt from the land revenue for more than 60 years, and 'provided it has been under some tenure recognized by the custom of the country,' this would be considered sufficient to establish title.[34] Only 12 years' prescriptive title was required if possession dated before the British conquest. Much of the regulations set out the details by which the collectors were to hear and settle suits on alienated tenures (chapter 10 of Regulation 17 of 1827).

When reading the procedure sections of the regulations of 1823 and 1827 it is clear that Elphinstone intended this legislation only for the old territories of the Bombay Presidency. The concession allowing 12 years' possession under a native dynasty to equal a prescriptive title of 60 years also indicates the limited application of the regulations. Elphinstone surely recognized that in the Deccan 12 years' possession of an inam prior to 1818 would have been difficult to disprove. His own provisional rules issued to the collectors were not nearly so liberal. Through legislation and practise Elphinstone and his successors in fact excluded the new conquests in the Deccan from the force of the regulations on alienated tenures. They did this simply by limiting the jurisdiction of the ordinary civil courts in the affairs of the Deccan sardars.[35] The Agent for Sardars was instead entrusted with the joint political–legal responsi-

---

[32] *Parliamentary Papers* 1826, xxv, 176–85.

[33] *Parliamentary Papers* 1829, xxii, 413–19.

[34] Regulation 17 of 1827, chapter 9, sects. 35–6.

[35] Regulations 29 of 1827, sect. 6 (for the Deccan) and 6 of 1830 sect. 2 (for the Southern Maratha Country) are the relevant pieces of legislation. See E. H. Townsend, Revenue Commissioner Southern Division to Government, 26 November 1847 in 'A Selection of Papers Explanatory of the Origin of the Inam Commission,' *Selections from the Records of the Bombay Government*, n.s. 30 (Bombay, 1856), pp. 70–2 (hereafter 'Selection of Papers'), The Revenue Commissioner noted that the Collector of Pune reported that by orders of 12 March 1840 government had specifically excluded his district from Bombay regulations on alienated tenures. At least, 'no investigation into Inams generally has ever been made in the Poona Collectorate' (p. 70). See also W. Hart, Inam Commissioner to Government, 30 December 1850 in 'Selection of Papers,' pp. 137–46 where the circumstances of the exemption of Deccan inams from the cognizance of the collectors are examined at tength.

bility for inamdars. Because the sardars could not launch actions in civil court to challenge a collector's decision on rent-free tenures, then the district officers could not in the first place issue decisions that would be binding. The Agent for Sardars was not a revenue officer; the extent of his interference in inams was to settle disputed legal title; the initial legitimacy of an alienation was not questioned. Only the Bombay government, by specific order of the Governor in Council, could resume an inam in the Deccan. Each case was unique.

It was against this unsatisfactory and cumbersome state of affairs that the Inam Commission was conceived. In fact, the prologue to Act XI of 1852 makes specific and pointed reference to the lacunae in legislation: alienated tenures in the new conquests were 'excepted from the cognisance of the ordinary Civil Courts, and incapable of being justly disposed of under the Rules for the determination of Titles.'[36]

Where the regulations of 1823 and 1827 were in force – mostly in the Konkan and Gujarat districts of the Presidency – it became apparent that the collectors had conducted a most desultory investigation of rent-free lands. The Collector of Thana, for example, even by 1847 reported that only 468 of 1900 cases had been decided in his district.[37] Furthermore, the collector raised numerous difficulties of procedure and interpretation of the existing regulations. He even doubted the necessity of investigating all inams.

It may be a question whether there can be any necessity of formally examining *all* such claims. According to Section XL, Regulation XVII of 1827, it would seem that it is only when the Collector has reason to believe that no sufficient title exists that it is competent to him to call upon the occupant to defend his claim. At any rate, in cases where Inam lands are held on duly registered deeds, granted by fully authorised public officers, which there are no grounds for calling in question, such a proceeding can scarcely be called for.[38]

Elphinstone's regulations thus had not proved to be a realistic means for dealing with inam. Apart from the fact that the regulations did not extend to a greater part of the Presidency, the collectors in those districts where they did operate did not perceive any legal or practical reason to be too enthusiastic in their inquiries.

In the 1840s, however, in the southern districts of the Bombay Presidency (the Southern Maratha Country) certain revenue officers

---

[36] Act XI of 1852, prologue in 'Selection of Papers,' p. 157.

[37] J. S. Law, Collector of Thana to D. A. Blane, Revenue Commissioner Northern Division, 22 October 1847 in 'Selection of Papers,' pp. 104–5. See also pp. 81–124 for a summary of correspondence on the types of inquiries conducted in the northern division of the Bombay Presidency under Regulation 17 of 1827.

[38] Law to Blane, 22 October 1847.

became increasingly concerned with apparently gross alienations of the public revenues. The Revenue Commissioner in 1843, for example, reported to Bombay that 'the extent of [inam] lands in the Southern Mahratta Country is shown to be enormous, and suspicions are entertained of a considerable portion being held in defective title. Of this, however, no intelligible estimate has yet been made.'[39] The opinion derived primarily from the revenue survey work of H. E. Goldsmid in the southern districts. It was Goldsmid, too, who recognized the worth of the Pune daphtar records for the settlement of inams. He successfully campaigned in Bombay to have this archive transferred from the control of the Agent for Sardars so that the revenue survey (and ultimately the Inam Commission) could put it to use.[40]

Goldsmid's apprehensions over the wasted revenue potential of the Southern Maratha Country were translated into the appointment of a committee for the investigation of all alienated tenures in certain restricted parts of the district. The Bombay government and the Court of Directors slowly permitted this committee to extend its inquiries throughout the Southern Maratha Country. In 1844 William Hart took over the lead of the committee.[41] And it was through the exertions of this one Bombay civil servant that the dilatory alienation inquiries in one district were transformed from a peripheral concern of the revenue survey into a full-fledged investigative commission working throughout the new conquests of the Bombay Presidency under the authority of Act XI of 1852. Hart in fact wrote the legislation; he devised the administrative machinery required to investigate inams; he must, therefore, even more than Goldsmid, be considered the founder of the Inam Commission.

In the early years of the alienation inquiries Goldsmid and later Hart worked under the close supervision of the Governor of Bombay and his council. The districts and talukas to be surveyed and settled were regulated through specific orders of government. Furthermore, each case proposed to be settled had to be separately reported to Bombay for approval. At first the Governor in Council had to issue the requisite orders; only later could Hart report his individual decisions to his nominal superiors in the Revenue Department.[42]

---

[39] D. A. Blane, Revenue Commissioner Southern Division to Government, 14 April 1843 in *Parliamentary Papers* 1857, XXIX, 483–4.
[40] See 'Correspondence exhibiting the Nature and Use of the Ponna Duftur,' *Selections from the Records of the Bombay Government*, n.s. 30 (Bombay, 1856), pp. 35–42.
[41] W. Hart, Inam Commissioner to Government, 1 July 1848 in 'Selection of Papers,' pp. 55–65, paras. 11–14.
[42] Ibid.

Without any formal legislative basis for his proceedings, Hart was, in his view, continually frustrated in his attempts to initiate a thorough-going investigation. He therefore strongly lobbied government for some legal basis for his 'Inam Commission' – as he began to refer to the inam committee in his correspondence. In 1848, for example, after having briefly enjoyed sole responsibility for his decisions in 1847, Hart again complained about the cumbersome necessity of reporting each case to Bombay:

government was obliged to revert to the course of procedure which it had already found to be inconvenient and unsatisfactory, – viz. one involving a separate review and a distinct order on a report of each case, which, though not really an *ex parte* decision, has seemed obnoxious to some of the objections to which such decisions are liable.[43]

Hart therefore took the liberty of forwarding a 'sketch' of an act, 'a very simple one,' which he thought would remove the administrative difficulties he was facing.

The Court of Directors ultimately sanctioned the establishment of an official Inam Commission through specific legislation. At the same time, the Court gave Hart some of the authority he wanted. To the Court it appeared

altogether unnecessary that the details of every case investigated by the Commission, in which the right of the Inamdar to hold his lands rent-free in perpetuity has been satisfactorily established, should be reported specifically for the orders of Government.[44]

Of course, where Hart proposed to resume an inam, the sanction of government would still be needed pending the enactment of legislation. Some two years would be required to prepare Act XI of 1852. But with these orders of the Court of Directors, giving Hart approval for a revenue inquiry with quasi-judicial powers over inams, came the root authority of the Inam Commission as it functioned in the 1850s.

To the present point, the rules under which Goldsmid's inam committee and Hart's nascent Inam Commission functioned have not been mentioned. There were certainly models that both could follow – the Bengal legislation in addition to Elphinstone's provisional rules of 1819 and his regulations of 1823 and 1827. Both men did, in some measure, adopt parts of these enactments. However, because they were not bound by Regulation 17 of 1827 in particular, Goldsmid and

---

[43] Hart to Government, 27 July 1848 in 'Selection of Papers,' pp. 125–8.
[44] Court of Directors to Bombay, 20 June 1849, extracts in 'Selection of Papers,' pp. 128–31.

Hart were free to develop their own proofs of the legitimacy of a tenure, and further, procedures for investigating and settling alienated tenures.

Hart considered the latter point as least as important as the former. Previous regulations had failed, he believed, because the district collectors had not time, even if they had the knowledge and inclination, to investigate inams. Bombay echoed Hart's views when reporting to Calcutta; unfortunately,

the inability of the regular revenue officers of this Presidency to spare time from their more urgent current duties has, the Right Honorable the Governor in Council regrets to have to admit, occasioned the knowledge of the titles of holders of alienated lands throughout the larger portion of the Presidency to have remained in almost the same imperfect state in which it was on our acquisition of the country.[45]

In the Southern Maratha Country, however, an efficient system had been established to judge inams. Hart reported that this had been found

most convenient to the claimants as well as the officers of Government. More than twenty thousand claims [by 1850] have been received and recorded ... and Government is aware how few complaints have been made by claimants (certainly not one for each thousand of inquiries instituted) regarding the mode in which their statements and evidence have been received and recorded.[46]

An examination of the details of Hart's system of settling inams is delayed until the cases of the Ranjangav and Cincvad Devs are considered in this and the following chapters. Here, however, it should again be emphasized that the Inam Commission was preeminently a *way* of handling alienated tenures. And as the cases of the Ranjangav and Cincvad Devs will show, questions of procedure were often uppermost in the minds of both commissioner and claimant.

With regard to the rules for determining the validity of an inam, Hart had, prior to the enactment of Act XI of 1852, adopted the rules of 1842 for claims to money and grain allowances for use in judging landed tenures. These were the same rules used for varsasans as detailed in Chapter 4.[47] Throughout the 1840s these provisions had been modified and amended through individual orders of government.[48] Eventually, it was this developed collection of rules and government orders that were to be incorporated, almost without further revision, into Act XI of 1852.

---

[45] Government of Bombay to Supreme Government, Calcutta, 7 January 1850 in 'Selection of Papers,' pp. 131–3.

[46] Hart to Government, 30 December 1850 in 'Selection of Papers,' pp. 137–46.

[47] See pp. 115–16.

[48] See Hart to Government, 1 January 1851 in 'Selection of Papers,' pp. 146–51 comparing the proposed Act XI of 1852 with the rules of 1842 and their amendments.

The specific provisions of the act will be noticed here when they affected the tenurial decisions of the Ranjangav and Cincvad Devs.

Hart and the Inam Commission did make one important contribution to the general development of British revenue policy on alienated tenures. The notion of title by prescription was refined: length of future possession was linked to length of prior possession. Regulation 17 of 1827 had, Hart informed government, recognized

a prescriptive title to exemption acquirable by 'any person, his heirs, or others deriving right from him,' who have held for sixty years under any 'recognized tenure'; but there is nothing to define the duration of the exemption for the future, nor to what heirs it is continuable.[49]

The Inam Commission had therefore developed, starting from the rules of 1842, a graduated definition of prescriptive title. Act XI of 1852 would define prescription in two stages: 60 years' possession before the introduction of British rule and two successions (to the grandson of the original grantee) would make an inam hereditary to the male heirs of the grantee; 40 years' possession and one succession would allow an inam to be held for one more generation.[50] Incidentally, Hart totally rejected the provision of Regulation 17 of 1827 whereby 12 years' possession under a native dynasty equaled 60 years' prescriptive title: 'such a clause would be wholly unjust to Government in a territory ... where for more than the twelve years in question all sorts of fraudulent acquisitions of land took place.'[51]

The Inam Commission's desire to give greater definition to prescriptive titles could only have occurred because they had access to records detailed enough to provide them with the requisite facts on the succession to inams under the Marathas. Previously, collectors had not been able to so exactly define prescription, and thus the early regulations in Bengal and Bombay had been left in general terms. However, in giving greater precision to prescriptive titles, the Inam Commission left itself open to many controversies over the interpretation of documents that were often not as complete or intelligible as imagined. How to read the evidence thus became another major concern of commission and claimant. In addition, by defining prescriptive title (and indirectly also title by deed) in terms of succession, and by in fact designating required heirs, the Inam Commission inadvertently intervened in the regulation of Hindu inheritance. This was perhaps the most serious defect of the

[49] Hart to Government, 30 December 1850.
[50] Act XI of 1852, B, 3–4.
[51] Hart to Government, 30 December 1850.

commission's legislative basis and one that would bedevil many of its settlements.

In preparing the legislation for the Inam Commission Hart had apparently hoped that the commission in the 1850s could function under the same informal rules of procedure and substance that it had in the 1840s. He consequently drafted an act that said nothing about how the commission would function, nor anything on the criteria for a valid rent-free tenure. Presumably, as it now appears, Hart wanted to keep his options open so as to be able to refine the workings of the commission as experience was gained in the large-scale settlements that were contemplated. The Supreme Government in Calcutta, however, was incredulous that it should be called upon to pass an act that merely established an Inam Commission, apparently without any legal restraints on its powers. Concerning

> the draft Act, the President in Council has felt a difficulty arising out of the ommission ... of all definition of a valid title to land wholly or partially free from assessment, and on account of the absence of any rules of procedure. The draft act merely provides that officers may be appointed to investigate and decide claims to hold lands free of assessment, and that these officers shall proceed according to such forms as may be laid down for their guidance by Government.[52]

Calcutta thought Regulation 17 of 1827 provided an adequate 'definition of a valid title'; the Supreme Government also recommended that some specific provisions as to appeal procedures be incorporated into the act.

Hart would not agree to the first suggestion. Instead, he redrafted the provisional rules of the Inam Commission and simply attached them to his draft act as 'Schedule B'. The commission's rules of procedure, with the suggested appeal mechanism, were added as 'Schedule A'. The impression remains that the redrafting of Act XI of 1852 was rushed to meet Calcutta's requirements so that the Inam Commission could function as an official body as soon as was possible. Perhaps, then, it is not surprising that Sir Charles Jackson later remarked that he had found the act's language 'very untechnical' when it was finally presented to the Calcutta council.[53] Hart had been somewhat lax in thinking through all the legal implications of his act. The subsequent failures of the Inam Commission can in part be traced to the haphazard manner in which its enabling legislation was created.

---

[52] Supreme Government, Calcutta to Government of Bombay, 11 October 1850 in 'Selection of Papers,' pp. 134–5.
[53] Jackson, *Vindication*, p. 68.

This interpretation is strengthened when the post-Inam Commission legislation on inams is considered. In 1863 the Bombay government passed two acts creating the 'Summary Settlement,' by which all inams and such, in all parts of the Presidency, were brought under one uniform set of rules.[54] All attempts to define title and regulate inheritance were now more or less abandoned, and what was already held as inam was to be confirmed simply by the payment of a moderate tax. The implement-ation of the najar and the abandonment of searching inquiries owes much, of course, to the post-Mutiny debates over resumptions as mentioned in Chapter 1.[55] The summary settlement, with its liberal provisions allowing already adjudicated inams to be improved in tenure (for example, from life to hereditary holdings), was a clear attempt to buy the support of the disaffected and powerful landed elements of rural society. But whatever its unstated intentions, the summary settlement was bound to prove more manageable, if not really more popular than the Inam Commission, because government had considered beforehand the consequences of its legislation. After coming close to adopting the model of the Inam Commission, the Madras Presidency too would create a type of summary settlement for its own inams.[56] Experience had taught the British that Hart's grand design for a commission minutely investigating all aspects of title and succession in alienated tenures was not practical.

The next section of this chapter examines how the Inam Commission actually operated when its inquiries were extended throughout the Deccan after the enactment of Act XI of 1852. Although at various intervals the commission presented reports and statistical results of its work, these tell us little about the settlements in action.[57] Most importantly, the official publications tell us nothing about how the inamdars perceived the commission. This chapter thus now considers the case study of the Devs of Ranjangav and the Inam Commission.[58]

[54] Etheridge, 'Narrative of the Bombay Inam Commission,' pp. 42–4. For the operation of the Summary Settlement, see *Annual Report of the Administration of the Bombay Presidency*, 1861/2, pp. 17–22, appendixes B and C, pp. 294–5; 1863/4, pp. 24–6.
[55] See pp. 4–5.
[56] Etheridge, pp. 41–42. For the Madras Inam Commission see BA: RD 1859; 95/66 concerning the character of the proposed inquiry with copies of correspondence between Madras, Bombay and London. Part of this correspondence, with extracts from the Madras revenue consultations, was published in *Parliamentary Papers* 1859 (sess. 1), XVIII, 501–88.
[57] See *Parliamentary Papers* 1857, XXIX, 486 (to 1856); Etheridge, appendixes A to R, pp. 73–90 (nearly complete statements).
[58] Published examples of case studies of Inam Commission settlements include 'Inam Commissioner's Report on the Claim of Mahadajee oorf Nago Punt Sadasew Baput to the Village of Modugay,' *Selections from the Records of the Bombay Government,*

Here is an example of one of the earliest inquiries, conducted by Hart himself, that the Inam Commission instituted in Pune District.

II. The Inam Commission in operation: an inam resumed

Among its critics, the purpose of the Inam Commission was to resume legitimate holdings to increase government revenues. According to Sir John Kaye it was 'that great confiscatory Tribunal.'[59] Apologists for the settlements attempted to rectify this persistent impression and show that outright resumptions, taxing land hitherto rent free, were comparatively rare. Certainly, the figures produced in the 1870s would indicate that far more inam was confirmed than revenue recovered: some Rs. 5.5 million against Rs. 3.7 million.[60] Perceptive critics might however argue that among the inams confirmed many had been reduced in the hierarchy of tenures. Nevertheless, the Inam Commissioners persisted in painting their activities in the best possible light: the commission's 'first duty ... was the confirmation of good titles,' which was, in fact, 'a real blessing to the country.'[61] Such assertions, although perhaps giving some assurance to the very selective reading public concerned with Indian affairs, could not completely disguise frequent denials of title. Physical eviction from the land, countered the commission, was not ever enforced when resumptions occurred. This was perhaps a moot point to those inamdars who had no rights, even if they had the inclination, to work the land and were essentially revenue collectors, not agriculturalists. Whatever may be proved about the extent of resumptions or the nature of inam, a denial of title was the worst possible judgment a claimant could receive from the British. Among all the Devs' inam, only the holdings of the Ranjangav Devs were subjected to this exercise of the Inam Commission's ultimate powers.

Although an ancient Ganesh shrine with inams for the support of the

o.s. 9 (Bombay, 1853) and 'Proceedings Relative to the Resumption of Certain Villages and Lands Held by the Late Anajee Nursew,' ibid., o.s. 15 (Bombay, 1855). Both concern resumptions in the Southern Maratha Country and were apparently published in justification of the need for the inam inquiries. The former report shows the rather summary proceedings of the first inquiries prior to Act XI of 1852. The latter well documents the commission's mature procedure, notably the appeal mechanisms. Without more information on the circumstances of the inamdars involved, both reports stand as isolated cases without much social or economic context. In addition, both reports are presented in the somewhat obscure manner of government proceedings.
[59] *A History of the Sepoy War in India*, 1857–1858 (9th edn, London, 1896), I, 175.
[60] Etheridge, p. 60 (table).
[61] Ibid., p. 2.

temple dedicated to Mahaganpati,[62] Ranjangav was a relatively late
acquisition for the Dev lineage. Chapter 2 has previously described how
Moreshvar, the youngest brother of the sixth Dev of Cincvad, obtained
part of the village in 1768/9. Thereafter, the descendants of Moreshvar
took on the dignity of being the Devs of the Ranjangav Samsthan. A
junior line of descent of the senior lineage segment had thus begun its
own process of inam acquisition to provide for the ever multiplying
shares in its revenue. However, with the intervention of the conquest the
Ranjangav Devs had not secured what the Inam Commission considered a good title to their lately created Samsthan.

Until 1852 the Ranjangav Devs had no difficulty in preserving their
inam. Shortly after the conquest the Collector of Ahmednagar, under
whose jurisdiction the village then fell, issued orders to continue the
holding to Moreshvar. Soon afterwards it routinely passed to his heir
Cintaman alias (*ūrph*) Appa Dev.[63] Similarly in 1848, when Appa
reported that he had lost his sight, was on the point of death, and had
retired from the active management of the Samsthan in favor of his son
Anyaba, Bombay sanctioned the inheritance when soon after the elder
Dev died.[64] Four years later Anyaba, also complaining about his failing
eyesight and sensing his approaching death, attempted to secure the
quiet transition of Ranjangav's management to his son Ganpat.
Reporting the inamdar's subsequent demise to Bombay, the Agent for
Sardars suggested the village be again continued to the 'legitimate son
and heir.'[65] The succession was in all respects routine and without any
additional problems. Ranjangav had taken the precaution, apparently
successful in 1848, of forewarning the British of the impending change in
title of their inam. The agent recalled Anyaba's sanad prior to issuing a
fresh document; the Collector of Pune wanted to know whether

[62] PA: Shahu daphtar, nos. 1030, 10180 for documents on these inams.
[63] Pottinger to kamavisdar of prant Junnar, 15 April 1818 (copy of original in PA: XII; 5/172, Marathi proceedings); kamavisdar to Shri Bapu (Moreshvar) Dev, Ranjangav, n.d., accompaniments to petition of Ranjangav to Government (translation), 8 December 1853, BA: RD 1854; 82/1257, pp. 249–50; see Inam Commission decision no. 91 (Ranjangav), 24 February 1853, PA: XII; 5/172, pp. 158–67.
[64] Appa Dev to Agent for Sardars (translation), 11 September 1818, accompaniment to Agent for Sardars to Government, 14 October 1848, PA: IX; 4/54, pp. 4–8 (kaiphiyat of Appa Dev in PA: XII; 5/172, Marathi proceedings); Anyaba Dev to Agent (translation), 16 October 1848 reporting death of his father, accompaniment to Agent to Government, 16 October 1848; Government to Agent, 31 October 1848 authorizing continuance of inam, PA: IX; 4/54, pp. 9–12.
[65] Anyaba Dev to Agent for Sardars, 14 February 1852; Ganpat to Agent, 17 February 1852 reporting death of his father; Agent to Government, 6 April 1852, PA: IX; 4/54, pp. 17–23.

Ranjangav should be continued on his inam register.[66] Bombay, however referred the question to the newly constituted Inam Commission for a report on the village's tenure.[67]

Generally, when such a request came from Bombay the commission first made a survey of the accessible documents bearing on the claim. Pending a formal decision of the inamdar's rights, a provisional recommendation was made on the issue at hand. The usual procedure was to settle inams in turn as recorded in the collectorate alienation registers with preference given to claims to the revenue of whole villages.[68] However, an impending succession required immediate attention. If a doubtful inheritance was recognized then the implementation of a formal decision might be delayed for a generation. Depending on the complexities of a case, a considerable time could pass before a claim was finally resolved. The interim period before a succession was recognized had important advantage for the commission. Closer scrutiny of the case, the representations of rival claimants, and the consequent appearance of contradictory evidence often brought to light irregularities of tenure or succession.

The great number of Marathi documents required for an alienation settlement, all of which had to be collected, edited, copied, read and interpreted, put a considerable strain on the commission and delayed its decisions. Ranjangav, one village, took nearly a year to settle; claims of multi-village inamdars often stayed pending for over five years. In the daphtar, the commission's Indian assistants undertook much of the tedious but basic research. Without the knowledge and labor of these largely faceless 'Subassistant Inam Commissioners' the wealth of documentation referred to in this and the following chapter could never have been found. Their work was relied on to such an extent that the head of the commission would later defend himself against criticism for letting a written judgment stand in the name of one of his assistants. The commissioner had found that

some of the native Sub Assistants are at this moment fitted in point of ability to conduct enquiries which very few European Officers could ... successfully prosecute ... [they are] some of the best specimens of the educated young men of

---

[66] Agent for Sardars to Register, Sadar Divani Adaulat, Bombay, 6 April 1852; Collector of Pune to Government, 8 April 1852, PA: IX; 4/54, pp. 15–16, 24.

[67] Government to Hart, 12 April 1852; Hart to M. G. Gordon, Assistant Inam Commissioner, 7 June 1852, PA: XII; 5/172, pp. 6, 9.

[68] Apart from the obvious efficiency of this practise, the Court of Directors had specifically ordered this procedure, see Court of Directors to Government of Bombay, 20 June 1849 in 'Selection of Papers,' pp. 128–31.

this Presidency... Very little of the work for which I have received thanks could have been performed without their assistance.[69]

Of course, fears were expressed about the possibility of corruption; and the subassistants had to be reminded, for example, not to communicate with claimants.[70] Perhaps the Indian most trusted was Gopalrav Hari Deshmukh, a scion of the family that produced Cinto Vaman Deshmukh, a noted minister of the last Peshva.[71] The tradition of service to the state, and to the daphtar, was in this case recognized and Gopalrav Hari rose to the position of Assistant Inam Commissioner, where his opinions perhaps carried a weight disproportionate to his rank. Although it is difficult to prove conclusively, what are here given as the opinions of the Inam Commissioner were probably often those of the Indian assistants, the real experts in the daphtar.

Initial research on Ranjangav's revenue history soon revealed that 'the case is a peculiar one and seems to have been irregularly treated,' in fact, 'half of the village of the whole of which it is proposed to make over to Gunput deo [Ganpat Dev] belongs to Government and has been apparently unauthorizedly held as Inam since 1803/04.'[72] Hence, the inamdar would not 'be put in possession of any part of the village Ranjungaon until he should establish his right to it before the Inam Commission.'[73] He could not so prove. And eventually the commission decreed only nine-twentieths of the net revenue of Ranjangav as a personal inam of the male descendants of Moreshvar Dev.[74] In other words, government resumed more than half of the claimant's revenue, money which three generations had collected over at least 50 years. Such, then, are the bare facts of one of the Inam Commission's many decisions. An examination of the evidence on which the judgment was based will give some indication of the technical complexities of procedure and interpretation continually facing the commission.[75]

[69] T. Cowper, Revenue Commissioner for Alienations to Government, 29 April 1857 (no. 1299); see also no. 1294 of the same date to Government with remarks on the characters of the Subassistant Inam Commissioners, PA: I; 40/35, fols. 15–21.
[70] Cowper, circular to Subassistant Inam Commissioners, 3 October 1855, PA: I; 40/35, fols. 9–11.
[71] G. S. Sardesai, *Historical Genealogies* (Bombay, 1957), p. 64. The family is konkanastha brahman. Gopalrav Hari is well known in Marathi literature under the pseudonym Lokhitvadi as an essayist of liberal tendencies.
[72] Hart to Government, 17 September 1852, PA: XII; 5/172, pp. 18–19.
[73] Hart to Government, 16 July 1852, PA: XII; 5/172, pp. 10–11.
[74] Inam Commission decision, Ranjangav, 24 February 1853.
[75] Based mainly on the decision of 24 February 1853 and M. F. Gordon, Assistant Inam Commissioner in charge of Pune daphtar to Hart, 14 July, 1852, BA: RD 1852; 116/1522, pp. 163–71. This latter document presents the results of the initial researches into the tenure of Ranjangav.

Supporting his claim, Ganpat Dev produced a copy of a sanad of July 1768 in which Madhavrav Peshva granted Moreshvar Dev half of Ranjangav less the *mokāsā* (here 25 percent of the svarajaya or Maratha assessment). The village inams and haks that already existed at the time of the Peshva's new grant were also deducted from the gross revenues. Apparently desiring to reinforce the authority of the sanad, Ganpat tendered copies of this document sent to the Ranjangav village authorities and to the officers and hereditary district officers of prant ('district') Junnar.[76] Although it was not explained how the Ranjangav Devs acquired the whole of their village's revenue, copies of Marathi memoranda from government issued in the successions of 1818 and 1848, which the claimant retained in his possession, demonstrated the uninterrupted enjoyment of the inam up to the time of the inquiry. The British had therefore, according to Ganpat, already recognized the whole village as inam. In essence, an estoppel was pleaded, a legal defence against the commission more fully developed in other cases.[77]

The Inam Commission conceded the authenticity of all the evidence produced by the inamdar. The four copies of the sanad directed to different recipients were found registered in the Peshva's diaries (rojkirds). However, a close examination of the central records clearly demonstrated how selective Ganpat had been in presenting his documents. It was found that almost simultaneously with the grant of inam, the Peshva had issued a sanad allowing Moreshvar the management, as a *kamāvīsdār* (revenue collector), of the non-inam half of the village's revenue. Government's dues, presumably somewhat less than what was actually collected, were supposed to be remitted to Pune in the normal course of the annual revenue settlements. The commissioners found Maratha accounts showing the revenue had been received until 1803/4. From that date until 1814/15, however, the accounts had this receipt as being due from Moreshvar but not paid. The bureaucracy therefore did not formally pass the annual estimate of revenue due and collected from Ranjangav. Similarly, a list of devasthans prepared soon after the conquest noted Moreshvar as managing half the village in *kamāvīs*. But this had been held without the benefit of a sanad, 'by the idol,' that is, as

---

[76] Copy of sanad of 25 July 1768 in PA: xii; 5/172, Marathi proceedings. The copies sent to the authorities in prant Junnar are dated 26 July 1768.

[77] See for example the pleading of the English solicitor for an inamdar and the answer of government in 'Proceedings Relative to the Resumption of Certain Villages,' pp. 89–91, 97–106. The Inam Commission maintained that the guarantees of William Chaplin and other officers under the Deccan Commission, after Elphinstone had become Governor of Bombay and assumed responsibility for the Deccan, did not constitute 'a specific and absolute declaration by the British Government, or any competent officer acting under it,' Act xi of 1852, b, 1.

a religious grant, since the disruptive incursions of Yashvantrav Holkar into the Deccan in 1803.[78] The clear implication was that the Ranjangav Devs, without the intervention of the central authorities, had neglected to send the due revenue to Pune and then simply appropriated it as inam. Apparently, the Peshva at first could not, and the Deccan Commission for political reasons later would not, enforce the legitimate fiscal demands of the state. What remained unexplained, however, was why both administrations would countenance such an apparent fraud on the public revenues when periods of comparative peace had been restored.

After identifying the discrepancy in the claim, the Inam Commission set out the history of Ranjangav's internal revenue divisions in the order to determine what share was due government In 1768 the village's proceeds had been fixed as detailed in Table 4. The amounts given appear to be the highest recorded assessments, the *kamal*, and indicate only the relative distribution of the revenue. Of particular note is the equal distribution of the assessment between the svaraj and moglai, the Maratha and Moghul shares. This is another case where villages to the north of Pune on the fringes of the Maratha homeland (svaraj) were nominally shared, and where the continued denomination of a moglai portion inhibited the northward expansion of the Dev's inam.[79] Although in the late eighteenth century the realities of political power and certain boundary adjustments with the Nizam of Hyderabad had rendered the distinction an anachronism, still the Maratha government felt some compunction in granting in inam what was not properly theirs to give. The Peshva was therefore obliged to grant Moreshvar only one-half of Ranjangav. If the niceties of Moghul claims at the height of Maratha power seem too improbable, there was also the title of a prior inamdar to consider. Provision was therefore made for the already existing ministrants of the village Ganesh shrine out of the mokasa (here a general term for government revenue capable of being alienated), which significantly was also part of the svaraj. In fact, the village inamdar felt aggrieved at the settlement – he demanded one-eighth of the basic village assessment (*ain jamā*) – and so later in 1768/9 obtained the entire mokasa. Moreshvar Dev therefore received only 44.98 percent of the gross revenue. But as kamavisdar for the remaining receipts he was well placed to control both the village inamdar's share and government dues.[80]

[78] Govind Sakharam Sardesai, *New History of the Marathas*, 3 vols. (Bombay, 1946–8), III, 368–75 for Holkar in the Deccan.

[79] For a full discussion of this point see pp. 43–4.

[80] At least once prior to 1803 Moreshvar Dev, when acting as kamavisdar, was at odds with some villagers, presumably the ministrants of the Ganesh temple. Although

Table 4. *Revenue of Ranjangav, 1768/9 (values in rupees)*

I.	Village Assessment (*ain jamā*)		4454.00
	A. Svaraj		
	1. *jilhā bāb*[a]	1670.25	
	2. *mokāsā*[b]	556.75	
		2227.00	
	B. Moglai		
	1. *Jagir*[c]	1620.25	
	2. *phaujdārī*[d]	556.75	
		2227.00	
II.	Sardeshmukhi (10% of I)		446.00
III.	Miscellaneous assessments (*sivay jamā*)		645.50
	A. *mahāl majkūr*[e]	245.00	
	B. *kharc paṭṭī*[f]	196.00	
	C. *sādilvārid*[g]	152.50	
	D. *bheṭ*[h]	1.00	
	E. *ciṭṭī masālā*[i]	1.00	
	Gross revenue		5545.50
Deduct	A. portion of mokasa as inam to Narayan Baba Pathak for village temple	318.00	
	B. balance of mokasa	238.75	
		556.75	
	Net revenue		4988.75

Half share to Moreshvar Dev:	half share to government:
2494.375	2494.375
	238.75 (mokasa balance)
	2733.125 (Total)

[a] Literally 'district tax,' perhaps *bābtī* for bab, in which case this refers to revenue for the Maratha state.

[b] A general designation for Maratha state revenues capable of being alienated, as detailed below.

[c] Generally, jagir refers to a political revenue assignment. In this instance it appears to be the Mughal state portion of the village, equivalent to jilha bab, an inference supported by the identical figures for the two designations.

[d] This appears to be the Mughal equivalent of the mokasa. Literally, the term refers to the office of a magistrate or head of police (Wilson, *Glossary*, p. 158), or perhaps a military leader (Molesworth, *Dictionary*, p. 559).

[e] Apparently, this is a general designation for subdistrict (mahal) general expenses (*majkūrāt?*, Wilson, p. 337) allowed to hereditary district officers.

[f] Either a general tax for public works (Wilson, p. 279) or a tax to defray the expenses of public officers visiting the village (Molesworth, p. 199) or incidental village expenses in general.

[g] Either incidental village expenses, for example for festivals, or any contingent charge above the village assessment (Wilson, p. 452; Molesworth, p. 844).

[h] Present given to superior, as when revenue of village settled; like a najar (Wilson, p. 80; Molesworth, p. 619).

[i] A fee levied for the *cit* ('note, chit') by person sent to collect village revenue (Molesworth, p. 636).

With the authority of the revenue documentation the Inam Commissioner could be confident in his decision; to him it was

perfectly clear that one half of the village Ranjungaum minus the Mokassa Uml [amal] is all that ever was granted in Inam . . . It seems most probable that during the last fifteen years of the disturbed rule of the last Peishwa, the original grantee appropriated to his own use the Government share . . . and it seems quite certain that since the conquest of the Deccan this family have by escaping any searching enquiry continued to enjoy what never belonged to them.[81]

Calculating what government should therefore receive, the commissioner decided that one-half the high kamal assessment would not be demanded, but neither would the inamdar be allowed to remit one-half of what he collected, 'for with the management in his own hands he would as a matter of course turn it to his own advantage, and as in all similar cases Government would not receive anything like the half of the realizations.'[82] Furthermore, the prior claims of the family which acted as *pujārīs* to the village Ganesh had to be protected: 'Government are bound to see that his [the pujari's] share as well as that of the Deo's is equitably calculated, and (what is of more consequence to him) *placed within his reach.*'[83] The Ranjangav Devs would lose the management of the entire village, including the right to collect their own inam revenue, and henceforth the Collector of Pune would calculate and distribute the various shares.

The substance of this decision, issued under the authority of the Assistant Inam Commissioner, was transmitted to the claimant in Marathi summary.[84] However, procedure required that the judgment could not become effective until an appeal had been received and considered or, alternatively, until after the time allowed for lodging an appealed had passed. Ganpat Dev not surprisingly lost little time in registering his dissent with the Inam Commissioner. His first appeal was rejected.[85]

Moreshvar was apparently removed from office in 1777/8, it is not clear whether the order to this effect was ever enforced. See *Selections from the Satara Rajas' and Peshwas' Diaries*, pt. 8, vol. 3, pp. 160–1.

[81] Decision of 24 February 1853.

[82] Ibid.

[83] Ibid., emphasis in original.

[84] *Phaisalnāmā* (decision document) by 'kaptan Kaupar saheb asistan inam kamishanar' (Captain Cowper, Assistant Inam Commissioner), 24 February 1853, PA: XII; 5/172, Marathi proceedings.

[85] Minutes of proceedings in appeal, C. J. Manson, Inam Commissioner, 18 May–5 July 1853, PA: XII; 5/172, pp. 40–2, endorsement to Marathi phaisalnama of 24 February 1853.

The inamdar could then petition the Governor in Council for redress. Because this course had been expressly allowed in Act XI of 1852, it was incumbent on Bombay not only to receive a petition but to actively investigate the complaints made. Government could, if it desired, change an Inam Commission decision for any reason, be it legal, political or humanitarian. There was thus every reason for an aggrieved inamdar to present a petition, no matter how seemingly hopeless his case. In the 1850s Bombay appears to have been innundated with paper. Provisions for special mailboxes, the translation of vernacular documents, and anonymous petitions (to be disregarded) had to be enacted. The increasingly common English petitions, it was decreed, would only be accepted 'if couched in intelligible language, otherwise they will be returned.'[86] To ease the mounting workload government relied heavily on the opinions of the initial Inam Commission decision in deciding these special appeals.[87] Only occasionally did Bombay itself make any important changes to a decision. Nevertheless, these special appeals often uncovered additional facts about particular cases; the correspondence with the commissioners elucidates the reasoning behind certain actions; and perhaps most important for our purposes, the petition to Bombay was a chance for the inamdar to express his own understanding of his rights. Much, of course, is rhetoric. Often, the righteous humility of the petitioner is unbounded. Occasionally, the representations had more to do with the factional feuds between rival claimants than with substantive issues. But even these complications only add to our understanding of the relations between the British and their privileged subjects.

Ganpat Dev exercised his right to petition Bombay because, as he informed the Governor:

I requested in my Appeal [to the Inam Commissioner] that I might be favored with being informed of the grounds, upon which it has been said that the half of the village was held by Government, as no reason has been given for such a statement in the decision, but as the above grounds have not been explained to me, I have no way but to submit a petition which I beg your Lordship in Council to take into consideration.[88]

---

[86] Notification of H. E. Goldsmid, Acting Chief Secretary to Government, 23 May 1854, PA: II; 1/14, fols. 8–11.

[87] In fact, Bombay requested that the commission make marginal notations on the petitions answering each specific complaint. This procedure was first adopted in the case of Ranjangav, see Government to Inam Commissioner, 6 October 1854, PA: II, 1/14, fols. 2–3.

[88] Petition of Ganpat Dev to Government (Persian Department translation), 2 November 1853, BA: RD 1854; 82/1257, pp. 289–307 and PA: XII; 5/172, pp. 108–32 (copy in Marathi proceedings).

To better attract the notice of government two petitions were submitted: the first, quoted above, is a lengthy Marathi document, some 22 closely written pages in the Inam Commission's modi copy; the second, dated only a month after the first, is in a very corrupt English and included translations, or rather brief abstracts, of all important documents that went to prove the Ranjangav Devs' uninterrupted possession of their inam.[89]

Both petitions, beneath all their verbiage, made only two points apart from a general complaint about the unfairness of the commission's decision. Procedure first occupied Ganpat Dev. As indicated by the above quote, he believed the commission had not given adequate reasons for their judgment. Furthermore, he objected to the entire method by which doubtful claims were investigated. The statements of a claimant or appellant should be given more credence. The Indian district revenue officers, who might be expected to have some knowledge of the Ranjangav case, should have been consulted. In short, the Inam Commissioners relied far too heavily on written evidence. It was true, conceded Ganpat, the Ranjangav Devs had originally been granted only half the village. The commission's documents were not disputed. But this was only part of the story. Apparently in 1803/4 Moreshvar Dev had approached the *divān* of the Peshva, Cinto Vaman Deshmukh, to have the government portion of Ranjangav converted into inam as the Dev's half share was not adequate for the Samsthan's expenses. Although the Maratha government did not subsequently make revenue demands, still no sanad was issued; apparently, Ganpat's

ancestors frequently reminded the said Deshmookh about the deed, but he said that he would obtain permission to grant me [Ganpat's ancestor] a title on finding a good opportunity, & that as I was not pressed for the payment of the income,why did I trouble him for nothing. Thus the above Deshmookh said, and without his having had furnished me with a sunnud he departed this life, a short time after the British rule was established.[90]

And the Deccan Commission, when told of this verbal arrangement, had allowed the entire inam to be continued. Ganpat's version of events 50 years before his time is plausible enough, though impossible to check from independent sources. Such an arrangement would have made no difference to the Inam Commission even if it had felt inclined to believe unsupported assertions. Vague promises from an officer of the Maratha

[89] Ganpat Dev to Government (English petition), 8 December 1853, BA: RD 1854; 82/1257, pp. 241–8 (enclosures, pp. 249–57).
[90] Petition of 2 November 1853. Cinto Vaman Deshmukh died 2 March 1817.

government, or possible underhanded deals with such functionaries, were no legal substitutes for a good title, a sanad, however obtained.

Ganpat also strenuously objected to the interpretations of the Marathi documents. How could the Ranjangav Devs receive nine-twentieths of the revenue when the original sanad specified one-half? The point was made again and again, apparently heedless of the logic in the analysis of the revenue distribution. This was perhaps a more rhetorical than real objection because Ganpat did in the same petitions state that the Peshva had granted half the village less the mokasa.

A more substantial point concerned British understanding of the nature of the Samsthan's tenurial rights. Whatever weight the commissioners may have put on the wording of the original sanad, which clearly granted the inam to Moreshvar Dev, the endowment was intended as a permanent devasthan for the village Ganesh. Because the revenue was intended for the support of the idol, it must belong to the idol; the Devs were only acting on behalf of the deity. As Ganpat's English petition inelegantly put it: the

sunnud was granted not to the Grantee but to the God and this man's name has only been noted as the receiver for the Deo [the deity]. It does not imply that should the descendants of the original Grantee die, the village is to revert [to government] and it is strange to see such a conclusion come to.

Moreshvar's name was included in the sanad 'only because no other strangers should interfere in the management.'[91] The management of an inam was the only thing hereditary to the Ranjangav Devs. Because they would not technically be in receipt of any money, then government could have no objection to adoption or any other private arrangement to continue this hereditary descent. Indeed, in no sense could the inam be considered the personal property of the Devs. In the absolute sense 'the Inam belongs to Government,' but it had been given to the deity.

and the idol does not lose its existence on the extinction of my [Ganpat's] family, but it remains as it is. If per chance, there shall be no male heir in my family, the conditions mentioned in the deed for the hereditary continuance of the worship to my family cannot be fulfilled without the adoption of a male child ... [but] there shall never be an occasion for adopting a male child, as I have a brother and we both have 4 sons and have 3 uncle's uncle [Ganpat's father's father's brother's sons].[92]

Ganpat's concern over the misinterpretation of his position was therefore theoretical – it made no difference to the income he would receive – but still the objection was serious and one which preyed upon

[91] Petition of 8 December 1853.   [92] Petition of 2 November 1853.

the inamdar. That Ganpat's opinions, if put into effect, would have upgraded his inam in the British hierarchy of alienated tenures (from personal hereditary inam to permanent devasthan) may or may not have been incidental to his petitions.

Nearly a year after these first two representations Ganpat was still waiting for Bombay's final verdict. Two rather obsequious English petitions were sent to government:

since this country has come under the powers of the English, all do enjoy justice and what delights most is that the poor get immediate redress for their grievances... In short all do enjoy perfect justice and peace under the sway of the British.[93]

Again the various injustices of the Inam Commission were pointed out to the Governor. But the situation was becoming desperate for the inamdar. Pending the resolution of his appeals, the Collector of Pune had attached the Ranjangav inam, that is, collected the entire land revenue and held it in trust.[94] For the appellant of moderate means the final recourse to Bombay could have unbearable financial consequences, a fact the British were not unaware of.

Government referred all Ganpat's petitions back to the Inam Commissioner, who in turn handed the problem to the officer who made the original decision.[95] Not surprisingly, the Assistant Inam Commissioner felt 'that every argument now brought forward has been already weighed & disposed of.'[96] Ignoring complaints about procedure, he particularly attacked the interpretation of the documentary evidence that Ganpat offered. In no way, the commissioner maintained, was Ranjangav a devasthan; the original sanad clearly specified an individual as the recipient of a hereditary half share (less the mokasa of course). The commission's decision was therefore strictly equitable and consonant with the Peshva's intentions. The inam, it was allowed, had been granted to Moreshvar Dev for service to the god, but government in effect recognized this when it declared the Ranjangav Devs hereditary inamdars. Surely such a concession did not create a permanent devasthan held in trust for an idol. In addition, the Assistant Inam Commissioner could not accept Ganpat's apprehensions over the unlikelihood of an adoption to maintain this supposed trusteeship ever

[93] Ganpat Dev to Government (English petition), 10 July 1854, BA: RD 1854; 82/1257, pp. 233–6.
[94] Ganpat Dev to Government (English petition), 29 August 1854, BA: RD 1854; 82/1257, pp. 319–20. Two reminders had already been sent in May: memorandum from Persian Department, 1 June 1854, BA: RD 1854; 82/1257, p. 317.
[95] Inam Commissioner to Cowper, 2 January 1854, PA: XII; 5/172, p. 43.
[96] Cowper to Inam Commissioner, 6 February 1854, PA: XII; 5/172, pp. 44–6.

being allowed. 'No allusion whatever to this question is to be found in the Assistant Inam Commissioner's Proceedings.'[97] Such hypothetical objections had nothing to do with the plain meaning of the original documents.

Not only were the inamdar's representations rejected, but a hint of fraud was detected in his petitions. Among the documents Ganpat had appended to his English petition was a Marathi yadi to his father from the Agent for Sardars that, so the translation went, continued the Ranjangav inam 'hereditarily.'[98] The assistant commissioner went to the trouble of having this memorandum searched out and read;[99] what he found was

a false translation; the *original* letter to the Appellant has been now examined & found to contain no allusion to hereditary continuance; It remains for decision how this, which would it is believed be severely visited in an ordinary Court of Justice, should be dealt with.[100]

Passing his assistant's report up to government, the Inam Commissioner noted the alleged fraud, but remarked that the petition writer was 'probably one of those men who make a livelihood by this means,' and he had to be shown to be equally fluent in Marathi and English and, less easy to prove, had conspired with Ganpat to submit a false translation.[101]

Finally, Bombay considered all the proceedings in the Ranjangav case. Government agreed with the Inam Commission interpretation of the facts and refrained from altering the original decision.[102] Ganpat Dev thus lost eleven-twentieths of his inheritance.

Questions of procedure and interpretation were the main causes of dispute when a verdict of the Inam Commission did not meet with the complete approval of a claimant. Substantial inamdars such as the Dev of Cincvad shared the same apprehensions as their junior colleagues over the way the British went about their work and their sometimes unaccountable views on the nature of inam. In many ways, such concerns united the greatest landed magnates and the holders of the meanest inam in their relations with the imperial administration. But as

[97] Ibid.
[98] Yadi of H. Newton, Assistant Agent for Sardars to Anyaba Dev, 17 November 1848, translation accompanying Ganpat Dev's petition to Government, 8 December 1853; copy of original in PA: xii; 5/172, Marathi proceedings.
[99] Cowper to Agent for Sardars, 4 January 1854; Agent to Cowper, 11 January 1854, PA: ix; 4/54, pp. 29–31.
[100] Cowper to Inam Commissioner, 6 February 1854.
[101] Inam Commissioner to Government, 20 February 1854, PA: xii; 5/172, pp. 38–9.
[102] Government judgment, 16 October 1854, BA: RD 1854; 82/1257, pp. 311–13.

the next chapter shows, the alienation settlements could be transformed into something much more than a confirmation of good titles and the resumption of bad. Within the great lineages of Maharashtra the Inam Commission brought into the open factional conflict over inheritance and succession, solved by negotiation and compromise under the Peshvas, but which now, because of the active or passive support of the British, could conceivably be fought to a successful conclusion.

7

Claiming an inheritance: the Inam Commission and the Cincvad Samsthan

Although seeking only to settle title to alienated revenue, the Inam Commission became inextricably involved with the regulation of Hindu inheritance. This was particularly so in three related areas: adoption, the rights of widows, and varieties of inheritance within particular lineages. Adoption was an issue that in the pre-Mutiny period pervaded all British relations with their privileged subjects. Although it was preeminently a problem in the succession to (and lapse to the state of) princely states, adoption also became the central issue in the settlement of the Cincvad Samsthan to be described in this chapter. A consideration of the rights of widows as heirs and managers of inam follows naturally from the issues surrounding adoption. In essence, what part did a widow have in adopting a son, advocating his interests, or acting as his guardian. The critics of the Inam Commission only occasionally considered this aspect of Hindu inheritance; secondary scholarship has paid scant attention to the widow; but here, her anomolous position in Hindu lineages, especially her possible access to real power within the lineage, is a crucial theme. Varieties of inheritance, particularly the distinction between partible and impartible estates, have been examined in the first part of this book in connection with the way the Peshva arranged the descent of the Devs' inam. The quite special features of the Devs' inheritance would bedevil the Inam Commission's efforts to make a straightforward settlement of the lineage's inam. Related to this last issue is the general problem of what constituted a permanent institutional grant, particularly a devasthan, and further, how the management of such inam was inherited in a particular lineage. Underlying much of the narrative in this chapter is a debate, between the Inam Commission and claimant and also within the Dev lineage, about the degree to which the Cincvad Samsthan was a devasthan inam and thus an impartible estate.

All these are legal questions, and this chapter shows how a revenue settlement created case law on some of the great issues of nineteenth-century Anglo-Indian jurisprudence. Still, however, the main interest remains with the inamdar and the practical effect such problems had on his affairs. Sometimes the legal issues were manipulated for personal, factional or family gain. At other times they became points of heartfelt protest against the Inam Commission's seemingly ignorant or biased decisions. Whatever the case, always an inheritance was the object. Often it was hoped to win approval for a change in title to an inam. Perhaps most commonly, the manner of an inam's descent – from father to son – was obvious to all. The inamdar then directed his efforts to preserving his holding and have the British confirm his title. Such was the situation at Ranjangav, though even there the particular type of inheritance became a point of contention, at least in the mind of the claimant. When it was unclear who would inherit an inam, then the opportunity arose for the possible heirs to use any strategy to acquire the coveted inheritance. Still the estate had to be protected from the inquiring energies of the British and possible resumption. But often, as this chapter shows for the Cincvad Samsthan, fundamental problems of Hindu succession became the real issues in the alienation settlements of the 1850s.

I. From the Peshva to the Inam Commission

The Samsthan was the inheritance of the Dev of Cincvad, and the regular succession to this divine dignity throughout the eighteenth century had provided an element of stability to Cincvad's affairs. Although the Peshva had in part recognized the personal claims of the junior Devs, creating a partible estate for their support, leadership in Cincvad remained with the acknowledged incumbents to the 'Devhood.' In Shaka 1727 (1805/6), however, the death of Cintaman III, seventh Dev of Cincvad, ended the mythopoeic descent of Moroba Gosavi's sainthood.[1] A prophecy Edward Moor recorded in 1800 was uncannily fulfilled:

the divine donation was covenanted to continue but for seven generations:–whence on the demise of Bawa Deo [Cintaman III], the present heir apparent ... the holy incarnation unless perpetuated by farther miracles will, as an emanation from God, be absorbed in him.[2]

Perhaps even at this time it was apparent the line of the saints would not be fruitful. Lord Valentia found the seventh Dev in poor health and suffering from eye disease. Answering Valentia's enquiries, the Cincvad brahmans denied that the divine succession would end with the seventh

---

[1] See petition of Nirubai Dev (widow of Cintaman III) to Agent for Sardars (English petition), 23 June 1854, PA: IX; 4/59, pp. 133–9.
[2] Account of an Hereditary Living Deity to whom devotion is paid by the bramins of Poona and its neighbourhood,' *Asiatick Researches*, 7 (1801), 385.

generation, but would instead carry on to the twenty-first. Valentia thought the brahmans had 'not acted with their usual prudence,' and 'ingenious as they are, would have some difficulty in carrying on the imposture [of the sainthood].'[3] Adoption was the only possible course. The inheritance had to be preserved in the person of the Dev, eldest member of the senior line of descent. But the natural succession was broken in 1805/6. No matter how apparently successful was the eighth Dev's adoption, in the sense that it preserved the Cincvad inam, henceforward the Samsthan would be open to the conflicting claims of those who sought its leadership.

The boy chosen to succeed as Dev, Sakharam later assuming the name Dharanidhar, fulfilled most dharmashastra strictures on who could be adopted: firstly, he was young being born *circa* 1796; secondly, he was a younger son and not his natal father's sole heir; and lastly, being the son of Cintaman's cousin (ego FFBS = adoptive father), the boy was closely related to his adoptive father.[4] For the Devs the last point was perhaps the most important. Sakharam belonged to the lineage segment closest to the descent line of the saints. Perhaps, then, his segment had the best claim to the leadership of the Samsthan. In addition, the adoption of so near an heir would keep the personal inheritance of the Dev of Cincvad – his portion of the Dev partible inheritance – within a close group of kin.

Contemporary observers saw the adoption as a purely economic transaction. Sykes thought it 'a laudable determination to preserve the valuable bequests of the temple, and not without hopes of still further profiting from the credulity of the public.'[5] Similarly, Maria Graham, while noting the Cincvad brahmans' desire to continue the sainthood, emphasized the same points:

as the piety and superstition of the Deo's neighbours has enriched the family by grants of lands, and towns and villages, the holy Bramins have decreed, that the god is still incarnate in the family of Maraba [Moroba]; and to the objection that

---

[3] *Voyages and Travels to India, Ceylon, the Red Sea, Abyssinia, and Egypt*, 3 vols. (London, 1809), II, 157. See also W. H. Sykes, 'An Account of the Origin of the Living God at the Village of Chinchore, near Poona,' *Transactions of the Literary Society of Bombay*, 3 (1823, rpt. 1877), 76 where the prophecy is said to have been derived from a curse placed upon the impious sixth Dev, clearly an indication that it was then obvious the direct line from the saint would end.

[4] Pandurang Vaman Kane, *History of Dharmashastra*, 5 vols. (Pune, 1930–62), III, 674–85. See *Pune-nagar samshodhan vrtta*, vol. 2, p. 112 (in *Bharat Itihas Samshodhan Mandal Quarterly*, 14, 1 (July 1943)) for a contemporary document referring to the adoption. This is a query regarding the performance of shraddhas (*māhālay* and *paksa*), ancestral funeral observances, by the widows of Cintaman.

[5] Sykes, p. 77.

the promise was only to seven generations, they answer, that as the deity was able to grant the favour to the immediate descendants of the holy Gosseyn [Gosavi], it would be impious to doubt his power of continuing it to their posterity.[6]

This materialist view of adoption is perhaps best expressed in the words of a nineteenth-century authority on Hindu law:

notwithstanding the spiritual benefits which are supposed to follow the practice, it is doubtful whether it would ever be heard of, if an adopted son was not also an heir. Paupers have souls to be saved, but they are not in the habit of adopting.[7]

When considering inheritance, religious motivations for adoption – 'the souls to be saved' through funeral obsequies especially – will not be given the prominence they properly deserve. The feelings of the nineteenth-century Dev kin should not be entirely assumed from the cynicism of outsiders, whether contemporary visitors or modern historian. Certainly, the orderly and decorous descent of the sainthood, howsoever it was achieved, was of real importance. And this was an importance that transcended the purely economic. Without the proper religious rites, the reputation of the Dev of Cincvad, with his ritual preeminence and social responsibilities, could not have been maintained. An adoption was both a religious and secular act, and the lineage saw no conflict between its twin aspects.

To all outward appearances Dharanidhar's adoption did not cause any controversy. At least the available sources give no hint of rivals to the Dev. Apparently the Peshva approved the adoption, and the Cincvad Samsthan survived intact the last troubled years of Bajirav. The Peshva apparently had no cause to interfere in the affairs of the lineage, either on account of the adoption or any other reason. Likewise, the Samsthan was untouched by the initial impact of the conquest and the institution of British rule. Being under the protection of Elphinstone's benevolent political policy towards inamdars, the Dev's landed interests were mostly ignored for upwards of 30 years.

In fact, Dharanidhar's adoption seems to have been a decided success with the Samsthan continuing to receive new inams throughout the first decades of British rule. Bombay only infrequently alienated any form of revenue. A very few inams were granted in the first years after the conquest as a reward for political loyalty (or rather, deserting the Peshva). So for example, the village of Pimple Saudagar near Cincvad,

---

[6] *Journal of a Residence in India* (Edinburgh, 1813), p. 71.
[7] J. D. Mayne quoted in Jack Goody, 'Adoption in Cross-cultural Perspective,' *Comparative Studies in Society and History*, 11 (1969), 65.

in which the Dev held a village land inam, was awarded to an individual for military service in Khandesh.[8] Cincvad could not expect such favorable treatment from the new rulers. Even in 1808 the shape of the new order was obvious to the classes receiving inam; a visitor to the Deccan reported that

the religious and learned Bramins complain that, in the territories subject to, or connected with the English, the general reverence is daily declining for a religion, no longer countenanced by the powerful. No new foundations or endowments are to be expected under the English government; and the begging Bramins even complain of a sensible decay of liberality in our dominions. These complaints and apprehensions are probably not without some foundation.[9]

Nevertheless, the need to expand inam holdings to support the growing lineage of an inamdar was as pressing as it had been before the conquest. Native states and princes in part assumed the burden of the Peshva. The Shindes of Gwalior, for example, granted Cincvad their jagir village of Tandli in Ahmednagar district. Miscellaneous grants, mostly cash allowances, were received from Baroda, other Hindu sovereigns and even the Nizam, all of which would later become part of a disputed inheritance.[10]

For the Dev perhaps the first significant effect of the conquest was in the realm of law and the inamdar's right to civil and criminal jurisdiction over the residents of his villages. Decrying the interference of the British, in 1825 Dharanidhar put the issue to government in practical terms:

the Ryots [*rayat*] of the Enam Gaons [*ināmgāv*]... are continually creating disputes and quarrels amongst themselves, and prefer complaints to the Sirkar [*sarkār*, 'government'], by whom the cases are investigated, by this proceeding our power over the Ryots is weakened, to our great detriment. It is requisite that the disputes which arise in our villages should be referred to us, and we will investigate them and decide accordingly to the rules of justice without partiality.[11]

---

[8] Harold H. Mann, *Land and Labour in a Deccan Village* (London, 1917), pp. 38–9, 164–8 for correspondence and Inam Commission decision on this case. Sir John Malcolm particularly favored the granting of inam to reward services to the British, see minute of 10 June 1828, 'Proposed levy of a nuzer, or fine, on the renewal of grants alienating the land revenue,' in *Parliamentary Papers* 1831/2, XI, Appendix, pp. 534–5 for one example of Malcolm's many exertions to preserve and create a 'native aristocracy.'

[9] Robert James Mackintosh, *Memoirs of the Life of Sir James Mackintosh*, 2 vols. (London, 1835), I, 463.

[10] *Shri Dhundiraj Ganesh Dev v. Ganesh*, ILR (*Indian Law Reports*), 18 Bom. (1894), 721–33 where these acquisitions figure prominently. See also note 126 below.

[11] Memorandum of Dev of Cincvad to Government (translation), 17 October 1825, enclosure in Government to W. Chaplin, Commissioner in the Deccan, 25 October 1825, PA: DC 82/4935.

The Collector of Pune could not accept the grievance, it being 'only brought into existence when the god [the Dev] refused or does not grant justice to his Ryots who are in the first instance recommended to endeavor to obtain it at his hands.'[12] At this time the British were unsure what legal rights the possession of an inam conferred. While attempting to define inam in its revenue aspects, the Deccan Commission asked the collectors to determine what legal powers the new government held in alienated villages as judged against Maratha practice.[13] Generally, the British were unwilling to make any legal concessions to inamdars, particularly in criminal matters, if they seemed to undermine political authority in the new conquests. Apparently, the Dev's legal aspirations were in consequence ignored. At least, the same complaints about interference continued to come from Cincvad.[14] Eventually, some of the more important sardars were given varying degrees of legal jurisdiction in their possessions. Dharanidhar asked for his power to be confirmed. His request was denied because government did not believe he had such authority under the Peshvas.[15]

Dharanidhar's representations about the legal control of the rayats in 'his' villages hints at the problems in studying the inamdar's administration of his lands. During the British period there are indications Cincvad was chronically short of money and ill administered. These belie the outward appearances of tranquility. As yet very little documentary evidence is available on the nature of Dharanidhar's administration or his character, though such is likely to be found in the British collected documents in the daphtar. The Dev himself was described in 1820 as 'a vulgar, uneducated looking lad of twenty-four,' but this visitor was decidedly unsympathetic to the spiritual presumptions of Cincvad and found the whole spectacle of the living god 'a paltry exhibition.'[16]

[12] H. D. Robertson, Collector of Pune to Chaplin, 9 December 1825, PA: DC 121/2557.
[13] Mountstuart Elphinstone, Commissioner in the Deccan to Political Secretary to Bengal Government, 1 October 1819 in *Selections of Papers from the Records at East-India House*, 4 vols. (London, 1820–6), IV, 207 ff., forwarding answers of collectors to queries. See numbers 65 and 66 on judicial powers of jagirdars and inamdars: Grant (30 April 1819), p. 224; Briggs (13 June 1819), p. 247; Chaplin (25 June 1819), p. 262; Pottinger (8 August 1819), p. 292. See also R. D. Choksey, *Twilight of Maratha Raj* (Pune, 1976) for these queries.
[14] Agent for Sardars to Judge of Pune, 3 May 1831, PA: IX; 4/59, p. 9.
[15] 'A regulation for vesting certain jagheerdars, surinjameedars and enamdars with the power of deciding suits within the boundaries of their respective estates,' Bombay regulation 13 of 1830 in *Parliamentary Papers* 1833, XXV, 276–7. For the Dev's request see Dev of Cincvad to Government (translation), 20 March 1838; Agent for Sardars to Government, 23 August 1838, PA: IX; 4/59, pp. 17–22.
[16] 'Diaries of Sir William Erskine, First Secretary of the Society (1804–15),' *Journal of the Bombay Branch of the Royal Asiatic Society*, 25 (1917–18), 375. Lady Falkland

In his dealings with the British Dharanidhar was quite shrewd – certainly his achievements in keeping the Samsthan intact and increasing its revenues must be credited. But still indications of problems at Cincvad reached the British through petitioners requesting the district officers to intervene with the Dev. In one example a creditor appealed to the Collector of Pune to have a mortgage on the village of Carholi continued so that Cincvad's debts could be liquidated.[17] Another odd case reaching the notice of government concerned the Dev's jewels, which had apparently been appropriated by the jewel keeper (*jāmdār*) and pawned in Pune for Rs. 5000. The offender was caught and jailed, but the Dev could not raise the money to redeem the jewels. The Samsthan stood to lose Rs. 15,000, the value of the jewels. The collector refused to give the Dev the money needed to reclaim the gems. The transaction was peculiar: the thief conducted himself openly; the jewels were pawned in a fair and above-board manner; and the Dev later requested that his servant be released so the matter could be settled privately. 'It now looks,' concluded the collector, 'as if the case had been got up for the purpose of making a petition to Government for 5,000 rupees.'[18] As in the above incidents, the inamdar's internal affairs only occasionally reached the notice of the British in the first years after the conquest. Although outside the scope of this study, the financial administration and embarrassments of institutions such as the Cincvad Samsthan, and hence the possible economic consequences of the conquest on the inamdars, are important areas for further research.

Prior to the advent of the Inam Commission, the inamdar must have believed that the new regime offered unlimited landed security for his holdings. Perhaps unaccountably for the inamdar, the British had chosen not to enforce its legislation on inam.[19] Furthermore, responsibility for the village revenue aspects of inam was supposed to fall on the collectors. Being more occupied with revenue producing government lands (*khālsā*), they had not the time, reason or authority to interfere much in the inamdars' domains. The necessary tools for any type of inam settlement – the documents of the Pune daphtar – were not even in the collectors' easy grasp. The Agent for Sardars in Pune guarded the

(wife of the Governor of Bombay, 1848–53) received a secondhand description of Dharanidhar: 'a little wizen-faced man, with grizzled beard and hair which had not been shaved for some days, and in the very scanty undress of a Brahmin.' The Dev complained 'that with the multiplication of the family and defection and illiberality of his disciples, he found it very hard to maintain himself in respectability.' Lady Amelia, Viscountess Falkland, *Chow-chow*, 2 vols. (London, 1857), I, pp. 295–6.

[17] Robertson to Elphinstone, 10 April 1819, PA: DC 94/296.
[18] Dev of Cincvad to Government, 17 October 1825; Robertson to Chaplin, 9 December 1825.
[19] Bombay regulations 1 of 1823, 17 of 1827, see 173–4.

archive but did not look too closely into the record of his privileged charges. In any case, the agent's duties were mainly political and judicial, even though the bulk of the daphtar concerned revenue matters. In short, here was a new government that had no officer charged with administering inam, which was a situation unparalleled in preconquest times or even under the Deccan Commission. Perhaps the British just did not care about title to Deccan inams.

A generation passed after the conquest; inheritances were mostly allowed; revenue was collected each year in inam villages with minimal interference from foreign *sāhebs*. Certainly the British attempted to regulate certain rights if they were seen to infringe on the authority of the state. The exercise of legal jurisdiction in inam villages is one good example. Others include the state's connection with religion and the regulation of commerce (examined in Chapters 4 and 5). But by 1852 most inamdars could probably feel confident that their prime inheritance – the right to receive the land revenue – had been implicitly acknowledged. Furthermore, the right to have the inheritance descend in the time-honored manner, as custom and circumstance demanded, was seemingly beyond question.

II. The Inam Commission, the adopted son, and the widow

When Dharanidhar died on 2 September 1852 there was again no direct heir to the 'Devhood'. His only son had died two years earlier; the Dev left a widowed daughter-in-law, three widows, and the two widows of his adoptive father. Another adoption was imperative. September 1852 was perhaps the most inopportune time to attempt such a succession to an inam tenure. The Inam Commission had recently extended its inquiries throughout the Deccan, and any inheritance would come under close scrutiny. This would be doubly so in cases of adoption as Bombay had just completed, after extensive correspondence with the commission and research in government records, an exhaustive report on the legitimacy of such successions.[20] On 14 September 1852 instructions were issued to the commission: while government agreed with the opinion that it had the sole right to sanction adoptions, all new cases would be allowed upon proper application, pending a final decision by the Court of Directors. However, if an inam was grossly

[20] Memorandum of H. E. Goldsmid, 15 June 1852 in 'Correspondence Illustrative of the Practice of the Peshwa's Government Regarding Adoptions and the Circumstances under which Adopted Sons could succeed to Property held from the State.' *Selections from the Records of the Bombay Government*, n.s. 28 (Bombay, 1856), pp. 1–26; note also the many individual cases discussed.

mismanaged, or where the circumstances of an adoption were obviously suspicious, such permission could be refused. In addition, heirs previously adopted without government leave were to be denied the right to inherit an inam. Bombay did not want to consider the claims of an endless number of heirs who said they had been previously adopted for now lapsed holdings. In all adoptions the guiding principle was to determine if a valid financial commitment would be created: 'whether or not there is any reason on the part of Government to admit the liability of the State to the demand against it of an adopted son.'[21] Government had no interests where such a succession only affected the sharers in an inam against each other.

The Inam Commission thus had wide authority for the retrospective authorization of succession by adoption. It had to determine whether some relative of a deceased grantee (perhaps even his adopted son) would have inherited the inam if the adoption had not been made. In this instance the religious and private act of adoption made no difference to government revenues. If, however, a man (or his widow) without permission adopted a son from completely outside his lineage, or from a lineage segment not in direct descent from an inam's original grantee, then the commission was to deny this attempt to pass on a revenue alienation. Such adoptions were, to the commission at least, fraudulent attempts to alter title to an inam. It should be mentioned here that the commission generally conceded the religious validity of any adoption, and moreover, such an heir could succeed to the private estate of an inamdar. What was a purely private possession and what was, in strict terms, alienated public revenue did, however, cause much debate.

If the Inam Commission denied the validity of the adoption that was necessary at Cincvad, then the Samsthan's inam would be in danger with the inamdar (presumably the adopted son, though official refusal of recognition would have created rivals) fighting outright resumption. For many reasons, as will be seen, the Dev's holdings were never so directly threatened. But almost every other state intervention at Cincvad would create difficulties. If government took the negative course and declined to interfere because the adoption did not in itself assert a revenue claim, then the way was open for discord among the Dev kin and the growth of factional aspirations to the position and inheritance of the Dev of Cincvad. Any previously silent opposition to Dharanidhar's administration would find a voice and a cause. The same disputes that led to the Peshva's tahanama would be revived, and the whole effort of the Maratha state to settle the affairs of the lineage undone. On the other

---

[21] Government to W. Hart, 14 September 1852 in ibid., pp. 27–8.

hand, if the Inam Commission recognized any legal heir apart from the adopted son, it could find itself in the invidious position of supporting one claimant against another. In effect, the commission would become a factional ally.

In their haste to provide an heir to Dharanidhar, the Devs not only failed to satisfy the British, but the proposed succession did not meet with the approval of a great number of Dev kin. The most satisfactory action for all concerned would have had government, in the manner of the Peshva, recognizing an appropriate and legitimate adoption after obtaining a consensus of all contending parties. Such an arrangement could take place even after the death of the adopting party – the Hindu legal tradition is flexible enough to permit a widow to arrange an heir for her deceased husband.[22] But the British had no inclination to interfere in the practical workings of adoption. Demanding only that permission be first requested, government left the legal validity of the facts of a case to the decision of the courts. At the same time, however, suspicious adoptions – those concocted much after a property transfer or not properly performed – were taken as an opportunity to negate the inheritance implicit in the act. An inamdar therefore had to steer a careful course in arranging for an heir not 'of the body.' At Cincvad the whole business was botched by those who managed it.

Urgent memoranda dated 1 September 1852 were despatched to Bombay, the Agent for Sardars, and the Collector of Pune stating that Dharanidhar was very ill and had therefore adopted his kinsman Ganesh. The authorities were requested to overlook the lack of prior permission – the illness had been quite sudden – and were implored to accept a *fait accompli*.[23] If the suddenness of this development occasioned surprise, then the arrival of a second memorandum on the same day as the first, which stated that the Dev had in fact died, must have raised suspicions of gross irregularities.[24] The Agent for Sardars, at this time the officer most familiar with the affairs of Cincvad, reported that the adoption had been made by 'friends of the late Dev,' and 'when the Dev was insensible.'[25] Several months after the event, Cinto Mangalmurti, then the senior living Dev and preadoption uncle of

---

[22] Kane, III, 668–74.

[23] Dharanidhar Dev to Government (Persian Department translation), 1 September 1852. BA: RD 1852; 117/1557, p. 163; to Agent for Sardars, PA: IX; 4/59, pp. 114–15; Collector of Pune to Government, 9 September 1852, BA: RD 1852; 117/1557, pp. 177–8.

[24] Moro Udhav, vakil of Cincvad to Government, 2 September 1852, BA: RD 1852; 117/1557, p. 165; to Agent for Sardars, PA: IX; 4/59, p. 116.

[25] Agent for Sardars to Collector of Pune, 21 September 1852; to Government, 24 September 1852, PA: IX; 4/59, pp. 124–7, 151–2.

Dharanidhar, described the deplorable situation while at the same time placing on record his interests; Cinto blamed the servants of the Samsthan:

Moro Oodhow [Moro Udhav] and Suckaram Muhipant Soodoomburraykur [Sakharam Mahipant Sudumbarekar]... brought a boy, who belonged to another family and without adopting him with proper ceremony, sent letters and sugar to the Agent, Collector and other officers intimating to them the fact of the adoption of the said boy... Though I am an heir to the State [i.e., Samsthan] yet the affairs of it are conducted by another person, which is contrary to the rules of my family. I therefore pray that your Lordship in Council will order the affairs of the said State to be conducted by the nearest relatives until the said boy has formally been adopted and a stop may be put to the management conducted by a boy not adopted with proper ceremony.[26]

Several years later when giving a brief description of the unusual circumstances of his adoption, Ganesh also emphasized the role of the Samsthan's karbharis (Samsthan's 'servants'):

when Shree Dhurneedhur Maharaj was on his death bed, Moro Punt Appa Vakeel [Moropant Appa vakil, Moro Udhav], gave me to him in haste, and distributed sugar and betel and nut in the mansion, and throughout the village in demonstration of the joy of having got a son. As it was night time, there was no opportunity for the observance of the requisite religious rites. The ceremony of adoption did not therefore take place. On the death of the Maharaj I performed his funeral obsequies as his son.[27]

Ganesh confirms many of the complaints common throughout the Dev lineage. Eighteen Devs residing in Pune, for example, in a petition likely produced at Cinto Mangalmurti's instigation, repeated the same points: the appropriate ceremonies were not performed; the Samsthan's servants managed the adoption; and Ganesh was not closely enough related to Dharanidhar.[28]

Though the adopted son would not, of course, admit the last point, it was probably the cause of much of the dissent among the Devs. Between 1650 and 1900, 22 of the 343 successions in the lineage were effected by adoption.[29] (This is an adoption rate of 6.4 percent, comparable to that

---

[26] Cinto Mangalmurti Dev to Government (Persian Department translation), BA: RD 1853; 114/761, pp. 293–5.

[27] Ganesh Maharaj Dev to Government (Persian Department translation), 2 August 1860, BA: RD 1860; 70/588, pp. 67–73.

[28] Petition of 18 Devs residing in Kasba *peth* (quarter), Pune to Government (English petition), 13 June 1853, BA: RD 1853; 114/761, pp. 299–300.

[29] Based on genealogical table (*circa* 1900), PA: Printed Index, vol. 11, p. 366 foldout; manuscript copies (*circa* 1860), PA: XIV; 28/322, fol. 195 (English) and PA: IC rumal 11 (Marathi/modi).

found in the few studies examining the issue.[30]) Of these 19 were within
the lineage, and on average the adopted son was removed 3.68
generations from the first ancestor held in common with his adoptive
father (here calculating the number of successions exclusive of the
ancestor's generation). Ganesh was distant six generations from the
fourth Dev of Cincvad, his common ancestor with Dharanidhar, which
was the remotest adoption ever made within the lineage.

It is now possible to reconstruct the bare outline of the way the
adoption was arranged and why it engendered so much opposition. In
preface it should be noted that adoption did not completely separate a
man from his original kin. The point is recognized in the dharmashastra
with regard to the possibility of the son adopted out performing, in an
exigency, religious rites for his natal family.[31] There were also very
practical benefits to placing a son in another family. As discussed
previously, it was one effective way of preserving an inheritance from
dividing into an excessive number of shares.[32] But in addition, and this
is an inference not easy to support with documentary or statistical
evidence, an adopted son's natal kin might reasonably be expected to
have exercised some control over his acquired inheritance. This would
be especially so if the boy was in any case closely related to his adoptive
father, say a nephew, or when the widow did not attempt to act as a
guardian. Even after the adopted son became established in his own
right, it is likely that a residue of obligation and connections with his
original kin would remain.

Ganesh belonged to the lineage segment of Umapati, son of the fourth
Dev of Cincvad. (Lineage segments are those issuing from the tahanama
of 1744/5 analyzed in Chapter 2.) However, Ganesh's father was
descended from Jagannath son of Vishvanath (fourth son of the third
Dev Narayan) and was adopted into the line of Umapati. The natal
segment of Ganesh's father had, by the terms of the tahanama, acquired
the svaraj of Sudumbare village, and later separately obtained its moglai
portion.[33] Among those who managed Ganesh's adoption was, accord-

---

[30] One example is Adrian C. Mayer, *Caste and Kinship in Central India* (Berkeley, 1960),
p. 243 where of 146 land transfers, 5.5% were effected through adoption.

[31] Kane, III, 691–7. The point is, of course, much disputed. Note also the retention of
natal sapinda relations for marriage purposes.

[32] See pp. 75–7.

[33] See sanad of 29 January 1754, *Selections from the Satara Rajas' and Peshwas' Diaries*,
II, 2, p. 103 for the moglai. The Inam Commission decision on Sudumbare has this
document dated in Rabilaval (31 December 1753) instead of Rabilakhar, PA: XIII;
55/740, pp. 422–9. Note also the comment of Frank Perlin, 'Of White Whale and
Countrymen in the Eighteenth-century Maratha Deccan,' *Journal of Peasant Studies*,
5 (1978), 228, n. 37, though it is unlikely the Peshvas only obtained the village's moglai
in the 1750s as stated.

ing to Cinto Mangalmurti, one Sakharam Mahipant Sudumbarekar. Though it is not completely certain whether this individual was a Dev, certainly because of his territorial epithet he was closely associated with Sudumbare and its inamdars. When the time came for the adoption to the 'Devhood,' apparently Sakharam Mahipant through the Sudumbare Devs called upon Ganesh's father to provide his younger son as an heir to Dharanidhar. Being at Cincvad, in close proximity to the dying Dev and apparently enjoying his confidence, Sakharam Mahipant was obviously much better prepared for the succession than any other interested party.

Ganesh was chosen because by virtue of his father's adoption he descended from the fourth Dev and so belonged to a segment closer to the saintly line than any Sudumbare Dev. Moreover, he was just barely included in Dharanidhar's *sagotra sapiṇḍas*, those kin being, to use Professor Derrett's words, 'agnate[s] within seven degrees [i.e., six generations, Ganesh's case] counting inclusively from the adoptee to the common ancestor.'[34] Among the Sudumbare Devs there were few if any eligible sons within the correct degrees of sapinda relationship, most candidates being only sons or already heirs in their own right. Possessing, however marginally, the dharmashastra's preferred requirements, presumably Ganesh was thought acceptable for the divine inheritance. He was not. The petition of the 18 Devs shows the breadth of dissatisfaction. Representatives of almost all lineage segments, except those of Umapati and Jagannath (Sudumbare), signed.[35] Prominent were members of the most senior lines who all held the inam of sacred sites: Cinto Mangalmurti and his nephew Bajaji Govind of Siddhatek, Dharanidhar of the Ojhar Samsthan; and Ganpat of the Ranjangav Samsthan.[36]

Many of the details of the adoption remain obscure. The origin and role of the vakil Moro Udhav, who figures prominently in later relations with the British, cannot yet be determined. Nevertheless, it seems clear the adoption was an attempt to seize the Samsthan's management from within the palace (the Cincvad vada), so to speak. The dissident Devs had reason for their complaints, however much an adoption was needed for the good of the whole lineage.

Most of the details of this factional dispute were unknown to the

[34] J. Duncan M. Derrett, 'Adoption in Hindu Law,' in *Essays in Classical and Modern Hindu Law*, 4 vols. (Leiden, 1976–8), III, 63.

[35] In passing it should also be recalled that Umapati had in the 1760s challenged the partition of inam in the senior lineage segment of the Dev of Cincvad, see pp. 81–2. Perhaps Umapati's descendants nurtured a longstanding grievance.

[36] Petition of 18 Devs to Government, 13 June 1853.

district officers. The British saw no more than contending parties to a suspicious adoption. Hence, the Agent for Sardars was concerned with the question of official recognition – he was opposed – and the Collector of Pune wondered whether the Dev's inam should now be attached.[37] If government disallowed the adoption then presumably the Dev's revenue would be resumed, thus applying to inams a version of Dalhousie's basically political 'doctrine of lapse.'

The Inam Commission did not see the issues in such stark terms. Adoption was but one way to effect a transfer of revenue; Dharanidhar's estate could possibly pass to other heirs even without an adoption. However irregular the proceedings, the real question was 'whether Government have an [financial] interest in either sanctioning or refusing to recognize the alleged adoption.'[38] There was little point in refusing if the revenue would, by the terms of Act XI of 1852, be continued to some descendant of the original grantees. An initial check of the Marathi records indicated all Cincvad's villages were 'alienated at the introduction of the British Government.'[39] Bombay was advised not to attach any of the Dev's revenues, there being 'no prima facie probability' that disallowing the adoption would gain the state anything.[40] On the other hand, the adoption could not possibly be endorsed given the suspicions raised and the lack of prior official permission. In the commission's opinion government should take no immediate action at all apart from having the inam entered in the accounts as before, 'merely adding the name of the person who may be the late Deo's recognizable heir.'[41] Dharanidhar's eldest widow was thought the most likely choice for this role.[42]

Creating a 'recognizable heir,' who would in reality serve as a temporary manager of the Samsthan, had several procedural benefits for the Inam Commission. Firstly, Ganesh's claim would be delayed until after the adjudication of the heritability of the inam. The question of who was to inherit could thus be subordinated to the terms of succession. Such a calculating arrangement, leaving the adopted son in administrative limbo, would not, the Inam Commissioner believed,

[37] Collector of Pune to Government 9 September 1852; to Agent for Sardars, 21 September 1852; Agent to Government, 24 September 1852, BA: RD 1852; 117/1557, pp. 151–2, 157, 177–8.
[38] W. Hart, Inam Commissioner to T. A. Cowper, Assistant Inam Commissioner, 11 September, 1852, PA: XIII; 55/740, p. 20.
[39] Cowper to Hart, 24 September 1852, PA: XIII; 55/740, p. 20.
[40] Hart to Government, 21 October 1852, PA: XIII; 55/740, pp. 182-7; see also Hart to Government, 11 October 1852, PA: XIII; 55/740, pp. 169-70.
[41] Hart to Government, 11 October 1852.
[42] Hart to Government, 21 October 1852.

recognize 'any right accruing from his adoption, as a right *thereby created against Government.*'[43] At least this would be the case for the present. Conceivably Ganesh's position might be eventually recognized, or if the Court of Directors altered Bombay's still provisional rules on adoption, he might succeed at once. And with the widow acting as heir, presumably without aspirations of her own, the adopted son would have someone to advocate his potential claim. By avoiding any decision on the adoption, the commission would not, in its view, be regulating inheritance at all.

Interests close to the heart of the bureaucracy would also be served. Allowing rival claimants to come forward to dispute the adoption would bring to light any deceptions that occurred. The petitions of Cinto Mangalmurti and the 18 dissident Devs certainly justified this hope. In addition, because the accounts of the Samsthan, needed to settle tenurial questions, were in the hands of those interested in having the adoption recognized, 'if the alleged adopted son's claims are at once absolutely and finally negatived, they are not likely to assist with the information which would otherwise be afforded by them.'[44] As always, the primacy of documentation set the course for the Inam Commission; in this case records might be concealed or destroyed, and as a consequence, all inquiries would be frustrated.[45]

Preserving the Samsthan's management in the hands of the 'recognizable heir' would save the British revenue officers from managing the Dev's affairs if his revenue was attached prior to a settlement of tenure. The Samsthan could not be dismantled when under attachment; it had fixed expenses that had to be properly disbursed; someone had to control its affairs. It was not merely a question of administrative convenience – the task was not beyond the British – but active management would necessarily have created an official connection with idolatry. This the British were unwilling to do. Temple trusts and other impartial bodies lay in the future.

The Bombay government approved the Inam Commission's proposals but wondered why the inam would not eventually revert to the state. Did the commission mean that the revenue would not escheat during the life of the widows?[46] Government had not been told of the

---

[43] Ibid., emphasis in original.
[44] Ibid.
[45] Such as the fears expressed in 'Correspondence regarding the Concealment by the Hereditary Officers and Others of the Revenue Records of the Former Government and the remedial measures in progress,' *Selections from the Records of the Bombay Government*, n.s. 29 (Bombay, 1856).
[46] Government to Hart, 6 November 1852, BA: RD 1852; 117/1557, pp. 172–3.

many direct heirs of the inams' original grantees, and Bombay supposed it was being advised on the capability of widows to inherit, a possibility well known in the dharmashastra.[47] The inam act itself made provision for such a succession: during the life of a widow a hereditary holding could not be resumed for lack of heirs.[48] But this was seen as a charitable concession. The Inam Commission defined heirs solely by the precise wording of sanads. A literal interpretation of terms such as *putrapautrādi* ('sons, grandsons and such') left no doubt that only lineal male descendants were intended. Furthermore, no case of female inheritance couls be found in the Marathi records, nor in the practises of the Maratha native states. Females could not succeed to any property let alone inam. To strengthen the commission's interpretation of customary practices in Maharashtra, the Inam Commissioner, Captain Cowper, had even called upon elderly shastris to swear (on oath) that they had never 'heard of a single case of succession by a Hindoo female to Inams or other grants held from the State.'[49] In practise a widow would never hold an inam if her husband had so-called reversionary heirs (brothers, brothers' sons, etc.; uncles, uncles' sons, etc.; in essence agnates descendent and ascendant in six generations, the sapindas of the *Mitākṣarā* legal tradition) who also descended from an original grantee.[50]

The Inam Commission had no intention of making Dharanidhar's three widows his primary heirs. However, many complicating implications issued from a course considered to be merely a temporary expedient. The widows were placed in quasi-possession of an inheritance they might wish to claim as theirs by right. Yet they were supposed to be acting on behalf of a son whose interests may have been quite different from their own. The widows were not principals in the adoption – Ganesh was supposed to have been adopted by Dharanidhar directly, not by a widow for her deceased husband – and it may have seemed that they were now usurping the claims of Ganesh, his natal kin,

[47] Kane, III, 701–12; see also Günther-Dietz Sontheimer, *The Joint Hindu Family* (New Delhi, 1977), pp. 51–3, 83–4, 134–5, 151–2 describing the diversity of theoretical and customary views on this subject.

[48] Act XI of 1852, B, 9 (1).

[49] 'Report of Captain Cowper (to the Bombay government) on the Evidence of Mr. Warden before the Select Committee of the House of Commons relative to the Inam Commission,' 22 October 1858, BA: RD 1859; 95/97, pp. 316–36, paras. 42–6. This report was reprinted in *The Bombay Standard*, 22 January 1859; and *Parliamentary Papers* 1859 (sess. 1), IV, pp. 347–65.

[50] Kane, III, 701, 711; Sontheimer, p. 52 for the position of agnatic kin. For the elaborate development of succession order in Anglo-India law, based on the slim foundations of Yajnavalkya III, 135–6, see Sir Dinshah Fardunji Mulla, *Principles of Hindu Law* (Calcutta, 1932), pp. 31-42.

and those who managed his adoption. Finally, the widows were now blocking the rights of Dharanidhar's agnatic kin, his nearest relatives, who, expecting to inherit by the terms of British legislation, found themselves frustrated by the very officers who framed the law.

Management of the Samsthan's inam in itself placed the widows in an anomolous position. The dharmashastra allows a mother to manage property for her minor son, though perhaps the agnates have a better claim.[51] But at Cincvad it was unclear whether the widows had really been given any such standing. Were they managing on behalf of Ganesh who had no recognized inheritance, or were they simply acting as his guardian with limited powers over his potential estate? Or further, were the widows managing only for themselves and government if no succession was allowed and the inam was resumed after the death of the last surviving widow? Complicating the situation and unknown to the commission was a precedent for a widow's management. Dharanidhar's adoptive mother Nirubai had done so during his minority. The widows were thus being placed in a position sanctioned by custom within the lineage, but without a clear understanding of the interests they were serving. With the precedent of Dharanidhar's adoption in view, they could only be driven into an alliance with the adopted son and his sponsors while actively hindering the agnates' aspirations to the inheritance.

Cinto Mangalmurti conceded in principle the widows' right of management. But such a tradition tacitly recognizing the adopted son was inimical to his position. He therefore attacked the arrangement for the same reasons he objected to the adoption: it was all due to the manipulations of the Samsthan's servants. They had 'obtained an order from Government for conducting the affairs in [the] widow's names,' an interpretation that must have surprised government.[52] The present situation was unfavorably compared to that which prevailed under the Peshvas: 'when the said Dhurneedhur was adopted[,] Niroobae the elder widow and who was Chief heir to the State [Samsthan] conducted the affairs of it without contracting any debts, but on the contrary liquidated those formerly contracted.'[53] Cinto therefore put forward the claims of Nirubai, and the elderly lady (then aged over 70) had been prevailed upon to again take up the management:

---

[51] Sontheimer, pp. 50–1; Derrett, 'May a Hindu Woman be the Manager of a Joint Family at Mitakshara Law,' in *Essays in Classical and Modern Hindu Law*, IV, 126–37 for the resistance to this power in Anglo-Indian law.

[52] Cinto Mangalmurti Dev to Government, 3 March 1853.

[53] Ibid.

[the] three widows having taken the above Lady [Nirubai] to the State [Samsthan] requested her to take upon herself the management of the State. Whereupon the said Karbharis [servants of the Samsthan] having sowed the seeds of discord among them [the widows] adopted such measures as prevented the said Lady from having her hand in the management of the State which is contrary to the customs thereof. From this it clearly appears that they intend to throw the State into confusion to cause a loss in lands and to profit themselves.[54]

In other words, the widows were being drawn into the factional dispute, and at least one was already in alliance with the karbharis. As will become apparent, this must refer to the second widow, Laksmibai, who eventually became the chief advocate for the adopted son.

Failing the claims of Nirubai, Cinto proposed that government appoint a trustee to manage the affairs of the Samsthan. The elderly lady herself, in a petition to the Agent for Sardars, proposed a similar course because she believed the karbharis' mismanagement was scandalous.[55] They had created disputes among the Devs, particularly concerning the payment of allowances to the remoter kin. The private ornaments of the Dev had been embezzled (this accusation apparently went back to the 1820s). The Samsthan's revenues were not being collected or they were appropriated by village officers. Even the charitable activities of Cincvad had been 'fraudulently' discontinued. The widows did not, according to Nirubai, question any of this, and it would be pointless for government to question them as they were so completely under the control of the karbharis. The Peshva had deputed an agent to help Nirubai during Dharanidhar's minority, and something similar should now be arranged. Indeed, government had a special responsibility to intervene:

this Suwusthan is not like other Suwusthans. It is specified in the Treaty of the Pashwah, and in the original sunnuds, which are in the Suwusthan, that if this Suwusthan is not properly managed by the holder thereof, the Government is obliged to put their hand in it.[56]

'Treaty' is a literal translation by Nirubai's English petition writer of the Marathi tahanama. Even if the significance of this reference had not completely escaped the British, it is unlikely they would have accepted the Peshva's settlement as a precedent for taking up the management of

[54] Ibid.
[55] Nirubai Dev to Agent for Sardars (English petition), 23 June 1854, PA: IX; 4/59, pp. 133–9; see also her petition to the Agent for Sardars (English petition), 8 December 1853, PA: IX; 4/59, pp. 130–2 where she invites the agent to her 'humble cottage, which I trust will tend to maintain my respectability, being myself the wife of a Surdar,' for discussions on the Samsthan's affairs. The request was ignored.
[56] Nirubai to Agent, 23 June 1854.

the Samsthan. Nirubai's reasoning was novel nevertheless, even if the circumstances had completely changed, and after all, the widows had been placed in charge precisely to forestall such a state intervention. Incidentally, the Inam Commission did not even receive a copy of Nirubai's petition and so had no opportunity to assess the importance of the Peshva's 'treaty'. The settlement of the Devs' inam in fact proceeded without any knowledge of the tahanama, the most important document in Cincvad's revenue history.

Before examining the Inam Commission's tenurial decisions and their effect on the Dev lineage, some consideration should be given to the actual power of a widow when placed in a position of management. Even though her titular position may have been recognized in law or by government, was she ever more than a cipher for ambitious male relatives? No doubt this question demands a close study of the position of women in Maharashtra, which is clearly beyond the scope of this study. A few historical examples perhaps give some hints of an answer. One of the earliest Europeans concerned with such matters, when writing of the preconquest society, remarked that brahman women in towns 'have the character of being mercenary and fond of intriguing with the men of their own caste.'[57] Quite a negative opinion, but despite the connotations of being 'mercenary' and 'intriguing', this description could apply to many prominent widows in Maratha history. Notable examples include Tarabai widow of Rajaram and for many years regent of Kolhapur, Ahilyabai Holkar the 'saintly' regent of Indore, and the widows of Mahadaji Shinde who took to the battlefield to claim their rights.[58] These were exceptional cases, but the standing of the female

[57] Thomas Coats, 'Account of the Present State of the Township of Lony,' *Transactions of the Literary Society of Bombay*, 3 (1823, rpt. 1877), 234.
[58] Govind Sakharam Sardesai, *New History of the Marathas*, 3 vols. (Bombay, 1946–8), Tarabai: I, 371–3, II, 20, 130–1, 284–5, 310–12; Holkar: III, 211–14; Shinde, III, 337–42.
  The case of Tarabai is particularly interesting, see Brij Kishore, *Tara Bai and Her Times* (Bombay, 1963), though the author never comes to terms with the main fact that his subject was a woman. See the revealing comments of Khafi Khan: 'she was a clever intelligent woman, and had obtained a reputation during her husband's lifetime for her knowledge of civil and military matters.' Also, 'Tara Bai... took the reins of government into her own hands. She took vigorous measures for ravaging the Imperial territory... She won the hearts of her officers.' H. M. Elliot and John Dowson, *The History of India as Told by its own Historians*, 8 vols. (rpt. Allahabad, 1964), VII, 367, 373–4.
  The point could be made here that the widows in these three examples were not brahmans, but rather Maratha and *dhangar*. Perhaps it can be argued that non-brahman widows had more freedom of action than their brahman counterparts. Apart from Coats' opinions above quoted, the case of Dharanidhar's three widows perhaps gives my argument some general validity.

regent was ambiguous enough that resourceful women could put themselves into positions of real power.

Perhaps the position of a widow reflected in part the power and status of the family from which she was given in marriage. Patrilineal descent, however, tends to obscure such connections. In the case of the Devs, the historical sources are almost completely silent on this point. Dharanidhar's widows appear to have come from the Hingne lineage, well known in connection with the religious center of Nasik and also as representatives of the Peshva in north India.[59] Presumably the Devs sought wives from such well-placed desashtha brahman families, so creating wide networks of influential social connections.[60] Evidence suggests a woman could call upon her original lineage for support during her widowhood. For example, Dharanidhar's eldest widow was at Nasik, apparently with the Hingnes, when she died; the second widow's brother resided in Cincvad and served as her adviser.[61] Making advantageous marriages created powerful widows who could not be dismissed as mere outcasts of the patrilineage. In this connection it is significant that documents such as the tahanama always make adequate, even generous provision for widows.[62] They were just too important to be passed over lightly.

Before 1857 Dharanidhar's widows appear to have been completely under the influence of the Samsthan's servants. In this year the eldest widow died and the second, Laksmibai, assumed the temporary management of the Samsthan on orders of government.[63] This lady emerges as a power and personality in her own right. Ganesh for one eventually (in 1860) expressed the strongest opinions on the character and actions of his guardian. Laksmibai had, he claimed, imprisoned Dharanidhar's third widow, widowed daughter-in-law and himself in

---

[59] According to Nirubai (petition of 23 June 1854) the widows were related to Amrtrav Purusottam Hingne, perhaps the grandson of Devrav Hingne, ambassador of Nana Phadnis to the Holkars. On the Hingnes see G. H. Khare, 'A Note on the Family Records of Peshwas' Agents at Delhi,' in *Select Articles* (Pune, 1966), pp. 103–9; *Hingne daphtar*, 2 vols. (Pune, 1945–7).

[60] Apparently Dev daughters were not in return much sought after. Moor, p. 389, observes: 'it did not occur to me to inquire if the females were peculiarly estimable [i.e. divine]–I judge not very highly so from never having heard of exalted personages seeking them as wives.' Perhaps this reflects the Devs' desire to create upward social links with more powerful inamdars and jagirdars, with such worthies not considering Dev daughters in return to be good matches for their lineage.

[61] Pseudonymous petition to Government (Persian Department translation), 3 October 1860, PA: XIV; 28/322, fols. 299–300, see also note 63 below.

[62] Four widows received between Rs. 56 and 300 each, then substantial amounts for the support of one person.

[63] Collector of Pune to Government, 15 April 1857 and further correspondence, PA: XIII; 55/740, pp. 127–30, 135–6.

the Cincvad vada. The rival widows were subjected to the greatest of 'privations as regarding wearing apparel, and even the use of the privies.'[64] What made this even worse was Laksmibai's lamentable personal conduct:

she has sold the wearing apparel, jewellery and gold and silver ornaments, and even the copper and brass pots, belonging to the Sunsthan, adopted the worship of Shuktee [*śakti*, source of female energy], and licentiously abandoned herself to liquor and other luxuries, as well as to fornication and other iniquitous indulgences in an unrestrained manner. This course she has secretly carried on for a length of time. She has now broken out openly, and spends thousands of Rupees... with a view to secure herself a continuance of the proprietorship of the Sunsthan.[65]

She could, moreover, strike down her opponents by sorcery or poison; it was common knowledge that such fates befell Dharanidhar and his only son. Ganesh feared for his life if his representations were made public. His situation was intolerable. 'Outwardly I am held forth as the proprietor; but at home I am not permitted to exercise the power of proprietorship in any matter whatever.'[66] Still he performed the requisite religious ceremonies in memory of his adoptive father and acted out the ritual of the Dev of Cincvad. Such could only be done by a male, and in Ganesh's opinion, 'ladies have no privilege beyond subsistence,' but the Samsthan's servants had given Laksmibai hope 'of becoming the sole proprietress of the Sunsthan.'[67]

Whether all these startling allegations are true is uncertain. Government refused to investigate if Ganesh would only publicly repudiate his petition. Perhaps he only intended the scandal to advance his own interests, which by 1860 were becoming increasingly separate from every other potential heir. Nevertheless, the tenor of this remarkable document lends some credence to an impression that Laksmibai's forceful dealings with the Inam Commission after 1857 reflect both the character of the lady and the striving of a widow to assert her rights as a legitimate heir and manager of an inheritance.

III. Inam, devasthan, and the lineal male descendant

In 1852 Bombay had been of the opinion 'that an early inquiry into the [Cincvad] case appears most desirable.'[68] But not until mid-1859 did the

---

[64] Ganesh (Ganpati Maharaj) to Government, 2 August 1860, BA: RD 1860; 70/588, pp. 67–73.
[65] Ibid.   [66] Ibid.   [67] Ibid.
[68] Government to Inam Commissioner, 6 November 1852.

Inam Commission take up the question of the succession to the Devs' inam. Although the Mutiny briefly suspended the alienation inquiries, nearly the whole of the seven years was needed to evaluate the massive amount of evidence on the tenure of 23 villages. These constituted most but not all of the major alienations. Revenues from fields, minor amals, holdings in the Konkan, and those granted by native princes were not at first considered. Even then, approximately 800 documents required examination. In addition, extensive extracts from the Peshva's rojkirds and the revenue accounts of the Maratha government had to be prepared. Copies of sanads and similar documents, depositions from claimants, village land summaries (*jāmīn jhāḍā va hiśeb*), and other proceedings for Haveli taluka alone occupy a manuscript volume of some 700 pages.[69]

Except in three cases, the Devs' villages were declared personal holdings to descend to the lineal male descendants of the original grantees. The tenure of Theur, Morgav and Siddhatek was interpreted to be devasthan, inam of the deities of those villages, but managed by the Dev of Cincvad. Even though the title to Cincvad's inam was solid – unlike that of the Ranjangav Devs – the decisions were bound to be unacceptable to the inamdar. Why should only sacred sites be devasthan while all other villages were considered personal holdings? Were not all grants meant for the support of the Samsthan, the Dev and hence the deity Ganesh? Cincvad in particular, with its renowned temple of Moroba Gosavi's samadhi, should have been declared a devasthan. The inamdar's objections are familiar. The Ranjangav Devs said much the same; similar points were made again and again in the inquiries into non-landed revenue, as described in Chapters 4 and 5.

However, two things distinguish the history of Cincvad's landed inam from these other examples. Firstly, the Samsthan did eventually succeed in having the British in part recognize its right to devasthan, even if the victory was only an example of administrative convenience. Secondly, the appeal for devasthan had implications quite beyond the solely religious, or even tenurial. It was one strategy to retain possession of the Samsthan argued by those who already held the inam. The reasoning behind this tactic will shortly become clear.

What remained obscure from the Inam Commission's tenurial decisions was the identity of the lineal male descendant. There were so many heirs tracing their ancestry back to the grantees of Cincvad's inam

[69] PA: IC rumal 11. For a summary of the results of the inquiry and bibliographic details, see Laurence Wade Preston, 'Land, Lineage and the State in Maharashtra: The Devs of Cincvad under the Maraths and the British,' (Ph.D dissertation, University of Toronto, 1984), Appendix B, pp. 400–04.

that the Inam Commission recognized the unlikelihood of Ganesh's adoption affecting the interests of government. No revenue could be expected through resumptions. Still, there were

good grounds... in declining to recognize the adoption

1st. The notorious bad character of the late Dhurneedhur Deo.
II. The distant relationship of the boy alleged to have been adopted.
III. The doubt connected with the ceremony itself.
IV. The objection to the adoption raised by many members of the family.[70]

The first point, mainly accusations about the profligacy of the late Dev, was irrelevant to the issue at hand. The other three, though important legal questions on Hindu adoption, also sidestepped the real issue of 1852–the lack of prior authorization. By accepting the objections of Cinto Mangalmurti and the dissident Devs and dwelling on the general dissatisfaction within the lineage, the Inam Commissiner could only recommend the Ganesh's position not be sanctioned as it would infringe 'the rights of the lineal male heirs.'[71] Bombay agreed. Bajaji Govind, the senior member of the lineage since the death of his uncle Cinto Mangalmurti, would be considered inamdar and his name entered in the public accounts as such.[72]

Within a week of the commission's decision being issued, Bajaji Govind made application to be put in possession of the Samsthan, and so to be recognized Dev of Cincvad. But only at the end of 1859 did the Collector of Pune respond to his request: it could not be done. In the collector's judgment, as it was communicated to Bajaji Govind, only a change in the accounts had been ordered, not a transfer of management. Laksmibai retained the inheritance, a situation Bajaji Govind abhorred: 'the ladies have no right to the Inam estate, they are at present in possession only in consequence of a temporary arrangement and not by virtue of any right.'[73] He would, of course, provide due maintenance for the widows. And he invited anyone who disputed his position as Dharanidhar's legitimate heir to launch a civil action and sue for possession of the Samsthan. Eventually Bajaji's demand for management of the Samsthan was approved;[74] surely, as the Inam Commissioner put it, 'Government did not... intend to confer on the Senior

---

[70] P. Dods, Inam Commissioner Northern Division to T. A. Copwer, Revenue Commissioner for Alienations, 31 May 1859, PA: XIII; 55/740, pp. 152–7.
[71] Ibid.
[72] Government to Cowper, 2 July 1859, BA: RD 1859; 6/844, p. 15.
[73] Bajaji Govind to Dods (English petition), 23 March 1860, PA: XIV; 28/322, fols. 351–4.
[74] Government to Cowper, 24 April 1860, BA: RD 1860; 70/588, pp. 62–3.

member of the family the empty honor of having his name entered in the Public accounts, but they meant that his rights should not be interfered with.'[75] Provision first had to be made for the widows, and after negotiations, not surprisingly Laksmibai 'expresse[d] the strongest objections to Bujajee's proposal to pay her Rs. four hundred.'[76]

One reservation that arose over immediately handing the Samsthan to the senior agnate concerned the distribution of revenues within the lineage. The Inam Commissioner had noticed (or perhaps was told) that 'several villages... are now and have been for generations managed by other branches of the family with the sanction of the Peshwa,' and therefore 'these [rights] must not be interfered with.'[77] For the moment this oblique reference to the tahanama was ignored, and the commission passed on to more pressing matters.

How could Bajaji's name be entered in the accounts, Laksmibai protested, if the tenure of Cincvad's inam had not been settled – 'final decisions have not yet been passed' – there remained the appeal process.[78] In mid-1860 the possibility of an impending change of the Samsthan's management became distinct. The widow (now describing herself as 'The Manager of the Grants to the Shree Deo') again asked that the transfer be postponed because she was at last ready to proceed with her special appeals to Bombay. Government acceded to her request. All previous instructions to the Collector of Pune were held in abeyance. The hopes of the lineal male descendant were again frustrated.[79]

The complex case Laksmibai put forward in appeal contains a convoluted argument meant in the end to show why her control of the Samsthan should not be disturbed. The key to her submissions was the use of the concept of devasthan in the inam act and its application to Cincvad's holdings. In summary, a religious endowment would not invariably descend to the lineal male descendant, it remaining in theory the eternal possession of a deity. The British had no interest in regulating the hereditary management of a devasthan because no financial liability

[75] Dods to Cowper, 30 March 1860, PA: xiii; 55/740, pp. 451–4.
[76] Collector of Pune to Dods, 26 June 1860, PA: xiii; 55/740, pp. 212–13.
[77] Dods to Cowper, 31 March 1860.
[78] Petition of Laksmibai to Government (Persian Department translation), 22 September 1859, BA: RD 1859; 6/844, pp. 17–26. This petition contains an explicit reference to the tahanama, but the petition was not forwarded to the Inam Commission. Instead, government was more concerned with denying the assertion that Ganesh's adoption had been recognized in 1852, see Government to Revenue Commissioner for Alienations, 12 December 1859, BA: RD 1859; 6/844, pp. 29–31.
[79] Petition of Laksmibai to Government (English petition), 1 June 1860; Government to Cowper, 16 June 1860, BA: RD 1861; 36/568, pp. 193–7; Cowper to Collector of Pune, 3 July 1860, PA: xiv; 28/322, fol. 363 verso.

was created, and further, because government had supposedly severed all connections with idolatry. Who managed a devasthan was therefore a matter of personal and customary law beyond the jurisdiction of the Inam Commission. Perhaps paradoxically, Laksmibai maintained that the Dev's management, which derived from custom and was sanctioned by partitions within the lineage, determined the tenure of his inam. The Cincvad Samsthan was devasthan because it was managed by the Dev.

We should not doubt the sincerity of the Devs when they described their inheritance as devasthan. The Ranjangav Devs, to cite another instance, made this claim when it made very little difference to the adjudication of their tenurial rights. But at Cincvad the short-term and distinctly Machiavelian object of the widow's appeal is clear. The Inam Commissioner understood this and was cynical: 'the principal object apparently in making this appeal is to prevent the senior male representative of the family succeeding to the village as a personal holding.'[80] In fact, the commissioner did not think any claim for devasthan had ever previously been registered from Cincvad. Laksmibai had no other alternative but to make such an appeal. The leadership of Cincvad was in the process of being removed from where, when judged against tradition, it probably rightly belonged. The British had to be convinced of the rightness of her cause in their own terms: through their own procedure, with evidence and argument couched in their legal framework, and with a real comprehension of the implications of Act XI of 1852. In the following paragraphs the way Laksmibai's appeals were constructed is examined in detail.

In common with most inamdars, Laksmibai thought the commission's procedures objectionable. An appellant had no hope of obtaining justice. In her case,

the decisions [were] passed by the Assistant Enam Commissioner Mr. Dods, I appealed to the Enam Commissioner, which also were examined by himself [Dods] having in the mean time been raised to that post, and thus it is no wonder that he confirmed his late decisions.[81]

Recommendations on the management of the Samsthan had been made without any consultations with the widow, and far too much reliance was put on petitions she was given no opportunity to answer. Important evidence was therefore ignored: 'decisions of the late Peshwa and present Government' had not been sought out. Because of these omissions, 'nobody has suffered so much wrong at the hands of the

---

[80] Inam Commission in appeal, 3 March 1860 attached to decision on Cincvad, 31 March 1859, PA: XIII; 55/740, pp. 289–303; PA: XIV; 28/322, fols. 109–14 (fair copy).
[81] Laksmibai to Government, 1 June 1860.

Enam Commissioners as we [Laksmibai and Ganesh] have now suffered.'[82]

The widow's appeals spent much effort in proving (or merely asserting) that there could be no objections to Ganesh's adoption. The religious ceremonies had in actuality taken place when the late Dev was alive. Ganesh performed all the requisite obsequies, the daily worship in the temple, and all the other duties of the Dev of Cincvad including the Morgav pilgrimage. At the time of the adoption there had been a hundred brahmans in Cincvad who raised no objections. Even Bajaji Govind, Laksmibai maintained, had no complaints at first and had even admitted as much in a letter to the Samsthan's karbharis. This elusive document had subsequently been seen by the mamlatdar of Haveli and must therefore be some place in the government records.[83] Pure opportunism, accomplished through the manipulation of the provisions of the inam act, was then Bajaji's sole motivation. If only government would recognize Ganesh's position, most of the widow's difficulties would be at once removed.

Whatever government or anyone else may have thought about the adoption in any case made little difference to the Samsthan's management. The Inam Commission could only determine the tenure of an alienation and pass judgment on the future length of possession. A revenue decision, according to Laksmibai, 'gives... no power to dispossess one incumbent, and transfer his right to another, in spite of possession... The Inam Commissioner nevertheless made such an attempt in my case three or four times, as indeed he admits in his decision.'[84] The facts of the situation were obvious: the widow held the estate in trust for the adopted son who was the *de facto* Dev of Cincvad. Anything the Inam Commission did could not dislodge him, for 'none but Civil Court has the power of determining the validity or otherwise of his adoption: in as much as it does not, either favorably or prejudicially, affect the interests of Government.'[85] A change in the Samsthan's management had therefore been mistakenly ordered at the instigation of officers not legally competent to make such recommendations.

Because the Samsthan was in Laksmibai's opinion a devasthan, there was even less reason for dispossessing its present proprietors. Citing

[82] Ibid.
[83] Petition of Laksmibai to Collector of Pune (Collector's translation), 23 June 1860, PA: XIV; 28/322, fols. 100–8. This document is an appeal on Cincvad village.
[84] Petition of Laksmibai to Government (Persian Department translation), 6 June 1860, PA: XIV; 28/322, fols. 100–8. This document is an appeal on Cincvad village. Similarly worded petitions were simultaneously submitted for Bhosri, Cincoli, Man and Carholi.
[85] Ibid.

regulations and circulars from Bombay, she pointed out that the Court of Directors had severed all connections with religious institutions and idolatry. How then could the British now interfere with the management at Cincvad? Left unsaid in all the widow's petitions, but surely understood in Bombay, was the fact that the inam act was quite vague on the manner of succession to the management of a devasthan.

Through the spirit and letter of the Samsthan's sanads, Laksmibai thought she could prove that Cincvad's inam was a religious endowment. Anyone could see that the first duty of the Dev of Cincvad was the worship of the deity Ganesh. The sanads had recognized this, and they often granted the inam for the support of the charities, worship and ceremonies of the Dev. Had not the Inam Commissioner himself in his decision on Cincvad village declared that the revenue had been given 'hereditarily for the support of the Ceremonies connected with the Chinchore Saosthan?'[86] In addition, the Maratha government accounts consistently debited the inam under the head of devasthan.

In Laksmibai's opinion, the commissioner had further misread the evidence when he insisted individuals and not the deity were referred to in the Marathi documents. In his original appeal proceedings he had 'treated the Estate as a personal Inam by employing an unreasonable argument that the grantee professed himself to be [an] incarnate [deity].'[87] Relying on popular traditions of the Dev's divinity, the commissioner believed grants had necessarily been made to a person because there was, in fact, no deity at Cincvad except the Dev.[88] Laksmibai easily dismissed this superstitious misapprehension: 'this erroneous decision has been passed simply because the name of my family happens to be 'Deo'.'[89] When the sanads said the inam was granted to śrī dev vāstavya (resident of) Cincvad or similar expressions, they were referring to dev in the sense of 'the Cincvad deity,' and the temple in the village where this god resided was known to all. For this reason there could be no possibility of the Dev having received a personal grant. Perhaps Laksmibai could have argued that because the Dev was a god, or at least considered as such by those who endowed Cincvad, then the inam had to be devasthan. Such a position, in many ways the Dev's own conception of his status, was probably thought

[86] Cincvad decision, 31 March 1859.
[87] Petition of Laksmibai to Government (Persian Department translation), 2 July 1860, PA: xiv; 28/322, fols. 89–97. This appeal encompasses nine villages.
[88] Act xi of 1852, B, 7(6) expressly states that grants to specific individuals 'for the performance of ceremonial worship' were to be treated as personal inams. It seems that Laksmibai misunderstood the Inam Commissioner's reasoning, or perhaps he was being facetious.
[89] Laksmibai to Government, 6 June 1860.

unlikely to appeal to the rational British. Instead, the widow countered the Inam Commission's somewhat facile dismissal of the Dev's divinity with her own rationalism.

The tahanama, which the commission had ignored, conclusively proved all the widow's contentions. It superseded all previous sanads, she maintained, and must be taken as the former government's definitive view of Cincvad's inam. When describing the provisions of the Peshva's settlement, Laksmibai emphasized the partition of the inam into Samsthan and lineage interests: much of the revenue was 'distinctly specified as the property of the temple; and assigned for the family, with a declaration that it should perform service in the temple.'[90] The management of the institution was entrusted to the line of the saints, now continued by adoption, and for this and all previously stated reasons government had no interest in the Samsthan's management.

Recognizing, however, that the tahanama could be construed as creating both personal and devasthan inam, the widow thus appealed most vigorously for those villages held entirely by the Samsthan. Individual and nearly identical petitions were submitted for each. All other villages and lands held or shared in different lineage segments came under one omnibus petition. Even here the Samsthan's rights were conceived as paramount; according to Laksmibai, 'the sum settled upon the different members [of the family was] entered in their respective names simply as a subordinate detail for practical purposes, so that the interest of the temple in the entire estate remained undisturbed.'[91] As we can now see, all other members of the lineage, except those who had separately obtained their own inam (for example, the descendants of Vinayak, brother of the third Dev[92]) were disadvantaged in the alienation settlements. Their names had not been recorded in the decisions, and they were thus not able to tender separate appeals to protect rights assigned to them in the tahanama. Laksmibai wanted the commission to retain at least this part of its settlement. Apparently she hoped the Samsthan and its managers would be allowed to continue dominating the junior Dev kin, including of course the rival agnates, whose holdings would now be part of a permanent devasthan.

While Laksmibai prosecuted her appeals in Bombay, the Revenue Commissioner for Alienations on his own initiative discovered the tahanama. Captain Cowper had hitherto left the Cincvad settlement to

[90] Ibid.
[91] Laksmibai to Government, 2 July 1860.
[92] Inam Commission decisions on Jamb, 15 February 1859; Hinjavadi, 31 March 1859, PA: XIII; 55/740, pp. 264–79, 325–43; Urali, 31 January 1859, PA: XIII; 1/6. Other examples include the villages of Akurdi, Ojhar, Ranjangav and Saste.

his subordinate Inam Commissioners. Even the various factual or provocative statements in the widow's petitions did not come to his notice until the appeal process was well underway. Procedure had these documents go from government to the Inam Commissioner (forwarded via Cowper's office) for report, and then back to the Revenue Commissioner for recommendation on appeal. Cowper had, however, taken specific notice of Laksmibai's petition to the Collector of Pune in connection with the provision of a widow's allowance. Seeing there explicit references to the tahanama, Cowper immediately called for all previous proceedings on Cincvad.[93]

The issues facing the commission that arose from the tahanama were, Cowper recognized, of crucial importance to the continued operation of the alienation settlements, which by 1860 was in any case much in doubt. British assumptions on the inheritance of inam were being called into question. Clearly, on the evidence of the tahanama, inam would not invariably descend to a sole lineal male descendant as an impartible inheritance. Through state intervention one inamdar's grants could acquire a dual character, becoming both partible and impartible. At the same time, one estate could be divided into personal and devasthan portions. Neither division depended on the original terms of a grant; the Peshva had made his partition on principles of financial equity for reasons of lineage harmony.

The widow, through the adopted son, was thus acting as agent for that part of the inheritance assigned to the Samsthan, surely a devasthan, which was all that was impartible. Furthermore, it could only be managed by the titular Dev of Cincvad, either in natural succession or adopted, because the Peshva had made separate personal provision for all the kin (including the Dev himself and especially the agnates) through partible shares. Creating a new Dev of Cincvad on the basis of tenurial decisions that lumped all the inam together, as if it was all impartible, would surely be a mistake. That the widow sought control over the whole estate, making it all the Dev of Cincvad's devasthan, and that she perhaps had her own aspirations as heir, were not critical issues for the Revenue Commissioner. Such were the natural consequences of the commission's own actions. More importantly, the tahanama highlighted the inability of legislation to separate an inheritance's tenure from the manner of its descent – each depended on the other.

Captain Cowper used all the resources of his office to discover more about the tahanama and why it had been so negligently overlooked. Not

[93] Dods to Cowper, 29 June 1860 (forwarding petition of 23 June 1860); Cowper to Dods, 7 July 1860; Dods to Cowper, 9 July 1860, PA: XIII; 55/740, pp. 202–3, 226–7.

only did he find several passing references to it in previous petitions and proceedings, but midway between the original decisions and the first appeals, Gopalrav Hari, the Assistant Inam Commissioner, had written an extensive memorandum attempting to convince his immediate superior of the justice of the widow's case and the relevance of the Peshva's partition of the Devs.[94] The widows had not, he thought, been put in possession of the Samsthan only to be deprived of it later. Government's original orders, which were for the 'convenience of the family,' in reality 'only prevented the widows from pleading possession against Government but they ought to be at liberty to plead it against anybody else,' and furthermore, 'the question then [in 1852] before Government was certainly not the rights of succession of any heir but the right of the family to hold the estate.'[95] Any precipitate moves by the Inam Commission would place the widow in an inequitable position. Government's own act allowed widows to hold an inam under certain circumstances, say if there was no lineal male descendant of a grantee. Hindu law, according to Gopalrav Hari, recognized the widow's absolute right to inherit. Therefore, enforcing the widow's removal from management would prejudice any future (and in his view probably successful) suit Laksmibai launched to have her position confirmed.

The Peshva's 'separation of the Deo family and division of their estate' (Gopalrav Hari did not use the term tahanama) could only reinforce the widow's rights. She was the legitimate representative of the senior, and separate line of the lineage; with the adopted son's position apparently being denied, she was the Dev's heir. Junior relations, to whom the Peshva had allowed their own shares of inam, could not preempt the Dev's divine inheritance and the control of the Samsthan entrusted to the direct line of saints. With an eye to the future the assistant commissioner also considered the consequences of ignoring the tahanama and summarily changing the Samsthan's management. 'One of the great objects [of the Inam Commission] ought to be to prevent litigation & this can only be attained by maintaining established rights of possession.'[96] The lineal male descendant should not get something he never expected. 'Suppose,' commented Gopalrav Hari,

under the old arrangement entered into by the family & which has been respected & recognized from generations, the eldest male descendant had a share of Rs. 500, he at once becomes rich & comes in possession of the Estate of 40,000 which the widows of the person who held that estate up to his death separately

94 Memorandum of Gopalrav Hari to Dods, 31 December 1859, PA: XIII; 55/740; pp. 471–9. See also notes of Cowper *circa* July 1860, PA: XIV; 28/322, fols. 311–12.
95 Memorandum of Gopalrav Hari, 31 December 1859.
96 Ibid.

from the members of the family, are deprived of & left to seek their remedy in ... impoverishing & never-ending lawsuits.[97]

The British, simply, should not cause such a 'revolution' in Cincvad's affairs. Although the question of succession through adoption was not explicitly examined in the memorandum, the thrust of Gopalrav Hari's thinking would not have supported interference in this or any other arrangement if the partition in the tahanama was altered.

Captain Cowper spent the latter half of 1860 in a voluminous and nattering correspondence with his subordinate Inam Commissioners attempting to discover why Gopalrav Hari had been ignored. Why had Captain Dods overlooked his assistant's and previous references to the tahanama? When did the commissioner first become aware of the document? Why was its existence not reported? Inevitably, these inquisitions moved the Inam Commissioner to defend his decisions. He could not, for example, accept that a widow had any right to succeed to an inam. The 'uniform practice' was to enter in the accounts, as possible heirs to hereditary inam, only the names of lineal male descendants. Widows and members of junior descent lines, if they felt themselves defrauded, had recourse to the courts.[98] Nor could the commissioner believe the Dev's inam was devasthan. Dharanidhar certainly did not act as if the revenue was the property of the Cincvad deity:

[he] was deeply involved in debt and several of the villages now claimed as Dewusthan were mortgaged by him; thus showing that whatever his opinions regarding their tenure were, he did not scruple to filch from the income of the Temple, when funds were required for carrying on his own debauchery.[99]

Although the power of an inamdar to alienate his own inam through mortgage was an interesting and controversial question, this had little to do with Captain Cowper's apprehensions. Generally, the defense of the previous decisions now given was merely a recapitulation of those same decisions, which were entirely logical and consistent when reading only Cincvad's sanads and considering them in terms of Act XI of 1852.

As for the tahanama, the Inam Commissioner had not thought it

seriously affect[ed] the decisions passed ... I considered it a document that would only be valuable in the Civil Courts in determining shares &c., & as it had never to my knowledge been brought forward before by the Agents of the Deo I naturally thought that they themselves did not lay much stress on it.[100]

[97] Ibid.
[98] Dods to Cowper, 27 July 1860, PA: XIII; 55/740, pp. 232–9.
[99] Dods to Cowper, 22 August 1860, PA: XIII; 55/740, pp. 461–6.
[100] Dods to Cowper, 8 October 1860, PA: XIII; 55/740, pp. 242–6.

On reconsideration he believed one-half of the holdings could be declared devasthan and one-half hereditary inam. But if all was considered a religious endowment and Laksmibai's appeals accepted, then the Samsthan would prosecute claims for the shares of the separated Devs.[101] Thus turning tahanama to his own advantage, Commissioner Dods maintained that his previous decisions would cause fewer disputes within the lineage. Moreover, the rights of the junior Devs, who 'for generations have probably contributed little or nothing to the support of the temple,' would be protected.[102]

While reviewing the commissioner's work, Cowper detected the unsavory presence of corruption and intrigue in the representations of Bajaji Govind:

enquiry... had disclosed so disgraceful an amount of unscrupulous falsehood on the part of his accredited agents... and has so completely satisfied me that these agents have been actively employed in intrigue which tho' perhaps not criminally punishable must nevertheless be discouraged by all practicable means.[103]

The details were apparently not committed to paper, but reading between the lines it seems Bajaji Govind had obtained the questionable help of a Subassistant Inam Commissioner and several clerks in advancing his case.[104] Through various devious means the tahanama had been withheld from the Inam Commissioner before his decisions were issued. In addition, Bajaji Govind had received first warning of the proposed transfer of the Samsthan's management. Laksmibai's agents only learned government's intentions when they somehow heard about the secret communications of their adversaries. Even when officially informed that she was to be ousted from the Samsthan, the widow had not been told all the reasons, but only that other family members questioned the adoption. What form of influence Bajaji Govind possessed to be able to systematically obstruct Laksmibai is not yet clear. Bribery, at least, does not appear probable. Captain Cowper nevertheless found the intrigues serious enough to permanently bar Bajaji Govind's agents from the Alienation Department. Thereafter the Revenue Commissioner became increasingly disenchanted with the claim of the lineal male descendant.

Similar allegations of corruptions were in turn made against Laksmibai. Bajaji Govind claimed the indomitable lady had

---

[101] Dods to Cowper, 22 August 1860.
[102] Dods to Cowper, 7 August 1860, PA: XIII; 55/740, pp. 455–8.
[103] Cowper to Dods, 26 September 1860, PA: XIV; 28/322, fol. 259.
[104] Cowper to Dods, 3 October 1860 & ff., PA: XIII; 55/740, pp. 247–61.

'poisoned . . . Captain Cowper's ears' because, as he told government,

it appears that Luximbaee has established an understanding with a very influential Member of the Revenue Commissioner for Alienation's office, through whom she gets information of every thing that transpires, and by whose assistance, she boasts, she would at last succeed in preventing the management of the Sousthan holdings from passing into your Memorialist's hands.[105]

The accusation, perhaps unfounded, appears directed against Gopalrav Hari. According to pseudonymous petitions sent to the commission and government, bribery was the source of the widow's influence.[106] Cowper thought these petitions were the handiwork of Bajaji Govind and his discredited agents, and he had 'not the slightest doubt that the accusations are without a shadow of foundation.'[107] Ganesh, when describing the iniquities of Laksmibai, made the same charges.[108] The details were sordid: Laksmibai had spent some Rs. 10,000 in Bombay to influence key members of the staff of the acting Revenue Commissioner for Alienations. A document with a guarantee for the money had been obtained from the adopted son (who claimed he was forced to sign), and government was urged to search the houses of Laksmibai's agents to secure the incriminating correspondence. Ganesh even forwarded as proof a letter which allegedly implicated the widow's agents in suborning the commission's Indian subordinates.[109]

Captain Cowper believed the accusations against the widow were primarily aimed at undermining the reputation of those who had uncovered Bajaji Govind's questionable schemes. If, however, Ganesh's petition is given some credence – Cowper never saw it – then conceivably Laksmibai paid Gopalrav Hari or others to advance her cause. Whatever the case, hints of corruption and a current of never-ending intrigue pervade all the proceedings of the Inam Commission.

When at length Cowper offered his recommendations to government on Laksmibai's special appeals, his opinions had undergone a remarkable change. Perhaps the tahanama most influenced the Revenue Commissioner, though the suspicion in which he held Bajaji Govind must have been a factor. Moreover, the practicalities of the situation

---

[105] Petition of Bajaji Govind to Government (English petition), 28 May 1861, BA: RD 1861; 36/568, pp. 221–9.

[106] Petition of 'Bhau Dev' to Government (Persian Department translation), 3 October 1860, PA: XIV; 28/322, fols. 299–300. Cowper received similar pseudonymous petitions on 27 and 30 September 1860.

[107] Cowper to Government, 8 February 1861, PA: XIV; 28/322, fols. 300–1.

[108] Ganesh to Government, 2 August 1860.

[109] Ganesh Hari Patvardhan, Bombay to Cintopant Bhide and Dhondopant Patvardhan, Pune, 29 June 1860, accompaniment to Ganesh to Government, 2 August 1860.

were obvious: in the first place, removing the widow from the Samsthan would not be easy; both the widow and the adopted son would undoubtably go to civil court if government ever succeeded in altering either's established position; likewise, Bajaji Govind would sue for possession if nothing was done and the widow left in her anomolous position. Ultimately Gopalrav Hari's 'never-ending lawsuits' would surely come to pass. Hence the only practical solution was to recognize Ganesh's adoption after the payment of a nominal najar. Then the Dev's inheritance and the management of the Samsthan would naturally pass to the adopted son. This was the course the Peshva had previously taken, and the precedent was particularly pointed out to government. As for the portion of the inam assigned to the Samsthan in the tahanama, this was beyond the claim of any other family member, and the adoption could not 'infringe the rights of any of them.'[110]

The particular merits of Laksmibai's appeals were not considered. What was devasthan in the light of the tahanama was left undecided. Cowper even avoided the word. Presumably all these difficulties, and also the rights of the junior Dev kin, would be settled if government simply suspended its skepticism on Ganesh's adoption. Moreover, if Laksmibai was accommodated in this manner and her special appeals withdrawn, then the inam would still officially be considered hereditary and personal to descend to Ganesh's heirs. In effect, the commission's tenurial decisions would remain unchanged; no mistake need be admitted. At the same time, the British would not be regulating inheritance, an exercise that gained the state nothing in revenue.

Bombay was not convinced. The Samsthan's management should be transferred as previously ordered, because to recognize the adoption 'certainly does infringe the rights of different members of the family.'[111]

By the time this resolution was issued and something of an impasse reached, the controversy over Dharanidhar's inheritance and Ganesh's adoption had effectively outlived the Inam Commission. Cowper had ended his long association with the inquiries, and William Hart (who made the original recommendations on Cincvad in 1852) was again supervising their operation in preparation for the introduction of the 'Summary Settlement.' Hart sought to apply the terms of these new acts to Cincvad while maintaining the nonrecognition of the adoption. Whoever was in possession of the inam would be offered the chance to have it declared devasthan on the payment of a najar of 25 percent of one

[110] Cowper to Government, 5 February 1861, PA: XIV; 28/322, fols. 373–4.
[111] Government to W. Hart, Officiating Revenue Commissioner Southern Division, 2 April 1861, BA: RD 1861; 36/568, pp. 209–17.

year's assessment. Government would now receive payment for its indulgence whereas a simple denial of tenure would produce no revenue. If Laksmibai accepted the offer her special appeals would be considered withdrawn. No action at all would be taken on the adoption. Aggrieved parties would have recourse to the civil courts. At any rate, it was not the intention of the alienation inquiries to change established rights of possession; such was 'wholly at variance with the principles on which the whole operations of the Inam Scrutiny have all along been conducted.'[112]

The inamdar had won a significant victory. The Inam Commission's tenurial decisions were to be overturned. The heartfelt conception of the Samsthan as a religious institution, whatever its inam was officially called, was at last to be conceded. But this was, in the end, the only way Hart could see to settle tenure while still not recognizing the adoption. Who actually managed the newly created devasthan would not be government's direct concern; Hart studiously ignored the whole problem. For revenue officers conducting a revenue settlement, Hart's proposal would have had the great advantage of ending their interference in matters of Hindu personal law, plus once and for all closing the tenurial investigation of Cincvad. For the various claimants to the inam it would have settled nothing. Still the same contending parties sought the same inheritance, and their relative positions remained the same as when the commission, in 1852, first intervened in the lineage. It remained to be seen whether the bait would be taken and Hart's solution accepted.

While still favoring the rights of Bajaji Govind, Bombay generally approved the proposed course. The Governor, George Clerk, in particular minuted that it was to be 'regretted' that the 'eldest male representative' had not been 'put in charge in 1852.'[113] Even though Laksmibai could not be dispossessed, Bajaji Govind would be recognized as heir, and the widow should be urged to voluntarily hand over the management of the estate. But only the courts could assist Bajaji Govind if Laksmibai adamantly refused. To further discourage the widow, government decreed she could only be offered the summary settlement when the acts became law – apparently it would not be binding otherwise – whereas Bajaji Govind could receive the concession whenever he gained the Samsthan's management.[114]

[112] Hart to Government, 3 May 1861, PA: xiv; 28/322, fols. 377–8.
[113] Minute of G. Clerk on Resolution of Government, 31 July 1861, BA: RD 1861; 36/568, pp. 233–9.
[114] Government to Hart, 4 September 1861; Hart to Bajaji Govind, 10 September 1861, PA: xiv; 28/322, fols. 384–5.

In 1863 and 1864 Laksmibai resisted all entreaties to come to terms. The 'friendly overture' was, she was told, the answer to her special appeals. Her only other course was to accept the original decisions.[115] But why should the widow pay a succession duty to obtain what she already possessed? What the commission now considered a devasthan was irrelevant. Government would not enforce a change in management. Removing both the widow and adopted son would be a difficult and lengthy task for Bajaji Govind. And it was by no means certain his litigation would be successful. In the foreseeable future the Samsthan would remain the inheritance of the Dev of Cincvad in direct father to son succession from the saint. For her part, the widow retained effective control over the inam, her position being once again given some form of official recognition. Her constant object attained, the summary settlement for the 12 villages under appeal was refused:

because as Luximeebaee says, she only requested that the tenure *already decreed hereditary* might be extended into permanent. She adds, that, if Government see fit to grant her request she will be glad; if not, she is content with the decisions already passed and will hereafter herself extend the hereditary tenure, into what will be equal to that of permanent by the payment of nuzzerana [najarana] or not, as she thinks best.[116]

Government took this as a withdrawal of the special appeals and closed the Inam Commission's proceedings on Cincvad.[117]

By any standard the alienation settlements were a failure. Possibly the tenure of a holding could be determined and the duration of its possession fixed. The British, like the Marathas, had ultimate power over the disposition of any inam. That which was granted could be resumed, and the criteria for either course rested entirely with the pleasure of the state. But the British found they could not impose their authority on matters of inheritance, a failing of revenue legislation eventually recognized in judgments of the Bombay High Court.[118] When they tried to intervene the results were disastrous: factionalism and litigation were the immediate consequences; in the broader sense, one of the fundamental structures of the Maratha society, the lineage, was under attack. Like the Peshva, perhaps all the Inam Commission

---

[115] A. T. Etheridge, Alienation Settlement Officer Southern Division to Collector of Pune, 17 December 1863, 14 March 1864, PA: XIII; 55/740, pp. 594–5, 623–4.

[116] Etheridge to W. Hart, Revenue Commissioner Southern Division, April 1864, PA: XIII; 55/740, pp. 627–9, emphasis in original.

[117] Resolution of Government, 21 June 1864, BA: RD 1862–64; 61/616, p. 181.

[118] *Vasudev Anant* v. *Ramkrishna and Shivram Narayan; Ramkrishna and Shivram Narayan* v. *The Government of Bombay*, ILR 2 Bom. (1878), 529–32.

could hope to effect was a lineage consensus consonant with custom and expediency.

Set within the context of almost classical problems of Hindu law – the respective rights of adopted son, widow, and agnates – the tenurial interventions of the commission revived long dormant divisions within the Dev lineage. By not immediately recognizing Ganesh, it forced the confrontation between Laksmibai and Bajaji Govind. The British never did settle the legal rights of widow and agnate, indeed they never completely understood the problem. What eventually became clear was that the adoption had to be accepted, however reluctantly, if lineage peace was to be preserved. The Peshva and his government had known this when they routinely approved adoptions (if nonpolitical of course). Captain Cowper, too, finally came to something of the same opinion. The fact was that adoption in traditional Hindu society was the only alternative to the threats to lineage solidarity inherent in the succession of either widow or agnate.

As basically a body established to investigate and settle revenue matters, the Inam Commission was unprepared to handle the intricate legal questions it created. Its original purpose, the investigation of tenure, became subordinated to succession. Who should hold an inam almost became more important than what was held. The exact status of the Cincvad inam was, in fact, never satisfactorily resolved. It was left as personal and hereditary inam, perhaps to be considered permanent devasthan, but neither decision could be enforced without disputes on the estate's possession and management. Further complicating the issue was the commission's inability to adequately delimit devasthan. Partitions such as the Peshva's tahanama, by so closely linking an endowment's tenure with the manner of its descent, in effect created devasthan. The creation of partible inam shares in addition to a devasthan was one more complication the commission never properly untangled. In summary, inam tenures could not be categorized simply on the basis of the wording of grants and such criteria, but were defined in the particular context of a lineage's customary mode of inheritance.

No act of government could hope to fashion the perfect synthesis that at once exactly defined inam while regulating its inheritance. Act XI of 1852 was particularly unsuccessful because it avowedly sought the former. Ambiguities on the latter abounded. When the opportunity arose, claimants soon perceived that the act could be used and manipulated in an attempt to claim an inheritance. We have seen the results: appeals and further appeals clogging the machinery of government; factional infighting in which the British became unwitting allies; and through all, an undercurrent of corruption and intrigue compromising claimant and government alike. An inam inquiry in these circumstances became a grimly fought contest, with a strategy being essential for the successful prosecution of a claim.

In the case of Cincvad, the widow prevailed in her dual course of securing the rights of the adopted son and the direct descent of the Cincvad saints while at the same time protecting and enhancing her own position. She was able, through argument and perhaps assisted by well-placed bribes, to convince the British that agnates and reversionary heirs could not take precedence over a widow and an adopted son. The lineal male descendant thus found the commission's initial views on Hindu inheritance, which he applauded and encouraged, transformed through the widow's use of the official interpretation of devasthan. For the moment his aspirations to the 'Devhood' were frustrated, and the widow could well believe her strategy to meet the challenge of the Inam Commission had been a success.

IV. Postscript: to the courts

Between 1863 and 1895 the Cincvad Samsthan was the subject of almost continuous court actions. The Bombay High Court considered four diverse cases: the 'charity suit,' or creation of a public temple trust;[119] the right of an inamdar to alienate his inam through mortgage and the consequent obligations of a successor;[120] the definition of a personal inheritance outside of a temple trust;[121] and finally, the right of a daughter-in-law to adopt, for her deceased spouse, an heir who would succeed to an estate already held by other heirs.[122] The intricacies of the pleadings involved and the acuteness of the judgments rendered will not here be examined in detail. Instead, these cases will be used simply to conclude the narrative on the affairs of the Dev lineage, which were left in such an incomplete and unsatisfactory state at the end of the alienation settlements.

As the inamdars moved into the courts, considerations outside the main interests of this study come to the fore. Firstly, the direct intervention of the state in questions of personal law subsided. The sources used here (those resulting from the administration of revenue and district officers) become concerned with only routine matters of tenure and revenue. The British recognized they could not hope to

---

[119] *Chintaman Bajaji Dev* v. *Dhondo Ganesh Dev*, ILR 15 Bom. (1891), 612–25.
[120] *Shri Ganesh Dharnidhar Maharaj Dev* v. *Keshavarav Govind Kulgavkar*, ILR 15 Bom. (1891), 625–43.
[121] *Shri Dhundiraj Ganesh Dev* v. *Ganesh*, ILR 18 Bom. (1894), 721–33.
[122] *Shri Dharnidhar* v. *Chinto*, ILR 20 Bom. (1896), 250–9.

control an inamdar's customary mode of inheritance, any more than they could directly legislate this for any other classs of society. The problem was best left to the indirect administration of the judicial system. In this respect the inam inquiries merge with the evolution of Anglo-Indian law in the later nineteenth century, a topic of sufficient complexity and interest to demand a separate investigation.

Secondly, the courts did not in themselves produce much new evidence on the affairs of the inamdar. Nor did they offer significantly original interpretations of indigenous documents. The Marathi sources, so much a part of this study, were in effect accepted as they were received from bodies such as the Inam Commission. In a way the situation was similar to that of Hindu law where in 1864 the study and translation of the Sanskrit dharmashastra for official legal purposes, and also the input of pandits into the judicial system, largely came to an end.[123] In both the revenue and legal fields acquired knowledge became sufficient for all future purposes. The era of discovery and interpretation of documentation had passed.

Finally, in their alienated revenue policy the primary concerns of the British changed in the latter half of the nineteenth century. No longer did they attempt a uniform interpretation for the many varieties of inam. Hence, less absolute faith was put in the precise wording of old documents. While the British still claimed to control the ultimate disposition of the state's grants, their perceived right as the successor to indigenous dynasties, now this authority was kept in abeyance. Pragmatic consideration in the settlement of each inam replaced the Inam Commission's dogmatism.

Government's dealings with religious endowments in particular take a very separate course. Whereas the Inam Commission was chary of treating religious holdings as essentially different from any other inheritance, subsequently these inams acquired a very distinct identity. They were seen as public property.[124] As such, supposedly independent bodies – temple trusts – were created to administer religious inams. They would, it was hoped, reform obvious abuses while distancing the British from the direct administration of religion. Temple trusts, their origin and workings, and the resulting litigation have been considered in

---

[123] J. Duncan M. Derrett, 'The Administration of Hindu Law by the British,' in *Religion, Law and the State in India* (London, 1968), pp. 316–17. 'In 1864 judicial knowledge of Hindu law was assumed.' (p. 317).

[124] Derrett, 'Religious Endowments, Public and Private,' in ibid., pp. 482–512 for this concept as it has evolved in modern India. Derrett's conclusion on the traditional right of the Hindu sovereign to interfere in religious institutions is sound, but we may doubt that a concept of a 'public' endowment existed.

other studies, notably for Madras.[125] Perhaps, however, the concentration on religious endowments in modern scholarship has been to the neglect of basic problems in Hindu personal law and their relation to revenue that apply to any inheritance, personal or religious, private or public.

In 1888 the charity suit, launched by junior members of the Dev lineage (the nominal plaintiff descended from the second Dev Cintaman), transformed the Cincvad Samsthan into a public religious trust and effected an arrangement for its better management. By this time Cinto, eldest son of Bajaji Govind, was in possession of the inam. In 1863, after the Inam Commission had abandoned its settlement attempts, Bajaji Govind filed suit against Laksmibai, an action not settled until 1874. Because of the separate interventions of Ganesh, the case was not even then decided on its merits. In 1871 the adopted son had sued Cinto and Venubai (widowed daughter-in-law of Dharanidhar) to be recognized heir and was initially successful. Cinto appealed, and for some unexplained reason Ganesh was persuaded to withdraw his suit without obtaining leave to reopen the case. This bar Ganesh was unable to remove even though he made repeated applications to superior courts. In 1873 he also sued Laksmibai. Again he was successful, but before he could execute this favorable decree and take possession of the Samsthan, Cinto won his case against Laksmibai. Because Ganesh had withdrawn his suit against Cinto, Laksmibai's plea – she claimed only to act on behalf of her adopted son – was no longer relevant. Cinto immediately took possession of the inam, obstructing Ganesh, and the aspirations of the lineal male descendants were at last realized.

At first glance Laksmibai emerges the clear loser in this litigation. But it appears that between 1871 and 1874 she abandoned her support for Ganesh, though still ruling in his name, and made common cause with her erstwhile rivals. She almost conceded the action Cinto launched against her, not producing a substantial defense. Ganesh was attempting to take his own course independent of both Laksmibai and Cinto. His 1873 action against the widow was apparently the culmination of an assertion of rights that started with his petition to Bombay 13 years earlier damning Laksmibai's iniquities. If he was successful in his own right, then the widow stood to lose her influence and control over the Samsthan's revenues. Such could only drive her into an alliance with the agnates. The courts and district revenue officers, however, did not

[125] See for example, Chandra Y. Mudaliar, *The Secular State and Religious Institutions in India* (Wiesbaden, 1974).

perceive the litigants' changes of position. Most thought the suit between the widow and the adopted son was amicable and meant only to counter Cinto by having the courts recognize Ganesh's adoption. However, Ganesh sued Laksmibai before he withdrew against Cinto and before Cinto was successful against Laksmibai.

In fact, by 1871 Ganesh was completely out of favor with the widow. In that year Venubai adopted Bajaji Govind's second son as heir to her late husband. This occurred some 21 years after her husband's death. While providing an heir to Dharanidhar's only son for religious purposes, it was also hoped government would favor this new lineal male descendant with the late Dev's inheritance. The courts considered it one more tactic by which Cinto could prosecute his case against Laksmibai. Perhaps it was. But at the same time there is some evidence that the widow approved the adoption, though the courts were skeptical and never investigated the possibility. Laksmibai's collaboration is most strongly indicated by the fact that the new heir (assuming the name Dharanidhar) at once undertook the ritual functions of the Dev of Cincvad previously performed by Ganesh. This could only have happened with Laksmibai's approval as she was then firmly in control of the Samsthan's management.

The fortunes of this new Dharanidhar were not particularly happy. When the charity suit was underway in the 1880s and Cinto suffered an initial setback from the proposed trustees, then this adopted Dharanidhar sued Cinto, his natal brother. This action, intended to circumvent the temple trust and obtain at least the personal inheritance of the Dev of Cincvad, was unsuccessful. The court ruled that what had already passed to other heirs could not be obtained through such a lately concocted adoption.

Having ousted Ganesh from the ritual status of Dev of Cincvad, then Laksmibai removed any possibility he could establish himself as Dharanidhar's personal heir. To do this she transferred the Samsthan's management to Cinto at the first practicable opportunity. There were no appeals, no protest, no petitions to government when Cinto won his suit – much out of character for the widow. Ganesh's only course now was to find some new grounds on which to sue Cinto or attempt (unsuccessfully) to reopen his former action. Surely the widow realized that when Ganesh was persuaded to withdraw against Cinto, then the latter would prevail against her. What form of promise or threat was employed on Ganesh is not at all certain. Perhaps he was offered a substantial settlement out of court, similar to one he would later obtain. Whatever the case, the widow's tactics had been effective. Once again she held the disposition of the Samsthan entirely in her hands. Laksmibai died in 1886 without taking any further active part in the Devs' affairs, though we may assume that her position and influence remained secure.

Ganesh attempted again and again to execute his decree against Laksmibai. He sued Cinto in 1878, but withdrew this suit when government reversed the decision Cinto obtained against the widow. Ganesh appeared to be on the verge of obtaining the Cincvad inam, but once again Bombay changed its mind and restored Cinto's position. Renewing his suit, Ganesh was in the process of appealing to the High Court when Cinto offered a compromise, which was accepted, whereby his rival acquired a portion of the inam but not the Samsthan's management. Apparently Cinto thought Ganesh had a good chance of ultimate success in the courts. Others shared the same opinion. For example, even in 1900 Ganesh was still looking for opportunities to have his adoption officially recognized. Government was then advised not to resume an inam thought to be personal to Laksmibai and hence to lapse on her death. Doing so would offer Ganesh the chance of making government a direct party to a suit, which it had not previously been, and 'the fact that on the only occasion on which Ganesh was called upon to establish his adoption he succeeded in doing so, is one that Government can scarcely overlook.'[126]

Increasingly a forlorn figure, having been manipulated throughout the inam inquiries and in the later court actions, Ganesh even lost the benefit of the compromise with Cinto. The trustees of Cincvad, after they ousted Cinto, turned against him. The compromise, alienating part of a public temple trust, was argued to represent a serious dereliction of duty on Cinto's part, which the trust was not responsible for. Either Ganesh was the adopted son and thus entitled to the Samsthan's management before the advent of the trustees, or he should have got nothing. Cinto was, the trustees argued, in effect a responsible representative of the Cincvad trust even though that status had yet to be accorded to the Samsthan when the compromise was made. As such, this

---

[126] Remambrancer of Legal Affairs to Government, 15 November 1900, PA: XIII; 55/740, pp. 649–60. This concerned Shinde's 'detached' jagir village of Tandli, which was granted to Cincvad. It was thought that when the village was transferred to British territory in 1861, in the course of territorial adjustments with the native princes, then the inam was converted into Laksmibai's personal holding. Ganesh also tried to obtain the village from Laksmibai, though the transfer of the Samsthan's management was thought to defeat the request, see Petition of Ganesh to Government (English petition), 2 May 1877; Collector of Ahmednagar to Revenue Commissioner Southern Division, 31 July 1877, PA: XIV; 28/322, fols. 418–20, 422–6. Apparently Laksmibai had agreed to transfer the village in the accounts when Ganesh succeeded in his suit against her, but she resisted any change in management, which was in any case held by a mortgagor. When Cinto obtained the Samsthan she denied Ganesh's claim entirely.

alleged squandering of public resources and Cinto's other abuses of power were used as arguments against the continued personal management of the Dev of Cincvad, whoever held that ritual status. Eventually, the new trustees were able to dispossess Ganesh from any claim to the inheritance of his adoptive father.

The charity suit creating the temple trust has been left to the last because it marks the effective end of the relations between those who previously sought the Dev inheritance. Laksmibai was dead; the lineal male descendants and the adopted sons now fell in front of the suit launched by the junior Dev kin. These were the lineage members who had been largely ignored in all previous settlements and court cases. The protests of their ancestors had led to the Peshva's tahanama and the creation of the particular form of inheritance in the lineage. The junior kin now used the new concept of a temple trust to secure their position and reassert their rights. Cinto had threatened the welfare of the entire lineage through his compromise with Ganesh and the mortgage of several inam villages (apparently to pay legal fees) and, if government would not intervene, then a new arrangement had to be created at Cincvad.

Cinto though, like all the managers of the Cincvad inam before him, thought his ritual position made him unassailable. He told the court:

I have been treating the devasthan as my private property. I and dev (i.e. the deity) are one. So I understand that I am the owner. I cannot say if we are separate. The estate is for both the private expenses and for charity... The ornaments on the idol are mine. We make no distinction between the god's property and mine. I understand I am Mangal Murti, the god of Chinchvad. We are not pujaris. It is not the case that Mangal Murti is owner and I am the manager. All the villages... I regard as my private inams.[127]

Such statements did not gain favor with courts considering devasthan, a religious institution and their concept of a public trust. Yet in his assertions Cinto was entirely consistent with the past view of the Cincvad inam. The Samsthan was the Dev's inheritance, and excepting the personal shares of all the Devs, no distinction could be made between what belonged to the Samsthan and what belonged to the Cincvad saints. Yet in this statement of the fundamental nature of the Dev of Cincvad's inheritance, Cinto, much to his own misfortune, and like his predecessors, had neglected the concurrent rights of the entire lineage.

[127] *Chintaman* v. *Dhondo*, 616–17.

8

Conclusion: an inamdar's rights and the authority of the state

On 27 July 1857 Benjamin Disraeli stood in the House of Commons to denounce the policies of the East India Company that, he maintained, had led to the recently reported disturbances in India. The Company was, he told the House, attacking the sanctity of property in India by establishing inquiries into the title of rent-free lands. In its arrogance the Company was questioning the validity of inam and jagir 'as proof of a powerful Government, a vigorous Executive, and a most fruitful source of public revenue.' This unprecedented course was totally at odds with previous British policy in India: when some tyrant had previously usurped these lands, 'we came in as vindicators of public right, and we invariably guaranteed the security of property, as in the case of jagheers and enams.' The end result of the Company's disregard of landed rights was that the British had 'estranged numerous and powerful classes from that authority which I think on the whole they were disposed to regard with deference.'[1] Hence, for Disraeli, it was no wonder than India was in revolt.

In this attack on British policy in India Disraeli effectively spelled the end of Company rule and of the Inam Commission (though both would struggle on for a time, heedless of any opposition). Although the motives for Disraeli's speech were political (he was then in opposition[2]), and whereas we may query his interpretation of Indian history, nevertheless he did isolate the major theme in the relations between the state and its privileged subjects. There was, on the one hand, the 'public right' issuing from the 'security of property.' Perhaps the notion of 'property' to describe rent-free lands, a not unnatural cross-cultural perception, was misapplied. But in essence Disraeli was referring to legal rights in land revenue, however this contract was defined. The 'security' of such rights depended on them being immune from capricious inquiries of govern-

---

[1] *Hansard*, 27 July 1857, 457–61.
[2] Robert Blake, *Disraeli* (New York, 1967), pp. 376-7. Karl Marx heard Disraeli on this occasion and believed the speech was made for political effect and posterity. It is, however, interesting to note that Marx, too, isolated the section on rent-free lands as the crux of Disraeli's argument; see *The First Indian War of Independence, 1857–1859* (Moscow, 1959), pp. 44–8.

ment. Moreover, they were secure because rights were heritable. (At least, within his own cultural framework Disraeli made the implicit equation of property and inheritance.) On the other hand, there was the 'authority' of the state to which its privileged subjects had to bow. Disraeli believed, rightly, that inamdars and others were prepared to acknowledge this authority and to avoid, if at all possible, unprofitable confrontations with government.

Disraeli's interpretation of the distressing situation in India was certainly culture-bound; all his misperceptions and rhetoric need not be corrected here. Nevertheless, his intuition of a delicate balance between the Indian state and its subjects has been at the core of this book. The two domains of rights and authority, separate but interdependent, go far to explain the history of the Devs of Cincvad. Further, these twin concepts help to give interpretative substance to the social and political history of early modern India, be it of the preconquest or British periods.

Rights, simply, are firstly what income the state's subjects held – the land itself on some direct basis (perhaps 'property'), the land revenue or similar claims on government revenue (inam and such), or some even more generalized control over sources of revenue (such as the largely fictive rights Maratha dynasties held from the moribund Mughal state). The domain of rights must therefore begin with the fact of items of revenue, the actual sources of income. How revenue was held, that is the technical description of its tenure, derives in part from the particularities of a right. But here is a more generalized way of describing rights. Conceptually, 'rights' extends to the manner wealth was transmitted, that is inheritance. The particular features of an item of revenue, or the conditions placed upon a variety of tenure, could influence matters of inheritance. The subject and process of inheritance thus were often formally related, though hard and fast rules should never be imagined. For the state's subjects the heritability of what was held was *the* critical issue. An item of revenue or a variety of tenure would be of little lasting consequence if it could not descend within a lineage. Inheritance, then, was the activating process within the domain of rights.

Rights, in all their manifold connotations, were guarded with all the legal, moral or even occasionally military power that could be mustered. Within the tripartite division of rights nothing could be conceded. If, for example, a fact of an item of revenue was challenged, then this implied a threat to the tenurial description of revenue rights, which ultimately and most seriously was an attack on inheritance. The vagaries of political change in India always made the possession of rights an uncertain matter. Any subject, great or little, and thus any subject's rights could fall before the tides of war and revolution. Mostly, however, rights had somehow to be insulated from the general authority of the state.

Authority, in this context, is the power of the Indian state to control its due revenue. Thus, the state could determine what rights were held and how they were held. I have argued that the Indian state had ultimate authority of these first two parts of the domain of rights. However – and this was the key point missed by the Inam Commission – this authority was lightly exercised. If legal title was maintained in relatively good order, the moral suasion (backed often by political or military power) a subject could bring to bear was enough for the state to allow its authority to be used to maintain rights. The Indian state had good reasons to play the part of the upholder of the moral order, as the guardian of dharma. Within the general sphere of the way rights were transmitted, however, the state's authority was much more circumscribed. The state did have a place in matters of inheritance if the process of transmission partly depended on the legal definition of what rights were held and how they were held. But this was a grey area, and the state would only impinge upon inheritance when it had the confidence and agreement of its subjects. Even then, the Indian state worked for a consensus that would harmonize rights of inheritance with its authority over the legal definition of rights.

In this book, the play between rights and authority in one lineage over time between two very different political powers, the Marathas and the British, has been examined. The continuities of Indian history between the eighteenth and nineteenth centuries exist precisely because the equation of rights and authority persisted throughout a period of great change, though, of course, the balance between the two was subject to any amount of alteration. Throughout the political transformation of India the domain of rights held firm. The state's subjects knew their rights had to be protected from whatever authority the state, be it Maratha or British, cared to exercise. Thus, for the Devs of Cincvad, maintaining the corporate unity of the kin eventually meant convincing the British of the legality of the lineage's revenue rights, and, at the same time, deflecting the new rulers' predilection to interfere in the way these rights were transmitted. If Indians were consistent in their perception of a subject's rights, political change transformed and often distorted concepts of authority. Being heirs to powers they only dimly understood, the British were seemingly fated to be a disruptive force as they attempted to administer their new subjects. Nevertheless, until at least the Mutiny, the British played out the part of the Indian state in its exercise of authority over landed magnates such as the Devs of Cincvad.

Having this idea of the play between rights and authority in view, the resulting conclusions derived from the history of the Devs of Cincvad offer the empirical evidence for interpretations of facets of early modern Indian history. Beginning with the revenue facts of a subject's rights, I have used privileged inam tenures and related revenues as a vehicle for my analysis of the Dev lineage. So, I described the acquisition of such landed rights in the context of the Maratha state's revenue granting process. Though inam was clearly a distinctive feature of Indian polities, and whereas we may ponder its special place in Indian social, political or economic organization, nevertheless I would downplay ideas of its essential uniqueness. Such revenue was but one form of landed rights among many; and, thus, but one aspect of rightholding that could form an inheritance in a lineage.

Still, as a right without obvious obligation, inam was a privilege eagerly sought. Consequently, it was a right the state granted with extreme care. Whatever the original reason for an inam grant, and no matter how highly esteemed a grantee, elaborate procedures were in force to assure the proper descent of an item of alienated revenue. No son could be positive he would obtain the wealth of his father. The state had to concur. Similarly, the change of granting power, even if it meant little difference in real political power, required the confirmation of all state grants. The involved state mechanisms for the administration of inam, so much in evidence in the documentary history of the Devs, may seem mere legal formalities. But it is obvious that the technical requirements of Maratha revenue policies masked the real power of the state. Nothing the state gave could not be taken back because no title deed was really permanent. Here was the means by which the Maratha state could exercise its authority over its privileged subjects.

The intricacies of the inam granting process call attention to certain features of eighteenth-century Indian polities that are only now beginning to receive some serious attention. Baldly put, the Maratha state was not, at least in its homeland, a predatory and rapacious military junta. Certainly, outside of Maharashtra the Marathas presented an unfavorable face to contemporary commentators, which subsequent historians have not much rectified. The British, especially, continued to perceive the Marathas as if ensconced behind Calcutta's 'Maratha ditch.' Although the eighteenth century was a time of political and military tumult, and in this the Marathas were central, this very confusion hides the formation of strong regional polities.[3] This process

---

[3] C. A. Bayly, *Rulers, Townsmen and Bazaars: North Indian Society in the Age of British Expansion, 1770–1850* (Cambridge, 1983) makes this general point; see also the comments of Burton Stein, 'State Formation and Economy Reconsidered, part one,' *Modern Asian Studies*, 19 (1985), 387–93.

was much advanced in the Maratha homeland. The documents relating to the Devs of Cincvad show a strong and ordered state, one which knew precisely how its territory was administered. Even after 1803, and the increasing British penetration of the Maratha state and the consequent compromise of its political power, it is not obvious that conditions had deteriorated as much as the first British administrators liked to believe. The Inam Commission, at least, came to believe that it could, from the Maratha state records, discover the truth of revenue alienations at any time, from the mid-seventeenth century right up to the conquest. Behind the wars and intrigues of the Maratha state and its enemies lies a century and a half of relatively stable government.

In part this stability was due to the way the Maratha state ordered its relations with its privileged subjects. If lineages such as the Devs would always bow to the authority of the state, they equally knew that the Peshvas would not easily interfere in internal lineage affairs. Here I have seen the preservation and descent of the Devs' inam rights partially in terms of the limits of state authority in the ordering of inheritance. The Maratha state would involve itself in the descent of inam for the corporate good of the lineage if it saw that disputes between the kin were compromising the integrity of state grants. Again, this was a duty that fell to the domain of state authority. Thus, the Peshva determined the half partible and half impartible character of the Devs' inam. Through this he fixed both the institutional nature of the Cincvad Samsthan and the actual patrimonies of the Dev kin. But the Peshva did not determine the actual mechanisms and principles of inheritance within the lineage once his settlement was made. Such clearly fell into the domain of rights.

The manner in which the Dev inheritance was finally settled in the eighteenth century suggests that Indian inheritance principles were as much influenced by pragmatism as by unvarying 'brahmanical' doctrine. Of course, in an elite brahman lineage such as the Devs succession was to males in patrilineal lines. I have no evidence of bilateral succession or such deviations from Hindu orthodoxy. Widows, however, were clearly possible heirs, even if their inheritance was supposedly only for their immediate maintenance. Furthermore, the instance of the Peshva's tahanama provides examples of enough variation from strict patrilineal inheritance patterns among the Devs to suggest that a principle of equity was often at work within the lineage. Further research on inheritance in India will, I believe, confirm how attuned lineages have been to particular and immediate circumstances when ordering the descent of their wealth.[4]

---

[4] Karen Isaksen Leonard, *Social History of an Indian Caste* (Berkeley, 1978), pp. 289–91 offers the most succint comparison for the case of the Devs. My impression is that

Pragmatic customary law at once preserved matters of inheritance and the management of rights to the responsibility of the lineage while allowing the Maratha state the ability to control the sources of a lineage's wealth and status. Adoption is a case in point that has often appeared in this study. The state had the authority to sanction or not any adoption that involved the descent of alienated revenue. This the Inam Commission would eagerly assert as it came to understand something of the state's authority. But in so managing adoptions the Maratha state could not dictate the manner in which an adoptee would receive his newly attained patrimony. Once the state had allowed the descent of an inheritance, it was within the lineage's rights to arrange the transmission of wealth in the best way possible. The best way was always any way that preserved the corporate unity of the kin and at the same time forestalled the state in exercising its final authority to resume landed rights. Thus, in matters of inheritance, and particularly so in adoptions, at least the appearance of lineage consensus had to be maintained if rights were to be kept. Such was notwithstanding the presence, as the evidence of the Devs amply suggests, of very dubious practises in managing successions.

When the British became interested in inamdar lineages the same themes of rights and authority clearly persist. At first, the British were most concerned with rights that compromised the self-imposed religious neutrality of the East India Company. Hence, through the investigation of varsasans and the Morgav pilgrimage the British sought to define their ritual obligations to the Dev and, equally as pressing, determine the cost. Similarly, with the Devs' interests in the commerce of Pune-Haveli the British needed to establish their exact legal and financial commitment to the lineage. Through tortuous inquiry in Maratha accounts and archives much effort was made to define the Devs' title to their mint and transit duties. Because the connection between these revenues and the landed basis of the Cincvad Samsthan – the cornerstone of the Devs' rights – was not grasped, a prolonged conflict between government and claimant was inevitable. The facts of the lineage's rights were under attack.

In the varsasan, mint and transit duty settlements the lineage tried to convince the new rulers that in the first place these rights were held under legitimate title. What rights the lineage held had to be proved. Further, as it was obvious, to the Devs, that the intent of all these grants was religious and charitable, then there was even less reason for the British to alter or eliminate them. Here the lineage sought to show how its rights were held. In the first phase of the settlement during the 1830s and 1840s

Leonard's case of the *kayasthas* is in many ways extreme, but this does not negate the principle here put forward.

the Devs did readily enough acknowledge the successor state's authority over its predecessor's grants. Unfavorable decisions from government were eventually if grudgingly accepted. However, now the manner and mechanism by which the British exerted this authority had changed. When offering compensation for a right about to be lost, the British seemed willing to separate the original intent of a grant from the money involved. The state now did not either confirm or deny the validity of an item of alienated revenue, but rather took some sort of intermediate course. In such a circumstance the lineage would certainly employ any strategy to prevent the loss of rights. Very soon the Devs became expert at deflecting the inquiring energies of the new government.

The changes in the Devs' tactics in dealing with the authority of the state hints at broader political developments in nineteenth-century India. Basically, the case of the Devs illustrates a change in perception of foreign rule. The petitions the Devs presented to government document a process in which Indian subjects gradually came not to accept the presumptions of the imperialists to act as the true successor state to preconquest dynasties. The British were seen to work by new rules and legal principles, and these could be learned and used to advantage. It was only a short step from understanding the philosophic basis and workings of British administrative and legal systems to a similar insight into the new political norms. The Devs themselves did not take this leap; that was left to new classes in Calcutta and Bombay who perhaps had more to directly gain from challenging the British in the political sphere. Changes in perception are not easy to document, but surely the historian should look towards those sections of Indian society that initially had the most to lose from a confrontation with the authority of the new state.

With the advent of the Inam Commission and its inquiries into landed revenue, the British became even more concerned with fixing the exact contractual relationship between the state and its privileged subjects. Again the state was exerting its authority over alienated revenue; so much was to be expected by the Devs; however, an inquiry into the core of the lineage's landed rights was the most serious challenge yet experienced from the British. But the time between the conquest and the inam inquiries had created a sense of landed security for the inamdar. Apparently, the new government had guaranteed alienated revenues through its own inactivity. Seeing in the 1850s that such was not the case, and the British had at last decided to exert the successor state's authority over its predecessor's grants, the Devs mounted a sustained effort to convince the British, in the new rulers' own terms, that Cincvad's inam was inviolable. Even with the severe factionalism that developed within the lineage, all the Dev kin were at least agreed that the British had no cause to either question the validity of Cincvad's grants or tamper with their apparently religious tenure. The prolonged method by which the British settled inams gave various lineage factions the opportunity to challenge the Inam Commission, and also each other. The language of government (both figuratively and literally) had been learned; no longer would the lineage accept as final any exercise of state authority.

At the same time, the Inam Commission had come to understand that the power to either confirm or deny revenue alienations was the key to political authority. The commission's own historian, when contemplating the accumulated insight of the alienation settlements, believed that

to confer grants of lands and pensions was, of all other rights of sovereignty, *the* privilege which the new ruler jealously exercised, and by which he knew he could best make the arm of his authority felt, as well as to retain that authority for any length of time.[5]

Such explicit assertions could only have been made because the Inam Commission had come to realize that in the preconquest society all relations between the state and its privileged subjects had been precisely recorded. The commission possessed the records of the Maratha state, and it actively gathered as many documents from the countryside as could in any way be obtained. With enough research, then, all contractual relations with lineages such as the Devs could be forever fixed. I have shown how, in fact, the commission was created precisely because the British had inherited the unique records of the Maratha state.

The settlement of the Cincvad Devs' inam has well illustrated the many failures of the Inam Commission. Several causes for this notable lack of success can be suggested. The first again concerns the nature of the preconquest documentation. The commission, by avowedly seeking all relevant documents when settling an inam, left itself open to charges of neglect. Certainly, as the instance of the tahanama illustrates, the commission did not always have the most important documentation at its immediate disposal. Moreover, a claimant could always maintain that such seminal documents remained to be discovered in the labrynthine Pune Archives.

However, the British failure to make the most of the preconquest documentation was more than a lapse of administration. The Inam Commission believed, as part of their British legal inheritance, that the documents themselves created obligations for the successor state. That

---

[5] Alfred Thomas Etheridge, 'Narrative of the Bombay Inam Commission and Supplementary Settlements,' *Selections from the Records of the Bombay Government*, n.s. 132 (Bombay, 1874), pp. 11–12.

is, sanads and such title deeds to inams had a binding force on all future relations between the state and its privileged subjects. Moreover, the documents put forth specific terms that spelled out the conditions regulating this relationship. Hence, the state's authority over alienated revenues could be fixed by statute; a set of rules would determine if any inam was to be confirmed or denied. The Inam Commission was part of that profound legal innovation the British brought to India, the concept of legislation, and the preconquest documents seemed most useful in making rule by statute work.

The truth of the situation was somewhat less absolute. At any specific time the documents fixed the relations between state and subject. An inamdar had to have current title; hence, the documents were kept in scrupulous good order. Certainly too, a sanad granting a specific inam created a variety of continuing legal title that any succeeding ruler or state would not lightly deny. But this did not mean that at any time new documents might not be issued entirely redefining the relations between subject and state. The exigencies of the moment, whether they were political, economic, social or religious, determined how the preconquest state would view its revenue alienations. We have seen how the Peshva did not hesitate, for broad social and religious reasons, to alter the terms under which the Dev lineage held its inam. Never did the the state abandon its authority to the legal letter of past circumstance.

The Inam Commission failed not only because it imperfectly understood the nature of the Indian state's authority over its privileged subjects, but also because even less real attention was paid to the concurrent domain of rights. Perhaps this might be understood as the limits to state authority that operated in two main arenas. The first concerned the actual items of revenue. If an inam was a precarious right, always open to redefinition or resumption, nevertheless the possession of a particular source of revenue created a claim based on tradition and sentiment. The Devs, in particular, were eager to convince the British of the inviolability of their inam because of its connection with the saints of Cincvad. Hence, the British had an inherited duty to maintain the finances and reputation of the Samsthan. If the British were to allow the Devs their ancient inams, then they should not tinker with the acknowledged purpose of the grants. The Devs' claim for devasthan, although often a legal strategy to use against British statutory law, was nonetheless based on real feeling.

But the rights of the subject, and hence the limits to state authority, had a second and more critical meaning than simply the question of what revenue a lineage held or how it was held. By creating legislation for inams based on the absolute authority of title deeds and such, the

Inam Commission created a situation wherein the state was forced into the regulation of inheritance. Attempts to identify the eldest male descendant of an inam grantee, or other such requirements of Act XI of 1852, put the British in the near hopeless situation of being arbiters of matters that could only be settled within inamdar lineages. Rather than simply recognize an heir or not, the British now had to identify that person. Inadvertently, the state had clearly transgressed to the very core of the rights of its privileged subjects. As for the Dev lineage, as Captain Cowper realized too late, the British could only confirm Cincvad's inam and recognize the suspiciously adopted son if government were not to deny title altogether. What was certain, was that by the 1850s the lineage would not invite the state to offer creative solutions to its internal factionalism in a way the Peshva had once undertaken. The new rulers were not to be trusted.

Finally, the question remains as to whether Disraeli's rights and authority have anything to do with the Mutiny. Considerable evidence exists to show that the Inam Commission caused extreme uneasiness in western India. Such would not be surprising if one imagines cases like that of the Devs of Cincvad multiplied thousandsfold. But apart from several isolated outbreaks, which perhaps can be explained by particular circumstances, little sustained rebellion occurred in those districts in which the Inam Commission operated. Perhaps, ultimately, inamdar lineages would never risk a final military confrontation with the authority of the state. Being dependent on the state for the granting and maintenance of rights, such could only be unprofitable. Further speculations on what could have happened in western India, or what Disraeli and other critics of the Company thought had happened, do not belong here. In fact, the operations of the Inam Commission continued unabated while north India was ablaze. Nevertheless, perhaps it can be suggested that the failures of the Inam Commission were part of a general phenomenon whereby the first phase of British rule in India collapsed when the authority of the Indian state came starkly into collision with the rights of its subjects.

BIBLIOGRAPHY

I. PRIMARY SOURCES

A. Marathi

1. *Pune Archives*

Ghadni daphtar
Inam Commission rumals and files
Jamav daphtar
Shahu daphtar

2. *Printed documents*

Aitihasik sankirna sahitya, Pune, vols. 1–12.

Apte, D. V. *Candracud daphtar*. Pune: Bharat Itihas Samshodhak Mandal, 1920.

Bendre, V. S. *Maharastretihasaci sadhane*, 3 volumes. Bombay: Mumbai Marathi Granthasamgrahalay, 1966–7.

Citale, V. S. *Pethe daptar*, 2 volumes. Pune: Bharat Itihas Samshodhak Mandal, 1948–50.

Garge, S. M. *Karvir riyasatici kagadpatre*, 3 volumes. Pune: S. M. Garge, 1970–3.

Gaykvad, Khanderav Anandrav. *Karvir sardaramcya kaiphiyati*. Kolhapur: Khanderav Anandrav Gaykvad, 1971.

Kale, V. G. 'Pimple Saudagar,' *Bharat Itihas Samshodhak Mandal Quarterly*, 11 (1930), 1–6.

Khare, G. H. *Hingne daphtar*, 2 volumes. Pune: Bharat Itihas Samshodhak Mandal, 1945–7.

Khobrekar, V. G. *Records of the Shivaji Period*. Bombay: Government Central Press, 1974.

Kulkarni, V. M., Kulkarni, A. R. and Deshpande, A. N. *Peshavyamci bakhar*. Pune: Deshmukh Prakashan, 1963.

Oturkar, R. V. *Maharastraca patrarup itihas*. Pune: n.p., 1941.

  Peshavekalin samajik va arthik patravyavahar. Pune: Bharat Itihas Samshodhak Mandal, 1950.

Pavar, Appasaheb. *Tarabai kalin kagadpatre*, 3 volumes. Kolhapur: Shivaji Vidyapith, 1969–72.

Poona Akhbars, 3 volumes. Hyderabad: Central Records Office, 1952–6.

Bibliography

Potdar, Datto Vaman. 'Moraya Dev samsthan Cincvad sambandhi kamhi junat assal kagad,' *Bharat Itihas Samshodhak Mandal Quarterly*, 2 (1922), 52–69.

Pune-nagar samshodhan vrtta, Pune. volumes 1–4.

Purandare, Krsnaji Vasudev. *Purandare daptar*. Pune: Bharat Itihas Samshodhak Mandal, 1929.

Rajvade, Vishvanath Kashinath. *Shivakalin gharani*. Pune: Bharat Itihas Samshodhak Mandal, 1915.

Shivakalin patravyavahar. Pune, n.p., 1912.

Sammelanvrtta, Pune. volumes 1–5.

Sane, Kashinath Narayan. *Aitihasik patre yadi vagaire*. Pune: n.p., 1889.

Sardesai, G. S., Kale, Y. M. and Vakskar, V. S. *Aitihasik patre yadi vagaire lekh*. Pune: Citrashala Press, 1930.

Selections from the Peshwa Daftar (*Peshave daphtaramtun nivadalele kagad*), ed. G. S. Sardesai, 45 volumes. Bombay: Government Central Press, 1930–4.

Selections from the Satara Rajas' and Peshwas' Diaries, ed. Ganesh Chimnaji Vad, 9 parts. Bombay/Pune: Poona Deccan Vernacular Translation Society, 1906–11.

Vad, Ganesh Chimnaji, Mawjee, Purshotam Vishram and Parasnis, D. B. *Decisions from the Sahu & Peshwa Daftar*. Pune: Purshotam Vishram Mawjee, 1909.

Kaifiyats, Yadis &c. containing historical accounts of certain families of renown in the Deccan and S.M. Country under the Mohammedan and Maratha governments. Pune: Purshotam Vishram Mawjee, 1908.

Sanads & Letters. Pune: Purshotam Vishram Mawjee, 1913.

Treaties, Agreements and Sanads. Pune: Purshotam Vishram Mawjee, 1914.

Vaidya, Shankar Laksman. *Vaidya daphtaramtun nivadalele*, 4 volumes. Pune: Bharat Itihas Samshodhak Mandal, 1944–9.

B. English

1. *Bombay Archives*

Revenue Department

1841; 56/218. 'Transit Duties. Proceedings respecting the grant of compensation to inamdars & jaghiredars, in lieu of,'

1842; 103/139. 'Zumindaree Hucks. Proceedings regarding compensation to be granted to Musjeeds, Temples & ca. for the loss of income from Transit duties under the operation of Act I of 1838'

1844; 138/578. 'Transit Duties. Poona. Moro Oodheo on behalf of the Deo of Sewusthan Chinchor. Proceedings regarding compensation due to the Sewusthan of Chinchore for the loss of Transit dues'

1845; 202/295. 'Proceeding regarding the abolition of Transit Duties in Jaghire Estates'

1846; 199/674. 'Transit Duties. Poona. Deo of Chinchore'

1847; 198/1145. re transit duties

1847; 200/1128. 'Transit Duties. Poona. Deo of Chinchore'

1848; 256/94. 'Transit & Town Duties; Appointment of Messrs. Ogilvy and Rose to investigate and settle all claims to compensation for loss sustained by the abolition of,'

1850; 218/634. 'Transit & town duties' (Dev of Cincvad)

1852; 116/1522. 'Inams. Poona. Gunput Deo son of Anneaba Deo' (Ranjangav)

1852; 117/1557. 'Inams. Poona' (Dev of Cincvad re Tulapur)

1853; 114/761. 'Inams. Poona' (Dev of Cincvad)

1854; 82/1257. 'Inams & Jaghirs. Poona. Gunputdew bin Anyabadew' (Ranjangav)

1858; 90/753. 'Inam Commission, Hon'ble Court's views regarding the operations of the, in Bombay'

1859; 6/844. 'Adoptions. Deo of Chinchore'

1859; 95/66. 'Inam Commission. Instructions to afford Mr. G. N. Taylor, Commissioner at Madras, information on matters connected with the,'

1859; 95/87. 'Inam Commission. Report by Captain Cowper on the Evidence of Mr. Warden before the Select Committee of the House of Commons relative to the,'

1859; 95/1291. 'Inam Commission. Letter addressed by Mr. Hart to the Chairman of the Colonization Committee regarding the,'

1860; 70/588. 'Inams – Deo of Chinchore'

1861; 36/568. 'Inams. Poona – Deo of Chinchore'

1862–64; 50/759. 'Inams & Jagheers. Poona. Bujajee Govind Deo alias Baba Deo Chinchwurkur'

1862–1864; 61/616. 'Dhurnidhur Deo of Chinchore'

Political Department

1848; 25–2030/1389. re Ojhar

2. *Pune Archives*

I; 40/35. 'Constitution of the Inam Commission'

II; 1/8. 'Adjustment of ancient land measures &c.'

II; 1/14. re method of appeal to Inam Commissioner

IX; 4/54. 'Deo of Ranjungaon' (Agent for Sardars' files)

IX; 4/59. 'Deo of Chinchwad' (Agent for Sardars' files)

XII; 4/156. 'Petitions presented to the Governor of Bombay during his tour in 1822'

XII; 5/172. 'Ranjangaon'

XII; 21/743. 'Correspondence regarding the definition of the term 'Inam''

XII; 21/753. 'Rules for regulating the manner and degree in which adoptions and alienations of Inams &c. are to be recognized on the part of Government by its Ministerial officers; also correspondence regarding the right of Inamdars to sell or permanently alienate Inams granted to their family; and the practice of the former Government regarding adoptions &c.'

XIII; 1/1. decisions of the Inam Commission, Haveli taluka of Pune district

XIII; 1/6. decisions of the Inam Commission, Haveli taluka of Pune district

XIII; 2/23. decisions of the Inam Commission, Bhimtadi taluka of Pune district

XIII; 3/29. decisions of the Inam Commission, Purandhar taluka of Pune district

XIII; 3/31. decisions of the Inam Commission, Purandhar taluka of Pune district

XIII; 7/132. re Ojhar Samsthan

XIII; 55/740. 'Chinchore Deo'

XIII; 58/786. 'Holdings & claims; Pant Sechew's Mouze Pirgut – lapsed kurans'

XIII; 67/923. 'Regarding the claim of the Deo of Suwusthan Chinchwur for the continuance as Inam of an income from the Village Toolapoor Bheemthurry Talooka in the Poona Collectorate'

XIV; 1/1. 'Mr. Elphinstone's letters'

XIV; 9/128. 'Management of the villages assigned to Devasthans'

XIV; 28/322. 'Holdings of Chinchore Deo'

'List of Cash Alienations in the Poona Collectorate as they stood on 1st July 1877,' printed lists.

'Note on the Alienation Office, Poona, compiled for the Committee appointed by Government Resolution No. 6099, dated the 27th July, 1905,' by A. C. Logan, Acting Commissioner, Central Division; in Printed Index, vol. 1, pp. 165–212.

Printed genealogy of the Dev lineage; in Printed Index, vol. 11, p. 366.

Volumes containing correspondence of the Deccan Commission, 1817–26.

3. *Government publications, printed documents and papers*

Arbuthnot, Alexander J., ed. *Major-General Sir Thomas Munro: Selections from his Minutes and other Official Writings*, 2 volumes. London: C. Kegan Paul, 1881.

Bombay Presidency, Government of. *Annual Report of the Administration of the Bombay Presidency*, 1861/2–1863/4.

Gazetteer of the Bombay Presidency, District Series, 25 volumes, ed. James Campbell.

Selections from the Records of the Bombay Government: no. 4, old series, 'Report on the Village Communities of the Deccan, with especial reference to the claims of the village officers in the Ahmednuggur Collectorate to 'Purbhara Huks,' or remuneration from their villages, independent of what they receive from government,' 1852.

no. 9, old series, 'Inam Commissioner's Report on the Claim of Mahadajee oorf Nago Punt Sadasew Baput to the Village of Modugay, in the Padshapoor Talooka of the Belgaum Collectorate, and the instructions issued thereon by government,' 1853.

no. 12, old series, 'Report on the Revenue Survey Settlements of the Hoobulee, Nuwulgoond, Kode, and Dharwar Collectorate, by Capt. G. Wingate... also an Extract from a Report of the History, &c. of the District of Chikodee, in the Belgaum Collectorate, by C. J. Manson...,' 1853.

no. 15, old series, 'Proceedings Relative to the Resumption of Certain Villages and Lands held by the late Anajee Nursew; and claimed as hereditary inams by his son,' 1855.

no. 28, new series, 'Correspondence illustrative of the Practice of the Peshwa's Government regarding Adoptions and the circumstances under which adopted sons could succeed to property held from the state,' 1856.

no. 29, new series, 'Correspondence regarding the Concealment by the Hereditary Officers and Others of the Revenue Records of the Former Government and the remedial measures in progress,' 1856.

no. 30, new series, 'I. Correspondence exhibiting the Nature and Use of the Poona Duftur, and the measures adopted for its preservation and arrangement since the introduction of British rule. II. A Selection of Papers explanatory of the Origin of the Inam Commission, and of its progress, from its experimental organisation in A.D. 1843 in one district of the Dharwar Collectorate, until extended to the whole of the Southern Muratha Country, the Deccan, and Khandeish, and constituted a judicial tribunal by Act XI of 1852. Comprising, also, correspondence relating to alienated land revenue generally throughout the Bombay Presidency,' 1856.

no. 31, new series, 'Correspondence exhibiting the Results of the Scrutiny by the Inam Commission of the Lists of Deccan Surinjams prepared in 1844 by the Agent for Sirdars, Mr. Warden, and revised under orders from Government in 1847 by his successor, Mr. Brown; containing, also, the proceedings which have taken place regarding these holdings from the introduction of British rule to the present period, and the rules by which their continuance is now regulated,' 1856

no. 38, new series, 'Correspondence relating to the Tenure of the Possessions in the Deccan held by His Highness Jyajee Rao Sindia under the Treaty of Anjungaum,' 1856.

no. 132, new series, 'Narrative of the Bombay Inam Commission and Supplementary Settlements,' by Alfred Thomas Etheridge, 1874.

Summary of the Law and Custom of Hindoo Castes within the Dekhun Provinces subject to the Presidency of Bombay, chiefly affecting civil suits, by Arthur Steele, 1827.

Bombay State, Government of. *Gazetteer of Bombay State*, Poona District, 1954.

Chaplin, W. *A Report exhibiting a View of the Fiscal and Judicial Systems of Administration, introduced in the Conquered Territories above the Ghauts, under the authority of the Commissioner in the Dekhan*. Bombay: Courier Press, 1824.

Choksey, R. D. *The Aftermath*. Bombay: New Book Company, 1950.

Early British Administration (1817–1836). Pune: R. D. Choksey, 1964.

The Last Phase, Selections from the Deccan Commissioner's Files (Peshwa Daftar), 1815–1818. Bombay: Phoenix Publications, 1948.

Period of Transition (1818–1826). Pune: R. D. Choksey, 1945.

Ratnagiri Collectorate (1821–1829). Pune: R. D. Choksey, 1958.

Bibliography

Twilight of the Maratha Raj, 1818. Pune: R. D. Choksey, 1964.

East India Company. *Selections of Papers from the Records at the East-India House, relating to the revenue, police and civil and criminal justice, under the Company's governments in India*, 4 volumes. London: Printed by Order of the Court of Directors, 1820–6.

Elphinstone, Mountstuart. *Report on the Territories conquered from the Paishwa, submitted to the Supreme Government of British India by the Hon'ble Mountstuart Elphinstone, Commissioner*. Calcutta: Government Gazette Press, 1821.

Forrest, George W., ed. *Selections from the Minutes and other Official Writings of the Honourable Mountstuart Elphinstone, Governor of Bombay*. London: Richard Bentley, 1884.

Gleig, G. R. *The Life of Major-General Sir Thomas Munro, Bart. and K.C.B., late Governor of Madras, with extracts from his correspondence and private papers*, 3 volumes. London: Henry Colburn and Richard Bentley, 1830.

Gurwood, John, ed. *The Dispatches of Field Marshall the Duke of Wellington, K.G., during his various campaigns in India, Denmark, Portugal, Spain, the Low Countries, and France from 1799 to 1818*, 13 volumes. London: John Murray, 1834–8.

Hansard, third series.

India, Government of. *Proceedings of the Legislative Council of India*, 1854–61.
Report on the Hindu Religious Endowments Commission (1960–1962), 1962.

Kaye, John William. *The Life and Correspondence of Major-General Sir John Malcolm, G.C.B., late envoy to Persia and Governor of Bombay; from unpublished letters and journals*, 2 volumes. London: Smith, Elder, 1856.

Kaye, John William, ed. *Memorials of Indian Government; being a selection from the papers of Henry St. George Tucker*. London: Richard Bentley, 1853.

Mackintosh, Robert James. *Memoirs of the Life of Sir James Mackintosh*, 2 volumes. London: Edward Moxon, 1835.

Madras Presidency, Government of. *Report on the Administration of the Madras Presidency during the year 1861–62*, 1862.

Maharashtra, Government of. *Census of India 1971; District Census Handbook, Poona*, 1974.

Memorandum of the Improvements in the Administration of India during the last thirty years, (by John Stuart Mill). London: East-India Company, 1858; reprinted Farnborough: Gregg International Publishers, 1968.

Philips, C. H., ed. *The Correspondence of Lord William Bentinck: Governor-General of India*. 1828–35, 2 volumes. Oxford University Press, 1977.

Sardesai, G. S., ed. *Poona Affairs (Elphinstone's Embassy) (Part II, 1816–1818)*. Bombay: Government Central Press, 1958.

4. *Parliamentary papers* (*House of Commons*)

Short titles have been taken from 'Annual Lists and General Index of the Parliamentary Papers relating to the East Indies published during the years 1801 to 1907 inclusive,' 1909, LXIV (89).

Bibliography

Firminger, Walter Kelly, ed. *The Fifth Report from the Select Committee of the House of Commons on the Affairs of the East India Company, dated 28th July, 1812*, 3 volumes. Calcutta: R. Cambray, 1918.

1821, XVIII (59), 195–292. 'Regulations passed by the Government of Bengal in 1819'

1826, XXV (158), 99–188. 'Regulations passed by the Governments of Bengal, Fort St. George and Bombay, 1823 and 1824'

1828, XXIII (129), 351–469. 'Regulations passed by the Governments of Bengal, Fort St. George and Bombay, 1825–26'

1829, XXIII (201), 195–522. 'Regulations passed by the Governments of Bengal, Fort St. George and Bombay in 1827'

1830, VI (646). 'Affairs of the East India Company and the trade between Great Britain, the East Indies, and China: Report from the Select Committee of the House of Lords, with evidence'

1830, XXVIII (60), 637–86. 'Regulations passed by the Governments of Bengal, Fort St. George and Bombay in 1828'

1831, V (65). 'Affairs of the East India Company: Minutes of evidence of Select Committee'

1831–32, VIII (734), IX–XIV (735 I–VI). 'Affairs of the East India Company: Report from the Select Committee, minutes of evidence and appendices'

1833, XXV (754), 245–84. 'Regulations passed by the Governments of Bengal, Fort St. George and Bombay in 1830'

1837, XLIII (357), 185–202. 'Religious Ceremonies (Madras): Memorial of the European population. Pilgrim Tax: Despatches'

1839, XXXIX (39), 189–90. 'Religious Ceremonies: Despatch, dated 8th August 1838, relating to the withdrawal of interference with the religious ceremonies of the natives of India'

1840, VIII (527). 'East India Produce (Select Committee): Minutes of evidence, with appendix and index'

1840, XXXVII (599), 199. 'Rent free land in Bengal, Behar, Orissa, and Benares: Establishment, salaries, cases, and appeals; statement'

1841 (sess. I), XVII (86), 739–52. 'Connexion between Government and religious institutions of the country: Correspondence'

1841 (sess. 1), XVII (232), 735–6. 'Religious Ceremonies of Natives of India: Despatch, dated 3rd March 1841, regarding withdrawal of Government interference, and relinquishment of revenue from temples, &c.'

1841 (sess. 1), XVII (328), 737–8. 'Religious Ceremonies of Natives of India (Separation of Government from all share in management of native temples): Despatch dated 31st March 1841'

1845, XXXIV (255), 47–82. 'Acts of the Government of India relating to imports, transit or inland custom duties, town duties, mookauts, and manufacture of salt'

1845, XXXIV (664), 321–400. 'Native Religious Institutions and Ceremonies, and payments to the support of Juggernath temple; Government connection and superintendence'

Bibliography

1846, xxxi (33), 33–92. 'Acts of the Government of India, 1844'

1852, x (533). 'Report from the Select Committee on Indian Territories'

1852–3, xxvii (426); xxviii (479); xxviii (556), 85; xxviii (692), 149; xxviii (768), 443; xxix (897); xxix (897 i–ii), 245. 'Indian Territories: Reports from the select committee'

1852–3, xxx (41); xxxi (627); xxxii (627 I); xxxiii (627 ii–iii). 'Indian Territories: Reports of the Select Committee of the House of Lords'

1857, xxix (341), 481–502. 'Titles of Land Commission (Bombay): Commission issued by the Government of Bombay for inquiring into the titles of resumption of land held in inam, or rent free, in hereditary occupation by native landowners; correspondence and statistics'

1857–8, vii (pt. 1) (261); vii (pt. 1) (326), 165; vii (pt. 1) (415), 373; vii (pt. 2) (461). 'Colonisation and Settlement of India: Reports of the Select Committee appointed to inquire into the progress and prospects, and the best means to be adopted for the promotion of European colonisation and settlement, especially in the hill districts, &c.'

1857–8, xlii (71 i), 305–38. 'Connection of the Government of India with religious ceremonies &c.: Further papers'

1857–8, xliii (75), 1–38. 'Improvements in administration during the past 30 years: Memorandum by Mr. John Stuart Mill'

1857–8, xliii (354), 85–92. 'Proclamation on the conquest of the Deccan, 1819 [sic], and instructions issued to the local commissioners'

1859 (sess. 1), iv (198); (sess. 2) v (171), 261–350. 'Colonisation and Settlement in India and the extension of commerce in Central Asia: Reports of the select committee'

1866, lii (226), 309–42. 'Land Tenures, Deccan: Report by the statistical reporter of the Government of Bombay'

5. Legal cases

Indian law reports

Vasudev Anant v. *Ramkrishna and Shivram Narayan; Ramkrishna and Shivram Narayan* v. *The Government of Bombay* (1878), 2. Bom. 1878, 529–32.

Narayan, son and heir of Sadanand Ramchandra, deceased v. *Chintaman and Moreshwar, sons and heirs of Balaji Natu* (1881), 5. Bom. 1881, 393–400.

Chintaman Bajaji Dev v. *Dhondo Ganesh Dev and others* (1888), 15 Bom. 1891, 612–25.

Ganesh Dharnidhar Maharajdev v. *Kesharav Govind Kulgavkar* (1890), 15 Bom. 1891, 625–43.

Shri Dhundiraj Ganesh Dev and others v. *Ganesh* (1893), 18 Bom. 1894, 721–33.

Dharnidhar v. *Chinto* (1895), 20 Bom. 1895, 250–9.

Annaji Raghunath Gosavi and another v. *Narayan Sitaram and others* (1896), 21 Bom. 1897, 556–63.

Ganesh Jagannath Dev v. *Ramchandra Ganesh Dev and another* (1896), 21 Bom. 1897, 563–67.

Bibliography

II. SECONDARY SOURCES

A. Works of reference (English and Marathi)

Annotated Bibliography on the Economic History of India (*1500 A.D. to 1947 A.D.*), 4 volumes. Pune: Gokhale Institute of Politics and Economics, 1977–80.

Boase, Frederic. *Modern English Biography*, 6 volumes. London: Frank Cass, 1965 (reprint).

Buckland, C. E. *Dictionary of Indian Biography*. London: Swan Sonnenschein, 1906.

Date, Shankar Ganesh. *Marathi grantha suci*, 2 volumes, Pune: S. G. Date, 1943–61.

Dictionary of National Biography

The East-India Register and Directory (title varies), 1831–58.

Ketkar, Shridhar Vyankatesh. *Maharastriya jnana kosh*, 23 volumes. Pune: Maharastriya Jnanakosh Mandal, 1920–9.

Khare, Ganesh Sakharam. *Khare jantri athava shivakalin sampurna shakavli* (*shake 1551–1649*). Pune: Oriental Buk Saplaing Ejansi, 1923.

Khobrekar, V. G., ed. *Shahu daptaratil kagadpatramci varnanatmak suci*, 2 volumes. Bombay: Government Press for Director of Archives and Archaeology, Government of Maharashtra, 1969–70.

Modak, Balaji Prabhakar. *Chronological Tables containing Corresponding Dates of the Hindu, Mahomedan and Christian Eras, from A.D. 1728 to 1889*. Pune and Kolhapur: Chitra Shala and Vidyavilas Presses, 1889.

Molesworth, J. T. *A Dictionary, Marathi and English*. Pune: Shubhada-Saraswat, 1975 (reprint).

Sardesai, G. S. *Hand Book to the Records in the Alienation Office Poona*. Bombay: Government Central Press, 1933.

Historical Genealogies. Bombay: Government of Bombay State, 1957.

Wilson, H. H. *A Glossary of Judicial and Revenue Terms, and of useful words in official documents relating to the administration of the Government of British India*. Delhi: Munshiram Manoharlal, 1968 (reprint).

Woodman, Joseph Vere. *A Digest of Indian Law Cases: Containing High Court Reports, 1862–1900 and Privy Council Reports of Appeals from India, 1836–1900*, 6 volumes. Calcutta: Superintendent of Government Printing, India, 1902.

B. Books and articles (Marathi)

Astavinayak. Bombay: Department of Tourism, Maharashtra State, n.d.

Avalsakar, S. V. and Apte, M. V., 'Pune shaharamtil jakat va vyapar,' *Artha Vijnana*, 6 (1964), 117–26.

Cincvadksetrastha Shri Moraya Gosavi-caritra. Cincvad: Shri Dev Samsthan, n.d.

Bhave, Vasudev Krsna. *Peshvekalin Maharastra*. New Delhi: Bharatiya Itihas Anusandhan Parisad, 1976 (reprint).

Dhere, Ramchandra Cintaman. *Mangalmurti Moraya.* Bombay: Vora and Co., 1958.

Gadgil, Amarendra. *Shriganeshkosh* Bombay: Vora and Co., 1968.

Joshi, Shankar Narayan. *Sambhajikalin patrasarsamgraha.* Pune: Bharat Itihas Samshodhan Mandal, 1949.

Shivakalinpatrasarsamgraha, vol. 3. Pune: Bharat Itihas Samshodhan Mandal, 1937.

Karandikar, J. S. *Shrigeneshotsavaci sath varse.* Pune: J. S. Karandikar, 1953.

Khare, Ganesh Hari. *Mandalamtil nani.* Pune: Bharat Itihas Samshodhan Mandal, 1933.

Khare, Vasudev Vaman. *Himmatbahaddar Cavhan gharanyaca itihas.* Kolhapur: L. D. Divan, 1967.

Lele, Ganesh Sadashiv. *Tirthayatraprabandha.* Nasik: Nasikvrtta, 1885.

Mujumdar, G. N. 'Ganeshyogikrt Ganeshvijay,' *Bharat Itihas Samshodhan Mandal Quarterly,* 12 (1932), 153–4.

'Shrimant Pantpradhan Balaji Bajirav urph Nanasaheb Peshave viracit 'Shriganeshkutukamrt',' *Bharat Itihas Samshodhan Mandal Quarterly,* 2 (1940–1), 46–7.

Potdar, D. V., 'Cincvad-Moraya Gosavi-Devalay kadhi bandhale?,' *Bharat Itihas Samshodhan Mandal Quarterly,* 21 (1940–1), 78–9.

Sadguru Shri Moraya Gosavi, Shri Cintamani Maharaj, Shri Narayan Maharaj, Shri Dharanidhar Maharaj yamcya padamca gatha. Cincvad: Shri Dev Samsthan, 1977.

Shaligram, Yashvant Vinayak. *Sriganpati-atharvashirsa-rahasya.* Pune: Shriganeshpith Prakashan, n.d.

Shri astavinayak stotra va mahatmya. Bombay: T. V. Parcure, Balvant Pustak Bhandar, n.d.

C. Books, articles, newspapers, and theses (English)

Ambirajan, S. *Classical Political Economy and British Policy in India.* Cambridge University Press, 1978.

Appadurai, Arjun. *Worship and Conflict under Colonial Rule, A South Indian Case.* Cambridge University Press, 1981.

Apte, M. D., 'The Nature and Scope of the Records from Peshwa Daftar with reference to zakat system,' *Indian Economic and Social History Review,* 6 (1969), 369–79.

Baden-Powell, B. H. *The Land Systems of British India,* 3 Volumes. Oxford: Clarendon Press, 1892.

Ballhatchet, Kenneth. *Social Policy and Social Change in Western India, 1817–1830.* London: Oxford University Press, 1957.

Banerjee, Anil Chandra. *The Agrarian System of Bengal,* 2 volumes. Calcutta: K. P. Bagchi, 1980–1.

Bayly, C. A. *Rulers, Townsmen and Bazaars: North Indian Society in the age of British Expansion, 1770–1850.* Cambridge University Press, 1983.

Bibliography

Bean, J. M. W. *The Estates of the Percy Family, 1416–1537.* London: Oxford University Press, 1958.

Bohannan, Paul. *Social Anthropology.* New York: Holt, Rinehart and Winston, 1963.

Bohannan, Paul and Laura. *Tiv Economy.* London: Longmans, 1968.

The Bombay Standard.

The Bombay Times and Journal of Commerce.

Bosher, J. F. *The Single Duty Project, A Study of the Movement for a French Customs Union in the Eighteenth Century.* London: The Athlone Press, 1964.

Cashman, Richard I. *The Myth of the Lokamanya.* Berkeley: University of California Press, 1975.

Cassels, Nancy Gardner, 'The 'Pilgrim Tax': A case study in the development of East India Company social policy,' Ph.D. thesis, University of Toronto, 1976.

Choksey, R. D. *Economic History of the Bombay Deccan and Karnatak (1818–1868).* Pune: R. D. Choksey, 1945.

Economic Life in the Bombay Deccan (1818–1939). Bombay: Asia Publishing House, 1955.

A History of British Diplomacy at the Court of the Peshwas (1786–1818). Pune: R. D. Choksey, 1951.

Mountstuart Elphinstone, The Indian years 1796–1827. Bombay: Popular Prakashan, 1971.

Clunes, John. *Itinerary and Directory for Western India, Being a Collection of Routes Through the Provinces Subject to the Presidency of Bombay.* Calcutta: H. Townsend, 1826.

Coats, Thomas, 'Account of the Present State of the Township of Lony: In Illustration of the Institutions, Resources, &c. of the Marratta Cultivators,' *Transactions of the Literary Society of Bombay,* 3 (1823, reprinted 1877), 183–280.

Cohn, Bernard S., 'The Initial British Impact on India, A Case Study of the Benares Region,' *Journal of Asian Studies,* 19 (1960), 418–31.

Colebrook, T. E. *Life of the Honourable Mountstuart Elphinstone,* 2 volumes. London: John Murray, 1884.

Conlon, Frank F. *A Caste in a Changing World, The Chitrapur Saraswat Brahmans, 1700–1935.* Berkely: University of California Press, 1977.

Courtright, Paul B. *Gaṇeśa, Lord of Obstacles, Lord of Beginnings.* New York: Oxford University Press, 1985.

Derrett, J. Duncan M. *Essays in Classical and Modern Hindu Law,* 4 volumes. Leiden: E. J. Brill, 1976–8.

Religion, Law and State in India. London: Faber and Faber, 1968.

Dirks, Nicholas B., 'The Structure and Meaning of Political Relations in a South Indian Little Kingdom,' *Contributions to Indian Sociology,* new series, 13 (1979), 169–206.

Divekar, D. V., 'The Emergence of an Indigenous Business Class in Maharashtra in the Eighteenth Century,' *Modern Asian Studies,* 16 (1982), 427–43.

Bibliography

Dobbin, Christine. *Urban Leadership in Western India, Politics and Communities in Bombay City, 1840–1885.* London: Oxford University Press, 1972.

Dutt, Romesh. *The Economic History of British India.* London: Kegan Paul, Trench, Trubner, 1902.

India in the Victorian Age, An Economic History of the People. London: Kegan Paul, Trench, Trubner, 1904.

Elliot, H. M. and Dowson, John, trans. *The History of India as told by its Own Historians,* 8 volumes. Allahabad: Kitab Mahal, 1964 (reprint).

Enthoven, R. E. *Folklore of the Konkan Compiled from Materials Collected by the Late A. M. T. Jackson, Indian Civil Service.* Delhi: Cosmo Publications, 1976 (reprint).

Erskine, William, 'Diaries of Sir William Erskine, First Secretary of the Society (1804–15),' *Journal of the Bombay Branch of the Royal Asiatic Society,* 25 (1917–18), 373–409.

Evans-Pritchard, E. E. *The Nuer, A Description of the Modes of Livelihood and Political Institutions of a Nilotic People.* Oxford: Clarendon Press 1940.

Falkland, Lady Amelia, Viscountess. *Chow-chow.* 2 volumes. London: Hurst and Blackett, 1857.

Fortes, Meyer. *Kinship and the Social Order.* London: Routledge and Kegan Paul, 1969.

'The Structure of Unilineal Descent Groups,' *American Anthropologist,* 55 (1953), 17–41.

Fortes, M. and Evans-Pritchard, E. E. *African Political Systems.* London: Oxford University Press, 1940.

Fox, Richard G. *Kin, Clan, Raja and Rule: State-hinterland Relations in Pre-industrial India.* Berkeley: University of California Press, 1971.

Frykenberg, Robert Eric. *Guntur District, 1788–1848, a history of local influence and central authority in south India.* Oxford: Clarendon Press, 1965.

Frykenberg, Robert Eric, ed. *Land Tenure and Peasant in South Asia.* New Delhi: Orient Longman, 1977.

Fukazawa, Hiroshi, 'Lands and Peasants in the Eighteenth Century Maratha Kingdom,' *Hitotsubashi Journal of Economics,* 6 (1965), 32–61.

'State and Caste System (jati) in the Eighteenth Century Maratha Kingdom,' *Hitotsubashi Journal of Economics,* 9 (1968), 32–44.

'A Study of Local Administration of Adilshahi Sultanate,' *Hitotsubashi Journal of Economics,* 3 (1963), 37–67.

Gallagher, John and Robinson, Ronald, 'The Imperialism of Free Trade,' *Economic History Review,* 2nd series, 6 (1953), 1–15.

Ghosal, H. R., 'Resumption of Rent-free Tenures for Assessment by the Company's Government (1819–1850),' *Indian History Congress, Proceedings of the Thirteenth Session* (1950), 316–19.

Ghurye, G. S. *Gods and Men.* Bombay: Popular Book Depot, 1962.

Goody, Jack, 'Adoption in Cross-cultural Perspective,' *Comparative Studies in Society and History,* 11 (1969), 55–78.

'Strategies of Heirship,' *Comparative Studies in Society and History,* 15 (1973), 3–20.

Bibliography

Goody, Jack, Thirsk, Joan and Thompson E. P. *Family and Inheritance, Rural Society in Western Europe, 1200–1800*. Cambridge University Press, 1976.

Graham, Maria. *Journal of a Residence in India*. Edinburgh: Archibald Constable, 1813.

Grant Duff, James. *A History of the Mahrattas*, 3 volumes. London: Longman, Rees, Orme, Brown and Green, 1826.

Gune, Vithal Trimbak. *The Judicial System of the Marathas*. Pune: Deccan College Post-Graduate and Research Institute, 1953.

Harnetty, Peter. *Imperialism and Free Trade: Lancashire and India in the Mid-nineteenth Century*. Vancouver: University of British Columbia Press, 1972.

Harris, Charles H. *A Mexican Family Empire, The Latifundio of the Sanchez Navarros, 1765–1867*. Austin: University of Texas Press, 1975.

Homans, George C. *English Villagers of the Thirteenth Century*. Cambridge, Mass.: Harvard University Press, 1941.

Jackson, Charles. *Vindication of the Marquis of Dalhousie's Indian Administration*. Allahabad: Chugh Publications, 1975 (reprint).

Joglekar, R. N. *Alienation Manual (Containing Information About All Kinds of Inams and Watans)*. Pune: R. N. Joglekar, 1921.

Kane, Pandurang Vaman. *History of Dharmashastra*, 5 volumes. Pune: Bhandarkar Oriental Research Institute, 1930–62.

Karve, Irawati. *Kinship Organisation in India*. Pune: Deccan College Post-Graduate and Research Institute, 1953.

Kaye, John William. *A History of the Sepoy War in India, 1857–1858*, 3 volumes. London: Longman, Green, 1896 (9th edition).

Kessinger, Tom G. *Vilyatpur, 1848–1968, Social and Economic Change in a North Indian Village*. Berkeley: University of California Press, 1974.

Khare, G. H., 'A Report on the Maratha Mints of the Peshwa Period Located at Poona, Chakan and Chinchavad, Both near Poona,' *Journal of the Numismatic Society of India*, 38 (1976), 102–9.

Select Articles. Pune: Bharat Itihas Samshodhan Mandal, 1966.

'Some Coins of the Peshwas,' *Journal of the Numismatic Society of India*, 4 (1942), 73–7.

Khatun, Monira, 'Some Observations on Maratha Coins,' *Journal of the Numismatic Society of India*, 22 (1960), 221–4.

Khobrekar, V. G., ed. *Sir Jadunath Sarkar Birth Centenary Volume; English translation of Tarikh-I-Dilkasha (memoirs of Bhimsen relating to Aurangzib's Deccan campaigns)*. Bombay: Department of Archives, Maharashtra, 1972.

Kishore, Brij. *Tara Bai and Her Times*. Bombay: Asia Publishing House, 1963.

Knight, Robert. *The Inam Commission Unmasked*. London: Effingham Wilson, 1859.

Kulkarni, A. R. *Maharashtra in the Age of Shivaji*. Pune: R. J. Deshmukh, 1969.

'Service-tenures under the Marathas: A study in inter-relationships,' *Indian Historical Records Commission, Proceedings*, 38 (1967), 100–7.

Kulkarni, G. T., 'Banking in the 18th Century: A Case Study of a Poona Banker,' *Artha Vijnana*, 15 (1973), 180–200.

Bibliography

'Land Revenue and Agricultural Policy of Shivaji,' *Bulletin of the Deccan College Research Institute*, 35 (1976), 73–82.

'Some New Light on Chauth and Chauthai Kul,' *Bulletin of the Deccan College Research Institute*, 36 (1976–7), 66–72.

Kumar, Ravinder. *Western India in the Nineteenth Century, A Study in the Social History of Maharashtra*. London: Routledge & Kegan Paul, 1968.

Laslett, Peter and Wall, Richard, eds. *Household and Family in Past Time*. Cambridge University Press, 1972.

Leighly, John, ed. *Land and Life, A Selection from the Writings of Carl Ortwin Sauer*. Berkeley: University of California Press, 1963.

Leonard, Karen Isaksen. *Social History of an Indian Caste, the Kayasths of Hyderabad*. Berkeley: University of California Press, 1978.

Macdonald, A. *Memoir of the Life of the late Nana Farnavis*. London: Oxford University Press, 1927 (reprint).

Malcolm, John, *Government of India*. London: John Murray, 1833.

A Memoir of Central India Including Malwa and Adjoining Provinces, 2 volumes. London: Parbury, Allen, 1832.

Mann, Harold H. *Land and Labour in a Deccan Village (Pimpla Saudagar)*. London: Oxford University Press, 1917.

The Social Framework of Agriculture: India, Middle East, England, ed. Daniel Thorner. New York: Augustus M. Kelley, 1967.

Mann, Harold H. and Kantikar, N. V. *Land and Labour in a Deccan Village (Study No. 2)*. London: Oxford University Press, 1921.

Mayer, Adrian C. *Caste and Kinship in Central India*. Berkeley: University of California Press, 1960.

Meskill, Johanna Menzel. *A Chinese Pioneer Family, the Lins of Wu-feng, Taiwan, 1729–1895*. Princeton University Press.

Metcalf, Thomas R. *The Aftermath of Revolt, India 1857–1870*. Princeton University Press, 1964.

Land, Landlords and the British Raj, Northern India in the Nineteenth Century. Berkeley: University of California Press, 1979.

Moor, Edward, 'Account of an Hereditary Living Deity to Whom Devotion is Paid by the Bramins of Poona and its Neighbourhood,' *Asiatick Researches*, 7 (1801), 383–97.

Oriental Fragments. London: Smith, Elder, 1834.

Moore, R. J. *Sir Charles Wood's Indian Policy, 1853–66*. Manchester University Press, 1966.

Mudaliar, Chandra Y. *The Secular State and Religious Institutions in India*. Wiesbaden: Franz Steiner, 1974.

Mulla, Dinshaw Fardunji. *Principles of Hindu Law*. Calcutta: The Eastern Law House, 1932 (7th edition).

Nayeem, M. A. 'The Working of the *Chauth* and *Sardeshmukhi* System in the Mughal Provinces of the Deccan (1707–1803 A.D.),' *Indian Economic and Social History Review*, 14 (1977), 153–206.

Patel, Govindlal D. *The Indian Land Problem and Legislation*. Bombay: N. M. Tripathi, 1954.

Perlin, Frank, 'Of White Whale and Countrymen in the Eighteenth-century Maratha Deccan. Extended Class Relations, Rights, and the Problem of Rural Autonomy under the Old Regime,' *Journal of Peasant Studies*, 5 (1978), 172–237.

Preston, Laurence W., 'Subregional Religious Centres in the History of Maharashtra: The Sites Sacred to Ganesh,' in *Images of Maharashtra, a regional profile of India*, ed. N. K. Wagle. London: Curzon Press, 1980, pp. 102–28.

Puntambekar, Shrikrishna Venkatesh, trans. *A Royal Edict on the Principles of State Policy, and Organization during the Sixty Years' War of Maratha Independence (A.D. 1646–1706) otherwise called Ramachandrapant Amatya's Rajaniti, dated A.D. 1716*. Madras: Diocesan Press, 1929.

Radcliffe–Brown, A. R. *Structure and Function in Primitive Society*. London: Cohen & West, 1952.

Raeside, Ian. 'A Note on the 'Twelve Mavals' of Poona District,' *Modern Asian Studies*, 12 (1978), 393–418.

Ramsbotham, R. B. *Studies in the Land Revenue History of Bengal, 1769–1787*. London: Oxford University Press, 1926.

Ranade, M. G., 'Currencies and Mints under Mahratta Rule,' *Journal of the Bombay Branch of the Royal Asiatic Society*, 20 (1897–1900), 191–200.
  Rise of Maratha Power and other essays. Bombay: University of Bombay, 1961 (reprint).

Raychaudhuri, Tapan and Habib, Irfan, eds. *The Cambridge Economic History of India*, volume 1, c. 1200–c. 1750. Cambridge University Press, 1982.

Richards, Eric. *The Leviathan of Wealth, the Sutherland Fortune in the Industrial Revolution*. London: Routledge & Kegan Paul, 1973.

Richards, J. F. *Mughal Administration in Golconda*. Oxford: Clarendon Press, 1975.

Robb, Peter, ed. *Rural India; Land, Power and Society Under British Rule*. London: Curzon Press, 1983.

Salahuddin Ahmed, A. F. *Social Ideas and Social Change in Bengal, 1818–1835*. Leiden: E. J. Brill, 1965.

Sahlins, Marshall D., 'The Segmentary Lineage: An Organization of Predatory Expansion,' *American Anthropologist*, 63 (1961), 322–45.

Sardesai, Govind Sakharam. *The Main Currents of Maratha History*. Bombay: Keshav Bhikaji Dhaule, 1933 (2nd edition).
  New History of the Marathas, 3 volumes. Bombay: Phoenix Publications, 1946–8.

Sarkar, Jadunath, trans. *Maasir-I-'Alamgiri, A History of the Emperor Aurangzeb-'Alamgir (reign 1658–1707 A.D.) by Saqi Must'ad Khan*. Calcutta: Royal Asiatic Society of Bengal, 1947.

Sen, Surendranath. *Administrative System of the Marathas (from original sources)*. Calcutta: University of Calcutta, 1925.

Shah, A. M. *The Household Dimension of the Family in India*. Berkeley: University of California Press, 1974.

Singer, Milton and Bernard S. Cohn, eds. *Structure and Change in Indian Society*. Chicago: Aldine Publishing Company, 1968.

Smith, M. G., 'On Segmentary Lineage Systems,' *Journal of the Royal Anthropological Institute*, 86, 2 (1956), 39–80.

Sontheimer, Gunther-Dietz. *The Joint Hindu Family*. New Delhi: Munshiram Manoharlal, 1977.

Stein, Burton., 'State Formation and Economy Reconsidered, part one,' *Modern Asian Studies*, 19 (1985), 387–93.

Stokes, Eric. *The English Utilitarians and India*. Oxford: Clarendon Press, 1959.
The Peasant and the Raj, Studies in Agrarian Society and Peasant Rebellion in Colonial India. Cambridge University Press, 1978.

Sykes, W. H., 'An Account of the Origin of the Living God and the Village of Chinchore, near Poona,' *Transactions of the Literary Society of Bombay*, 3 (1823 reprinted 1877), 69–78.
'On the Land Tenures of the Deccan,' *Journal of the Royal Asiatic Society*, 2 (1835), 3205–33.
'Special Report on the Statistics of the Four Collectorates of Dukhun, under the British Government,' *Report of the Seventh Meeting of the British Association for the Advancement of Science*, 6 (1838), 217–336.

Tone, William Henry. *A Letter to an Officer on the Madras Establishment; being an attempt to illustrate some particular institutions of the Maratta people; principally relative to their system of war and finance. Also an account of the political changes of the empire, in the year 1796, as published in the Bombay Courier*. London: J. Debrett, 1799 (reprint).

Tulpule, Shankar Gopal. *Classical Marathi Literature from the Beginning to A.D. 1818*. Wiesbaden: Otto Harrossowitz, 1979.

Valentia, Lord. *Voyages and Travels to India, Ceylon, the Red Sea, Abyssinia, and Egypt in the years 1802, 1803, 1804, 1805, and 1806*, 3 volumes. London: William Miller, 1809.

Vashista, V. B. *Land Revenue and Public Finance in Maratha Administration*. Delhi: Oriental Publishing, 1975.

Wagle, N. K., 'The Ordeal in the Mosque of Ranjangav: An Aspect of Dispute Resolution in 18th Century Maharashtra,' in *Islamic Society and Culture, Essays in honour of Professor Aziz Ahmad*, ed. Milton Israel and N. K. Wagle. New Delhi: Manohar, 1983.

Wagle, Narendra and Kulkarni A. R. *Vallabha's Parasharama Caritra, an eighteenth century Maratha history of the Peshwas*. Bombay: Popular Prakashan, 1976.

Washbrook, David, review of *Social History of an Indian Caste* by Karen Isaksen Leonard. *Pacific Affairs*, 52 (1979–80), 735–7.

Wrigley, E. A. *Population and History*. London: Weidenfeld and Nicolson, 1969.

Index

Act XI of 1852, 177, 178, 179, 219,
225–6; and inheritance, 208, 231–2,
247; origins, 164–5, 172–3, 175, 176,
179
adoption, 198, 203, 228, 243; and Devs
of Cincvad, 82, 191, 192–3, 196–8,
220; and Inam Commission 195,
202–3, 208–9; and kinship, 206, 232;
and lineage, 198, 205–6, and lineage
factionalism, 197; and lineage
segmentation 74, 197, 203, 207; and
partible inheritance, 197; and
widow, 204, 206
advamarg, 141
Afghans, 50
Agent for Sardars, 89, 173–4, 175,
201–2; and commerce, 127–8, 134,
153–4; and Devs of Cincvad, 182,
193, 208, 294; and inamdars, 87, 89;
and Morgav pilgrimage, 112–13, 114
agnihotri, 106
Agra Presidency, 148
agriculture, 15, 30, 79, 80
alienated revenue, 10–11, 173–4, 238–9;
and authority of state, 46–8, 245;
and British policy, 77, 90, 201–2,
238–9; and Mountstuart Elphinstone,
169–74; extent of, 12–13;
settlements in Bengal, 165–9;
settlements in Bombay, 172–7
Ahmednagar city, 108, 109–10, 142
ain jama, 186
Ajnapatra, 47
ajnapatras, 41, 45
Akurdi village, 38
Alandi village, 17, 141
allowances. *See* varsasans
altamgha, 166
amanatdars, 128, 129
Ambar, Malik, 30
Ambi Budruk village, 39, 81, 83, 98
Amended Rules of 1842, 115–16, 117
Amini Commission, 165–6
Anglo-Indian law, 195–6, 198, 199–200,
232–3

Anglo-Maratha war (1802–3), 108
ankushi rupee, 123, 131
annasatra, 32, 40, 126–7, 128, 137–8, 152
anusthan, 50, 105
astavinayak, 16
Aundh village, 39, 62, 66–7, 139, 140
Aurangzeb, 37, 51, 137
authority of state, 240; and alienated
revenue, 46–8, 245; under British,
233, 238–9, 240; and Inam
Commission, 244–5

Bajirav Peshva, 54, 108, 109–10, 198
Bajirav Ballal Peshva, 43–4, 55
Ballhatchet, Kenneth, 104
Banaras, 105
Banere village, 38–9, 81
Banerjee, Anil Chandra, 167
banking, 51
Baroda, 199
Bassein, Treaty of, 3, 54, 108, 171
Bassein campaign, 52, 81
Bengal, Regulation 2 of 1819, 167–9
Bengal Presidency, 113, 148–9, 165–6,
170–1
Bentinck, Lord, 149
Bhor ghat, 2, 139
Bhosri village, 39, 79
bigha, 60
Bombay, 51
Bombay, Regulation 1 of 1823, 173
Bombay, Regulation 17 of 1827, 173,
176
Bombay Missionary Conference, 120
Bombay Presidency, 88, 92, 140, 148–9,
169–74
Bombay–Pune routes, 6, 54, 139–40
Bopegav village, 58–9
Briggs, John, 88n, 172
British, 3, 4, 54–5, 77, 87, 88; and
alienated revenue, 201–2, 238–9;
and coinage, 127; and commercial
reform, 90, 159–60; and inheritance,
230–1; and lineage factionalism,
207–8; and mints, 134; and

Index

religious endowments, 90, 114–15, 120–1; and rights, 243–4; and transit duties, 152–3; and varsasans, 92, 99–100, 113, 115–16, 242. *See also* Deccan Commission; Inam Commission

British conquest: of the Deccan, 83, 84, 87–8, 99, 169, 198; and law, 199–200

British rule: and authority of state, 233, 240; nature of, 4–5, 89, 132, 244; as successor to Marathas, 90, 92, 162

Cakan village, 44, 140
Calcutta, 241
Candracud, Gangadhar Yashvant (Gangoba Tatya), 81
Candvad mint, 125
Carholi village, 39, 79, 201
Caskar lineage, 150
caste, 18
cauki, 141
cavar, 31
Ceul (Chaul), 39, 137n
Chaplin, William, 63, 87, 88n; and Morgav pilgrimage, 112, 119; and transit duties, 146–7, 148; and varsasans, 110–11
chatrapati, 37, 41
Cikhli village, 36, 66, 67, 79, 140, 141
Cincoli mahal, 136, 138–9, 140, 148
Cincoli village: as inam, 28–31, 38, 39; and Moroba Gosavi, 29, 30–1; and transit duties, 138–9, 140
Cincvad mint, 1, 51, 90, 122; and the annasatra, 126–7, 128; and British, 128–35, 243; and Marathas, 124, 127–8, 129–31; and Marathi documents, 128, 129–31, 133–4; and varsasans, 124, 135
Cincvad Samsthan: and adoption, 195, 197–8, 202–3, 203–8, 235; and British, 54–5, 200–2, 215–16, 228–9; character of, 15, 83–4, 160, 236–7, 243; and inam acquisition, 35–9, 80; and inheritance, 55, 195, 196, 222, 232; lawsuits, 228, 232–7; location, 16, 34–5, 136; and Marathas, 31–2, 35, 53–4, 57, 66, 79, 82–3, 212; and Mughals, 53; and politics, 53–5, 56, 68–9; and religion, 27–8, 32, 93, 116, 185
Cincvad transit duties, 1, 90, 137–8, 149; and British 149–50, 153–9, 243; duty posts, 139–41; and Marathas,

136–7, 155; purpose of revenue, 137–8, 151–3, 155–6, 158
Cincvad village, 2, 3, 28, 53, 140; and Ganesh cult, 27, 28, 93; as inam, 30, 36, 58, 59; location, 1, 17–18, 34–5, 38; and Moroba Gosavi, 30, 31
citpavan brahmans, 49
Citrav, Bapuji Shripat, 43
Citrav, Shripat Bapuji, 43
Clerk, George, 155, 229
Clive, Robert, 165, 166
coinage, 124–6, 127
Collector of Pune, 100, 200, 201, 204, 208; and Cincvad mint, 132, 133, 134; and Morgav pilgrimage, 114, 116; and Ranjangav Samsthan, 182–3, 192; and transit duties, 149–50, 153–4, 157–8. *See also* H. D. Robertson
Collector of Thana, 174
commerce, 90, 122–3, 159–60
Commissioner for Claims, 151, 154, 156–7
compensation, 132
Cornwallis, Lord, 166
Court of Directors: and adoption 202, 209; and alienated revenue, 168, 175, 176; and religious endowments 113; and transit duties, 145, 149; and varsasans, 120
Cowper, T. A., 117–18, 222–7, 228, 231, 247

Dapodi village, 155
daksina, 104–5
Dalhousie, Lord, 165, 208
daphtardar, 112–13
dastak, 64, 122, 137–8
dayabhag, 56
Deccan, 12–13, 35, 37, 47, 87, 88
Deccan Commission, 46, 87, 88, 160, 200; and alienated revenue, 169–72; and mints, 124–6, 134–5; and Ranjangav Samsthan, 186, 190; and transit duties, 137, 149; and varsasans, 99–111, 119
Deccan sardars, 173–4
Dehu village, 17, 140, 141
Derrett, J. Duncan M., 207
deshasta brahmans, 18, 49, 214
Deshmukh, Cinto Vaman, 184, 190
Deshmukh, Gopalrav Hari, 184, 224–5, 227, 228
deshmukh of Pune, 31
deshpande of Pune, 119

265

Index

Dev, Anyaba (of Ranjangav), 182
Dev, Bajaji Govind, 297, 217–18, 220,
    231; and fraud, 226–7; and lawsuits,
    228–9, 230
Dev, Cintaman (I), 31, 32, 50, 57, 58
Dev, Cintaman (II), 80–1
Dev, Cintaman (III), 196–7
Dev, Cintaman (Appa) (of Ranjangav),
    182
Dev, Cinto (son of Bajaji Govind),
    234–7
Dev, Cinto Mangalmurti, 211–12, 217;
    and adoption of Ganesh, 204–5,
    207, 209
Dev, Dharanidhar (I), 56–7, 82
Dev, Dharanidhar (II): adoption of,
    198–9, 211, 212; death of, 116
    202–5, 294; described, 200–1, 225;
    and Ganesh Dev, 206–7; widows of,
    208, 210, 214–5
Dev, Dharanidhar (of Ojhar), 207
Dev, Dharanidhar (son of Bajaji
    Govind), 235
Dev, Digambar, 67, 75, 77
Dev, Ganesh, 208–9, 214–15, 227, 231,
    234–7; adoption of, 204–8, 210, 228
Dev, Gajanan, 66, 71–4
Dev, Ganpat (of Ranjangav), 182,
    184–5, 189–92, 193, 207
Dev, Heramb (Bunyaba), 81, 82
Dev, Jagannath, 49, 206, 207
Dev, Laksmibai, 202, 212, 234–7; appeals
    of, 218–22, 229; and British, 219,
    230, 231; character of, 214–15; and
    fraud, 226–7; and Morgav
    pilgrimage, 116–17, 118
Dev, Lambodar, 66
Dev, Moreshvar, 82–3, 182, 184–5, 190,
    192
Dev, Narayan (I), 36, 39, 46, 61–3, 206
Dev, Narayan (II), 53, 82, 83
Dev, Nirubai, 211–13
Dev, Sakharam, 197. *See also* Dev,
    Dharanidhar (II)
Dev, Umapati, 81–2, 206, 207
Dev, Venubai, 234–5
Dev, Vighneshvar, 39, 67, 72
Dev, Vinayak, 36, 64; and lineage
    segmentation, 71–4; separate
    acquisitions, 39, 63, 222
Dev, Vishvambhar, 50
Dev, Vishvanath, 66, 72, 206
devasthan, 10, 47, 109–10; and British
    policy, 99, 100–2, 216, 229–30; and
    Cincvad Samsthan, 58, 116, 218–19,
    220–2; and inheritance, 195, 231;

and Morgav pilgrimage, 117; and
    Ranjangav Samsthan, 185, 191–2;
    and tahanama, 223, 228; and transit
    duties, 115–16
Dev of Cincvad, the, 52–3, 80–3,
    112–13, 193, 201; adoption of,
    196–8; divinity and ritual status,
    1–3, 158–9, 235, 237; and religion,
    49, 215, 220, 221–2; social status,
    49–55
Devs of Cincvad, 14, 15–18, 19, 66; and
    commerce, 51–2, 122, 129, 136–41,
    148, 160–1; and inam, 82, 116, 186;
    and Maratha state, 50–1, 83–4; and
    rights, 240; and religion, 15, 16, 18;
    social status, 11–12, 46
Devs of Ranjangav, 164, 216, 219
dhanyajakat, 137
dharma, 64
dharmadan, 103
dharmashastra, 197, 206, 210, 211, 233
Disraeli, Benjamin, 238–9, 247
Diwani, 165, 166
'doctrine of lapse', 208
Dods, P., 219, 225
Dongargav-Mhase village, 55

East India Company, 87, 88–90, 122–3,
    165, 238, 243. *See also* Court of
    Directors
Elphinstone, Lord, 120
Elphinstone, Mountstuart, 87, 89; and
    commercial rights, 123–4, 130, 146,
    160; and inam, 169–74, 198, 171–3;
    and Morgav pilgrimage, 111–12,
    119; and Proclamation of Satara,
    99–100; and varsasans, 104, 107–8,
    111, 117
English: petitions, 189, 193; sources, 8–9,
    13
estoppel, 185
Evans-Pritchard, E. E., 70

Falkland, Lady, 200n
festivals, 16–17
Fortes, Meyer, 70
frauds, 193, 201, 212, 215, 226–7
French, 49, 50

Ganesh, 50, 158; and Devs of Cincvad,
    1, 16, 53, 94, 221; and the Peshvas,
    49, 94; used by Tilak, 17
Ganesh caturthi, 94
Ganesh cult: Cincvad, 27; Morgav, 27,
    93

Index

Ganeshkhind, 94
Ganesh sacred sites, 15, 16, 50, 82–3, 93,
  181–2, 186, 207. *See also* Morgav;
  Ojhar; Ranjangav; Siddhatek; Theur
Ganpati, *See* Ganesh
ganpatya, 49
genealogy, 69, 71
Ghod river, 53
Goldsmid, H. E., 175, 176
gotra, 18n
Govindji, Dulabshet, 128
Graham, Maria, 2, 3, 197–8
Grant, James, 88n, 170
Gujarat, 174

hagiography, 25–7
hak, 150, 153, 154–5, 185
hakdar, 151, 156
Hart, William, 118–19, 175–6, 228–9
Hastings, Warren, 165
Haveli taluka, 15, 31, 137
Hingne lineage, 214
Hinjavadi village, 36, 141
'Holder of an Ultra Regulation Estate',
  157
Holkar, Ahilyabai, 213
Holkar, Yashvantrav, 53–4, 186
hundikari, 142, 143
Hyder Ali, 48

idolatry, 90, 113, 114, 120, 219, 221
inam: acquisition process, 24, 32, 37–8,
  77, 80, 83; and British, 169, 170–2,
  198–9; and commerce, 10, 122, 135,
  137, 155–6; defined and character, 5,
  10, 12–13, 48, 84, 241; and Devs of
  Cincvad, 1, 11, 32–9, 57–61, 199;
  granting process, 40–5, 47; and
  inheritance, 46, 70–1, 81, 163,
  202–3, 210; location, 33, 34–5, 38,
  39, 65–6; mortgage of, 201, 225,
  232, 237; resumption of, 38–9, 46,
  91, 164, 170, 181, 196; and villages,
  23–4, 77–80, 83
inam amal, 123–4, 135
Inam Commission: and adoption, 195,
  202–2, 208–9, 216–7, 228; Amended
  Rules of 1842, 117; and authority of
  state, 5, 240, 244–5; Bengal origins,
  165–9; character of 4, 162–4, 195;
  and Cincvad Samsthan, 90–1,
  203–8, 215–17, 220; and
  Elphinstone, 169–74; end, 238; and
  inamdars, 87, 89–91; failings, 230–2,
  245–7; and Indian Mutiny, 4–5,

247; and inheritance, 195, 196, 210,
  225–6, 246–7; legislation, 164–5;
  and lineage factionalism, 194, 229,
  247; and Marathi documents, 14,
  162, 163, 183–4, 209, 216, 245–6;
  and Morgav fair, 117–19; and
  Morgav pilgrimage, 116–21; and
  Parliament, 5; petitions and appeals,
  189, 192; and prescription, 166–7,
  178; procedure, 177–8, 179, 183–4,
  190, 192–3, 209, 219–20, 223, 231;
  Ranjangav appeals, 189–92;
  Ranjangav decision, 184–8; and
  resumption, 181; and rights, 246; in
  Southern Maratha Country, 174–7;
  and tahanama, 212–13, 218, 222–6;
  and varsasans, 116, 121; and
  widows, 195, 210–11
inamdars, 60, 84, 122–3, 201–2; and
  British, 87, 198, 201–2, 204, 243–4;
  and Deccan Commission, 87, 88, 89,
  198; and Inam Commission, 162–3;
  and law, 199–200, 232–3
India, Government of: Act XXIII of
  1871 (Pension Act), 111
Indian Mutiny, 4, 87, 162, 240, 247
Indrayani river, 44, 139, 140
infant mortality, 74
inheritance, 18, 19, 61, 63, 68, 106, 152,
  239–40, 241; and Act XI of 1852,
  208, 247; and adoption, 222;
  bilateral succession, 242, and
  British, 163, 164, 178–9, 180, 202,
  224–5, 230–2, 247; of brothers,
  62–3; and Cincvad Samsthan, 196,
  232; impartible, 55, 56, 68–9, 195,
  222, 223; and lineage, 74–7, 91, 242;
  under Marathas, 242–3; and
  Marathi documents, 231; partible,
  55, 58, 67–8, 80, 84, 195, 196, 197,
  223, 231; and Ranjangav Samsthan,
  191, 196; reversionary heirs, 210,
  232; and tahanama, 223, 231;
  unilineal descent, 9; and widow, 208,
  209–10, 214, 223, 231

Jackson, Charles, 165, 179
jagir, 11, 46, 81, 122, 166
jagirdars, 11
jakat, 67. *See also* transit duties
jakatdar, 151n
Jamb village, 36
jamdar, 201
jamindar, 167
Jejuri village, 98, 101
Jinji, 37

267

Index

Morgav village, 33–4, 79, 100, 101, 117–18, 216; and Devs of Cincvad, 27–8, 34–5, 36, 57, 66, 81; and Ganesh cult, 27, 30–1, 93
Moroba Gosavi, 1, 26, 49; and Cincvad, 3, 28, 30, 31, 216; inam grants to, 28–31, 57; life of, 25–30; and Morgav 27, 30–1, 93
Moshi village, 140, 141
Mula river, 139, 141
Munro, Thomas, 46, 47–8, 88n, 99–100, 146
Mughals, 36–7, 43–4, 51, 53, 124
Muslims, 48, 60, 99

najar, 53, 128, 228
najarana, 117
naka, 138
Nana Phadnis, 49, 50, 54, 82
Narayanrav Peshva, 105
Nasik town, 140, 214
Nasik district, 125
'native aristocracy', 4
nemnuk, 103–4
Nizam of Hyderabad, 94, 186; grants of, 199; and Pune district, 23, 43–4, 137; and Sambhaji of Kolhapur, 44–5
Nizam Shahi sultanate, 30
north India, 50, 139, 247
Nuer, 69

Ojhar Samsthan, 83
Ojhar village, 83
opium, 144
Orissa, 113

paisa, 60n
Palkhed, Battle of, 44n
Panipat, Battle of, 49, 50, 52
Pant Saciv of Bhor, 41, 42–3
Parlikar, Shripat Sesadri, 18n
partition, 56, 82–3. See also inheritance; tahanama
parva, 101
Parvati temple, 100
patil, 40
patilki, 52
Pavna river, 139
pensions, 92
Peshva daphtar. See Marathi documents, Pune Archives
Peshvas: and alienated revenue, 39, 42–3, 108, 124, 170; and Devs of Cincvad, 1, 84, 212; and lineage, 57, 91, 196; political relations of, 3, 23, 35, 42–3,

45, 57, 88; and Pune city, 17, 35; and religion, 47, 93–9
Pethe, Trimbakrav, 98
petitions, 189, 193
phutgav, 140
pilgrim tax, 113
Pimple Saudagar village, 198–9
Pimpri-Cincvad Municipal Corporation, 17
Pirangut village, 52
political change, 244
political sovereignty, 58
Portuguese, 52
Potdar, D. V., 29
Pottinger, Henry, 88n, 108–10, 170; on transit duties, 143, 144, 146
Povla family, 52–3
prant, 15
prasad, 51, 95
prescriptive title: in Bengal, 166–7, 168; in Bombay, 115–16, 171, 173, 178
Pringle, R. K., 102
Pune Archives, 13–14, 201–2; and Devs of Cincvad, 35–6, 95–8, 129–30, 136–7; and Inam Commission, 175, 245. See also Marathi documents
Pune city, 16–18, 87, 139; and Devs of Cincvad, 35, 38, 205; under Marathas, 17, 35, 54; mint, 125; temples, 16, 100; and trade, 17–18, 79, 138–41, 158
Pune district, 13, 30, 43–4; commerce in, 122, 130, 137; varsasans in, 100–2
Purandhar taluka, 33
Purandhar town, 49
Purandhare, Trimbakrav, 101
Puri, 113

Radcliffe-Brown, A. R., 69
rahdari, 141
Rajaram, 36, 39, 40
Rajputs, 7
Rajvadi village, 98
Ramcandrapant Amatya, 47
Ramdas, 26
Ramraja, 45
Ranjangav Samsthan, 82–3, 181–2, 193; and Inam Commission, 181, 184–8, 189–92; and inheritance, 182–3, 196; sanads of, 185, 191
Ranjangav village, 91, 185, 186–7
rasum, 151n
Ravet village, 31, 37, 39, 66n, 82, 139
regionalism, 15–18
rent-free tenures. See alienated revenue; inam

269

Index

revenue: accounts, 31–2, 186–7; policy 6; rights, 239–40; system, 23, 31, 60. *See also* alienated revenue; inam
Revenue Commissioner, 132–3, 134, 175
rights, 25, 238–40, 243–4
Robertson, H. D., 88n, 171; and commerce, 123–4, 130, 144, 146; and Morgav pilgrimage, 111–12; and varsasans, 100–1, 102–3, 104–5, 106–7
rojina, 104
rojkird, 119, 185
ruka, 31

Sadashivrav (Bhausaheb), 49, 50n
sagotra sapinda, 207
sahotra, 40, 41
salt duties, 137
samadhi, 3
Sambhaji II (Shambhu) of Kolhapur, 40, 44–5, 136–7, 155
sanad: and commerce, 127, 136–7, 152; and Devs of Cincvad, 35–6; definition and form, 24, 41, 45, 47, 166; and Ranjangav Samsthan, 185, 191; and Vakad village, 40–1; and varsasans, 107–8, 109, 115–16
saranjam, 11, 46
sardeshmukhi, 40, 66–7, 136
sargaudki, 40
sarpatilki, 40
Saste village, 39, 78
Sasvad town, 101, 103
Satara, 51, 55–6
Satara, Proclamation of, 99–100, 102, 107, 152, 169
sati, 49
Sauer, Carl O., 16n
segmentary state, 70
Shah Alam, 165
Shahu, 39, 46, 51; and Devs of Cincvad, 35, 36–8, 40–1, 42–3; and Peshvas, 35, 57; tahanama of, 57; and transit duties, 136–7, 140
Shinde, Mahadaji, 213
Shindes of Gwalior, 199
shingoti, 142
Shivaji, 1, 40, 41, 137
Shore, John, 166–7
Siddhatek village, 39, 57, 81, 83, 100, 101, 216
Siddhivinayak, 83
social anthropology, 8, 68
social conservatism, 6–7
Solapur, 126

Southern Maratha Country: alienated revenue settlement, 174–7; coinage and mints, 126, 130; transit duties, 146
Sudumbare village, 44, 72, 206
Sudumbarekar, Sakharam Mahipant, 205, 207
Summary Settlement, 180, 228–9, 230
svaraj, 186
svayambhu images, 27
Sykes, William Henry, 2–3, 197

taha, 56
tahanama, 58–9, 62, 66–7, 80–1; and adoption, 203, 228; defined, 55–6, 58; and Devs of Cincvad, 57, 61–3, 65–6, 81, 222; and Inam Commission, 117–19, 212–13, 218, 222–6; and inheritance, 223, 231; issued, 55, 56–7; and land, 59, 60, 61; and lineage, 57, 72–3, 206, 237; principles of, 55, 59, 60, 61, 62, 64, 83; and sardeshmukhi, 66–7; and transit duties, 64, 67, 136; and widows, 62, 214
Taiwan, 7
taka, 31
Talegav, Battle of 51, 53
taluka, 15
Tandli village, 199, 236n
tankha, 71, 78–9, 136; defined and use, 59, 60–1
tankshal, 131
Tarabai, 213
tarph, 15
tea, 146
temple trust, 17, 209, 232, 233–4, 236–7
Thackeray, St. John, 144–5, 147
thalbharit, 141, 153
thalmod, 141, 153
Theur village, 36, 57, 66, 98, 100, 101, 216
Tilak, B. G. ('Lokmanya'), 17
Tipu Sultan, 48
Tiv, 69
Tone, William H., 23
transit duties, 67, 122, 136–7, 139, 140, 146, 152; abolished, 148–9; administration of, 139, 141–3, 144–5; as alienated revenue, 10, 137, 143, 146, 147, 153, 156; and British policy, 135–6, 143–4, 144–6, 152–3; and British reforms, 146–9; on commodities, 137–8, 144, 146–7; compensation for 150–1; and

270

Index

CAMBRIDGE SOUTH ASIAN STUDIES

These monographs are published by the Syndics of Cambridge University Press in association with the Cambridge Centre for South Asian Studies. The following books have been published in this series:

Cambridge South Asian Studies